W9-CDP-003

PRAEGER LIBRARY OF AFRICAN AFFAIRS

ZAMBIA

PRAEGER LIBRARY OF AFRICAN AFFAIRS

The Praeger Library of African Affairs is intended to provide clear and authoritative information about the historical, political, cultural and economic background of modern Africa. Individual countries and groupings of countries will be dealt with, and also general themes affecting the whole continent and its relations with the rest of the world. The library appears under the general editorship of Colin Legum, and each volume is written by an acknowledged expert on its subject.

ALREADY PUBLISHED

ETHIOPIA: A New Political History, *Richard Greenfield*

SOUTH AFRICA: A Political and Economic History, *Alex Hepple*

THE LITERATURE AND THOUGHT OF MODERN AFRICA, A SURVEY, *Claude Wauthier*

ZAMBIA: *Richard Hall*

Richard Hall

ZAMBIA

FREDERICK A. PRAEGER, *Publishers*
New York · Washington · London

To my mother

FREDERICK A. PRAEGER, *Publishers*
111 Fourth Avenue, New York, N.Y. 10003
77-79 Charlotte Street, London, W.1, England

Published in the United States of America in 1965
by Frederick A. Praeger, Inc., Publishers

Second printing, 1967

Library of Congress Catalog Card Number: 65-18325

Printed in the United Kingdom

Contents

ABBREVIATIONS USED IN THE TEXT

(A further list of abbreviations, mainly of literary and other sources, is given at the head of *Notes and References*)

AAPC	All-African People's Conference
AMWU	African Mineworkers Union
ANC	African National Congress
BAN	'Build a Nation' Campaign
BASMO	Barotse Anti-Secessionist Movement
BNP	Barotse National Party
BSA Coy.	British South Africa Company—(the) 'Charter' or 'Chartered' (Company)
CS	Chief Secretary
DC	District Commissioner
MLC	Member of the Legislative Council (Legco)
NPP	National Progress Party (formerly UFP, *q.v.*)
NRG	Northern Rhodesia Government
PC	Provincial Commissioner
PDC	People's Democratic Congress
RST	Rhodesian (later Roan) Selection Trust
SNA	Secretary for Native Affairs
SPC	Senior Provincial Commissioner
UAC	Urban Advisory Council (Committee)
UAU	United Anti-UNIP Movement
UAWA	United African Welfare Association
UFP	United Federal Party
UNIP	United National Independence Party
UTUC	United Trade Union Congress
ZANC	(Zambian) African National Congress

Preface

IT has been said by some African scholars, such as M. Sekene Cissoko of Mali, that national or ethnic histories merely crystallise a narrow pride in one country at the expense of continental unity; this Pan-Africanist argument is not without force, because the period of effective colonial rule has been so short that cultural and other distinctions are much less marked between neighbouring states in Africa than they are in Europe. However, the political realities cannot be denied by idealism; new African countries such as Zambia exist within the boundaries imposed by colonialism and rely primarily on national pride for their dynamism.

This having been said, it is none the less true that one can only write a national history in Africa covering about seventy years. 'Pre-European history' must be viewed regionally. For example, I have treated the Lunda empire of Mwata Yamvo in some detail, because although it lay outside the boundaries of modern Zambia, it was the source of Zambia's principal tribes during the seventeenth and eighteenth centuries and exerted a powerful influence until long after the migrations. Similarly, the Portuguese and Arab slave-trades which were so disastrous for the people of Zambia, must be viewed on a canvas stretching from Zanzibar to Benguela. In more recent times, the overthrow of Lobengula was directly interlocked with the progress of Rhodes north of the Zambezi.

For ten years of this century, Northern Rhodesia (as it was then called) belonged to a now defunct political structure, the Federation of Rhodesia and Nyasaland. Here again, it has been necessary to deal at some length with events in a larger arena. I should add that because the Federation was the subject of so much dispute and so many contrary views, I have thought it wise to use quotations extensively in recording that period. In a number of instances, it has not been possible to reveal the sources of information garnered during my nine years in Central Africa.

This book generally proceeds chronologically, but for clarity it has seemed best to place at the end the chapters dealing with the Copperbelt and the country's economy.

Many people have been generous with information and advice. Although none of them should be held responsible for errors or opinions expressed in the book, I must particularly thank the following : Mr Denis Acheson, Mr G. Chindele, Mr Trevor Coombe, Dr Brian Fagan, Dr Prosser Gifford, Mr Ivor Graham, Sir Stewart Gore-Browne, the Hon. Mwansa Kapwepwe, President Kenneth Kaunda, Mr Godwin Lewanika, Miss Mutumba Mainga, Mr David C. Mulford, Mr Harry Nkumbula, Mr John Sokoni, and Miss Norma Wright. I should like to mention my indebtedness to Mr Clifford Little, who has made many useful suggestions and given me access to his library of Africana. Mr John Dodgson has provided, in the final two chapters, much valuable material on Zambia's economic development. Mrs Pauline Hodgson and Miss K. Krishnamurti compiled the index.

R. H.

ZAMBIA

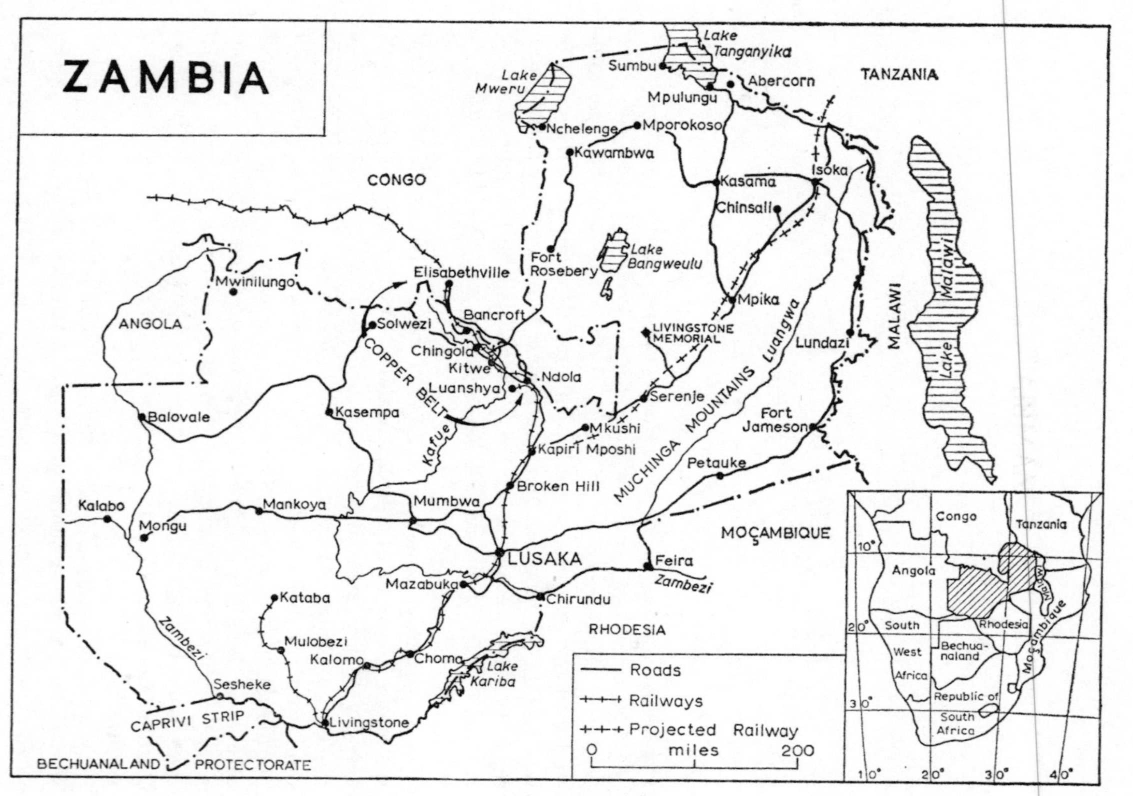
ZAMBIA
Lake Tanganyika
Sumbu
Abercorn
TANZANIA
Lake Mweru
Mpulungu
Nchelenge
Mporokoso
Kawambwa
Isoka
Kasama
CONGO
Chinsali
Lake Bangweulu
Fort Rosebery
Elisabethville
Mwinilungo
Mpika
Solwezi
Bancroft
ANGOLA
LIVINGSTONE MEMORIAL
Chingola
MALAWI
Lake Malawi
Lundazi
Kitwe
Ndola
COPPER BELT
Luangwa
Luanshya
Serenje
Balovale
Kasempa
MUCHINGA MOUNTAINS
Fort Jameson
Mkushi
Kafue
Kapiri Mposhi
Petauke
Broken Hill
Kalabo
Mankoya
Mumbwa
MOÇAMBIQUE
Mongu
LUSAKA
Feira
Zambezi
Mazabuka
Kataba
Chirundu
RHODESIA
Zambezi
Mulobezi
Kalomo
Choma
Lake Kariba
Sesheke
CAPRIVI STRIP
Livingstone
BECHUANALAND PROTECTORATE
Roads
Railways
Projected Railway
0 miles 200
Congo
Tanzania
Angola
Malawi
Rhodesia
Moçambique
South West Africa
Bechuanaland
Republic of South Africa
10°
20°
30°
40°

1. *Zambia*

1

The Land and Its Peoples

I GENERAL FEATURES

ZAMBIA arouses little enthusiasm among visitors with an eye for scenic beauty. After serving for a while in what was then Northern Rhodesia, Sir Charles Dundas, a colonial administrator of the old days, wrote in his autobiography that the country was 'almost nothing but flat, featureless bush and low forest land' separating two beauty spots, the Victoria Falls in the south and the Kalambo Falls dropping 700 feet over a precipice 1,000 miles to the north.[1]

Certainly, land-locked Zambia cannot compete for natural splendours with neighbouring Malawi. Perhaps also its size (vast even by African standards) makes modern travellers hurry from one place to another and miss the fascination beyond the roadside. The impression of barren emptiness is reinforced by the sparsity of population. In an area (290,000 square miles) far larger than that of France, Belgium and the Netherlands combined, it has three and a half million people; about one third of these are concentrated on the Copperbelt and along the line-of-rail. Compared with Malawi, Zambia has about the same population and eight times as much land surface.

In the north-east, the scarcity of inhabitants is brought home sharply as one drives along the Great North Road, the dirt highway into Tanzania. Although most villages cluster beside the road, it is possible to travel for forty miles at a stretch and see hardly a sign of life. The scenery is so monotonously unchanging that in the rainy season motorists have been known to spin around several times in the mud and then drive for miles before realizing they were going back the way they had come.

The natural character of Zambia becomes more evident if one follows the courses of its four great rivers. Three of these—the Zambezi, the Kafue and the Luangwa—drain the south and east of the country. The fourth, the Luapula, rises in Lake Bangweulu and empties its flood into Lake Mweru in the far north-west after forming a long boundary with the Congo. These rivers and their innumerable tributaries flow through valleys sometimes clothed with dense tropical forests, the remains of a vegetation which once covered most of Zambia. The rivers make imposing waterfalls (which in former days were considered to be the homes of spirits). When possible, the makers of the territory's few main roads have followed the watersheds—the easiest but least interesting routes.

This is the surface of Zambia, part of the world's greatest plateau stretching for 3,000 miles down the African continent. Almost all of the country undulates at a level above 3,500 feet, with the average altitude being rather greater in the northern 'wing'. Abercorn, overlooking Lake Tanganyika, is 5,400 feet above sea level, and so ranks as Zambia's highest town. A 'spine' of higher ground including the Muchinga mountains, runs north-east from the middle of the country to the Tanzania border. On the eastern border of the country, near Lundazi, the Nyika mountains rise to 7,400 feet. The lowest parts of the country are the flood-plains of the Kafue river and the Zambezi. The town of Livingstone, near the Victoria Falls, is below 3,000 feet.

The country's distinctive red soil is powdery and light. As a rule there is not much topsoil and apart from occasional pockets, the ground is not naturally fertile, quickly becoming deficient in nitrogen and other elements needed for high farm yields.[2] In many places there are outcrops of granite rocks, which with quartzites and shales form the main geological foundation of the region. Only in Barotseland is the soil markedly different, changing to sand of the type found in the adjoining Kalahari desert. In the *dambos,* the open patches of swampy ground found throughout Zambia, the soil is black, but experiments have shown that it is not especially fertile and the main value of *dambos* is for dry season grazing. In the extreme south, around Livingstone, there are patches of lava left by long past volcanic activity; there has been no volcanic activity in Zambia in modern times, although there are occasional mild earth tremors and hot springs are found in various parts of the country, especially the Zambezi valley.

The hundreds of miles of woodlands vary greatly according to the altitude and rainfall, which is much heavier in the north than in the south. Over most of Zambia the trees are tough, cross-grained types with smallish leaves and long thin branches. Scientifically they are referred to as the *Isoberlinia* and *Brachystegia* types, which renew their foliage in the months of September and October.[3] These trees, which include a number of species called 'Mixed Mutondo' cover the Copperbelt and their tough timbers make ideal props for the mines. Barotseland has valuable forests of teak and mahogany and in the low sweltering valleys grow palms, rough-barked mopani trees and the grotesque baobabs with swollen trunks and short branches; cream of tartar is made from the fruit of the baobabs.

Until recent times, Zambia was rich in game of nearly all species found in tropical Africa. Early European travellers such as Livingstone made constant mention in their writings of the amount of wild life in the region. A Baptist missionary, Clement Doke,[4] wrote:

> Game of almost every kind abounds, though with the advent of the white hunter and the increase of muzzle-loading guns in the hands of the natives it is fast diminishing. In 1913, when I first visited the country, portions of the Kafue plains were still teeming with herds of big game, and one could stand on an ant-hill and chose one's breakfast from any ten or more species feeding with apparent unconcern.

Doke was writing of what is now the Copperbelt, where it is unusual today to see any wild animals apart from the occasional duiker (a small fleet-footed antelope). In the game reserves and remoter districts, where the human population is small, animals are still numerous.[5]

More than 100,000 square miles of bush are infested with tsetse fly (*Glossina morsitans*), which cause the fatal trypanosomiasis in unprotected cattle.

For nearly three-quarters of the year Zambia has no rainfall. The wet season lasts from November until April and a rain shower outside that time is regarded as phenomenal. In June and July the weather is sunny but distinctly sharp : ice has been known to form on a dish of water left in the open and frost can be a hazard for crops in the valleys. When the rains break in November with the southward movement of the inter-tropical zone there is an immense feeling of relief, despite the violent thunderstorms which accompany the torrential downpours. The Copperbelt area has one of the highest incidences of lightning in the world.

II OUTLINES OF GEOLOGY

For more than 500 miles the Zambezi river forms the southern boundary of Zambia, separating it from the Caprivi Strip and

Southern Rhodesia; then it runs through Mozambique to the Indian Ocean. Once, however, it flowed westward, emptying itself into a vast drainage area to the south. That was about 150 million years ago. The geologists are able to look back still further. About 500 million years ago, there was a mountain range stretching from the country's present north-west boundaries, through what is now the Western Province, to the Lusaka area and on to the south. The roots of these long-vanished mountains are scientifically known as the 'Katanga arc'. They contain the mineral wealth which is now the Copperbelt.[1]

These mountains were planed down even before the period about 220 million years ago when Zambia entered an ice age. As the great shield of ice melted, what is now Zambia became covered with swamps. The surface of the earth was still slowly moving, and as rifting took place the valleys filled with softer rocks. This was the prelude to the Mesozoic Era, the age of reptiles living in shallow freshwater lakes. The Kafue basin was such a lake as this 200 million years ago; so were Barotseland and the Luangwa valley. Fossil remains of the creatures of that time have been discovered throughout Zambia. During 1963, an expedition from the British Museum of Natural History found in the Luangwa valley the skull of a reptile not unlike a crocodile. Its teeth were nearly five inches long. The animal, related to the earliest dinosaurs, was living about 200 million years ago in what is now the Lundazi District.

After the distant period when reptiles began to crawl from the lakes on to the land, the climate became completely arid. Lakes dried up and their beds filled with wind-blown sand; Zambia became a true desert. Then, about 180 million years ago, fissures opened in the earth and lava poured out. These floods of lava were greatest in what is now the Zambezi valley and their traces can still be seen at the Victoria Falls and near Chirundu. Tilting and warping of the earth's crust caused major changes in the drainage system of the region. The Luapula, which earlier had been joined to the Kafue, became that oddity, a river rising from one lake and emptying itself into another. The present complex was created whereby the Chambezi (now generally called the Chambeshi) starting only fifty miles from Lake Tanganyika, runs south-west to Lake Bangweulu; the Luapula flows out of the lake and forms an irregular arc before feeding Lake Mweru. Consequently the land north-west of the Muchinga Escarpment is in the basin of the Congo river, to which Lake Mweru is linked by the Lualaba. While the northern wing of the country drains westward, ultimately into the Atlantic, the Zambezi and its tributaries go to the Indian Ocean.

This is the more remarkable since the Chambeshi and Luapula are several hundred miles farther east than the source of the Zambezi.[2]

III TRACES OF EARLY MAN

Apart from the efforts of Dr J. Desmond Clark and a few others, archaeological fieldwork in Zambia so far has been fragmentary.[1] Any outline of pre-history must be tentative, since future finds are likely to necessitate major reassessments. However, scientists are generally agreed that the world's first humans developed in Africa. Discoveries recently made in Tanzania by Dr Louis Leakey add weight to this theory. Man in the accepted definition is a creature able to make and use tools. In the Olduvai Gorge of Tanzania, Dr Leakey found the remains of a human being scientifically called *Homo habilis,*[2] who was living about 1·8 million years ago. This primitive man, who was about four feet tall, used pebbles for hacking up bones and stripping meat from the animals he had caught. *Homo habilis* also probably made himself crude windbreaks in which to live. Although no fossilised remains of this species and the contemporary *Zinjanthropus boisei* have yet been found in Zambia, the same kind of pebble tools were discovered some years ago not far from Lusaka.[3] Since Zambia lies across the main route which men, ancient and modern, have travelled up and down Africa, it is not unreasonable to assume that *Homo habilis,* the earliest human being known to the world, lived also in Zambia.

Life in the forests of Central Africa a million years ago was violent, the first men living at war with wild beasts, competing with the bigger carnivores for their common food. Many species then living in Zambia are now extinct: sabre-toothed tigers, a type of wolf, a huge baboon, the ancestors of the giraffe (with a shorter neck and bigger antlers).[4] Also there were the most typical of African animals, the forerunners of modern elephants. The *Dinotheres* ('terrible beasts') were as big as modern elephants and had powerful tusks pointing downwards. In the rushing rivers lived crocodiles and other reptiles, the type of life which had dominated the earth for more than 100 million years.

Gradually man progressed to the 'Hand-axe' culture. Many hand-axes have been found in Zambia—some in the far north at the Kalambo Falls and others near the Victoria Falls.[5] The men who made these hand-axes lived as long ago as 300,000 BC. Their homes were close to the rivers and they used stone tools for skinning animals and for digging up grubs to eat.

The huge number of these tools found at the Kalambo Falls

suggests that the 'hand-axe' men must have lived in large communities. Gradually, about 50,000 years ago, man began to make a wider variety of stone tools and learned how to use fire. Dating from this period are the first discovered fossil remains of man himself in Zambia. He is the famous 'Broken Hill man'—*Homo rhodesiensis*. The discovery of his skull was made by accident.[6] Blasting at the Broken Hill lead and zinc mine forty years ago uncovered a small cave. On a ledge in the cave was the skull, which after 25,000 years was still formidable enough to terrify the labourers on the job. When the gang returned, the white man in charge stuck the skull on a post to keep everyone 'on their toes'. It was only after several days that the skull was noticed by a doctor and sent off to the British Museum in London.

Broken Hill man (who was obviously of a general type spread all over Central Africa), was much more like modern humanity than *Homo habilis,* but his face was far different from our own. The Zambian of 25,000 BC had almost no forehead and heavy bone ridges under his eyebrows. His mouth was large and his neck short and thick. However, the leg, hip and arm bones found near the skull prove that the body of man has changed little in many thousands of years. It is not possible to know the skin colouring of Broken Hill man : his hair was probably long and coarse. The skull found in the cave had a hole in it, and it has been suggested that the man may have been killed with a spear.

Middle-Stone-Age men went naked, but possibly plastered their bodies with a mixture of red mud and fat. They could perhaps talk in a language of grunts and clicks, but existence remained basically a battle for survival. In the grass and woodlands there were giant pigs and buffalo (now both extinct) and herds of savage elephants. The nearer we get to modern times, the greater our knowlege becomes of pre-historic man in Zambia. In a cave at Mumbwa and another site at Victoria Falls, examples of tools from what is known as the 'Stillbay culture' have been found. These tools, skilfully made from quartz, show the increasing intelligence of the men who made them. From what we know of these people, they had big brains and were almost as tall as modern man. *Homo sapiens* was about to appear in Zambia.

About 10,000 years ago, there was a movement into southern Africa from the east and north of the continent.[7] The migrants brought new techniques for making weapons, such as arrows which were barbed so that once the head struck home it would not fall out. Ivory and bones were also used—but much more cleverly than when employed by Broken Hill man thousands of years before.

The Later Stone Age is generally considered to have begun

6,000 years ago in Central Africa and its people were of the bushman type, who lived in caves, or on sandy banks alongside rivers. They were small folk, on an average no more than five feet tall, and it is believed that changes in climate made them shorter than their ancestors. The modern Bantu tribes found these bushmen types still in much the same Stone-Age conditions as those of 6,000 years earlier.

Recent excavations at Gwisho Hotsprings on Lochinvar Ranch in the Southern Province have given a clear picture of life at this time. The bushmen hunters lived in family bands, on small camping sites on the edge of the Kafue Flats. Their houses were merely small windbreaks of grass and sticks, and their dead were buried within the settlement. Over thirty skeletons are known from the three Gwisho settlements investigated between 1960 and 1964. The hunters subsisted on a wide range of game and fish, as well as gathering wild produce and fruit from the *Acacia* woodland. The Lochinvar sites date to the third millennium BC.

It is believed that the Twa, who live in the swamps of Bangweulu and Lukanga are the pre-Bantu who fled there for safety. The name Twa seems to have been applied throughout Southern Africa by the modern tribes to the more primitive Stone-Age men they drove before them. The pigmies of the Congo are called Twa by their neighbours (who also describe them as 'coming from the root of the world'). The bushmen in South Africa are given the same name by the Xhosas. The Boers identified the people they fought in Namaqualand nearly 300 years ago with the name Twa.

The very first messages out of Zambia's distant past are mysterious scratchings and paintings found on the walls of caves in the northern parts of the country. These geometric designs peculiar to the region are in definite patterns, rather like the absent-minded drawings people make on note-pads while sitting round a conference table. There are circles, rectangles, hooks, dots and straight lines crossing one another. At one time it was believed that these symbols were a debased form of Arabic script, but this is now discounted. Such schematic art, which was coloured by the artists in red, yellow, brown and white, has been dated by the C^{14} method to more than 4000 BC through associated material found in a cave beside the Chifubwa Stream near Solwezi, in the North West Province. Until at least 5,000 years after this, Arab influence would be out of the question. The Stone-Age culture connected with the strange geometric art is called Nachikufan, after the caves in the Muchinga mountains where many examples were examined and photographed by Dr Desmond Clark in 1948.[8] In some places the rock paintings are twelve or more feet above ground level, so ladders must have been used by the inhabitants of the caves. Why they took such trouble with apparently meaningless squiggles is unknown, but one theory is that they were considered protection against evil spirits.

Other places in the territory where pre-historic art exists are : *Nsalu Cave,* forty miles north of Serenje in the Central Province; *Na Chitalo Hill* in Mkushi district, close to Msofu Mission; *Mwela Rocks,* three miles east of Kasama; *Zawi Hill* and *Rocklands Farm,* both close to Fort Jameson.

IV THE FIRST FARMERS

Present evidence suggests that about 2,000 years ago a new type of people came to Zambia. Perhaps they were little different from the Stone-Age people. The vital contrast was that these people made pottery.[1] The significance of this is that in southern Africa pottery-making is always associated with farming because deliberate food production calls for the use of storage vessels. The pattern is clearly established in archaeological discoveries made farther north in Africa. These primitive pottery makers, Zambians of the time when Jesus Christ was alive, made thick pots with a distinctive channelled decoration. Some of these vessels have been excavated at Situmpa, close to the Machili river which forms the eastern boundary of Barotseland, and at Lusu on the Zambezi. It is thought that the people who made them were immigrants from East Africa, because the decoration on early dimple-based pottery found there is similar.[2]

The discovery of 'Situmpa-ware' in the remains of Stone-Age settlements suggests that pottery-makers who could also smelt iron, mingled or traded with the earlier inhabitants. This must be guess-work, however, in the same way as we can only guess at the reasons why pottery decorated in Situmpa style has also been found at the Kalambo Falls—and dated by the C^{14} method to between 500 and 1,500 years ago. Since the pottery-makers came from the north, it would be reasonable to expect later dates in the south. In Southern Rhodesia, similar ware has been found near the Zimbabwe ruins and dates to around AD 300.[3] On the other hand, it became known in mid-1965 that an Iron Age site in Southern Rhodesia has been dated to as early as 300 BC.

We can assume that the first farmers grew cereals such as sorghum and millet, kept sheep and goats, fished in near-by rivers and possibly spoke a Hamitic language. The Hottentots also have some words of Hamitic origin, and it is possible that the first farmers continued their wanderings right down to the southern-most tip of Africa.[4]

V TRADE WITH THE EAST

On the plateau between Lusaka and Livingstone are the remains of villages dating from approximately a thousand years ago. People of the Iron Age occupying these villages lived by farming and hunting. In the south a number of skeletons have been found, buried in the tightly doubled-up position that was customary. One skeleton of a woman, perhaps the wife of a village ruler, was lavishly adorned. She wore round her neck thousands of beads of glass and shells; there were also two big *mpande* shells. At her waist more beads were hanging in rows. The wrists and ankles of all the skeletons were decorated with many ivory and metal bracelets. In these early Southern Province villages archaeologists have also found shells and copper ornaments.[1]

The *mpande* and cowrie shells and beads prove that in AD 900 the people in what is now the Southern Province of Zambia had trade links with the Indian Ocean. The beads came from India itself. For many centuries the *mpande* shell was the basic currency of Arab traders in Africa. A hundred years ago, two *mpande* shells bought a slave; five bought a medium-sized elephant tusk.

The East Coast of Africa has been in contact with the Arab world from early times. Even earlier, the Romans are thought to have sailed down as far as Cape Delgado, and a Roman coin dating from the second century was reputedly found in a gold working in Southern Rhodesia. The port of Sofala, near the modern Beira, existed for the gold trade in the sixth century, perhaps before; and so did Kilwa.[2] From Kilwa, a well-defined track leads to Manda on Lake Nyasa. Under the rule of a Persian prince, Ali Ibn Hassan, Kilwa became a town of great importance in the tenth century. The historian Masudi has left details of gold exploitation still farther south in the same period. Even the Chinese had a fair knowledge of East Africa more than a thousand years ago.[3]

In view of the long history of coastal trade it is hardly surprising that its effects were felt far inland, north of the Zambesi. One obvious means of access was the Zambezi itself which is navigable for almost 400 miles as far as the Quebrebasa Rapids. Another route is up the Rovuma valley to Lake Nyasa—a way to the interior which Livingstone used in 1866.

A vivid picture of this early Arab trade was provided by the discovery in 1960 of Ingombe Ilede ('Where the cow sleeps').[4] Ingombe Ilede was found on the north bank of the Zambezi less than thirty miles upstream from the confluence of the Kafue. Excavations have revealed a wealth of material. Dating by the C^{14} method shows that Ingombe Ilede was occupied from AD 650 or earlier to as late as AD 950. The graves contained copper crosses, gold beads and bangles, beads of many colours, iron-work, gongs, leather amulets of possible Arab origin, *mpande* shells (one set in a gold mounting) and tools for making copper wire. It is clear that these people were middlemen in the ivory and copper trade channelled from both banks of the river down the natural highway of the Zambezi, for there is no copper deposit near Ingombe Ilede itself. We also know that copper was being smelted by Balubas of the north-west, in what is now the Congo, as early as AD 900, and that the Lomagundi mines in Rhodesia were also being worked as early as this. The graves of Ingombe Ilede also revealed that people wore a variety of cloth, some perhaps imported, and pottery spindle whorls found there show they wove their own cotton. Along the Zambezi a word for cotton is *tonje* (Bemba—*tonge*) which linguists believe is derived from the Arab word *qutuniyyah* meaning cotton-thread. Although weaving wild cotton is now a lost art in the Southern Province, it was much practised until eighty years ago. In 1860, Sekeletu the Kalolo ruler sent a message to Queen Victoria through Livingstone, inviting her to send out settlers and in it he said: 'I shall cut off a country for them to dwell in . . . a country of cottons and the Batoka tribe weave it. Subject tribes and the Banajoa also sow cotton and use it.'[5]

The people of the Southern Plateau area of Zambia who knew the earliest Arab traders seem to have been of a negroid type, although their origins are not known for certain. Like the modern Tonga, they were great cattle-owners. Their beasts were of the indigenous Sanga variety, small and short-horned. Clay models of these animals have been found. Like the earlier 'Situmpa ware' farmers, they grew millet and ate wild fruits. In the Southern Province the musulu (*uapaca Kirkiana*) and mpundu (*parinarium mobola*) are both common trees and their fruits are pleasantly edible. In the old days, this area had vast quantities of wild animals including lions and elephants, and their bones found around the villages of the inhabitants of AD 1000, show that they were successfully hunted; elephants were probably trapped in pits, which is a time-honoured African method.

The first discoveries of the villages of these early farmers were made a few years ago near Kalomo, ninety miles north of Livingstone. A mound called Kalundu (Tonga for 'little hill') was uncovered in 1957 during a realignment of the main road. Later, another village was excavated by Dr Brian Fagan at a place called Isamu Pati ('big tree'). Several other villages have also been found, showing evidence of the same 'Kalomo culture'. About 150 miles north of Kalomo, near Mazabuka, more recent diggings have exposed a village with the name Kangila. A study of pottery excavated at Sebanzi Hill near the Gwisho Hotsprings has proved that the Tonga settled in Zambia at least as early as AD 1200.[6] A clay pot from the hotsprings area is known to date back to the very earliest Zambia farmers of 2,000 years ago.

At present, there are no known remains of the 'Kalomo culture' people north of Choma. Perhaps these simple farmers were few in number and rotated several village sites as the soil became exhausted. Remains found at Isamu Pati have been dated by the C^{14} method and show that the site was occupied intermittently for more than 500 years. The people lived in round pole-and-dagga huts on top of the hill, and their dead were buried right in the village—still a common custom. Bones that have been found show that cattle became more common in the later years of occupation. Around AD 1250–1400, the 'Kalomo culture' came to an end. Perhaps the people moved on elsewhere or died out through a plague. Most likely, the ancestors of the modern Bantu-Botatwe tribes (Tonga, Ila, Lenje) arrived on the scene and the earlier inhabitants merged with them.

VI THE LEGENDS OF THE TRIBES

There are more than seventy recognised tribes in Zambia.[1] Many are small and almost impossible to distinguish in language and culture from their neighbours. It is difficult to separate legend from fact when investigating the origins of the tribes, but it is certain that many have an inter-connected history. Until recent years the legends were related reverently, with much detail, even among the smallest tribes.

The Lamba people, who live in the area of the Copperbelt (and also across the border in the Congo) say that God (Lesa) came down to earth with the name of Luchyele.[2] With many helpers he arrived from the east, to allot places to all the tribes and give them rivers, hills, trees and grass. Strange markings on sandstone near Ndola are said by the Lamba to be footprints of Luchyele and his assistants.[3] Luchyele went back to his heaven, high in the sky, but promised his children he would return. When there is thunder and lightning, the Lamba say: 'God is scolding us'! From heaven, Lesa sent a chameleon with a message to the earth; the message said: 'When people die, they will live again.' But the chameleon walked very slowly, and Lesa then sent another messenger, the lizard, saying: 'When you die you die for ever.' So

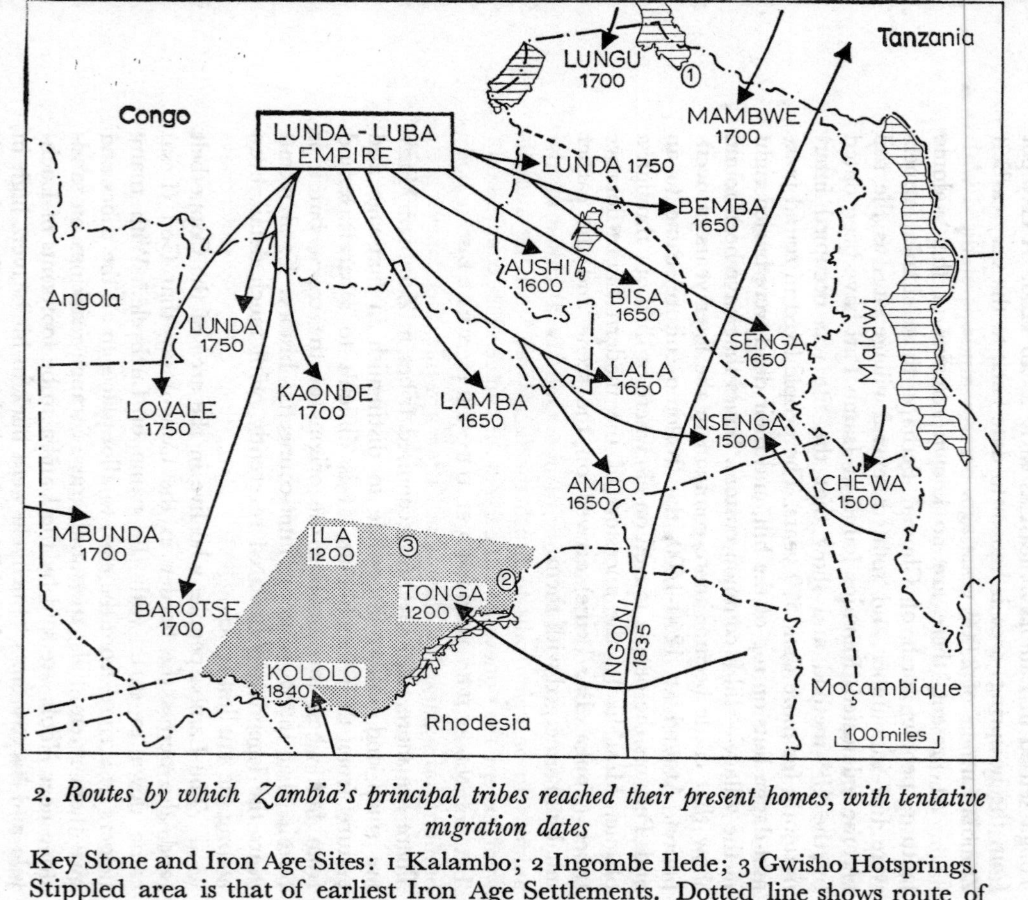

2. *Routes by which Zambia's principal tribes reached their present homes, with tentative migration dates*

Key Stone and Iron Age Sites: 1 Kalambo; 2 Ingombe Ilede; 3 Gwisho Hotsprings. Stippled area is that of earliest Iron Age Settlements. Dotted line shows route of Lacerda to Mwata Kazembe Ilunga in 1798.

the quick lizard reached the people first and cast them into despair with his grim tidings. That is why the chameleon is a hated creature—for failing to bring Lesa's good news in time.

After Luchyele, say the Lamba, a man came to visit them called Chipimpi. He came from the west and with him was his sister Kawunda. She was also his wife. Kawunda is credited with having obtained vegetable seeds for the people by hiding them in her long hair while planting for a Luba chief by the Lualaba river. Chipimpi had a son, also called Kawunda, who killed his father and became ruler of the Lamba in his stead.

The neighbours of the Lamba, the Lala to the north-east,[4] tell the story differently. 'There was a woman with only one breast to suckle two children; it was this woman who caused the human race to fill this world. From her were born two children, Mushili, a woman, and her brother, Lesa.' The brother and sister were married and from their incestuous union sprang good and evil. They had two children, Luchyele and Kashindika. It was Luchyele who went to the home of his father to be given two packages containing the sun and the moon.

There is also a Lala story of how God (Lesa) called all the animals to be given tails to brush the flies away.[5] All the animals went except the coneys and the *georychus* mice. The coneys said: 'Let somebody who is going get our tails for us.' But nobody brought tails back for them and after a while the coneys grew anxious and complained, 'Surely somebody must be bringing tails for us—perhaps they cannot find any to fit us!' At that, the mice grew alarmed and rushed off to Lesa. They found all the tails had gone and had to be content with stumps. Then the coneys went to Lesa and said, 'Where are the tails for us?' And Lesa replied, 'You did not come when all the rest came. It is because you are conceited. Hit them, somebody—send them off!' So the coneys went off in anger to a thicket, peering to see if anyone was coming; and they still have no tails!

All the tribes have their own myths and fables. These are part of the country's heritage even though today they are being lost in the rush of modern life. They can sometimes provide clues to origins of Zambia's people, especially the recurrent theme of incest in the Creation. This theme even appears in the mythology of the Lozi, who live hundreds of miles away from the Lamba and Lala; the Lozi tell the story of the Great God Nyambe, whose wife was his daughter, Mwambwa.[6]

It is a reasonable assumption that all the tribes who possess the 'incest-myth' are harking back to a common ancestry in some misty past. Anthropologists look for the answer in the 'Sudanic

States' which existed more than a thousand years ago in the northern parts of black Africa. Some look even further back to the royal incest of ancient Egypt. In the Sudanic States, the roles of Queen Sister and Queen Mother were deeply revered. They still are in Barotseland. It is interesting to note in this connection that the elders of the Lunda of the Luapula valley (a people with a keen regard for history) begin their written tribal history with an emphatic sentence, 'The Lunda are a tribe of the Bantu who came from the north, from Sudan'.[7]

VII MIGRATION AND CONQUEST

The migration of the peoples of Zambia has continued for at least the past 500 years and continues to this day. In the west and east, refugees still cross the border to escape from Portuguese rule in Angola and Mozambique. There is also migration from the south, away from Southern Rhodesia and South Africa.

To achieve a coherent picture, it is necessary to draw a line at the last tribal migration into Zambezia in pre-European times, that of the Ngoni warriors who crossed the Zambezi in the east in 1835 and the Kololo who arrived in Barotseland at about the same time. Both groups came from South Africa and were uprooted in the wars sparked off by Chaka.

The Ngoni and Kololo found the rest of the Zambia peoples already well established. The forerunners among the tribes were the Tonga, Ila, and related groups of the south. They had come into Zambia from the north-east around 1200, probably through the gateway of land between Lake Tanganyika and Lake Nyasa. Although the Tonga lost all their legends in the slave-hunting holocaust of the late nineteenth century,[1] the Ila are emphatic that their ancestral home was beside Lake Tanganyika and there are cultural links to support this claim.[2] In the Southern Province and nowhere else in Zambia the chiefs are always addressed as 'Mwami'; a thousand miles to the north, in Burundi, chiefs are given the same title. However, the Bantu Botatwe ('three people'—Tonga, Ila, Lenje) through contact, often enforced, with their neighbours such as the Kaonde and Lozi, have acquired many cultural traits which are essentially Congo-rooted.

It is believed that a section of the Tonga people were known several hundred years ago as the Mbara, and that they occupied an area both north and south of the Kafue river before 1500. In a map by Bartholomeu Velho dated 1561, they are marked in that area.[8] It has been suggested that they also spread across into what is now Southern Rhodesia and people with Tonga features are still called Mbara by the Shona. In 1514, the Portuguese explorer Antonio Fernandes described 'Chief Mobara's country' which he said was 'a journey of seven days from Monomotapa . . . there lies a great river between this king and the king of Monomotapa'.[4] Fernandes says that the people of Chief Mobara had 'tails like sheep' (ox skins, with tails hanging down?), but otherwise his record makes a great deal of sense. He writes: 'And from there they bring copper to sell it to Monomotapa in ingots like ours and also through the other land.' He describes how the people came in canoes across the 'great river' (obviously the Zambezi) and left their copper and ivory on the bank. Then the Arab traders would put their cloth down in exchange, beside the copper and ivory and go away. Chief Mobara's people would again canoe across the Zambezi to see if the offering of the Arabs was fair. Fernandes goes on: 'If they are not content they go away and leave it and do not return until more has been laid down, or they are brought back by signs.' According to Fernandes, the people living in this area were cannibals: 'And if any of them dies, they eat him and bury a cow.'

To the east of the Mbara (Tonga) country, other people who had arrived at a very early date in Zambia were the Nsenga and the Chewa.[5] The latter belonged to the Malawi (Maravi) group of peoples who were welded into a powerful empire several hundred years ago. Legends tell us that the Chewa came from the north-west, from the Luba empire of Chief Cawalamakumba in what is now the Congo. Led by Chief Kalonga they came on to Zambian territory near Lake Mweru, then went north to Lake Tanganyika and south-east to the Lake Nyasa region. The Nsenga,[6] who are now centred on the Petauke area of the Eastern Province, have similar origins, but Chewa claims that the Nsenga are just an offshoot of themselves set up by Chief Undi are probably untrue. Although Undi did install Chief Kalindawalo over some of the Nsenga about 1780, this was late in the history of the tribes.

Undoubtedly both the Chewa and the Nsenga came very early to the east of Zambia. When they arrived, the simple bushmen or Twa people were so hard to make contact with, that they were given the name Mwambonelakwisa ('Where have you seen me?'). There is a traditional story among Zambian tribes that the Twa always asked people they met: 'Did you see me before I saw you?' If the answer was negative the Twa were delighted but if told they had been seen first, they jumped up and down with rage.

The Nsenga went on to settle along the Zambezi east of the

confluence with the Luangwa, and soon made contact with the empire of Motapa in present-day Southern Rhodesia. Tradition says that Nsenga chief Nyambende of the Elephant (Nzou) clan was conquered by Samarengu, son of the first Motapa—and this is datable to about 1450. It is also related that other Nsenga clans (Mumba and Mvulu) were along the Zambezi at this time. There can be no doubt that like the people higher up the river Ilede, the Nsenga were trading with Arabs and Portuguese, then active in exporting ivory and gold from Central Africa; the Nsenga were perhaps too far east to act, like the Mbara, as middlemen in the copper trade.

VIII THE LUNDA EMPIRE AND THE PORTUGUESE

It is only the Bantu Botatwe tribes of the Southern Province and the nineteenth-century invaders who do not share a common origin with the rest of the Zambians. Even the Tonga and Ngoni are now closely integrated with the rest: many Tonga are permanently settled in Barotseland, where they were taken as slaves, and the Ngoni have adopted from the women of conquered enemies the local languages and customs. Although the Lozi and Bemba are now 800 miles apart, they both sprang from the great Lunda-Luba empire in the Congo. The Lozis (like the Kaonde, Lovale and Luapula valley Lunda) trace their history to the Lunda. The Bemba, Bisa, Lamba, Aushi and related groups belong rather to the Luba people.[1]

As early as AD 900 there had been a powerful Luba kingdom along the Lualaba river. The people were skilled coppersmiths and used copper ingots as currency.[2] Further west, near the Kasai river, the matrilineal Lunda people lived in a country they called Nkalanyi.[3] Little is known of the Lunda until about 1500, when they had their headquarters at Kapanga, a little to the east of the Kasai. The empire became great after a merger between the Lunda and Luba shortly before 1600. The cause of the merger we are told, was a love-at-first-sight meeting between Luweji, chieftainess of the Lunda, and Chibinda Ilunga, a chief of the Luba. This is how the Mwata Kazembe's tribal elders relate the story in the records of Zambia's Lunda people:[4]

> There came a man from the country of the Luba, and by tribe he was a Luba of Mbiti Chiluwe. In his occupation of hunting game he wandered about in many lands. He came to the country of the Lunda where Makwe Luweji reigned; he

had with him many peoples; he found a stream in the bush and built a rough shelter there and settled down to kill many animals. He went out in the morning and killed an eland which died some distance off, near the village of Makwe Luweji. He followed the trail of the animal a long way and found a well-worn path and realised there were people near. He had come a long distance so he followed the path which took him to a spring, where he sat down, very tired.

Then came women from the village to draw water, and he asked: 'Who is chief of the village?' and they answered: 'You who are asking about our village, where do you come from?' He replied: 'I am a stranger in this land.' The women went straightway off to the village, being very anxious to inform their husbands. They told them how they had found a man at the spring who said he was a stranger, and said they should go and talk to him. At once the men went and questioned him; and he told them where he had come from and all about himself. And he said he had come with many followers who had remained behind where he had built his shelter. The men said they were going to take him so that the Makwe could see him. They took the hunter to Makwe Luweji, and as soon as the Makwe saw him she loved him for he was handsome.[5]

And so they were married, and that is how the Lunda and Luba peoples joined together. But tradition tells us that some of Luweji's brothers were annoyed that their sister had chosen Chibinda Ilunga, a stranger, as her husband. They set off with followers to start a kingdom of their own. One of the brothers, Chikundi, headed west, and made contact with the Portuguese who had already been established around the mouth of the Congo since 1485.[6] This contact with the Portuguese in about 1600 was to have far-reaching effects, vestiges of which can be recognised today in two early Portuguese statues of the Virgin Mary among the relics in the sacred grove of Paramount Chief Chitimukulu of the Bemba. It is also thought that the iron-work bow stands used by certain chiefs, mainly in the North-Western Province, are half-remembered imitations of the candelabra used by sixteenth-century Jesuit priests in Angola.[7] It was from the Portuguese on the west coast that the central African hinterland received such crops as maize and cassava; these were introduced from Portugal's other colonial interest in South America, 1,500 miles across the Atlantic, and greatly increased the agricultural potential of the land.[8] These crops may have led to population increases which would have provoked migrations.

Far more profound, however, was the effect of the slave-trade which the Portuguese developed in the sixteenth and seventeenth centuries to stock the plantations in their new American colonies.

By the middle of the sixteenth century, the Portuguese were already probing inland. Cannibal mercenaries brought from Java in the East Indies were going as far as the Kwango river. Tribe was set against tribe. The slave-hunters were armed for their work with match-lock guns—primitive weapons but sufficient for spreading terror among unworldly people. A chain reaction was set off in places the Portuguese never had the forces to conquer and administer, but which they regarded as within their grasp. A Portuguese royal charter had declared that Angola was to be 'occupied and exploited in the name of God and the king'.[9] The *conquistadors* dreamed of the day when they would link hands across Africa, from the Congo to the Zambezi. In the east, even before 1600, they had reached Zumbo, 1,500 miles up the Zambezi on the borders of modern Zambia. In 1663, the Mozambique historian, M. C. Pereira, recorded that Portuguese traders had penetrated more than 700 miles inland from the Indian Ocean, 'to Boeca towards the kingdom of Angola'.[10] Authorities identify the Boeca as the BaWisa, living between the Chambeshi and Luangwa rivers of Zambia.

Thus, when the Lunda-Luba empire was penetrated by the Portuguese slave traders from the west, peoples of Luba origin who had earlier migrated into what is now Zambia, were meeting Portuguese adventurers from the east, looking for ivory and gold.

IX THE COMING OF THE BEMBA

It is generally accepted that weaker tribal groups explored eastward first into what is now Zambia from the Lunda-Luba region and as the stronger migratory movements developed the early arrivals were pushed farther and farther from their homeland. Then it became impossible to return westward; there were too many opponents in the way. It is said that the Chewa, who live east of the Luangwa, wanted to return home at the end of the eighteenth century to the Luba domain of Chief Cawalamakumba. But when they reached the Lenje country of Chief Mukuni (around the present Broken Hill) they were told about the fierceness of the Bemba across their projected route, and gave up the idea.[1]

The migrations into the 'northern wing of the Zambian

butterfly' in most cases involved a crossing of the Luapula river, now the boundary with the Congo. The Luapula valley itself is densely populated and the river is rich in fish—not to mention crocodiles and hippopotomi. The first people in the valley are said to have been the Bwilile and Shila who lived by fishing and were not averse to catching a hippo with harpoons if the need arose.[2]

Various small groups crossed the river until in the seventeenth century the Bemba appeared. The exact reason for their migration is not clear, although there is a probability that the stimulus of contact with the Portuguese played a part. Bemba tradition says that the Mukulumpe (tentatively identified with Chibinda Ilunga who married the Lunda chieftainess Luweji) punished his sons Chiti and Nkole for causing many deaths through some scheme of theirs. He made them sweep the royal yard and in anger they went off with their followers.[3]

What the ill-fated scheme of Chiti and Nkole was we do not know. However, the Bemba-speaking Lala people have their own tradition :

> In Lubaland the chief's sons met to drink beer and when they had drunk well one of them said : 'It is not good for us to live like we do in this country, it is too flat and if fighting men were to come, they could easily attack us and we should all be killed; let us build a high platform which will reach to heaven, then if the fighting men come we shall be able to climb to the top and shoot arrows at them.' His companions agreed : 'Yes, let us build.'
>
> At daybreak they began to build and they worked day after day and they had many workmen. One day, when many of them were on the top, and others were climbing up, some with poles and some with bark-rope, the whole thing fell down with a crash because the poles at the bottom had been eaten away by termites. Many people were killed, all those whom they had forced to work. Their father the chief was enraged : 'You sons of slave women, you have killed off my people to a man.' The chief's sons were terrified and there was a great scattering. . . .[4]

The Bemba crossed the Luapula well before 1700, (possibly as early as 1640) at Kashengeneke, and then moved eastward, setting up villages or camps as they went. They crossed the Chambeshi river at Safwa and then turned south-east between the Lala and the Bisa. On the journey, say some sources, the leaders Chiti and Nkole sent back a half-brother to fetch a sister, Bwalya Chabala, from the Congo, but on the way the half-brother committed incest with her. This anecdote may be true or perhaps a revival of the legends of 'Sudanic' ritual incest. The Bemba invaders moved on south-east to the country of the Nsenga, where Chiti is said to have seduced the wife of Mwase, and been killed with a poisoned arrow for his behaviour.[5] Nkole then killed Mwase, and his unfortunate wife, and burnt their bodies by the Katongo river. But the smoke from the fire made Nkole ill, and he died too.[6] After this gloomy series of events, the Bemba stopped their advance towards the Zambezi and turned back across the Chambeshi to settle on the plateau and consolidate their position. (It was not good farming country, but the Bemba have never been particularly interested in farming.)

As the eighteenth century arrived, the Bemba began to acquire territory at the expense of the people around them. These included the cattle-keeping Sukuma (Fipa), the Lungu iron-smelters, the Beba and the Mambwe, also called the Nkondo. The Mambwe in particular were worthy opponents of the Bemba and many fierce battles were joined with them. Later the Bemba were to become locked in combat with the Bisa.[7]

Not all the Bemba stayed on the plateau, however; one section of them headed westward towards the Luapula and established a domain there under Chief Nkuba. Today in the Congo, to the west of Lake Mweru, is a powerful Chief Nkuba who belongs to the *bena ngandu* (royal crocodile) clan like the Bemba rulers in Zambia.[8]

X THE LOZI ENTER THE VALLEY

Well before 1700, another group detached itself from the Lunda-Luba empire. Unlike the Bemba and their associates, this people did not cross the Luapula river but headed south and then south-west to the upper regions of the Zambezi. There are indications that it was a slow journey, extending over as many as twenty years, until the migrants established themselves in the flood-plain beyond the Luena confluence. These were the nucleus of the Lozi people, destined to become as supreme in the south as the Bemba in the north. It used to be asserted that the Lozi were an offshoot of the empire of Monomotapa in what is now Southern Rhodesia (and indeed Rozvi elements may have crossed the Zambezi to settle) but it has now been established that the Lozi are essentially akin to the Lunda.[1] Places with identical names (Imuba and Namayula) are found in both Lozi and Lunda territory, the dress of the rulers is similar and there are cultural parallels. Both Lunda and Lozi rulers wear feathers as part of their headdress, and like Mwata Yamvo, the Litungas wear a special necklace of white stones known to the Lozi as *mande*. The fact that the two groups revere their rulers, present and past, in the manner of Sudanic-type states is perhaps not so conclusive as is sometimes claimed, because the same structure exists to the south. Yet the evidence that the Lozi have blood ties with the Lunda appears overwhelming. Ecologists say the distinctive Lozi system of flood-plain farming must have been derived from the north-west. Finally, many words in Luyana, the old Lozi language, resemble Bemba.

When the Lozi first reached the Zambezi, they were given the name Luyi or Luyana, (foreigners) by the existing inhabitants, who called the country Ngulu. These people were Twa or Kwengo, who it is said talked a click language and were pale-skinned, and were driven away to the south-west to the edges of the Kalahari, or according to other tribal authorities, set to doing iron-work for their new masters. It is not clear whether the Nkoya people to the north-east arrived in what is now Zambia before, or after, the Lozi, but the two groups are now closely connected and despite some disagreement the baNkoya were incorporated in Barotseland under colonial rule.[2] So also were the Lovale, although the Lovale were later 'liberated'.[3] On linguistic and other grounds the Kaonde farther north are regarded as much nearer the Bemba, although Kaonde history makes it clear that the tribe owed allegiance through Chief Musokantanda, who lived in the Congo north of Solwezi, to the Lunda ruler Mwata Yamvo.[4]

The Lozi were ruled by women when they first made their home by the Zambezi. Their queen was Mwambwa, whose daughter Mbuya succeeded her and gave birth to numerous sons and daughters who established themselves around her domain. There is a story that Mwambwa's followers began to plot against her, so she handed power over to her son Mboo.[5] There is also the tale that Mwambwa's daughter committed incest (the recurrent theme) and that the father of the children will remain a secret for ever. The Lunda of the Luapula valley declare that the Lozi were the followers of Mutanda Yembeyembe, younger brother of the first Lunda Mwata Yamvo. They say that Mutanda fled to the Zambezi after killing two chiefs in a quarrel over a discovery of salt on the Lualaba river,[6] but this story does not feature in Lozi tradition.

When the Lozi reached the plain in the Libonda-Lealui area they found conditions ideal for a settled, highly-organised life. There was excellent pasture for their cattle, which were driven up into the woodlands during the floods, fish was abundant in the Zambezi and could be easily trapped in the shallow lakes, honey was readily available from the forests and the area was rich in game, especially the red lechwe. There seems little doubt that the Lozi were at least as fortunate as any of the immigrant tribes in their choice of a new homeland. For more than a hundred years they lived unchallenged and untroubled, while extending their sway over a score of 'lesser' tribes around them.[7] The plain, eighty miles long by twenty miles wide, with woodlands around it, provided for all their needs. Over all, the Litunga reigned supreme: when a ruler died, his most revered *indunas* (chiefs) committed suicide by drowning. Every morning the people followed the Litunga in the rite of prostration to the rising sun.[8]

XI MWATA KAZEMBE AND LACERDA

About half a century after the Bemba and Lozi had migrated to Zambia, another movement eastwards from the Kasai river took place. Several sons of Mwata Yamvo ('Lord of Death') Mukanzo were sent out to conquer new lands to the south and east. One of the sons was Kanyembo Mpemba, and after a long and slow journey he reached the Luapula river south of Lake Mweru, close to the place where the Bemba had crossed before.

The reasons for the second Lunda exodus are not clear. According to one account, Kanyembo Mpemba was on an expedition to collect slaves for trading with the Portuguese at Luanda.[1] The official record of the Eastern Lunda is, however, far more heroic. It tells how Kanyembo travelled from the west in a *muselo* (a zebra-skin litter borne by eight men) surrounded by drummers and dancers and many troops, with axe-men to cut a swathe through the bush before his path.[2] One story says that the Lunda were shown where to ford the river by a chief's daughter they found digging for edible roots; they tied a rope around her waist so that she could not escape and used her as a guide.

Mwata Kazembe Kanyembo had little trouble in conquering the local chiefs along the east of the Luapula; his men were, for one thing, equipped with guns, probably match-lock or flint-lock muzzle-loaders obtained from half-caste traders in exchange for slaves or ivory. There is also a recurrent legend that they were greatly helped in finding a way through the country by Namfumu na Chituti, sister of Nkuba, who was the most powerful chief in the area. Apparently Nkuba's sister wanted to be revenged, because Nkuba had killed her son and used his skin as a doormat.[3]

Kanyembo died soon after the Luapula crossing in 1740 and was followed by Mwata Kazembe Ilunga Lukwesa, who was to rule for nearly fifty years and spread the fame of the Lunda far and wide. According to Lunda history, the tribe conquered as far as Lake Nyasa to the east, and received tribute in the form of cattle from as far south as Barotseland.[4] These claims would appear to be excessive, but there can be no doubt that Mwata Ilunga soon managed to dominate the trade to both east and west from his capital beside the Mofwe Lagoon. The Angolan half-castes at the court of Mwata Yamvo learnt of Kazembe; so did the Mozambique half-castes and Goans at Tete.

The names of the first Europeans to enter the land that has become Zambia can be uncovered from a study of old Portuguese documents. The knowledge we have is fragmentary but it seems certain there were illiterate traders wandering through the heart of Africa in the early eighteenth century whose experiences were never recorded. In the east, one natural route was up the Luangwa river from its confluence with the Zambezi. At the confluence, Zumbo was settled in 1714 and early records talk of gold mines to the north.[5] In 1732, Feira ('Market') was founded on the far side of the Luangwa on Zambian soil. The most prominent Portuguese figure of the time was a Jesuit monk, Father Pedro da Trinidade, who owned a gold mine near Zumbo called Chipapa.[6] The lure of gold doubtless drew other Portuguese into the upper Zambezi region: there are numerous references to such mines, worked by 'negresses' under the command of the *prazeros.*[7] Father Pedro was known to the local Nsenga and Soli people as *'Pai',* (father) and also as *'Khoma nyundo'* (to strike with a hammer) because he fed the Africans during a severe famine, in return for which they worked with picks and hammers to build the church and convent at Zumbo.[8] He was Captain of the Zumbo-Feira Settlement and died in 1751.

Between 1754 and 1756, Feira was attacked and sacked by Changamire's tribesmen and the governor at Sena, farther down the Zambezi, sent an army officer, Joao de Souza, to investigate the affair.[9] Souza was later appointed the commandant at Feira. However, Feira remained a hazardous outpost and did not compare in importance with Tete, which in 1788 became the seat of government, and had a garrison of eighty men, with two churches, a hospital, a prison and a factory. It is important not to exaggerate the extent of Portuguese colonialism in Central Africa, up to the eighteenth century, and it has been established that the total non-African population of Mozambique was rarely more than a thousand, a large proportion of whom were Indians from the Portuguese colony of Goa.[10] Portugal lacked the resources to administer or colonise its empire properly, and it was primarily concerned with clinging to its rich plantations in Brazil. When it came to supplying slaves for Brazil, Angola was the closest hunting-ground, although many ships did take human cargoes from the Zambezi valley around the Cape from 1645 onwards.[11] Portuguese African colonisation between latitudes 6° and 20° south was a frail thing, mostly existing in name only, but it had little competition.

The first official attempt to open an overland route from coast to coast across southern Africa by way of the capital of Mwata Kazembe, although planned more than thirty years earlier by Coutinho, governor of Angola, did not in fact take place until 1798. The attempt was made by a half-caste Brazilian scholar, Dr Francisco José Maria de Lacerda e Almeida.[12] We first hear of Lacerda in 1797, in Angola, where he proposed a chain of fortified posts in the interior to 'explore the copper mines'. He also sent a memorandum to the Minister of State in Lisbon, advocating an expedition from east to west across Africa. Lacerda declared:

> Iron which abounds in the interior is an article which interests us not a little. The negresses smelt this metal from the stones everywhere containing it, and considering the lack of tools it is astonishing how well and how cheaply they make their *assegais,* chains and similar articles. . . . There is an even greater abundance of excellent copper which they convert into ornaments, collars, wristlets and anklets.[13]

It is not clear why Lacerda did not attempt a crossing from west to east, since he was already in Angola. Several years before he wrote to Lisbon, two *pombeiros* (half-caste bondsmen) from Luanda, Alexandre da Silva Teixeira and José de Assumpçao Mello, had entered the Zambezi valley from the west and bartered with the people in what is now Balovale District.[14] They were well received and 'business was prosperous'.

It is plain from what Livingstone was to report fifty years later that Mulambwa (also called Santuru), the Lozi Paramount Chief who reigned from about 1780 to 1830, had regularly sent canoes up the river to the Lovale to buy European clothes, crockery and beads.[15]

Lacerda's proposal for an east-west rather than a west-east crossing was one that met with approval from Lisbon. The British occupation of the Cape in 1795 had given a new urgency to the project. There was a possibility that the Portuguese sea routes to the East Indies might now be imperilled. Lacerda suggested another danger too. 'The new possessors of Table Bay require careful watching, or our want of energy will enable them to extend themselves northwards. Who will prevent these new colonies from selling slaves of our southern interior, thus probably injuring our trade?'[16]

In 1798, Lacerda had sailed around Africa and been appointed governor of Sena. Speedily he assembled his expedition, which has been described with some justification as 'an amazing cavalcade'. It included 400 African porters, fifty men-at-arms, two envoys, a chaplain (Father Francisco Joao Pinto) and three guides. Two of the guides were Gonçalo Caetano Pereira, a half-caste from Tete who had visited Mwata Kazembe two years earlier, and his son Manoel.[17] So on July 3, 1798, Lacerda and his great company set out westwards from Tete. But the ambitious Brazilian was never again to see the Atlantic Ocean that washed his homeland.

XII 'THE INSOLENCE OF THE CAFFRES'

A great disadvantage facing Francisco de Lacerda as he advanced towards the heart of Africa was the reputation of the Portuguese. By this time they had been completely identified with slavery and repression, so the unfortunate explorer was unable to command any loyalty from his over-large retinue and had to have the porters flogged repeatedly. From his diary it is clear that the porters 'worked to rule' at best. He was soon faced with mass desertions and had to employ 200 women to carry the loads. Lacerda wrote miserably: 'My sleep is lost and my days are spent in thinking how to obviate the delays, the slow marches and the insolence of the Caffres. . . . When I send a command to be executed, all cry out and do nothing'.[1]

He was soon to fall victim to malaria and had to be carried in a *machila* (a type of palanquin carried on poles). After six weeks of laboured progress, he crossed into what is now Zambia on August 18, 1798. He had passed by many small mines being worked by the inevitable 'negresses' and shortly after crossing the Chambeshi river wrote in his diary: 'Many Muizas (Bisa tribesmen) passed us yesterday, coming from King Kazembe, with ivory and copper bars for sale'.[2] It is plain that the Lunda had a strong grip on the export of copper from Katanga to the east coast.

It is also obvious from his diary that there was a busy traffic across the plateau to the Luangwa river. On September 21, 1798, Lacerda refers to the 'high road' along which were many villages. He went on:

> To the northward lies the Uemba [Bemba] nation, between the Muizas [Bisa] and the Mussucuma [Sukuma], who reach

> the banks of the Chire [Shire] or Nhanja [Lake Nyasa]. Also they assure us that the Uemba and the Mussucuma are mortal enemies to, never sparing, the Kazembe's people; but they are equally so with the Muizas, whom they know by their combed heads. On the south are the Arambas [Lamba] and the Ambos, peaceful friends of Kazembe, who trade, they declare, with the Caffres near Zumbo.[3]

This is the first written record of several Zambian tribes, showing that they were living approximately in their present homes more than 160 years ago.

After a disastrous journey of three months from the Zambezi to Lake Mweru, the hungry remnants of the expedition staggered into Mwata Kazembe's presence. Lacerda was at the end of his resources and died a fortnight later. The Jesuit chaplain, Father Francisco Joao Pinto, took over command, but bitter quarrels immediately broke out. The thousand-mile journey westwards to Luanda must have appeared impossibly daunting; even to the half-caste Pereiras it was completely unknown territory. There is also reason to think that the Lunda were lacking enthusiasm for the whites and half-castes who for months afterwards hung around the capital.[4]

In twos and threes the Portuguese left Kazembe and took the highway through Bisa country back to Tete. Then on July 26, 1799, Father Pinto himself turned back. The following excerpts from his diary show how the party fared:

> The Caffres of the expedition having refused to carry me, I begged Lieutenant-Colonel Pedro Nolasco to lend me nine of the slaves of D. Francisca, settling that their loads should be committed to my wild Caffres, who each walked in chains. . . . This day we passed by the village of a Murando Caffre, when our soldiers began to rob poultry. . . . José Rodrigues Caleja was marching so fast that he would not trouble himself with the sick slaves of the Crown, and whenever one could not walk his head was cut off. . . . At 10 a.m. we reached the Chambeze [Chambeshi] river, which was not fordable, as before. We were, therefore, obliged to bargain for canoes, and the Caffres kept us till 3 p.m. We were obliged to give up to them all our remaining cloth, copper and calaim, our beads, copper bracelets and ivory. . . . The provisions were dear; apparently the Muizas [Bisa] had passed on the word to starve us. They were envious of our ivory and slaves, and they looked upon us as their rivals in the trade. Here begins a regular system of blackmail, and Gonçalo Caetano Pereira,

> having finished his cloth, gave a small slave girl. . . . After a short distance we reached a village where they robbed us of two other hoes and a tusk. They also wounded a Caffre with a poisoned arrow. . . .[5]

From then on the journey became a rout, with constant fighting with the Bisa villagers and insubordination from the slaves. Once the wretched priest was deliberately dropped in a river by his bearers and food became so short that he had to barter 'a little negress' for a few ground-nuts and some millet. Supplies were abandoned in desperation. At last the remnants staggered to the outskirts of Tete, where Father Pinto waited until after dark before entering the town because of his ragged condition.

Seven years later, the authorities in Angola gave two *pombeiros* orders to cross the continent from west to east. The two were Pedro Joao Battista and Amaro José; the former could write a little and kept a diary.[6]

Following the accepted route inland, the traders went first to the court of Mwata Yamvo and with many halts from there followed the well-worn track to the Luapula and the court of Kazembe. By the time they arrived, the old ruler, Ilunga Lukwesa, had died and been succeeded by the much inferior Chibangu Keleka. The Lunda kept the *pombeiros* prisoners for four years and only released them when a trade mission arrived from Tete and discovered the unfortunate pair; after being escorted to Tete, the *pombeiros* gave an account of their experiences before trekking back to Angola. Thus they achieved a double crossing.

Battista made a number of interesting observations about the journey. At the village of Chamuguiga in Katanga 'natives dig the copper; in the midst of the country is where they dig the bars'. Two Africans owned the deposit and were assisted by their children and slaves. 'To the west of the Luapula, greenstones (copper-bearing malachite) are found in the ground called Catanga.'

In the first quarter of the nineteenth century, the power of the Kazembes was in decline, but still retained enough magic for the Portuguese to make them send another expedition from Tete in 1831. Captain Antonio Candido Pedroso Gamitto was second-in-command, and described the eastern Lunda capital as 'a good market for buying ivory, copper and slaves'. The expedition itself was equipped with 120 slaves as porters.

Gamitto's chief was Major José Maria Correa Monteiro, who later became the commandant of Feira. The two soldiers, who were accompanied by half-caste traders with fifty more slaves of their own, reached Mwata Kazembe in November 1831. Just before they arrived, one of the traders died and Gamitto expropriated his donkey. He rode on it into the Lunda capital, and by his own account was a remarkable spectacle, with his beard and hair grown long, and dressed in a blue jacket, white trousers and scarlet sash.[7] Gamitto says that the people were impressed, describing him and the donkey as 'a man with six legs' and being astounded when it brayed. In the Lunda account of Gamitto's visit, the attitude of the Portuguese to Africans is well revealed by the information that the traders flung handfuls of beads among the people in front of Kazembe's palace. Quarrels soon broke out between the expedition and its hosts.

After the abortive journey of Monteiro and Gamitto, the Portuguese appear to have abandoned their dream of straddling the 'interior' between Mozambique and Angola. Until much later in the nineteenth century, almost their only contact with the people of the future Zambia was through wandering slavers known as Mambari in the west and Chikunda in the east. Yet between 1830 and 1840, new and crucial influences were already converging on the Zambia region. The first was coming from the far south, where powerful warrior groups were migrating in search of new homes. The second was from the north-east, from the slave-hungry sultanate of Zanzibar. The last was to come from the offices of the London Missionary Society in early-Victorian England. All three forces—African, Arab and European—were soon to meet and inter-act in the vast unmapped tract of country between the Zambezi and Lake Tanganyika.

XIII THE NGONI INVADERS

On November 20, 1835, a few miles from Feira, Zwangendaba crossed the Zambezi river from the south with about 1,000 followers and many head of cattle. The date is known precisely, because tribal history records that while the crossing was in progress there was an eclipse of the sun.[1] The Ngoni's reputation spread before them and drove fear into the hearts of the Zambian tribes. In Chief Chinoyi's area, three days from the river, Zwangendaba had ordered some truculent opponents to be flung head-first down a deep hole in the ground (the caves near the town called Sinoia).[2] The Ngoni were formidable warriors, attacking in a tight arc and using short stabbing spears instead of bows and arrows. When they took captives, they did not sell them into slavery, but either made them grow crops or absorbed them into the tribal regiments which were formed frequently; the new warriors were accepted as Ngoni and had equal opportunities to reach positions of authority. Later, the captors even adopted the local languages from the women they took in war.[3]

By the time the Zambezi was reached, only a small élite could claim to be Ngoni (the name derives from Nguni which the true Zulus called themselves). Yet the discipline instilled by this élite was to make the Ngoni feared as far north as Lake Tanganyika for the next twenty years. Zwangendaba led his people forward slowly, forming new regiments as he did so. Rather than fight it out and meet defeat and death, many villagers 'joined up' voluntarily. The original thousand increased many times over. By 1845, the Ngoni had reached the northern end of Lake Nyasa. Then Zwangendaba died and the Ngoni split up, some pressing farther in their astounding migration until they reached Lake Victoria, 3,000 miles from Natal. One of Zwangendaba's sons, called Mpezeni, decided to turn westward towards the country of the Bemba. This led to violent war between two tribes equally renowned for military prowess.[4]

For several years the Ngoni under Mpezeni raided the fringes of the Bemba people to the north and east of the plateau and a number of minor chiefs submitted to them. They also played havoc among the Bisa, who had become subservient to the Bemba after a series of battles earlier in the century.

By 1850, the Ngoni were established along the Muchinga Escarpment, where they sent out *impis* in every direction. Their nearest victims were the Lala in the Serenje area, but they also went as far as the Lamba country in what is now the Copperbelt and attacked the Lenje along the upper Kafue. One group entered the Tabwa country near Lake Mweru but were repulsed by Senior Chief Nsama.[5]

To the south-east, the Ngoni met stiffer resistance from the Chewa, who were well armed with flint-lock muzzle-loaders obtained from the Chikunda slave-traders of the Zumbo area. Mpezeni's warriors also fought and defeated a marauding group called the Bapule and drove them off towards Lake Nyasa; there is some mystery about the Bapule, but it is thought they were a splinter group of the Kololo (also from Natal).

For the Bemba, the activities of the Ngoni newcomers were far from welcome. They regarded slave-raiding between the Luapula and the Luangwa as their own prerogative, and on occasion had made sorties as far south as present-day Broken Hill, to prey on the Lenje. Under the leadership of Chitimukulu Chileshe Chepela, the Bemba united to oust the Ngoni.[6] The decisive collision began in about 1855, when a series of battles were fought. It was gunpowder which decided the issue, for the Bemba had many firearms provided by the Arabs in exchange for slaves. The fighting ranged as far north as Isoka district, where today there is still to be seen a monument to a Bemba 'company commander' who fell victim to the Ngoni stabbing spears; a pair of elephant tusks were placed on his grave by a former Chief Nkula.[7]

In 1865 the Ngoni under Mpezeni retired across the Luangwa and by 1870 had settled permanently in their present home around Fort Jameson.[8] Seven years later, another Ngoni army under Ngonomo and Chidumayi met the Bemba west of the Muchinga mountains and the fighting lasted three days, but Chitimukulu's supremacy remained unchallenged in the plateau.[9] Yet Mpezeni's Ngoni were to remain a powerful force in the east for another twenty years, until they were crushed and impoverished by opponents of another kind and another colour.

XIV SEBITUANE CONQUERS BAROTSELAND

Three or four years after the Ngoni had crossed the Zambezi into Nsenga country, another group of invaders crossed the great river, 500 miles to the west. These were the Kololo, led by a remarkable Basuto commoner called Sebituane. The Kololo were in many ways similar to the Ngoni: their wanderings began through the upheavals caused in Natal by Chaka, and their long migration had included many battles in which elements of other tribes had been absorbed.[1] It was the tough, light-skinned Basuto nucleus which kept Sebituane's company together as it struggled stubbornly from the Limpopo to the Chobe and then towards the Zambezi. At first, the Kololo did not enter the heart of Barotseland. After halting to fight at Linyanti,[2] they crossed the southern extremities of the kingdom. Then they went north-east into Batokaland (near the site of the present-day Kalomo) and might have remained there but for an invasion by the Matabele under Mzilikazi, himself a warrior who had fled north from Natal. This provoked Sebituane to begin a new journey to the west, through the lands of the Ila (Mashukulumbwe).[3]

By this time, estimated to be 1840 or shortly before, the Lozi people had established a powerful state to which tribes all around the flood plain paid tribute. There were still connections, both in custom and language, with the old Lunda empire to the north, but the Lozi had acquired a character of their own through the absorption of new elements. These included Mbunda peoples who had migrated from the west (probably to avoid the Portuguese slave-traders at the turn of the century).[4] There were also minor incursions by Bechuana peoples from across the Zambezi. One ruler who had been largely instrumental in building up the tight administration and military structure of the Lozi had been Mulambwa, Litunga since about 1780.[5] His slaves had enlarged the mounds dotted around the plain and had planted trees for shade. Mulambwa had pushed out the bounds of his domain by war and laid down a series of laws by which justice was to be done. He made contact with the outside world through the Mambari half-castes who were penetrating the valley in growing numbers.

The Lozi must also have had contact with Arab and Portuguese traders to the east. The Tonga peoples, whom the Lozi by now dominated, had long maintained trade links with Zumbo, Tete and Monomotapa. Livingstone wrote that Mulambwa had a canoe 'of planks sewn together, which was so large it required twenty men to paddle it'. Gervas Clay makes an interesting observation upon this description: 'It is curious that canoes of planks sewn together should be the type used in the Indian Ocean and not, apparently, indigenous to Africa.'[6] Certainly it is surprising that Mulambwa did not find it easier to have nails made by the renowned iron-workers of Kalabo. Could it be that Mulambwa had employed itinerant Arab traders who had wandered far up the Zambezi, to make his royal craft for him?

It seems that Mulambwa had died by the time Sebituane attacked the Lozi in the flood plain. There is still a conflict of opinion both as to the date of the attack and as to whether Sebituane temporarily settled in the Batoka highlands (finding them healthier) after and not before he overwhelmed the established power. However, even if Mulambwa was still living, he must by then have been an old man with less enthusiasm for war than he had in his prime; according to James Chapman, who travelled through the Zambezi valley in 1862, Mulambwa fled 'into Central Africa' from Sebituane without fighting or even meeting the foe.[7] There is certainly no doubt that the Kololo (who like the related Ngoni fought with stabbing spears and carried large ox-hide shields) were too formidable in battle for the Lozi. The latter were also weakened at the time by a power struggle between the sons of Mulambwe; an uncle called Selumalumi was holding the throne. Sebituane and his general Bololo swept all before them. Some of the Lozi chiefs took service under the Kololo, while others fled to the north and west and retained their independence.[8]

Sebituane set about consolidating his power and increasing

the wealth of the Kololo-Barotse kingdom. He achieved the former by installing his own people all over the domain, so that one family occupied a dominant position in every village. Kololo became the *lingua franca* to such an extent that within a few years the old Luyana tongue had been almost forgotten. Sebituane also won the loyalty of the offspring of Mulambwa by his kindness: 'So we found him, with even the sons of the chiefs of the Barotse closely attached to his person . . .' wrote Livingstone in 1851. The Kololo had also brought with them from the south cattle of a larger type than those which existed previously north of the Zambezi; these served to improve the Barotse herds.[9]

Yet Sebituane was not able to devote himself to husbandry and the improvement of his kingdom undisturbed. He had to fight off repeated attacks from other predatory hordes who originated, like himself, from beyond the Limpopo. One of these was the Zulu plunderer Nxaba, who had crossed the Zambezi about the same time as the Ngoni, but somewhat farther west, and had long been causing havoc along the Kafue. Sebituane met Nxaba (or Ngabe) in battle, killed him and wiped out his force. More troublesome were the Matabele hordes, who took it as their right to seize slaves from the subject people of the Barotse.

One encounter with the Matabele was near Linyanti and when Sebituane suspected a plot to kill him, he decided to meet treachery with treachery. The Matabele had asked for a parley, pretending that they were quarrelling among themselves and wanted the Kololo to support one faction against the other. Sebituane told his men to shorten their spears into daggers and hide them in their clothing. When the parley began, the Matabele were told to leave their arms behind. 'Which one is Sebituane?' they demanded. The Kololo pointed out not Sebituane but one of his lieutenants. The Matabele answered, 'That is not the man', and identified Sebituane correctly. At this, the Kololo brought out their daggers and wiped out their enemies.[10]

On another occasion the Matabele raided Sebituane's temporary capital in the Batoka country and captured many women and cattle. Sebituane, who had been away at the time, hurried after the raiders when he heard what had happened, caught up with them south of the Zambezi and successfully freed the women and recaptured the cattle. Probably the most famous story of Sebituane's military cunning concerns his destruction of a Matabele army on Beta Island, just south of Senanga. There are several variations, and this is Gibbons's account:

> The army was allowed to advance a considerable distance

without opposition, but also without the means to replenish their supplies, for everything edible was transferred to the many islands in the river. At length their route took them past an island from which the bleating of a goat was heard. In the reeds they discovered a man in a canoe, apparently in hiding. In answer to questions, he stated that many Makololo with their women and cattle were on the island, and under penalty of death he was ordered to ferry them across. The canoe plied backwards and forwards until a sufficient force was concentrated on the island to advance from cover to the attack. The Makololo [sic] now upset the canoe and swam away to safety, drowning the Matabele who guarded him. To their discomfiture, the warriors found they had been outwitted, for the only living creature on the island was a tethered kid bleating for its mother. Those on the island died of starvation, and few of the remainder, if any, survived to tell the tale.

2

Contending Forces of the Nineteenth Century

I LIVINGSTONE, 1851–60

THE idea that the white travellers of the nineteenth century really 'discovered' the lakes, rivers and mountains of Africa's interior has become increasingly discredited and unpopular. Yet it is true that the journeys of the European explorers a century ago marked the beginning of a new era in the heart of Africa. The long isolation of history was at an end.

Supreme among these white travellers was David Livingstone, who first set foot on Zambian soil at the age of 38 and was to die on it nearly a generation later. He pursued a myth derived from the writings of Herodotus, the Greek 'father of history', that the Nile had its source in a series of fountains. Livingstone's obsession that they bubbled out of the earth somewhere beyond Lake Bangweulu drew him to his death at Chitambo's village, 130 miles north-east of the Copperbelt. In his 10,000 miles of tramping, Livingstone crossed and recrossed Zambia, visiting places where probably no white man had been before; if they had, they had left no records.

Livingstone's unique role in the history of Zambia was that by the account of his journeys he brought mysterious Central Africa into the forefront of attention in Victorian England. He signposted the way which other men of quite different character and motives were to follow, while he himself epitomised the questing ideals of his century.

Livingstone had decided, while he was studying medicine in Glasgow, that he would become a missionary in China, but had to abandon this aim because of Palmerston's 'Opium War'. Then through the London Missionary Society he met Robert Moffat, who since January 1817 had been working for that body in southern Africa. Livingstone was drawn by the challenge of the 'dark continent' and early in 1841, soon after he became a doctor, he arrived at Moffat's missionary headquarters in Kuruman (now in Cape Province, South Africa). Shortly afterwards, the London Missionary Society decreed that its representatives should move farther into the interior and Livingstone heard the news with 'inexpressible delight' and immediately advanced into what is now Bechuanaland.[1] After four years at Mabotsa he had collected much information about the country beyond the Kalahari desert; Griqua traders had gone on ahead and the migration of the Makololo to Barotseland had opened up lines of communication; many rumours about the interior were also coming back from those Boers who had extended the Great Trek across the Orange river to the Limpopo and even beyond. Livingstone, who always detested the Boers for their treatment of the Africans (they in turn hated him and plundered his mission at Kolobeng),[2] wrote, 'Who will penetrate Africa?'

In 1849, Livingstone crossed the Kalahari for the first time and in August reached Lake Ngami, that unpredictable stretch of water 200 miles south of the Zambezi; with him were two English big-game hunters, William Oswell and Mungo Murray.[3] It was a decisive event, for the former mill-boy had begun his historic journeys. Next year he went back across the Kalahari, taking with him his wife Mary (Robert Moffat's daughter) and their young children. His objective was the Barotse valley, where the Kololo ruler Sebituane was waiting to receive him. But his hopes were frustrated when the children and the Livingstone's servants were attacked with fever beside Lake Ngami. Mary Livingstone had obviously been seriously affected by the rigours of the journey because she was expecting a baby (which died only a few weeks after it was born in Kolobeng) and she herself was paralysed in the face. Livingstone was not deterred, however, and resolved to take his family (his wife, pregnant again), with him on a third expedition.

The expedition got under way in April 1851. The Livingstones and their children (Robert, five, Agnes, three and Thomas, two) were accompanied by their wealthy friend William Oswell and his Jamaican servant, George Fleming. There was difficulty in obtaining guides for the route to Sebituane, because the intervening chiefs had sent back the Kololo messengers. They were reluctant to open the way, over which they had a monopoly, along which ivory came down from the Barotse valley.

On June 18, the expedition reached the Chobe river, where it was greeted by one of Sebituane's senior *indunas,* Ponwane, a Lozi and not a Kololo. 'Many of the people were clothed in European manufactures, one had a dressing-gown on, and a red worsted nightcap.'[4] The extent to which their hosts were wearing European clothes in the 'far interior' astonished the expedition at first. William Oswell pointed out: 'Many of Sebituane's followers were dressed in green baize, red drugget, calico and cheap gaudy cloth. . . .'[5] It was only later that Livingstone realised that Mambari slave-traders were very active in the Zambezi valley, selling goods brought from Angola, and even making shoes for the Kololo. Long before Sebituane arrived on the Zambezi, the region had obtained trade goods from the west.

Portuguese and Arabs were visiting the Zambezi valley; the caravans of Syde bin Habib were travelling right across the continent from Zanzibar to Benguela seeking slaves and ivory. Approaching from Bihe in the west, an Hungarian called Magyar Laszlo had passed through Lovale and Lunda country in 1849–50 and Joaquim Graca took much the same route a year or two earlier. The notable adventurer Francisco da Silva (usually called Silva Porto) made several journeys into Barotseland around the middle of the century. Livingstone was to meet Porto at Naliele in 1853, and although calling him the 'headman of the Mambari' admitted rather reluctantly that the Portuguese did his utmost to be friendly; Porto was trying to cross the continent at the time, but turned back and sent some of his *pombeiros* across to Mozambique by way of the Copperbelt and Chewa country.

All accounts agree that the visitors made a tremendous impression on Sebituane when he met them on the Chobe on June 21, 1851. He was genuinely interested in the skills of the whites and also felt that their presence would safeguard him from the constant raids of the Matabele. His capital was established on the north bank of the river to watch out for raiders, and it was only when it proved impossible to transport Livingstone's waggons across to him that he moved his headquarters to the south bank to be with the visitors.[6] Livingstone greatly disapproved of Sebituane's habit of smoking *dagga* (hemp).

Ironically, the visit of the whites was probably fatal for the intelligent and friendly Sebituane. According to Livingstone, the Kololo chief died (a mere sixteen days after the expedition arrived) from pneumonia caused by the flare-up of an old wound, 'just over the region of the liver', received in battle thirty years before.[7] The

African story is that Sebituane had ridden horses in his youth in Basutoland and was anxious to try the saddle again. Livingstone and Oswell had travelled on horse-back, so the missionary let Sebituane ride his own mount. It was a lively animal and the chief, who by this time was grown old and emaciated, fell off and suffered serious hurt. He quickly became desperately ill.

Livingstone was cautious about trying to cure the chief, who had several African doctors treating him: 'I saw his danger, but, being a stranger, I feared to treat him medically, lest, in the event of his death, I should be blamed by his people.'[8] There was also the difficulty that Mrs Livingstone was pregnant, and tribal superstition held that a sick person could be made worse by a visit from the husband of a woman in such a condition.[9] On the day before Sebituane died, Livingstone and his son Robert went to see him, standing at the door of his home. The chief's last words before the whites were when he told a servant to take little Robert to his wife Maunko, to 'get some milk for him'. Livingstone wrote: 'Poor Sebituane, my heart bleeds for thee. . . . Little didst thou think, when in the visit of the white men thou sawest the long cherished desires of years accomplished, that the sentence of death had gone forth. . . .'[10]

Rather astonishingly, the Kololo remained equally affable towards Livingstone after Sebituane's death. They said: 'Do not leave us, though Sebituane is gone. His children remain and you must treat them as you would have treated him. No blame can be attached to you.'[11]

At the beginning of August, Livingstone and Oswell crossed the Linyanti (Chobe) leaving Mrs Livingstone behind with the waggons, she being only a few weeks from her confinement. The two men, with the guidance of the Kololo, made their way on horseback towards the Zambezi (which they knew as the Sesheke, after the town at the point where crossings were usually made). With increasing excitement they drew nearer the river and reached it on the afternoon of August 4.[12] 'All we could say to each other was, "How glorious! How magnificent! How beautiful!"' They crossed on to Zambian soil briefly and heard about the Victoria Falls from the local chiefs, Mwanamwali and Monibothale. 'Four days below Sesheke is situated the waterfall of Mosiotunya, or "resounding smoke". It is so named because of the spray rising with great noise so high as to be visible ten or twelve miles off.'[13]

In 1851, the Luyi and other pre-Kololo people were in the grip of domestic slavery, and Sebituane had also exchanged fourteen-year old boys with slavers for old guns (a gun for a boy). This made him even stronger as a ruler, and he then acquired English muskets by selling captives to the Arabs.[14]

Yet Livingstone made a prophetic observation about the moribund Kololo, who soon were to be wiped out by their own subjects. They had suffered severely from malaria in the marshy Linyanti area, while the Lozi did not seem so susceptible. The Kololo were 'all sickly looking and yellow' when compared with their powerfully built subjects.[15] It would seem they were also suffering from syphilis, caught from the Ila tribe.[16] Under the shrewd Sebituane, the Kololo could maintain their position, but when he died they were doomed. Sebituane told his daughter Mamochisane that she should become the chief after him; and in the way male chiefs constantly took new wives, so she must have many husbands. This did not appeal to Mamochisane, who abdicated, and gave the throne to her younger brother Sekeletu, who was barely seventeen years old. With his Kololo aides dying round him, and the Matabele worrying him from the south, the boy ruler had too much strain imposed upon him.

After a trip to Capetown to send his wife and four children home to England, Livingstone came back to Zambian soil in the middle of 1853. Sekeletu and some of his followers were by this time riding around on oxen, following advice given by the missionary to the ill-fated Sebituane. With a group of porters (described as Kololo, although few of them were) Livingstone began his journey late in 1853 to Luanda on the west coast.

The missionary's intentions in making the journey through Angola were to seek an easy route by which doctors, teachers and missionaries could reach the hinterland north of the Zambezi; he had decided that the long trek through Bechuanaland was too hazardous, because of both the lack of water and the hostile Boers. But after seven months of struggling through the barbaric wilds of Angola, its people half-crazed by centuries of the slave-trade, he realised that this again was no gateway to Zambia.[17] At the Atlantic, Livingstone turned back with his porters and retraced the way he had come from the Zambezi. As he walked (with stubborn Scottish pride, he nearly always walked, despising the Portuguese way of being carried in a *machila*)[18] the missionary doctor again saw the grim evidence of 'the trade' everywhere. His mind burned in anguish and he was to write: 'The strangest disease I have seen in this country seems really to be broken-heartedness, and it attacks free men who have been captured and made slaves.'[19] In later life, especially after his wife had died of malaria on the lower Zambezi in 1862, he became irascible and quarrelsome; few of his fellow Europeans could get on with him, and he preferred to travel only with Africans. Yet in his deep sympathy, his 'human kindness' as the Lunda called it, his failings were enveloped and became nothing.

On November 16, 1855, during the west-to-east march across the continent, the Kololo took him to see the world's most awe-inspiring waterfalls, which he promptly named after Queen Victoria: 'I decided to use the same liberty as the Makololo did and gave the only English name I have ever affixed to any part of the country.'[20]

He went by canoe down the wide river from Kalai, and when he was about half a mile from the falls, transferred to a lighter craft. The canoists sang a song: 'The Leeambye! Nobody knows/Whence it comes and whither it goes.'[21] The Zambezi is at its lowest in November, the rains having just begun and the flood-waters from the Barotse valley having not yet built up. So Livingstone was able to go down to the very lip of the cataract and land on the island now named after him. Gingerly, he and his guides went to the edge and looked over: 'I peered down into a large rent which had been made from bank to bank of the broad Zambezi, and saw that a stream of a thousand yards broad leaped down 100 feet and then became suddenly compressed into a space of fifteen or twenty yards.'[22]

A few days later, Livingstone set off across the Batoka plateau, crossed the Kafue south-east of modern Lusaka, and reached Quelimane on the Indian Ocean in May 1856. Several of the Barotse were keen to go with him to Britain, but through lack of money he could only take one, and chose the headman Sekwebu. This Sekwebu was by all accounts a remarkable man, whom Livingstone greatly admired for his 'great prudence and sound judgement'.[23] As a small boy, Sekwebu had been captured by the Matabele and taken to the neighbourhood of Tete, but somehow made his way home again. On the journey down the Zambezi, he had proved invaluable to the missionary. 'Indeed, but for his good sense, tact, and command of the language of the tribes through which we passed, I believe we should scarcely have succeeded in reaching the coast.'[24] In very rough weather, the two boarded a Royal Navy vessel, the *Frolic*. Sekwebu had never seen the sea before and was terrified. When they reached Mauritius, Sekwebu was seized by a temporary fit of madness. The ship's officers suggested that in case he threw himself overboard he should be put in chains. Livingstone refused: 'Being a gentleman in his own country, I objected, knowing that the insane often retain an impression of ill-treatment, and I could not bear to have it said in Sekeletu's country that I had chained one of his principal men, as they had seen slaves treated.' The next night, Sekwebu again lost his mind and flung himself overboard. 'And though he could swim well, pulled himself down hand under hand by the chain cable. We never found the body of poor Sekwebu.'

In London, Livingstone was handed the gold medal awarded him by the Royal Geographical Society the year before. He was famous and his book, *Missionary Travels and Research in South Africa* became a best-seller. Less than two years later he was back again on the Zambezi, at the head of a powerful expedition to which the British Foreign Office had contributed £5,000. Its aim was to see if the Zambezi could be opened to 'trade with the natives' and most important in Livingstone's eyes, to look for ways of wiping out the slave trade in Central Africa; in a burning phrase, he had described this as the 'open sore of the world'.

The expedition lasted for five years, and in general it was a failure.[25] Livingstone's white companions, especially his brother Charles, could not keep up with him, and he became morose at the repeated disasters and delays. Most of the five years 1858-63 were spent around Lake Nyasa, but in 1860, Livingstone took his brother and John Kirk the botanist up to the Victoria Falls. From there they went on to Linyanti to see Sekeletu. It was not at first a cheerful reunion, although the people were happy to see 'Monare',[26] with many of the Lozi porters he had taken with him to the east four years earlier.

Sekeletu, ulcerated with leprosy, his kingdom far from secure, his elders hazy with beer and *dagga,* had become distrustful of all outsiders.[27] A white hunter called William C. Baldwin who had walked from Bechuanaland to the Falls (steering himself with a small compass), was being held prisoner. Possibly he was suspected of being a Boer, a race the Kololo detested. Livingstone secured Baldwin's release, but it was too late for him to help the Helmore-Price London Missionary Society expedition, which a few months earlier had been almost wiped out near Linyanti. One of the two missionaries, both their wives and several children had died, perhaps through being poisoned. All their goods were looted by the Kololo. Livingstone stormed: 'You have killed and plundered the servants of God, whom you invited to your country, and the judgment of God will fall on you!' This sombre prophecy soon came true. Late in 1860, Livingstone left the Zambezi valley, never to return, and two years later Sekeletu was dead. By 1864, the Lozi under Sipopo had swept down from the unsubdued north and slaughtered the remnants of the Kololo almost to a man.

II THE ARABS AND THE YEKE

Between the sixteenth and eighteenth centuries, the trading supremacy of the Arabs along the African east coast had been challenged by the Portuguese. Yet it is clear that the ancient contact with Zambia's people was never completely denied to the Arabs. In a letter dated March 22, 1798, the Brazilian explorer Francisco de Lacerda told the Lisbon government: 'The dry goods hitherto imported into this country [the Bisa area] have been bought by the Mujao [Yao], indirectly or directly, from the Arabs of Zanzibar and its vicinity. Hence these people received all the ivory exported from the possession of the Casembe [Mwata Kazembe of the Lunda].'[1] Later he said: 'I now think with reason that the great number of tusks which once went to Mozambique, and which certainly came from these lands, now goes to Zanzibar.'

From Antonio Gamitto, the Portuguese army captain who visited the Lunda in 1831, there is even more specific evidence. When he arrived at the court of Mwata Kazembe two 'Moors' were there, and he was able to pick them out immediately from among a great crowd of Africans.[2] These Arabs, whom Gamitto called Impoanes, told him they came from the east coast, which was at least 800 miles away by the shortest route. When the arrogant Portuguese expedition began quarrelling with the Lunda, they were told bluntly by a court spokesman that Mwata Kazembe would have no compunction in cutting off their heads; the Lunda had little need of Tete, because they obtained all the cloth they needed from either the Zanzibar coast or Angola.[3]

The two Arabs Gamitto met beside Lake Mweru 130 years ago were in the van of a great wave of traders who ruthlessly scoured the heart of Africa throughout much of the last century. From 1750 to 1820 the coastal Arabs had been weakened by internecine fighting, although despite this the Zanzibar slave market was busy with the buying and selling of enslaved Africans brought from the interior.[4] There then appeared on the scene the remarkable Seyyid Majid bin Said, through whose inspiration the Arab renascence was to begin. At the age of 16, in 1806, Seyyid Said killed his uncle, Kis bin Ahmed, Imam of the Persian Gulf state of Oman;[5] the Omanis had long dominated Zanzibar and Mombasa, and Seyyid Said soon moved southward to establish himself as Sultan of Zanzibar as well.

One of the supreme ironies of the career of Seyyid Said is that while his subjects were the lords of the slave-trade, which aroused such loathing in Victorian England following Livingstone's revelations, the sultan was helped and protected by the British. They had signed treaties with him in Oman and the Royal Navy had wiped out pirates interfering with the Omani sea routes. When he extended his domination to the African coastline, the British decided to back him as a counter-balance to increasing French activities in the Indian Ocean.[6] To act through the sultan and assist in the extension of his empire was much cheaper than direct British control. In 1841, Britain posted Lieut-Col. Atkins Hamerton to Zanzibar to become consul, and the power behind Seyyid Said's throne. A British official called Robert Cogan declared hopefully that Zanzibar could be used as a gateway through which 'education and morality' might be directed to a wide expanse of Africa. In 1845, the sultan agreed under pressure to sign a treaty banning the shipment of African slaves from Zanzibar to Oman; in return for the loss of taxes, on slave exports, Britain bound herself to pay him £2,000 a year. The treaty was a soporific for British consciences, but was easy to circumvent. None-theless, Seyyid Said remarked gloomily to Queen Victoria's representative: 'You have put on me a heavier load than I can bear.'[7]

The caravans still set out from Zanzibar for long expeditions to the interior, and to each one Seyyid Said gave a blood-red flag to show that it had the blessing of the sultanate. Hindu and muslim merchants from British India (the forerunners of today's numerous Indian community in East Africa) would give the Arabs credit on goods for bartering. Since the caravans might be away for more than a year at a time, it was natural that staging posts should be set up inland, and these posts developed into permanent Arab settlements. The town of Kazeh (now Tabora) was founded in about 1830;[8] 500 miles from the ocean, it was on the main caravan route to Ujiji beside Lake Tanganyika. By 1850, many slave-traders were regularly coming down from Ujiji to the northern regions of Zambia, while others were using the more direct route across the top of Lake Nyasa or through Kota Kota.

It is important to realise that the adventurers, paying a certain allegiance to the Sultan of Zanzibar, were rarely pure Arab. Almost all the Arabs had some proportion of African blood, for just as slavery was permitted by the Koran, so racial mixing was not subject to any taboos. Arab aristocrats had no hesitation in taking African wives, and as the British explorer Sir Richard Burton pointed out with some relish, the ladies of Zanzibar used their slaves for more than cooking. Livingstone remarked of two Arab traders he met in Barotseland in 1853 that they were 'quite as dark as the Makololo'.[9] Whatever the colour of the invaders, however, they were usually referred to by the tribes with whom they came into contact as Balungwana or Bangwana, which had the broad meaning of 'outsiders'. The name Swahili has sometimes been applied to Arabs of inferior standing and comes from the word *sawahil,* the plural of *sahil,* meaning 'the coast'. Closely allied to the Arabs were the Yeke or Yongo, who were Africans of the important Nyamwezi tribe.[10] The Nyamwezi became involved in the slave-trade because their home was close to Tabora and many of them found employment as carriers between the lakes and the coast. From this experience the Nyamwezi learnt enough to begin ivory and slave-trading on their own, usually selling captives to Arab middlemen at Tabora, Ujiji and elsewhere.

Balungwana dispersion over Zambian soil quickly became widespread. Livingstone first met Syde bin Habib at Naliele in 1853; this wealthy trader had come from the Lake Mweru area and reached the Zambezi valley through the Katanga.[11] He was the same Syde bin Habib who had a house at Mpweto, where the Luvua flows out of Mweru. The Lala people of Serenje say in their history that the Swahili came 'selling flint and steel for making fire' and traded for 'slaves and handmaids'.[12] Livingstone also met around Lake Nyasa Arabs who had travelled far across the Luangwa. Yet it was not the Arabs who first caused devastation on a wide scale, but the Yeke.

Since early in the nineteenth century, the Yeke had been travelling around Lake Tanganyika and had come into contact with the tribes east of Lake Mweru. One of the most prominent of these adventurers was Kalasa-Muzwiri, who led a well-armed expedition to Katanga in search of copper and slaves. Kalasa-Muzwiri formed alliances with several Katangan chiefs and on his second journey beyond the Luapula took his son, Ngelengwa, aged twenty, with him.[13]

This son was to become the notorious Msidi, also variously known as Msiri, Mushidi, Mushili and Mwenda.[14] Msidi went to the court of Mwata Kazembe Chinyanta in the 1850s, and asked for permission to cross into Katanga; this was a request which Kazembe was reluctant to grant, and according to one source, Msidi bribed him with a musical instrument and medicine for smallpox. Another Yeke who was at the court said: 'Chief, don't let this Msidi cross; don't let him go to Katanga'. To his ultimate cost, Kazembe ignored the warning.

The Lunda version of the arrival of Msidi is as follows:

> Msidi was a Yeke of the Nyamwezi tribe. He came from the land of Busumbwa [Ushirombo] beyond Lake Tanganyika. He

was a trader. He traded ivory, copper and slaves. He had with him many Yeke. The things in which they traded they sold to the Balungwana or Arabs of Tabora and Zanzibar. When he arrived at Mwata Chinyanta's capital, he said to the chief: 'O chief, I have come from far, and I am going to Katanga, your subject chief who was a friend of my father Kalasa; I want to be ferried over the Luapula'. Mwata Chinyanti answered him: 'The place where you are going is my country, and I desire that you do no harm there, for the copper is my copper and the people are all my people.' Msidi agreed to this and he was given people to ferry him across. He went off with his followers. They were well received by Katanga, but soon Msidi began to cause disturbances and sent people off with guns to capture men as slaves. Mpande, the chief of the Sanga, was an old man with leprosy, and his people did not care for him, but Msidi did, and helped him because they would not do so; and Mpande asked Msidi to fight on his behalf because his people did not respect him. He asked him to kill men and spare the women. Msidi did this, and when Mpande was about to die, he put the bracelet of chieftainship upon Mwenda's [Msidi's] arm and said: 'There will be no other chief here to succeed me except you.' This is how Mwenda came to settle there.[15]

Cunnison says: 'This was the first stage in the disappearance of Kazembe's wide empire. Msidi's capital lay just slightly north of the route linking Kazembe and Mwata Kazembe.'[16] For more than thirty years, Msidi ruled his powerful Garenganze empire, which was one of the most remarkable phenomena of nineteenth-century Africa. His lieutenants with Ruga Ruga mercenaries spread devastation in every direction in the hunt for slaves and ivory,[17] which he sold to the Portuguese in the west and the Arabs in the east. The Portuguese gave him a white wife to gratify his pleasure-loving nature. The Arabs also presented a bride; the latter was strangled for being a witch, which provoked a war.[18]

Although Msidi had his capital in what is now the Congo, his activities had a dire effect on the peoples of Zambia. Yeke bands either working for Msidi or imitating his success, pillaged the Kaonde, Lamba, Lima and Lala to the south, and the Aushi, Bisa, Chishinga and Shila to the east. Tribes such as the Aushi were reduced to the status of subject peoples.[19] Some groups, such as the Bisa, were simultaneously trying to fight off attacks from the Ngoni and Bemba at the same time. The Lamba and others nearer the Zambezi were also being ravaged by Chikunda raiders led by Portuguese half-castes from the Feira area; Lala records tell of a 'war' against the 'children of the Portuguese' at this time.[20]

Towards the end of his career, Msidi left a permanent mark on one of the Zambian tribes, when in 1885 he sent an ivory and slave-trading expedition into the Lamba country, which is now the Copperbelt. The expedition was led by the ruthless Chimfumpa, and many of the people fled in terror.[21] Katanga, the chief on the Kafulafuta river, escaped with his followers into Lenje country. Mputu of the Lamba, who had succeeded Nkana, was overwhelmed by Chimfumpa's Ruga Ruga, and to show that he had surrendered, he adopted the name Mushili, a title by which Msidi was commonly known. Mputu also showed his submission by sending Msidi gifts: two female slaves and a *mpande* shell (although some legends say he sent fifty elephant tusks to the tyrant of the Garenganze). The name of the slaver Mushili has been retained to this day for the senior Lamba chief in Zambia.[22]

III TIPPOO TIB

In the year 1867, the north-west of Zambia was invaded by the most renowned Arab slave-trader of them all. His real name was Hamed bin Muhammed,[1] but he was always known as Tippoo Tib, or Pembamoto (Swahili *moto,* fire). The origin of the name Tippoo Tib has remained something of a mystery. According to Livingstone, the slave-trader himself invented it, after conquering the Tabwa chief Nsama and seeing all the loot he had won: 'Now I am Tippoo Tib, the gatherer of wealth!'[2] But etymologically this is obscure. Tippoo Tib always claimed that he earned the title because his muskets made a sound like 'tip, tip'. A third suggestion is that the name came from the nervous twitching of his eyelids, although Tippoo Tib himself did not like this interpretation.[3]

Tippoo Tib was a plunderer who showed no mercy to his African victims. Most African accounts do not paint him in any favourable light at all. But on the whites who met him, Tippoo Tib made a remarkably favourable impression. Alfred J. Swann, one of the earliest missionaries in the Lake Tanganyika region of Rhodesia, went so far as to call him a 'frank, manly character'.[4] Henry Stanley took him on the disastrous and flamboyant expedition to rescue Emin Pasha; King Leopold II named the Arab as provisional governor of the Upper Congo. In his old age, Tippoo Tib retired quietly to his native Zanzibar and died there of malaria in June 1905. The year after his death, his biography[5] appeared, written by the German consul in Zanzibar, Heinrich Brode, and based upon Tippoo Tib's own records in Arabic.

Read in conjunction with other accounts, Tippoo Tib's description of his two journeys through Zambian territory shed a remarkable light on the activities of the Arab slave-traders there. Not long after the middle of the century, the Arabs and the Yeke were powerful enough in the northern part of the country to cause a fundamental change in the relationship between neighbouring tribes. It was a change for anything but the good. Enmity was fostered between rival chiefs and they were supplied with guns to wage wars. In this way, the supply of slaves was maintained at a profitable level; elephant hunters were kept stocked with powder and shot and in exchange for cloth and beads their ivory was bought for the slaves to carry to the coast. The system was simple and effective. When a slave-trader decided to settle down, he would usually attach himself like a parasite to a convenient chief. What happened in such situations has been described as follows:

> There they traded, and when ivory and slaves were sufficient they sent off caravans to the coast, which brought back guns and powder and other trade goods. After a time of peaceful penetration, having ingratiated themselves with the people and having built a walled village, the armed Arabs one morning would suddenly attack their erstwhile hosts and friends, killing their men and carrying off women and children. Other villages around, seeing the futility of fighting such strong foes, would to 'save their heads', as they put it, carry slaves and ivory to them and obtain whatever peace terms the Arabs cared to impose. From then on, raids in the more distant villages were the order of the day, while the locals, turned into Arab servants, shared in the plunder. Thus mushroom Arab kingdoms were brought into being, and built up throughout Central Africa.[6]

While still a young man, Tippoo Tib came to Zambia from the east, leading a caravan including more than a hundred men with guns.[7] He traded first in 'Urori', a region north of Lake Nyasa, where he bought a large quantity of ivory. From there he marched south to 'Ruemba', the Bemba country. He was 'amicably received by the sultan, Chief Mwamba, but was unable to make any profitable bargains'. Tippoo Tib left his brother Muhammed bin Masud behind with fifteen Ruga Ruga to trade with the Bemba and to maintain his lines of communication. The caravan then advanced cautiously towards 'Itabwa', the Tabwa country, which 'bore a very bad reputation'. The old chief Nsama was 'powerful and bloodthirsty'. According to Tippoo Tib, the Bemba and the Lungu paid tribute to Nsama—a claim which is almost certainly incorrect but was designed to make his subsequent victory sound more heroic. The Arab freebooter related that people all along the route tried to dissuade him from crossing the Lofu river into Itabwa. 'Moreover, an old Arab named Amer bin Said esh shaqsi, who has spent years in the country, frightened him with an account of an expedition which he had made a considerable time ago with other Arabs, but from which few had returned with whole skins. But our wanderer was powerfully attracted to this rich country, for all accounts agreed in affirming that there were untold treasures of ivory there.' (It should be mentioned that at this period, the late 1860s, ivory prices in Europe were at an unprecedented high level.)

According to Tippoo Tib's imaginative account, Nsama's capital east of Lake Mweru was 'a great city' surrounded by trenches and thorn hedges and standing at the foot of a mountain. Old Nsama, described by Tippoo Tib as being 'between eighty-six and ninety', had a large storehouse full of ivory but refused to give him any in return for the presents of the visitors. Fighting soon started. Tippoo Tib was not the man to let a fortune slip through his clutches because of a stubborn old African ruler. In three days of battle, about 2,000 Tabwa were wounded or killed. The Arabs, using guns against men armed with bows and spears, suffered few casualties, although Tippoo Tib was wounded in three places by arrows. The booty seized by the Arabs was immense : 1,000 slaves, 30 tons of ivory,* 10 tons of copper and 'an untold number of goats'.

Tippoo Tib then retired to the Lungu country at the lower end of Lake Tanganyika and the local chief immediately came to an agreement with him, offering to join in more fighting against the Tabwa. 'With his help a deliberate war of extermination was carried on against Itabwa, which, after two months, ended in Nsama's entire overthrow. He was granted peace in return for a large tribute.' Having achieved, according to his lights, a great success, and having used, in classic fashion, one tribe to smash another, Tippoo Tib went back to Zanzibar. There the sultan was duly impressed with the 'rich spoil' and loaded the slave-trader with honours.

Tippoo Tib was not done with Zambia, however, and a few years later he was back again in search of more booty. In the Tabwa country the old chief had died and his son was ruling. Perhaps not surprisingly, the new chief refused to see Tippoo Tib, but sent him forty elephant tusks. The caravan, 4,000 strong, had

* Worth at least £13,000 then—equal to about £70,000 today.

brought with it a team of Fipa hunters who busied themselves with shooting expeditions. According to local tradition, one of them called Sefu also busied himself fathering many children in the Tabwa country.[8]

While the hunters stayed on in Nsama's area, Tippoo Tib went south-east to the Bemba country and visited the chiefs, including the paramount Kitimkaro (Chitimukulu). 'For but a small amount of goods he obtained a great deal of ivory, wherefore he bears witness that they [the Bemba] were good people.'

The next foray after returning to the Tabwa country was across the Kalungwisi river against the Lunda of Mwata Kazembe Muonga Sunkutu. Since the mid 1850s the Lunda had become more and more harassed by Arab and Yeke traders; the whole area round Lake Mweru was infested with them and two nephews of the chief had been slaughtered in Katanga on the orders of Msiri. The Lunda history relates how Mwata Muonga had become incensed at this and declared : 'Now I shall kill all the Arabs who are here because they are the same family as Mwenda's Ngalaganze.'[9] It would appear that Muonga carried out his threat and the Arabs who survived fled northwards into Tabwa country to take refuge with the forces of Tippoo Tib (who was usually known as Pembamoto in that area). This threatening situation gave the chance he had been awaiting to Lukwesa Mpanga, a Lunda aristocrat who had been Kazembe but was deposed through refusing to go through the traditional circumcision ceremony. Lukwesa had been living in exile at Mpweto, and immediately linked up with Tippoo Tib to assault the Lunda domain.

From two accounts we have,[10] it seems that two attacks were made : first, a battle was fought on the Kalungwisi in which, according to the Lunda version, Tippoo Tib outflanked the defenders and the survivors fled back to the capital at Mofwe. Tippoo Tib's account is rather different. He told Brode that his caravan approached the Lunda country slowly during the rainy season and had to travel far upstream before finding a place to cross the swollen Kalungwisi. Then as the crossing began, the Lunda attacked, killing several men and seizing guns and merchandise. When Tippoo Tib asked why this 'unexpected hostility' should be shown to him, the Lunda answered that they would demonstrate they were different from Nsama's people and could not be beaten by him. In fact, they were determined to kill all intruders. Tippoo Tib's version goes on : 'This impudent reply demanded immediate retribution'. Even Said bin el Hinawi, a 'pious and forgiving man', advised fighting. So reinforcements were ordered up from Itabwa, there was more warfare, and before long the Lunda were broken. This is typical of Tippoo Tib's accounts of how uncompromising African rulers provoked him and had to be taught manners by his muskets. In fact, his liaison with Lukwesa, who was duly installed on the Lunda throne with his backing, shows considerable similarity to the use of the Lunda chief against Nsama a few years previously. Perhaps this time, though, Tippoo Tib was disappointed with the loot: the Lunda had only tattered traces of their former glory, and according to Livingstone the principal functionary at the court was Katamatwi, a man who was kept busy cutting off the ears, noses and hands of people unlucky enough to displease the Kazembe.

Having swept all before him on the shores of Lake Mweru, Tippoo Tib went on to the west, where he acquired a great empire on the upper Congo. Yet many Arabs stayed behind in what has become Zambia, one of the most prominent being Abdullah ibn Suliman, who settled down in the Mporokoso area and died there in 1916. His village was marked on most maps of the country produced before the 1939–45 war, and in very recent years people of the district still spoke Swahili and read the Koran—an island of Mohammedanism which had withstood for seventy years the Christian missionaries and Bemba language all around.[11]

A Swahili called Teleka settled on the Zambezia shore of Lake Tanganyika around the turn of the century, near the small port of Sumbu. He was quoted in 1959 as saying that business in the area was still scarcely as good as it had been in the old days of the slave-trade.[12]

IV LIVINGSTONE AND HIS FOLLOWERS

From the very beginning, the scent of death hung over Livingstone's last journeys in Zambia. After the personal tragedies and defeats of the Nyasaland expedition he seemed to be a man in pursuit of oblivion. Gone were the high spirits so evident in his first book, *Missionary Travels.* Now he was left with a relentless courage, which for seven years drove the emaciated body of a hero prematurely aged. Everything was against him: he suffered constantly from dysentery and internal bleeding, his uncontrolled servants deserted him, and in a futile experiment, his baggage animals included six camels and three tame Indian buffaloes. Much has been written about Livingstone's final years in Africa but one fact is undeniable: but for the help constantly given him by his lifelong enemies, the Arab slave-traders, he would almost certainly have died six years before he did.

Livingstone entered the Luangwa valley from the east at the end of 1866 and journeyed northwards towards the Bemba country. By the time Livingstone reached Lake Mweru and arrived at the court of Mwata Kazembe he had been struggling for more than a year across the plateau. While at Kazembe's, he stayed with the Arab traders and talked with an old man called Perembe who was reputed to be 150 years old. Perembe said that when the Portuguese expedition led by Lacerda had reached Kazembe in 1799, he himself was married and already had forty children; the Lunda had conquered his ancestors, the old man told Livingstone.[1]

Towards the end of 1868, Livingstone was waiting, after a journey to Lake Bangweulu, to travel northwards to Ujiji with a party of Arabs led by the notorious Mohamed Bogharib. The caravan included a vast accumulation of copper, ivory and slaves, and when some slaves escaped fighting broke out with neighbouring Bemba tribesmen, whom the Arabs accused of hiding the runaways. Livingstone watched a furious battle which lasted for two days when the Bemba attacked the emcampment at dawn. He was astonished by the courage of the Africans, who rescued their wounded while the Arabs fired at them. The fighting over, the caravan moved off, with Livingstone being carried in a litter by the Arabs. He left Zambian soil, to begin his wanderings around the Lualuba river and the shores of Lake Tanganyika, to meet Stanley, and then return once more to Lake Bangweulu as though drawn by a fatal magnet.

In the months leading up to his death in the Lala country, Livingstone received little help from the villagers as he wandered through the swamps in the rains. A reason may have been his close connection with the slave-traders four years earlier; also the loss of his medicine chest had destroyed the 'magic' which made him revered. Time and again he wrote of the delays put in his way, especially by Chief Matipa whose village was close to the point where the Chambeshi entered the lake. With one excuse after another, Matipa kept him waiting weeks for canoes, until in desperation Livingstone went and fired a shot through the roof of the chief's hut. 'Thanks to the Almighty Preserver of men for sparing me thus far on the journey of life. Can I hope for ultimate success?' he wrote in his journal. It was his sixtieth birthday. Kneeling beside his bed six weeks later, Livingstone died. An African servant who could read and write, and who had been given the name Jacob Wainwright at a mission school for freed slaves in India, intoned his burial service.

Within two decades of Livingstone's death, missionaries of

many societies began to penetrate the land that is now Zambia.[2] From the south came the Jesuits, who after numerous deaths among their numbers managed to establish themselves in the Bantu Botatwe country. Other Catholics, the White Fathers, were able to win favour with the Bemba sub-chief Makasa in the far north and despite the initial opposition of Chitimukulu, soon spread their influence across the plateau. The Plymouth Brethren set up stations in the north and north-west, while in Barotseland the French Protestants of the Paris Missionary Society established themselves among the Lozi. Around the shores of Lake Tanganyika the London Mission Society was active by 1880, and in the bitter fighting at the time between the Bemba and the Mambwe, the mission stations became places of refuge for people fleeing from raiders. Yet the Bemba always took care to avoid damaging the goods of the missionaries and would pile up the white man's property neatly before attacking a village. Such regard was not shown in the south by the Ila, who at first threatened to kill any Europeans who entered their territory. Near where Lusaka now stands, an Austrian missionary named Emil Holub and his wife Rosa lost all their possessions and barely escaped with their lives when the Ila surrounded them; one of their party, Oswald Zoldner, was killed.[3]

Yet it was not occasional hostility from the people which presented the greatest obstacle to missionary penetration. Malaria and blackwater fever were the enemies which killed scores of Europeans north of the Zambezi in the last decades of the nineteenth century. For that reason, increasing use was made of African preachers and teachers. One of the first of these to arrive came from the Church of Scotland headquarters at Livingstonia, in Nyasaland. His name was David Kaunda, and he settled at Chinsali. His youngest son was to become Zambia's first Prime Minister and President.

V 'NORTHERN ZAMBEZIA' AND THE SCRAMBLE FOR AFRICA

When in the 1880s the partition of the African continent began, the European powers advanced cautiously towards the interior from their footholds on the coast. Thus it is not surprising that the remote and land-locked region between the Zambezi and the bottom of Lake Tanganyika came only late into the reckoning; both politically and economically it did not evoke any considerable interest. Because of the fanciful reports by travellers such as

Mauch and Baines of goldfields in Matabeleland, the Cape politicians were able to persuade Britain to resist Portuguese demands on 'Southern Zambezia', but beyond the river the great powers saw little worth having. The narratives of Livingstone and other travellers suggested that white settlement was out of the question and if natural wealth existed, little was known about it. The Berlin Conference of 1885 was concerned mainly with West Africa, where 'The Congo Free State and the French Congo had emerged as recognised political entities, though as yet with no trade and with nebulous frontiers'.[1] In East Africa, British and German commercial interests were competing on the coast, although their respective governments had far less enthusiasm for imperialistic ventures there than is commonly supposed;[2] it was feared, with some reason, that 'protecting' such lawless territory would involve much expenditure on administration without offering immediate rewards. Abhorrence of the slave-trade was not considered adequate motive for saddling the metropolitan country with regions several times bigger than herself.

Against this hard-headed attitude the missionaries pleaded in vain. In one of his lectures on Central Africa in 1857, Livingstone had told a distinguished audience at Cambridge: 'Do you carry on the work I have begun! I leave it with you!'[3] The religious societies answered his call, enduring much loss of life among their members. Individual idealists were prepared to devote their fortunes to fighting slavery: such a person was Mr James Stevenson of Ayrshire in Scotland, who gave £15,000 to build the 'Stevenson Road' (along what is now the Zambia-Tanzania border) to link early mission stations of Lake Nyasa and Tanganyika.[4] Such private endeavour was a far cry, however, from official responsibility.

Even in Nyasaland, the British government was reluctant to intervene in the struggle between the well-established missions and the Arab slave-traders. Lord Salisbury said in May 1888: 'I feel that a consul represents a compromise between the desire of the missionaries to obtain protection and the desire of the Home government not to be involved in extensive operations. To please the missionaries we send a representative of the government: to spare the taxpayers we make him understand that he will in no case be supported by an armed force. The only weapon left to him is bluster.'[5] It was a precise statement of British policy towards Northern Zambezia.

On the other hand, the Portuguese began adopting a much more positive policy towards Central Africa in the 1880s. They saw their vast, if neglected, African empire being snatched from them after 400 years. Colonial patriots were pressing the government in Lisbon to obtain international recognition of Portugal's historic right to the interior between Mozambique and Angola, and the army officer Serpa Pinto made a bold trans-continental journey, passing through Barotseland on the way. In Lisbon, scholars produced the diaries of such early explorers as Lacerda. As far as the northern region was concerned, Britain was never disposed to argue, and in October 1888, her ambassador in Lisbon put forward suggestions for an agreed partition. Apart from the Nyasa mission field, '. . . Her Majesty's government would not object to recognise the territory north of the Zambezi as falling exclusively within the Portuguese sphere of influence'.[6] Needless to say, neither side had any regard for what inhabitants of the area might have felt.

If Portugal had agreed to a settlement at that moment, there is no doubt that all the land between the Zambezi and Katanga would have become a Portuguese possession, but the British proposals were rejected, because Portugal felt she would soon be able to take Mashonaland, and Nyasaland as well, by force. Yet within six months the situation was to change. New forces (to be described in the next chapter) appeared on the scene and Britain was finding a way to extend its influence without distressing her taxpayers. The partition offer to Portugal was hastily withdrawn, and on December 27, 1889, Sir Henry Ponsonby wrote to Queen Victoria: 'Lord Salisbury utterly rejects the archaeological arguments of the Portuguese, who claim half of Africa on the supposed cession to them in 1630 of the empire of Monomotapa, of which event Lord Salisbury can find no account whatever in this country.'[7]

When it became known that Portugal had lost Central Africa, there was a bizarre sequel in Angola. In despair, the aged Silva Porto, the 'Mambari headman' who had met Livingstone on the Zambezi nearly forty years before, wrapped himself in a home-made Portuguese flag, sat on twelve barrels of gunpowder and blew himself through the roof of his house. Despite the best efforts of a Dr Fisher, a Plymouth Brethren missionary, his life could not be saved.[8]

3

Concession Hunters and a Queen's Protection

I ORIGINS OF THE BRITISH SOUTH AFRICA COMPANY

IN the second half of the 1880s, the British government had been quite content to see northern 'Zambezia' pass into the hands of Portugal, but Cecil Rhodes was not.[1] The member of the Cape Parliament for Barkly West near Kimberley had long nurtured his grandiose if sometimes incoherent ideas of the role he felt destined to play in Africa. At twenty-four he willed his entire estate to the founding of a secret society which would be devoted to 'the occupation by British settlers of the entire Continent of Africa' as part of a design to spread British power throughout the world. By the time he was thirty-five, such student fantasies seemed a little closer to reality. Already Rhodes had amassed a vast fortune by winning control of the mining interests in the Rand;[2] he was a dominant figure in the Cape Parliament and was to become Prime Minister within two years; opposition to his schemes for opening the 'road to the north' had been forced aside and as early as 1884 he had himself replaced the Reverend John Mackenzie,[3] a redoubtable missionary in the Livingstone tradition, as Imperial Deputy Commissioner for Bechuanaland.

When Rhodes took his first decisive action north of the Limpopo in 1888, his immediate objective was not Barotseland, but Matabeleland. This domain was ruled by Lobengula, a merciless but intelligent ruler whose Zulu people had been driven northwards under his father Mzilikazi, by the Boers in earlier years. The Matabele were rich: their cattle numbered more than

250,000. They were terrible in war, feared by the Bamangwato to the west, by the Mashona to the east and by their old enemies the Barotse to the north.[4]

Early explorers had brought back tales of fabulous wealth in Lobengula's kingdom. It was said that there were great reefs of gold waiting to be exploited. It was also widely known that the high veldt lands of the subject Mashona offered great prospects for white settlement. For years it had been Rhodes's dream to bring Matabeleland and Mashonaland under his personal sway—'the land of Rhodes'.[5] Now the moment seemed at hand, and if he did not act swiftly, the Transvaal Boers of President Paul Kruger might forestall him.

It is essential to relate in some detail how Lobengula was handled (with the aid of missionaries) because this illuminates much that was to happen soon afterwards, when Rhodes reached across the Zambezi into the Barotse kingdom of Lewanika. The two operations were closely connected since the rival African kings were played off against each other with consummate expertise. Moreover, without the concession wrung from Lobengula, there would have been no foundation for the subsequent granting of a royal charter to the British South Africa Company, which has been so central to Zambian affairs for more than seventy years.

To speed his progress in Matabeleland, Rhodes was able to manipulate several people in key positions. One was Sir Hercules Robinson, High Commissioner in the Cape, and senior Imperial representative in southern Africa; Sir Hercules was not very 'correct' and had acquired shares in De Beers, the diamond empire controlled by Rhodes.[6] Next, there was Sir Sidney Shippard, the administrator of Bechuanaland: Shippard had first become friendly with Rhodes at Oxford, had been an executor of the 'secret society' will, had become attorney-general of Griqualand West (in which Kimberley was situated) and was later to be a director of the British South Africa Company.[7] Others in the network included Captain Francis Newton, private secretary to Sir Hercules, and Ralph Williams, Her Majesty's representative in Pretoria.

Finally (somewhat unwittingly) there was John Smith Moffat, brother in law of the late David Livingstone. Moffat had spent his childhood in Lobengula's land and was trusted by the king. Rhodes had slipped him into the position of deputy to Shippard—a useful move because Shippard was not liked by the Matabele and had earned for himself the title of *marana maka*, 'father of lies'.[8]

When it was learnt in Capetown at the end of 1887 that a Boer emissary named Pieter Grobler (later mysteriously murdered) had obtained some sort of treaty with Lobengula, Moffat was ordered to obtain one as well.

By this date the king at Bulawayo was surrounded with concession seekers. He was harassed, but determined to hang on to the rights of his people at all costs. So John Moffat found Lobengula adamant. If the king wanted to put himself 'under the protection' of Queen Victoria, he would do so. But he had no wish to take that step. It took Moffat five weeks to make any progress. Then at last on February 11, 1888, he managed to persuade Lobengula to put his royal elephant seal on a treaty of 'perpetual amity'.[9]

The treaty's main stipulation was that Lobengula would never make further agreements with any power except Britain without the 'previous knowledge and sanction of Her Majesty's High Commissioner for South Africa'.[10] Next followed a full-scale deputation to Lobengula, and Rhodes chose Charles Rudd to lead it. Rudd had been his partner in diamond speculations, and had sat in the Cape Assembly for one of the Kimberley constituencies. With him went Rochfort Maguire, later to become a director of the British South Africa Company, and Frank Thompson, a 'native compound manager'.[11]

In September 1888, the party reached Bulawayo. Rudd's main opponent was an agent of the Buchuanaland Exploration Company, a syndicate directed by Lord Gifford. Ten other organisations were on the scene as well. To add to Lobengula's bewilderment, the Bishop of Bloemfontein suddenly appeared in Bulawayo. Next came Sir Sidney Shippard with a platoon of police. The king looked anxiously for an adviser he could trust, and settled on the Reverend Charles Helm, who recommended the party led by Rudd. Rudd promised again and again that Lobengula was not being asked to surrender his land, but merely to give permission for the digging of 'one hole'. Large numbers of the Matabele had trekked down to Kimberley to work, and they had seen the 'one hole' that Rhodes had dug there for diamonds.

At long last, Lobengula succumbed, and on October 30, 1888, he put his mark to the 'Rudd Concession', the origin of British power in Central Africa.[12] Helm wrote on the document that he had 'interpreted and explained' the concession to the king and his council.

In return for handing over the complete mineral rights of his 'kingdom, principalities and dominions', Lobengula was promised £1,200 a year, 1,000 Martini-Henry rifles, 10,000 rounds of ammunition and a 'steamboat with guns' on the Zambezi, which Lobengula was very keen on because it would give him a chance to destroy the canoe fleets of his enemy Lewanika.

Lobengula was never to get his gunboat, and the rifles were in a dubious condition. But the king did get £1,200 a year, while he lived.

Immediately the Rudd concession was in his hands, Rhodes began to use it to further his schemes for a company with a royal charter, but ranged against him were determined critics led by the Reverend John Mackenzie, the former deputy commissioner. Mackenzie was alarmed at the prospect of vast regions falling under the sway of a tycoon whose friendship with the Boers in the Cape seemed extremely ominous. The answer, as Mackenzie had always seen it, was to put Matabeleland and the areas northward under direct Imperial administration. This was precisely what Rhodes did not want.[13]

Mackenzie tried desperately to thwart Rhodes and for a time it looked as though there would be no royal charter. The Prime Minister, Lord Salisbury, Joseph Chamberlain, Lord Rosebery and others listened to Mackenzie's arguments. The government expressed disapproval of the Rudd Concession and nobody was much convinced by the suggestion, originating from Shippard,[14] that the Matabele did not know how to use rifles and so would do less damage with them than with assegais. One of Rhodes's leading critics was the Duke of Fife, son in law of the Prince of Wales.

When Rhodes reached England in April 1889 he immediately set about placing bribes where they might do good,[15] and began talking to everyone in authority he could meet.[16] An introduction to high social circles finally turned the scales—it was arranged by none other than Charles Helm, the 'interpreter' of the Rudd Concession. This culminated in a party with the Prince of Wales; he was entranced with Rhodes's plans for Africa and reported back to Queen Victoria, who then spoke favourably to Lord Salisbury. Rhodes also had another trump: where was the money coming from to make Central Africa red on the map, if Mackenzie's scheme for direct Imperial protection was adopted? The British taxpayer would have to contribute, and that would make the Tory government unpopular.

At the same time, Rhodes was dealing with his business adversaries. Lord Gifford and several others were strong enough to challenge his claims in Matabeleland: a united front would be essential when petitioning for the charter. By the end of April, Rhodes was in control of all the different groups, with Lord

Gifford as his principal. Gifford was very suitable, for apart from being an aristocrat he had won the VC for gallantry in the Ashanti war and had been colonial secretary for Gibraltar.[17]

On the last day of April, 1889, Lord Gifford wrote to Lord Knutsford, who was secretary of state for the Colonies in the current Conservative government, and outlined the plans for a charter company. It would be responsible for 'development of the Bechuanaland Protectorate and the countries lying to the north', which in the mind of Rhodes already embraced what was to become Zambia. Gifford ended a letter to Knutsford by declaring that such a chartered company would 'be able peacefully and with the consent of the native races to open up, develop and colonise the territories to the north of British Bechuanaland with the best results both for British trade and commerce and for the interest of the native races'.[18]

Lord Knutsford wrote a fortnight later to the Marquis of Salisbury, in an approving vein. One sentence reveals how well Rhodes played his hand: 'The example of the Imperial East India Company shows that such a body may to some considerable extent relieve Her Majesty's government from diplomatic difficulties and heavy expenditure.' The next shows how little Lord Knutsford realised the extent of the territory which Rhodes intended the royal charter should embrace: 'In Lord Knutsford's judgement such a company as that proposed for the *Bechuanaland Protectorate,*[19] if well conducted, would render still more valuable assistance to Her Majesty's government in South Africa.'

In the meantime Lobengula was learning the significance of the Rudd Concession. On January 18, 1889, there appeared a notice in the *Bechuanaland News*: 'I hear it is published in the newspapers that I have granted a Concession of the Mineral in *all* my country to Charles Dunnell Rudd, Rochfort Maguire and Francis Robert Thompson. As there is a great misunderstanding about this, all action in respect of the said Concession is hereby suspended pending an investigation to be made by me in my country—Lobengula.'[20] In April, the king wrote to Queen Victoria, protesting that the Concession was a trick, as it 'contained neither my words nor the words of those who got it'. In August he wrote again to the Queen: 'If the Queen hears that I have given away the whole country, it is not so.' This second letter was intercepted by Shippard and did not reach Britain for more than three months (the normal transit time was six weeks), and by then the charter had been granted.

On July 13, 1889, the formal petition to the Queen was made. It concluded:

Your Majesty's petitioners believe that if the said concessions, agreements, grants and treaties can be carried into effect, the condition of the natives inhabiting the said territories will be materially improved and their civilisation advanced, and an organisation established which would tend to the suppression of the slave trade in the said territories, and to the said territories being opened to the immigration of Europeans, and to the lawful trade and commerce of Your Majesty's subjects and other nations.

The charter was publicly granted on October 29, 1889.[21] A few days later, Mackenzie fell ill, utterly exhausted.

Rhodes had returned to South Africa some weeks before, and was busy arranging to send a powerful vanguard of white farmers into Mashonaland, which was controlled by Lobengula. The Rudd Concession had said nothing about land rights, so there could be clashes with the Matabele during this 'occupation'.[22] A pioneer force which had to fight its way into Mashonaland would need heavy protection, and this would be a serious drain on the £1,000,000 capital of the Charter Company. Also, such an invasion would provoke complaints from outsiders, one of whom was Sir Henry Loch. Loch was the new and quite incorruptible high commissioner in Capetown, Sir Hercules Robinson having been recalled for making a speech so biased in favour of Rhodes that an outcry had followed.

Late in 1889, a plot was hatched in Kimberley with two young adventurers called Frank Johnson and Maurice Heany. The latter was an American, who had fought against the Red Indians. They were promised £150,000 and 100,00 acres in Mashonaland, in return for making 'sudden assaults on all the leading strongholds of the Matabele nation'. This would be done with 500 European horsemen. The scheme was agreed and signed by Rhodes, Johnson, Heany and Rutherford Harris, secretary of the Company. The 500 mercenaries began to collect in Bechuanaland and success seemed certain; then Heany became drunk and let the story slip to the Rev E. A. Hepburn, a missionary with King Khama. The story filtered through to Sir Henry Loch, who immediately sent for Rhodes. For a lesser man this exposure might have spelt ruin, but Rhodes blustered and somehow convinced Sir Henry that all the talk from Bechuanaland was 'vastly exaggerated'. It was only in August 1959 that the details of this still-born 'Johnson Raid' were first made public, by a Rhodesian newspaper.[23] Johnson had become Colonel Sir Frank Johnson, a leading citizen of Rhodesia, and in 1940 he wrote his autobiography, entitling it *Great Days*. When the book was in proof form one chapter was deleted. It was headed 'Kidnapping of Lobengula', and told the whole story, including Johnson's account of how he would personally assassinate the Matabele king if need be. The documents are now in the National Archives of Southern Rhodesia, together with a typed copy of the secret Kimberley agreement.

By 1892, occupation of Mashonaland had turned out to be more expensive and less rewarding than Rhodes had imagined. Before long the British South Africa Company was in financial straits and a quick *coup* was needed to restore its shares.[24] Matabeleland had to be seized.

The chance came in 1893.[25] Some Mashona villagers had stolen 500 yards of the British South Africa Company's telegraph wire, and paid the fine imposed with cattle. Lobengula sent warriors to punish the thieves, both for stealing the wire and for paying the fine with cattle he regarded as his own. The warriors appeared near a white settlement called Fort Victoria, and killed some Mashona. They did not molest any Europeans, but the settlers regarded such behaviour as an intolerable liberty. In charge at Fort Victoria was a Captain Lendy, who not long before had been censured for torturing a Mashona chieftain to death.[26] Lendy's patrol pursued the Matabele and shot thirty of them dead. The settlers now demanded war against the 'troublesome kaffirs'. Dr Starr Jameson, the administrator of Mashonaland, gave the idea every encouragement.

In August 1893, Lobengula knew the final crisis was at hand. He refused the monthly instalment of his £1,200 a year saying that it was 'the price of his blood'. He also returned most of the rifles given him under the Concession. He wrote to the Queen: 'Your Majesty, what I want to know from you is this: Why do your people kill me?' His tenses were muddled but the meaning was plain, and the Queen replied: 'You can tell the king from me that I have no intention of invading his country.' This message was sent through Sir Henry Loch, at whose invitation the king dispatched three emissaries to Capetown. But as soon as they entered the Bechuanaland Protectorate, two were murdered and the third, Lobengula's brother, fled back to Bulawayo.[27]

Jameson next made his secret 'Fort Victoria Agreement' with the settlers and enlisted nearly 1,000 men for the onslaught on Lobengula. Each was promised 6,000 acres of land and twenty gold claims, and the agreement contained this sentence: 'The loot shall be divided half to the British South Africa Company and the remainder to the officers and men in equal shares.'[28]

At last, under constant pressure from Rhodes, Loch gave permission for two punitive expeditions on the fringes of Matabeleland. Rhodes and Jameson were ready and early in October the whites set off for Bulawayo, with the Bishop of Mashonaland among them.[29] It was a triumph. With their maxim guns, seven-pounders and magazine rifles the settlers killed more than a thousand Matabele for the loss of six men. When Jameson led his army into Bulawayo the king had blown up his capital and fled north, towards the Zambezi. Before going, Lobengula had made sure that the white traders around Bulwayo would be safe.[30] Patrols were sent out to capture the king but he was never caught and is said to have died of smallpox in the bush early in 1894. His last act was to dispatch to Rhodes, who had now reached Bulawayo, a bag holding more than 1,000 sovereigns as a sign of surrender. But the money was stolen by two white troopers.[31]

An enthusiastic account of the Matabele War (one satisfying result of which was a share-out of the 250,000 head of cattle) can be found in Marshall Hole's *The Making of Rhodesia.* Hole was a senior administrator for the British South Africa Company, and took part in the destruction of Lobengula. Here is his epitaph on Lobengula: 'So passed from the stage a remarkable figure, whose misfortune was that he lived to become an anachronism.'[32]

North of the Zambezi, the Charter Company's use of force to gain control might not be so uncompromising, yet as Colonel Colin Harding, another senior official of the British South Africa Company, was to write in later years: 'Truly the pen is mightier than the sword, and in the hands of experts . . . achieved more in Barotseland than the most potent lethal weapon in many of our less fortunate dependencies.'

II THE LOCHNER CONCESSION OF 1890

On March 22, 1948 Roy Welensky addressed an admiring audience in the Northern Rhodesia Legislative Council. The representative for Broken Hill was attacking the British South Africa Company.

> The first point I want to make is that these agreements, if you can call them that, were negotiated in the early part of the nineties. On the one side you had a Company-cum-government which was negotiating with African chiefs. I have no doubt that the Company knew what it was after; I certainly question whether any African chief, whether he was the king of the Barotse or any other African chief, knew what he was

> disposing of in parting with the mineral rights. I question whether any African chief, including the King of the Barotse, without consulting his people, had the right of disposing of the mineral rights. As a matter of interest, if Hon. Members care to read the *Pim Report* they will see that Yeta III petitioned the king direct, expressing surprise that the Company should have thought that any mineral royalties ceded were ceded to them in their capacity as a Company; his suggestion was that they had obtained the mineral royalties in their capacity as the government of the territory.[1]

Welensky was speaking in support of his own motion challenging the British South Africa Company's mineral rights and urging that they should be acquired for Northern Rhodesia.

Seconding Welensky was Colonel Sir Stewart Gore-Browne, who had known the Protectorate for nearly forty years.* He declared:

> I have spoken before on this subject. I have spoken of the iniquity of these royalties, while at the same time paying a tribute to the British South Africa Company for the work they have done for this country in the past, work for which they have now been amply recompensed. I have spoken of the manner in which these royalties were obtained: that indeed takes one back into a somewhat murky past.

The debate was adjourned and was not resumed. Two days later the financial secretary of the Northern Rhodesian government, G. E. Thornton, announced that the second part of Welensky's motion, urging that mineral rights should be acquired for Northern Rhodesia, would be 'energetically pursued'.[2] It would be anticipating to discuss the result of this pursuit, or the reasons why Welensky's demand for challenging the validity of the concessions in Northern Rhodesia was refused.

For the moment we must follow these threads back to King Lewanika sitting with his advisers both black and white at Lealui beside the Zambezi.

About the time that the missionary François Coillard had arrived in Barotseland with Lewanika's permission, the latter had the disconcerting experience of being deposed. He fled to Khama of Bechuanaland for protection, then returned at the end of 1885 to defeat his usurpers and their youthful 'puppet' king, Tatila Akufuna. Although Coillard had at first established an amiable relationship with the Akufuna group, Lewanika did not seem to

* See p. 109.

resent this permanently.[3] Coillard told him that as a man of God he was above politics. In fact, the missionary was tireless when politics could advance his evangelical aims, and for fear that the Portuguese Catholics would acquire his Barotse parish, he persuaded Lewanika again and again to hurry in obtaining 'British protection'.

Lewanika did not need much urging, in view of his own uneasy throne and the threat of Lobengula's *impis*. With the British behind him he would be safe from within and without. In 1887, Lewanika wrote to Khama :

> I understand you are now under the protection of the great English Queen. I do not know what it means. But they say there are soldiers living at your place, and some headmen sent by the Queen to take care of you and protect you against the Matabele. Tell me all as a friend. Are you happy and quite satisfied? Tell me all. I am anxious that you should tell me very plainly, your friend, because I have a great desire to be received like you under the protection of so great a ruler as the Queen of England.[4]

It is worth noting that Bechuanaland was under direct Imperial administration. When, in 1895, small parts of it were handed over to the British South Africa Company, there were bitter protests from Khama.[5]

In the first week of January 1889 (eight weeks after the signing of the Rudd Concession), Lewanika was in deep gloom. He asked Coillard to write a letter for him to Sir Sidney Shippard asking for the protection of the British government.

The letter went on to say that many of the Barotse had already trekked to Kimberley to work in the diamond fields and had come back much impressed. This had led their chiefs and countrymen to 'yearn after the protection of Her Majesty the Queen's government'.[6]

The real motive for Lewanika's urgency was put forthrightly. The Matabele were boasting, as they had done before, that they were shortly going to overcome and destroy the kingdom of Lewanika. They had made pacts with the Batoka tribes north of the Zambezi, who were nominally subject to the Barotse and suffered from their raiding for slaves. Coillard wrote : 'The King Lewanika has heard that Lobengula, the King of the Matabele, is under Her Majesty's government. He therefore respectfully asks whether such a raid could be made without the sanction of the Queen's government.' The fact that even in Barotseland the Rudd Concession was regarded as having put Lobengula 'under Her

Majesty's government' is a revealing sidelight on the way Rhodes's concession hunters went about their work.

The letter from Lewanika was forwarded to the Colonial Office and finally arrived in England in August—a delay of more than seven months. Negotiations for the royal charter had by then been virtually completed and Rhodes had returned to Africa. Lord Knutsford, the colonial secretary, sent a vaguely encouraging answer to Lewanika and passed the application for 'protection' over to Rhodes. It is, however, significant that Knutsford's reply to Lewanika stressed that the Rudd Concession did not qualify as having put Matabeleland 'under Her Majesty's government'.[7]

Lewanika grew more and more anxious. The first consignment of Rudd Concession rifles for Lobengula had arrived in Bulawayo in April 1889. At that moment there appeared in Barotseland a certain Harry Ware, who was well travelled in Central Africa and had visited the Victoria Falls in 1885. For some years he had prospected for gold in the region south of the Zambezi; he was after something bigger now. In Kimberley he had been given instructions to obtain a concession from Lewanika for the mineral rights. Behind this move was a syndicate, outside the Rhodes consortium, headed by two speculators called H. J. King and C. E. Nind. In his negotiations Ware made great play with the 'protection of the Great White Queen', as all other concession hunters were doing, and Lewanika (who could write) signed what was later to become known as 'the Ware Concession'.[8] This granted 'the sole and absolute and exclusive right to dig, mine and quarry for precious stones, gold, silver and all other minerals and metals of whatever description for the term of twenty years, with the option of renewal . . .' over the whole of the subject Batoka country; this was detailed as 'extending east from the river Machile, the boundary to the north to be the cattle path leading to the Maccikulumbo (Ila), the boundary to the south to be the Zambezi river . . .' This loose description covers perhaps 10,000 square miles. Lewanika was to get £200 a year and a royalty of four per cent on all minerals or precious stones that were mined in the kingdom. It doubtless seemed better than nothing.

Coillard had supported Ware in his negotiations, and he gives an account of the way they were handled :

> A Mr Ware, representing a mining company, has come to solicit a concession from Lewanika for exploiting gold, which is supposed to abound in certain parts of the country. The thing was so novel that the king and his councillors, taken at a disadvantage, found themselves greatly embarrassed. They

feared a trap, and yet at the same time were fascinated by the considerable presents of Martini-Henry rifles, of ammunition, blankets and garments which Mr Ware by no means forgot to bring with him.[9]

Some of Lewanika's people questioned whether the presents were honourable and whether the king was not 'selling his country' in accepting them. Coillard tells of another unnamed company which was trying to win a commercial monopoly from Lewanika, and adds: 'So there are the first waves of the invading ocean of European immigration crossing the Zambezi. Where will it stop? What will be their result for the nation itself, and for the tribes of Central Africa?'

With the precious document in his pocket, Ware did not linger to search for minerals but hurried back to Kimberley. He got there some weeks later and formally ceded his concession to Nind and King on October 11, 1889. His task was done and he never appears on the stage again.

When Rhodes returned from England after arranging the royal charter he received the vexing news that he had been forestalled in Barotseland. Earlier in 1889, when Coillard's letter petitioning for 'protection' on behalf of the king had been received, it had looked as though making an agreement with Lewanika would be completely straightforward. However, one of Rhodes's tenets was that every man has his price. There was no doubt that Nind and King would have theirs. He was so confident of this that he dispatched an expedition to parley with Lewanika some weeks before buying the Ware Concession. According to the various authorities, the expedition set out from Kimberley in October 1889. Marshall Hole, in *The Making of Rhodesia,* at one point says it was November but later specifically mentions 'early in October'.[10] In *Coillard of the Zambezi* by Coillard's niece Catherine Mackintosh,[11] it is stated: 'Two months later (September 1, 1889) Sir Sidney Shippard informed Mr Coillard that Mr Rhodes had written to the Board of the British South Africa Company supporting Lewanika's petition.[12] Without fully knowing its greatness and importance, he had seen and grasped the opportunity. Almost immediately afterwards, the envoy of the Company, Mr. Elliot Lochner, left for Barotseland to open negotiations.'

Certainly Rhodes did not get control of the Ware Concession until December 23, 1889,[13] and some months later he wrote:

When I came out from England I found that a syndicate here

> had obtained the concession of the Barotse Kingdom, and their concession was prior to the granting of the Charter. I tried in every way to make terms with them, and after an immense amount of negotiation the lowest they would take was £9,000 and 10,000 shares. As the concession gave the whole of the minerals of the Kingdom,* I did not think it excessive, and I communicated the facts to London.

These words of Rhodes are interesting in various ways. First, they show his concern with the mineral rights, which likewise had been the main acquisition of the Rudd Concession in Matabeleland. Second, they show that the men behind Ware understood full well the coup they had achieved. Lastly, they suggest that Rhodes felt the royal charter had in effect given him absolute power as a maker of British concessions north of the Zambezi.

The expeditionary team sent by Rhodes to treat with the Barotse was led by Frank Elliot Lochner, a former member of the Bechuanaland Police, which was an official British force. Lochner knew King Khama well and was regarded by him as a friend.[14] Khama was Lewanika's ally, and it was obvious that this might be the crucial factor in negotiations. After a disastrous journey, Lochner reached the Zambezi at the end of December, some way from Lewanika's capital of Lealui. With no assistance from the Barotse tribesmen, the party was stranded. Lochner, a man of courage, doggedly waited by the river, until at last, in March 1890, canoes were obtained and the last stage of his journey was completed.

Coillard was expecting Rhodes's agent, and took him to his house at Sefula, not far from Lewanika's capital. Here Lochner slowly recovered his strength. After a few weeks he asked the king for a meeting. Lewanika granted this, but was so suspicious that he refused to call a Council of Barotse people to consider Lochner's overtures. Lewanika was still sitting uneasily on his throne, and feared that any further sign that he was 'selling his country' might be enough to provoke a full-scale revolt.[15] Yet he felt that if only he could get 'protection' he would be safe from both his own people and from Lobengula too. From the opposite point of view the document which Lochner was finally to take back has been described as 'by far the most important treaty with Africans concluded by the Company in Northern Rhodesia'.[16]

In the negotiations for the treaty, the three central figures were of course, Lewanika, Lochner and Coillard. But there was also a fourth person whose role was to be of great importance—a

* This, in fact, was far from correct.

trader, George Middleton. Until the end of 1887, Middleton had been a member of Coillard's mission party as a lay helper. A young Englishman, with a long solemn face and powerful physique, he had won Coillard's devotion.

Middleton had left Coillard with the intention of returning home but before 1890 was back in Barotseland as a trader, representing a firm in Mafeking.[17] In this role he began to replace the ivory-trader George Westbeech, for after nearly twenty years on the Zambezi, Westbeech had died little more than a year before Lochner's arrival.[18]

With Lochner living under his roof, Coillard was heavily committed to help in the negotiations. Moreover, Rhodes was always quick to solicit the aid of a strategically placed missionary, and he made a powerful assault on Coillard's sympathies. He had offered Coillard the position of British resident in Barotseland in October 1889,[19] although he had not yet bought the Ware Concession and had no rights whatsoever north of the Zambezi beyond the general terms of the royal charter. Coillard refused the offer in a letter of April 8, 1890,[20] saying: 'You enquire of me whether I can accept the residency. Well, I cannot serve two masters. But if without any official title I can be to your Company of any service as a medium of communication, and until you get a proper man, I willingly place myself at your disposal.'

Some years later, in her biography of Coillard, Catherine Mackintosh insisted that 'apart from his services as interpreter to both sides impartially, the only action M. Coillard took was to secure as far as possible the interests of the natives and the rights of the king and chiefs'.[21] But both Coillard himself in his letters and Lochner writing to the British South Africa Company contradict this.

Notwithstanding the help of Coillard, Lochner had been assigned a delicate task. He threw gifts around, and Lewanika's aides took everything offered without being as gullible as Lochner imagined.

Lewanika himself refused to accept any presents at all, though Lochner never stopped offering them But the king showed politeness to his guest in traditional manner by giving him fourteen oxen for slaughter. However, Rhodes's man was after more than cattle and grew impatient. In a letter to Shippard he told of his difficulties and forecast: 'I think it will take at least another two months before it is finally settled.' That was on April 9, 1890.[22]

Although it was to be expected that Lochner would invoke the name of Queen Victoria, in fact he went much further. He told Lewanika he was an ambassador from the Queen and had been sent to offer her protection for Barotseland. He was not merely seeking a concession, but an alliance between the Barotse nation and 'the government of Her Britannic Majesty'.[23] If the king chose to reject such an offer it would be taken as an unfriendly act.[24] Then Queen Victoria might even be driven to *force* her friendship on Barotseland. Any hints that the British South Africa Company was not quite the same thing as the British government were quickly glossed over, and it was pointed out that the president of the Company was the Duke of Abercorn, whose Duchess was a member of the Royal Household, and that another director, the Duke of Fife, had a father-in-law who was the heir to the British throne.[25] Lochner was relentless in using this line of approach and there is evidence that Coillard accepted it. This is not surprising—he was a Frenchman and had no great understanding of British politics. Later, when he realised what had been done, he protested bitterly to the Company that 'If the British Protectorate has been used simply as a blind, I emphatically protest against it and regret if I have unwittingly been a dupe and an accomplice in such transactions.'[26]

Whenever Lochner wrote to Lewanika from Coillard's house at Sefula, he used an envelope stamped 'OHMS'.[27] In notes Lochner wrote to the king, any mention of the Company was carefully tucked away. For example: 'If you and your councillors accept the protection of the Queen of England, etc. . . . the Company will send traders into your country who will deal fairly with you and your people, the same as is being done now at Khama's town.' An essential distinction (that the Company did not administer Khama's country) was evaded. While the word 'protectorate' has a precise meaning and must involve direct administration by the imperial power, 'protection' is a vague generalisation with no legal force.[28]

Early in June, Lochner suddenly decided it was time for a celebration for the Queen's birthday. The king and a number of chiefs came to Sefula for the occasion and Lochner slaughtered several oxen. Coillard did his best with a magic-lantern show but the real excitement was to follow because Lochner had a box of fireworks. The effect was tremendous. Lewanika was gaining confidence that he could come to terms with Lochner without being deposed and he had been thoroughly deluded into believing that Lochner was Victoria's ambassador. The king decided to call a *pitso,* or national assembly.

When the Barotse national assembly was gathering, Lochner set out from Coillard's house by canoe, the plain being still flooded from the rains. Coillard and another missionary, Jalla, followed some days afterwards. As Coillard wrote later, it was important to avoid anything which might—'in the eyes of the natives'—identify the concession-hunter with his well-meaning host and advocate.[29] The assembly was opened on June 22. In the centre of a large gathering Lochner and Lewanika sat facing each other.[30] The king wore European clothes topped by a bowler hat; around about were the royal musicians with drums and xylophones. Coillard and Jalla acted as interpreters and when possible spoke in favour of the draft concession in Lochner's pocket.[31] But many of the Barotse were still suspicious. Middleton was warning them against accepting the concession, declaring that Lochner was 'an adventurer like Ware, and that his mission was a bogus one'.[32]

After the national assembly had lasted for several days, a 'remarkable coincidence' gave Lochner the advantage he needed. On the scene appeared Makoatsa, from Bechuanaland. He was the regular messenger between Khama and Lewanika and he had a message for the Barotse people.[33] The messenger walked into the middle of the gathering and shouted Khama's words: 'Barotse, I have tasted delicious food and I have shared it with you! What have you done with it? I have sent you messengers like Makoatsa. How have you received them? Today, I hear sinister rumours, you speak again of revolution. Take care! Lewanika is my friend: and if you dare to make attempts against his life or power, I am Khama! You will see me with your eyes and hear me!'[34] Makoatsa went on to urge the Barotse to put themselves in the hands of the Great White Queen. He told them that the Chartered Company was made up of the 'Queen's men' who had been given the job by Her Majesty of spreading civilisation to all people in the heart of the continent.

III THE MEANING OF THE CONCESSION

On June 27, 1890, the Barotse Concession was signed.[1] The speech by Makoatsa had turned the scales and subdued conspirators among the Barotse who wanted to throw out Lewanika and Lochner with him.[2] For that reason it warrants examination. Marshall Hole and others like Sir Kenneth Bradley who have adopted his line,[3] assert that the cryptic phrase 'delicious food' was a reference only to 'British protection' as offered by Lochner. But a footnote to Coillard's eye-witness account says that it 'related to the Chartered Company *as well as* the missionary'.[4] But this is scarcely satisfactory, because Bechuanaland was not administered by the Company, and for an ardent convert like Khama, 'delicious food' might equally well have been an expression to describe Christianity.

Be that as it may, Makoatsa's own remarks about the Great White Queen take on a new significance when one realises that he had been 'hired' by Lochner. Writing to Rutherford Harris, secretary of the Company, a few days after the signing, Lochner had this to say: 'Macquetsie,* Khama's messenger, was of the greatest possible help to me, as of course the Barotse listened to him more readily than they did to me; he made an excellent speech. . . . I told him that if I was successful, some time back, I would ask the Company to make him a good present; he stated that if the Company would give him a waggon, nothing would please him more.'[5]

The signing of the Concession was, in the words of Coillard, 'a curious spectacle'.[6] A small table was set up in the middle of the council arena and those present who were able put their signatures to the document. Only five came in this category; Coillard and Jalla as witnesses, and Lochner, Lewanika and his eldest son Litia as interested parties. Then nearly forty councillors, chiefs and headmen put their marks below. Many of those who made their marks had only a vague idea of what they were doing, but felt that if the Concession was inevitable they might do well to share in it. 'I believe that the good people imagined that they would thus secure their quota of *mali*—that is, money!' wrote Coillard afterwards.

The signing was followed by speeches and the exchanging of gifts. Lochner handed to the king four cases of gunpowder, two cases of cartridges, fifteen muskets and five rifles, together with a saddle and 162 cotton blankets.[7] All these were formally presented to the Barotse nation by the 'Gambella' (*Ngambela*), Lewanika's prime minister. In return, Lewanika gave two huge elephant tusks which when held upright formed an arc more than six feet high.[8] These were to go to the Queen, through the Dukes of Fife and Abercorn, to prove to her that the king's heart 'was white towards her' as the tusks themselves.[9] Although the traditional Barotse ideas on private property were different from European concepts (as can be seen from the manner of acceptance of Lochner's gifts) a man like Lewanika understood the European concept well enough. Consequently the tusks were later to become a cause for much acrimony, when it became known that Victoria never received them.

Two versions of the Concession are accessible, both in Colonial Office papers.[10] The version Lochner took back to Rhodes

* Lochner's version of 'Makoatsa'.

contains several paragraphs which were left out of the copy which the king retained. However, the net result was the same—the king had unwittingly given the Charter Company absolute rights to win the vast regions north of the Zambezi. The concession was described as covering the 'whole of the territory of the said (Barotse) nation, or any future extension thereof, including all subject and dependent territory'. Immediately after the signing, Coillard prepared a map showing the extent of this; in the north-west the boundary was said to reach the Zambezi-Congo watershed, and further east to follow the course of the Kafue river. It is clear that Lewanika could not delimit his kingdom by reference to frontiers, but had a firm idea of the tribes which fell within his authority. Never at any time did he claim jurisdiction over the Lamba tribe living in what is now the Copperbelt. The importance of this was not to become apparent until long after, when the Chartered mineral rights over the Copperbelt were subjected to anxious scrutiny.

Most important from Lewanika's point of view was a clause in the text: 'this agreement shall be considered in the light of a treaty between my said Barotse nation and the government of Her Britainnic Majesty Queen Victoria.' It was as near as Lochner dare go to putting himself up as a government-appointed ambassador, empowered to make treaties for a region bigger than Britain itself. Later, the colonial secretary, Lord Knutsford, felt constrained to pass this censure: 'Mr Lochner may have made too free a use of Her Majesty's name in communicating with Lewanika.'[11]

The promise of the Company that it would civilise the people by the provision of 'schools and industrial establishments' rings slightly hollow when one realises that the Company hardly gave the slightest thought to native education during all the years it administered Zambia. Such educating as did take place was done by the missions. In 1924–5, when the Colonial Office was taking over the administration, expenditure on native education was £348 for the whole of Zambia. 'The administration manifested little or no interest in education prior to 1925', commented the *Journal of the African Society* in 1931.[12]

Finally, there is the matter of the £2,000 subsidy promised to 'the said chief or king, and to his successors in perpetuity'. The king had been insistent upon that figure, although Lochner was most worried about what his superiors in Kimberley might say. But Lewanika had a powerful case: if Lobengula had been promised many rifles and a gunboat, the least he should receive was enough money to buy guns from the Portuguese traders. For the reason why Lewanika could not be armed like Lobengula one must look back to the Treaty of Berlin in 1885: Barotseland was

6—Z

in the area covered by that treaty, and under it, the introduction of large quantities of rifles was strictly forbidden; but Matabeleland was beyond the treaty area. Lochner had done his best to appease the king by giving him four cases of gunpowder, which would be invaluable for making ammunition.

Lochner wrote to Rutherford Harris: 'The subsidy, you will see I have fixed at £2,000: you will no doubt consider this very large. . . .'[13] He then blamed Coillard for naming the sum, and said it would ensure the loyalty of the chiefs under Lewanika, since they would get some of it. This was doubtful—and in any case, nobody got the £2,000. In November 1894, Coillard wrote to his sister-in-law about the Company: 'They have no communication whatever with Lewanika. It pays them, for they have secured the country, but they don't speak of paying him his annuity of £2,000. More than £6,000 is now due to him.'[14] By the time Lewanika did start getting a regular annuity it had been cut to £850 and a clause about honouring the royalty from the Ware Concession had been removed. There is evidence that Rhodes was not anxious to have the Lochner concession sanctioned—perhaps because of the £2,000, but also because he had concluded that Barotseland itself was poor in minerals.

Even in 1890, Coillard's feelings about the Concession were confused. Before it was signed he had written to his friend, the Reverend J. Smith: 'I have often wished that I had nothing to do with such transactions . . . the king did not seem anxious to face the question of the so-called protectorate.' He wrote to his wife, Christina, on the day before the signing: 'We are working on the treaty—terrible business.'[15] Immediately afterwards he scribbled in his diary: 'At present, I must abstain from comments. We have our fears, we also have our hopes.'[16]

One cannot help having a suspicion that one of his keenest emotions after the signing was relief that he would be seeing the departure of Lochner. On August 5, 1890, a letter to Christina Coillard says: 'Mr Lochner has left at last.'[17] It went on to contrast the calculating generosity shown by Rhodes's man towards the natives, and his meanness, with the missionary's attitude. 'Mr Lochner has exploited the generosity which my vocation imposes on me, and he exploited my hospitality.'

Yet there is no doubt that the missionary made great efforts to push the Concession through. Lochner told Harris: 'I am sure the Company owes much, if not more, to Mr Coillard than to myself in having secured the Barotse country; he is heart and soul with the Company, and there never need be any fear of things going wrong as long as he takes the same interest in the country's work as he has done heretofore.'[18] This responsibility was the cause of Coillard's distress in the years ahead, when he had come to realise that he had not helped Barotseland to come under the 'Queen's protectorate' but had assisted the British South Africa Company to cast its shadow across the Zambezi.

Apart from Lochner, a share of the responsibility must rest on another man, Sir Sidney Shippard. While Lochner had been on his way to Lewanika, Sir Sidney added the weight of his official position to the mission. He told Coillard: 'The Dukes of Fife and Abercorn are on the Board of Directors of this great Company, and the fact that the Duke of Fife has just married the Queen's grand-daughter—the eldest daughter of the Prince of Wales —gives great importance to his position.'[19]

One person by no means deceived in all this was George Middleton, the missionary worker-turned-trader. During his trips to Mafeking for supplies he had come to learn just what the British South Africa Company amounted to—'a simple mining association' was his own description. He branded the Concession as 'an immense sale of the whole country' and immediately Lochner had left Barotseland he began to urge his views on the king.[20] According to protagonists of the Chartered Company, Middleton poured poison in the king's ear; Lochner accused him of trying to obtain a concession for himself, but this hardly stands up to examination because Middleton was very highly regarded by the king, who listened to him as he had formerly done to Westbeech,[21] and it is hard to believe that he could not have obtained a concession if he had seriously wished it.

Catherine Mackintosh, in her *Coillard of the Zambezi,* took a consistently pro-Company line and sneered at Middleton as being 'a working man of little skill or education'.[22] But Middleton was most definitely a man of intelligence. His letters have clarity and vehemence, even if it was a vehemence which later turned to bitterness.

The first letter he wrote after the signing of the Concession was on behalf of Lewanika. It was addressed to the prime minister of Britain, Lord Salisbury, and was a long and carefully worded repudiation of the Concession.[23] The first paragraph reads:

> At the request of Lewanika, paramount chief and ruler of the Barotse kingdom, I have the honour to forward to you the following protest against the concession which has been lately obtained from him by a Mr Frank Elliot Lochner on behalf of the British South Africa Chartered Company. He [the king] states that the objects of the Company were not explained to

> him at the time as they were written in the document purporting to be the concession as agreed upon. The king is very indignant at the sweeping nature of the agreements, and the very exclusive terms of the rights said to have been conceded by him to the Company, and he further states that he repudiates the document in question in its entirety, as he did not understand the meaning of the terms employed.

Middleton's letter in the name of the king went on:

> Not being able at the time to analyse these statements clearly, and, like most African chiefs, having the utmost confidence and trust in the goodness and goodwill of Her Gracious Majesty the Queen, he simply consented to sign any document whatever, under the firm impression that it at once secured to him personal protection of Her Majesty the Queen and Her government, never for a moment suspecting that the document was nothing less than a gigantic monopoly of the entire natural resources of his country, as well as the cession of the administrative, commercial and industrial rights to a trading and commercial association, and consequently quite at variance with his expressed desires and the wishes of his people. . . . The king further adds that he would not trouble your lordship with this protest, but that he feels he has been taken advantage of . . .

The letter stressed how much the Queen's name and the name of her son-in-law (sic) had been used 'to persuade him to sign away his mineral and other resources for ever, for a paltry £2,000 a year, and he decidedly objects to the deception practised upon him'. The first instalment of money for the Ware Concession would be sent back. Finally, Middleton pointed out that he had read the charter of the British South Africa Company to the king, who protested under Clause Seven, which empowered the secretary of state to arbitrate in any disputes.

It may be recalled that the Rudd Concession was repudiated by Lobengula three months after it had been signed. Lewanika had delayed four months before taking the same action. He also turned to Coillard, and asked him to write to Queen Victoria for him. To 'give an insight into Lewanika's mind', the missionary translated the king's words literally, leaving them in their 'crude native shape'.[24] Once again it was stressed that the use of the Queen's name had been used to gain his consent. 'What I wanted was not money but protection: not the protection of a mining and mercantile company but the protection of Your

Majesty and Your Government, nothing else. . . . I bring my tears to you, great and gracious Queen, the mother of men. I earnestly pray that Your Majesty may extend over me the cloak of your protection.'

All this seems at variance with the telegram sent by Lochner to the Company on September 8, while he was on his way to Kimberley: 'Lewanika, his chiefs and nation, at full *pitso,* have accepted protectorate of Chartered Company. They understand the right of the Company is to govern the people through the king and chiefs.'[25]

Because Coillard knew of the protest Middleton was sending, he decided to hold his own letter to the Queen for some while and it was not forwarded from Barotseland until April 1891—a delay of six months. However, for reasons not clear, Coillard's letter reached London first.[26] Possibly Sir Sidney Shippard had performed one of his intercepting acts in Bechuanaland, although he admittedly had been heavily engaged in helping the Company in various other ways at this time—so much so that questions were being asked by his superiors about reports that he was countersigning British South Africa Company cheques.[27] At any event, in July Sir Henry Loch forwarded to the colonial secretary Lewanika's second letter, together with Coillard's pleas that the British government should 'formally proclaim the Queen's protectorate over the country'.

This set off a series of exchanges between the Colonial Office and the Foreign Office. On August 3, 1891, Knutsford suggested that Lewanika should be told that he was 'under the Queen's protection'.[28] On August 12, the Foreign Office wrote back attempting to compromise on the problem.[29] It suggested Lewanika should be told that the Company was acting on behalf of the Queen under royal charter, but also recommended that the Company should not be allowed to exercise powers of government or administration in Barotseland. The proposal was that Her Majesty's Commissioner for British Central Africa, Harry Johnston,[30] should handle Barotseland's administration from his headquarters in Nyasaland. This was in line with the Command Paper of February 1891,[31] which tried to lay down a basis on which the Company could operate north of the Zambezi; Johnston was to administer on behalf of the Company, at the Company's expense.

Finally Knutsford told Loch to assure Lewanika that he was 'under the protection of the Queen' and that he should make contact with Johnston in Nyasaland—a somewhat difficult exercise when one considers the state of communications at that time.[32]

The king was to be promised that Johnston would visit him. Not entirely surprisingly, Her Majesty's commissioner never did find time to trek across from Lake Nyasa, since he was busy coping with Arab slave-traders on one hand and Rhodes on the other.[33]

When Middleton's letter reached London it was almost entirely ignored. Knutsford passed it to the Foreign Office with a mild stricture on Lochner's methods and a suggestion that Middleton was not an entirely disinterested party.[34] Nobody took the trouble to reply to Middleton, who was still fuming at his inability to achieve for Lewanika what he described as 'a treaty of amity and political preference with Her Majesty's government'.[35]

So as 1891 wore on, the mood of anger and bewilderment possessed Lewanika, while Middleton blamed Coillard for everything, and the two men had constant arguments, sometimes in front of Lewanika.[36] Although it may be that Middleton was too harsh in his attacks on the man for whom he had previously worked, it must be remembered we have only Coillard's side of the story, since no diaries or private records by Middleton have survived.

Sometime in April 1891, Coillard wrote sadly in his notebook: 'Thus we have been scratched in the thorny field of policies',[37] and on June 10 he wrote to the British South Africa Company, addressing his letter to Rutherford Harris, the secretary: 'This message will bring you a message from King Lewanika and Mr Middleton will remit to you from him through me the £200 paid to the king by Mr Lochner as the first annual payment of the Ware Concession. You are aware that three years ago the king applied for the protectorate of the British government. He was assured of the friendship of the government, of his request being seriously considered, and that the reply should be conveyed to him at once. That reply has never come.'[38]

Coillard then described the visit of Lochner and the means by which the Concession had been obtained. He warned of Lewanika's feelings and related how Middleton had accused the missionaries of wilfully deceiving the king. After saying that he emphatically protested if he had been made 'a dupe and an accomplice' in the use of the British protectorate as a 'blind', Coillard ended by declaring: 'Matters having assumed such a threatening aspect, and being, as far as our safety and our mission are concerned, in so grave a position, I must decline having in the future any more to do in these matters.'

Middleton took this letter with him on one of his trips to the south for trading supplies, but what answers were made by the Company to Coillard and the king is not known. All that can be certain is that they took no steps to prove their honourable intentions—presumably because they had so much to deal with in trying to establish the Mashonaland settlers.

When at last, towards the close of 1891, Loch's message arrived,[39] Coillard for a moment believed all troubles were ended. It seems he did not really grasp the all-important difference between 'protection' and 'protectorate'. This can be seen by his assertion that Loch's message meant 'the definite establishment of the British protectorate over the Barotse country'.[40] But Lewanika could read between the lines of the British government's sophistry. He knew what he had wanted, and before long the atmosphere was gloomy as ever.

IV REVELATIONS OF JOHNSTON AND THOMSON

While the distrust between Coillard and Lewanika was still smouldering at the end of 1891, a traveller arrived from Angola. He was Dr James Johnston,[1] a Scots settler in Jamaica who had decided in 1890 to walk across Africa. With him were several Jamaican negroes who he vainly hoped might settle down in Central Africa to evangelise. Johnston was an unorthodox man who wrote in the historic present and played '*Way Down upon the Swanee River*' on his cornet to divert African villagers. He had, however, a shrewd and penetrating mind.

With food supplies nearly exhausted, Johnston reached the Barotse valley at the start of December 1891. He had sent messengers to Lewanika asking permission to enter the king's domain and although they reported back that the king had forbidden any white man, on pain of death, to enter Barotseland, Johnston had nowhere else to go. The messengers had failed to reach Lewanika himself, so Johnston went alone to the capital at Lealui. As he crossed the Zambezi in a canoe, 'Hippopotami were bathing in cool waters just above where we crossed, but I was too preoccupied to take much notice of this.'

The first person to greet Johnston was George Middleton, who was living near the king, and later they went across to the *lekhothla* or royal courtyard. Lewanika made an immediate impression on the doctor: 'I was graciously received and could not but feel that at last I was face to face with a real African king . . . Lewanika was plainly dressed in English clothes, and sat on an ordinary cane-bottomed chair: his manner was affable and free. In front of him were his band of drummers and *marimba* players.'

In the days that followed, Johnston and the king talked together for many hours. The king gave two huts in his own village to his guest (Johnston shared these with his Jamaican companions, Frater and Jonathan), and sent an ox as a gift. He dispatched warriors to bring in Johnston's dilatory carriers, and invited the doctor to dine with him one evening. It was 'a very good attempt and in English style, but for the slave-waiters who bringing in or removing each dish did so crouching on their knees (no native is allowed to stand in Lewanika's presence)'.

After being at Lealui for ten days, Johnston asked to be allowed to go to Coillard's mission station, and the king provided him with a horse and carriers for his baggage. At the end of the brief ride across the plain, Coillard stood waiting with his helpers, the carpenter William Waddell and a young Swiss teacher called Elise Kiener who had arrived in Barotseland the year before. Coillard wrote later: 'One ray of sunshine has, by God's grace, shone in the midst of all these clouds—the visit of Dr Johnston of Jamaica.'[2]

Coillard showed Johnston his mission work and invited him to preach in the Sefula church, to 'the rawest looking lot of natives I ever met inside a place of worship'. Both men were keen photographers and they spent days together planning and taking pictures. One of the most remarkable pictures Johnston took was of the wedding of Litia, Lewanika's eldest son, on New Year's Day 1892. The ceremony was performed by Coillard because Litia was one of the very few converts among the Barotse.

Johnston's picture shows Litia and his bride arm-in-arm. Both are wearing European clothes; she has a veil and he is carrying a Bible. On the left are Waddell and Elise Kiener and in the background is the heavily-bearded Coillard. A group of small Barotse girls in ankle-length dresses are grouped behind the bride, and a score of formidable matrons stare at the camera from a safe distance. The scene has a strange pathos, typifying Coillard's struggle to bring his vision of civilisation to a far corner of Africa.

By mid-January, having been given permission to leave Barotseland, Johnston set off down the Zambezi by canoe. At one stage he was somewhat dubious about obtaining the king's permission, for his medical skill made him a valuable member of the community. Lewanika was slow in collecting carriers for him, and it was only after Johnston had formally served notice of his departure by presenting a Winchester rifle that he got away. The rest of his journey need not concern us, although his commentary on the administration in Southern Rhodesia was biting.

Yet it was not a wasted journey. Johnston's *Reality versus*

Romance in South Central Africa appeared in 1893, more than 350 pages long and illustrated with fifty of the author's photographs—some of the most outstanding pictures taken in southern Africa before the turn of the century. The book was a sensation, both for its caustic observations on missionary work and its revelations about the British South Africa Company. Johnston told the world about Lewanika's anger over the fate of the elephant tusks presented to Lochner for the Queen. The king learned that these were in the Company's London board-room from the book *Zambezia,* written in 1891 by E. P. Mathers.* It can be assumed that Middleton had brought *Zambezia* back to Barotseland from one of his trips to Mafeking, for Johnston reports that the facts had been translated to the king from the book in 1892, so that afterwards 'his anger was white heat'. The British newspapers decided that elephant tusks were news, and after quoting Johnston's account the *Daily Chronicle* branded the whole affair as 'the meanest form of embezzlement'.

A few years after the controversy caused by Dr Johnston's book, an even stronger indictment of the Chartered Company was produced by H. C. Thomson in his book *Rhodesia and its Government.*[3] An experienced traveller and a professional writer, Thomson summed up his findings bluntly :

> But though the settlers deserve generous treatment, the Charter Company itself, as a government, has no claim whatever to indulgence. It has caused terrible bloodshed . . . it has cruelly wronged and oppressed those natives placed under its control. It is due to ourselves as a governing nation that it should be deprived of its powers, and that we should take over charge of the territories and peoples it has misgoverned, just as we took over charge of India.[4]

Thomson was writing some years before the British South Africa Company began to administer north of the Zambezi, and his investigations were necessarily confined to Southern Rhodesia, where he travelled widely and interviewed a wide cross-section of the white community. His book (which Rhodes did all in his power to suppress) is a damning record of forced labour, flogging and even murder.

Thomson was no left-wing sentimentalist, and believed with his age that Britain had a God-given duty to extend its empire. But he was emphatic that Rhodes had too much of Africa :

* The whereabouts of the tusks are unknown today. Possibly they were destroyed when the Chartered Company's offices were bombed in 1940.

> The failure of the Company to govern rightly has arisen from weakness of administration and extent of territory. They have acquired more land than they can govern—that is the truth of the matter; and instead of contenting themselves with what they have, and trying to administer it properly, they are now anxious to acquire yet more land beyond the Zambezi. In that lies the danger of the situation. If Central Africa is to be opened out, let it be done by the Crown direct, and let it be primarily for the introduction of better government, and not for the exploitation of gold; and by direct dealings of Imperial officials with other chiefs, and not through the medium of concessions, otherwise we shall lose altogether among the Central African tribes the reputation for English fair dealing and humanity which Livingstone and Moffat spent their lives building up.[5]

One of Thomson's comments on what he had seen might well have been written about François Coillard, who was at that time pondering as to whether he had done right in helping the Charter Company: 'First the missionary goes up, and if he is a good man, his influence becomes so great with the tribe that he seems to it almost like a god. An entrance having thus been obtained into the country, and white men received with cordiality and friendship, the chief is wheedled into giving a concession, by which, before long, the ruin of the tribe is effected. . . .'[6]

V WINNING THE NORTH-EAST

Simultaneously with the Charter Company's acquisition of the ill-defined kingdom of Lewanika,[1] there was a desperate contest in progress for control of the region farther north between the Luangwa valley and the Luapula river. In Barotseland the rival interests had been British and Portuguese (at the signing of the Lochner Concession an unnamed Portuguese had looked silently on from the crowd). But around the northern plateau, the leading contestants were British, Belgian and German, the Portuguese having long since abandoned their efforts to advance up the Luangwa.* British penetration was from the east, where the fumbling African Lakes Company had been operating since 1879 in support of the Scottish missionaries around Lake Nyasa.[2] Ten

* For a brief period there had been a fort in the Luangua valley in the 1820s; but since the Monteiro expedition to Kazembe, Portuguese penetration had been restricted to Chikunda slave-trading.

years later, Harry Johnston, the consul, arrived with the support of Lord Salisbury for his schemes to obtain 'preliminary treaties with the native chiefs'. In spite of the danger of being cut off in the rear by Serpa Pinto's expeditionary force on the Shire river, Johnston hurried westward.[3] He was inspired by the visions of Rhodes, whom he had met in London while the latter was pressing for his royal charter; they both agreed fervently that there must be an 'all-red' Cape to Cairo route,[4] so it was essential to grasp territory south of Lake Tanganyika. Also, Rhodes had his eyes fixed on the possibility of winning Katanga, whose mineral wealth was already known: in 1884, a German explorer named Paul Reichard had brought back specimens of Katangan copper, to substantiate the earlier reports of Livingstone, Cameron and others. Rhodes gave Johnston £2,000 to help him pay his way in the interior.[5]

By the end of 1889, Johnston was along the Stevenson Road, where the missionary Alfred Swann met him riding on a donkey. The consul obtained twenty-four concessions from chiefs or other persons who passed as such, and reached Mweru before having to turn back to deal with Pinto on Lake Nyasa. One immediate effect was to halt the German advance southwards, because in July 1890 his treaties were taken into account when the Anglo-German boundary between Lakes Tanganyika and Nyasa was drawn.[6] (Also taken into account were the two African Lakes Company's trading posts, shrewdly called Fife and Abercorn, set up on the Stevenson Road.)

The two other principal concession-hunters in the region were Alfred Sharpe,[7] magistrate from Fiji, who had originally come to Central Africa to shoot elephants, and Joseph Thomson,[8] a young geologist-cum-journalist fresh from scaling the Atlas mountains in Morocco. Sharpe had been taken on by Johnston, who had met him accidentally beside the Shire, while Thomson was hired by Rhodes to replace a German called Keppal Stier who had been told to arrange a treaty with Msiri but had been sacked for some unknown reason, before even starting his journey.

The ultimate prize for the concession-hunters was undoubtedly Msiri,* because even though Britain had agreed at the end of 1889 that the Congo Free State should include Katanga,[9] Rhodes for long hoped that a treaty with the Yeke tyrant might swing the balance. In 1891, he was still ordering Thomson: 'I want you to get Msiri's. I mean Katanga. . . . You must go and get Katanga.'[10] Sharpe and Thomson, who were each surprised to find the other in the field, did not get on well, and each agreed to take

* See below for various chiefs of this name (p. 84).

different routes to this goal. Sharpe first saw Mpezeni, chief of the Ngoni, who refused to sign a treaty. Then he went across the Luangwa and took it on himself to declare the whole of the country to the west to be 'under British protection'.[11] This empty gesture both ignored the wishes of the people in the region and could have done nothing to establish Britain's rights at an international conference. Next, Sharpe travelled north-west, making treaties where he could; one of these was with the Tabwa chief, Nsama, who was preposterously entitled 'Paramount Chief or King of the Bemba People and of the Itawa country'.[12] (It is worth noting that no treaty was ever signed with Chitimukulu, the genuine Bemba paramount.) Nsama was given various promises in return for giving the Charter Company the right to 'search, prospect, exploit, dig for, and keep all minerals and metals', to carry on a wide range of business including the manufacture and import of 'arms and ammunition of all kinds' and 'to do such things as are incidental or conducive to the exercise, attainment, and protection of all or any of the rights, powers and concessions hereby granted'. One of the promises made by Sharpe was that Nsama would be given 'a British resident, with a suitable retinue and suite of British subjects, and an escort of British police. . . .' Rather bathetic after this was the promise to give Nsama £25 a year 'or the equivalent thereof in trade goods'. The wording of this agreement, and of those made with other tribal rulers, was identical at many points with the terms of the Lochner Concession. All may have derived from an original draft supplied by Rhodes.

Sharpe had reached an analogous agreement with Kazembe of the Eastern Lunda,[13] and as with Nsama it was to be considered 'in the light of a treaty or alliance made between the said (Lunda) nation and the government of Her Britannic Majesty Queen Victoria'. Nine years later came a sequel, when an Imperial force arrived from Nyasaland to attack Kazembe's capital; the force was sent by Sharpe himself, who was by then Sir Alfred, and had risen to be commissioner. Two accounts of this incident offer a revealing contrast. One is in Gelfand's *Northern Rhodesia in the Days of the Charter,* which was published with the financial help of the British South Africa Company. Gelfand says :

> There still remained Kazembe, another powerful chief, who opposed the advent of the white man. It was anticipated that sooner or later settlement would have to be made with this chief, who lived on the south-east side of Lake Mweru. Several times he had attacked tribes living at peace with the administration. He taxed villagers living near Kalungwesi and

refused to allow Dr Blair Watson into his domain to discuss the question of submission to the administration. It was known, too, that he harboured Arabs in his territory. . . . Accordingly, in October 1899, a contingent of European officers and Sikhs, with Dr Gray as its medical officer, arrived at Kazembe's with a seven-pounder gun, only to find the village deserted and the Arabs fled. The whole affair was over and no further trouble occurred in the Mweru district.[14]

The other account appears in the tribal history of the Lunda.[15] 'The Europeans came with troops and powerful guns, and Mwata Kanyembo ran off to Kabimbi across the Luapula. He stayed there for a while, then made for Mambulima. At this time the Europeans burnt the capital and many people died in it.' The African account goes on to describe how the chief told the missionaries at Mambulima he would submit to white rule and was brought back to the remains of his capital by a woman missionary (a Mrs Anderson), who gave him a metal hat in recognition of his chieftainship: 'On the hat which the lady gave us was the writing: *"Sapeurs pompiers de Paris"*.' That a Paris fire-brigade helmet had reached the Luapula valley in 1899 is interesting. Even more interesting, perhaps, is the treatment meted out to a chief who only a few years earlier had signed what he presumed was a treaty of 'amicable and friendly relations' with Queen Victoria.

Sharpe had managed (in the last stages of exhaustion and deserted by most of his porters) to reach Msiri, but had failed to obtain a concession. He was followed by a Belgian expedition, commanded, ironically enough, by a young Canadian, Captain William Stairs. In 1891, the Belgian flag was run up after a brawl in which Msiri was shot by Captain Bodson, who was killed himself a moment later. Msiri's head was cut off to show the populace that he was really dispatched,[16] and Stairs hurried back to the coast, where he died of malaria. Until quite recent times, to mention the name of Stairs to history-conscious white settlers in Zambia was enough to provoke anger. He has been called the 'traitor to the Empire'[17] who stopped Rhodes from obtaining the Katanga mines in addition to the Copperbelt.

While Sharpe was on his abortive journey to the north of Bangweulu, Joseph Thomson was taking a more southerly course,[18] accompanied by Charles Wilson and John Grant and 145 porters.[19] The caravan carried smallpox with it, and a third of the porters died of the disease. Even worse, in villages where a halt was called to sign a treaty, the people became infected as well. At the farthest point reached, the court of the eastern Lamba ruler,

Mushili (Msiri), the chief's son became a victim. Thomson wrote: 'Regretting sincerely that Mshiri's [sic] hospitality should have cost him so dear, we hurriedly completed our preparations, and on November 18 [1890] commenced the long return journey to Nyasa.'[20] The Lamba well remember the visit of the three and recall that Thomson brought a Union Jack and that the smallpox (*ichingwali*) epidemic lasted for a long time after the caravan had gone.[21] Thomson became stricken with a stomach illness which was ultimately to prove fatal and he had to be carried in a hammock; when they reached the capital of chief Mpezeni the travellers were ambushed by Ngoni warriors and narrowly escaped being wiped out; shortly afterwards, while Grant had been sent hurrying down to Rhodes in Capetown with copies of the treaties, Wilson died of malaria.

For all this chronicle of disaster, the concessions obtained by Thomson were a ludicrous confusion. Although he never reached the significant Msiri, he did his best by making agreements with two other Msiris—one a person oddly described as 'Paramount Chief of the countries of Bausi and of Ilala and of Kawende'—and the other with the chief whose son caught smallpox. There were a dozen more Thomson treaties, two with so-called 'sultans of Iramba'. In return for trade goods, men who could neither read nor write, and whose very existence in most cases seems quite forgotten, handed over most extensive rights. One treaty he signed was with Nansala, called 'a chieftainess of the Lobisa country of Mbalala'. In fact, Nansala was merely a village headwoman who was pushed forward by the people because they did not want to disclose the real chief. She has never been regarded as a chief. Thomson's book was full of errors and he inexplicably called the country near the Hook of the Kafue 'Manicaland'. The consul, Johnston, said frankly that many of the documents were 'absurdly worded'. Moreover, in offering 'protection' on behalf of the Queen, Thomson went beyond his authority. The Foreign Office complained that the treaties contained 'engagements' beyond the powers of the British South Africa Company to contract on behalf of Her Majesty's government and which the government would not accept.[22]

A contemporary historian, L. H. Gann has written:

> It should, however, be noted that neither Thomson nor Sharpe ever penetrated into the mineralised regions of the present Copperbelt or Broken Hill. . . . Nevertheless Johnston, in his capacity as Her Majesty's commissioner, sanctioned the country's [sic] mineral rights as extending to the Kafue.[23]

Dr A. J. Hanna has remarked:

> The treaties made by Johnston and his agents Sharpe and Buchanan appear to have been made as far as possible in good faith, but the same can hardly be said of the transactions between Thomson and chiefs who had never before had any dealings whatsoever with any white man. As a result of these transactions, Thomson claimed with pride that 'over an area of about 40,000 square miles the entire political, trading and mineral rights have been acquired at a very small expense and with few future liabilities'. But the Thomson treaties are the only legal title which either the Crown or the British South Africa Company has ever obtained to the region of the upper Kafue, the economic heart of Northern Rhodesia.[24]

Early in the twentieth century, the boundary of North-Western and North-Eastern Rhodesia (the two administrative entities into which the territory was divided in 1899) was moved from the Kafue river. On the demands of the Company, it became an approximately north-south line across the hundred-mile 'waist' of the territory. The overt grounds for the change were claimed to be ease of administration (yet it was found possible to run the whole of Zambia as one from Livingstone by 1911) and also the desirability of putting 'the principal mining properties' under a single administration. After the change had been gazetted by the Imperial government on September 29, 1905, the Board of the Charter Company declared that its policy was to recognise Lewanika's authority over the whole of North-Western Rhodesia 'thereby gaining stronger economic rights than it previously possessed'. Although by this time the Company was skilfully whittling away Lewanika's authority even in Barotseland proper, and it was patently ridiculous to suggest that his sway had ever extended to and beyond Ndola and Mkushi, the pressure for the new boundary indicates that Thomson's treaties were seen to have a minimal validity.

In March 1904, the secretary of the British South Africa Company, Wilson Fox, wrote to Codrington, the administrator of North-Eastern Rhodesia, to explain why some of his territory was being removed: 'Under the Lewanika Concession our rights to minerals are very clear, but in North-Eastern Rhodesia our rights are founded upon a very large number of contracts made with personages whose existences today are somewhat mythical . . . had we ever to prove our title to any of these rights we should not be in quite so favourable a position in your territory as in Barotseland.'[25] Codrington answered: 'Your rights to minerals may be very clear under the Lewanika Concession, but to contend that any such concession or agreement whatever with Lewanika has any connection with territory or natives further east than Sitanda (near the Kafue river) is beyond all reason. If you are going to hold your rights on a fiction they will rest on a less secure basis than at present.' Codrington went on to admit that there was 'a lot of humbug' about the Thomson treaties but there was nothing so 'fictitious' as to suggest that Lewanika had any influence in the region being transferred to North-Western Rhodesia. Later, Coryndon, the administrator for North-West Rhodesia, tried to make Stephenson, the Chartered official for what is now the Copperbelt area, agree that Lewanika's sway extended that far. But he was unsuccessful.

Apart from rare (and invariably derogatory) comments in academic works,[26] Thomson's Zambian journey has remained under a shroud of silence for more than seventy years. In many quarters it seemed preferable that the details should be left in that condition. Yet it would be wrong to underestimate Thomson himself, who apart from being a man of considerable literary and scientific achievement at an early age, refused to accept uncritically the general adulation of his employer. He wrote in a letter: 'You mustn't imagine that I am an out-and-out admirer of Rhodes. He is a man with terribly grave faults and many weak points. He is unscrupulous to a degree in carrying out his schemes, although no-one who knows him properly can fail to be struck with intense admiration at the greatness of his plans and ideas. . . .'[27]

4

Three Decades of Chartered Rule

I THE FIRST WHITE ADMINISTRATORS

IN the last ten years of the nineteenth century, the first isolated outposts of white administration were set up in the vast regions of 'Northern Zambezia'. Initially, Harry Johnston had authority from the Zambezi to Lake Tanganyika and from Lake Nyasa to the disputed boundaries in the far west—an area of about 300,000 square miles. His headquarters were in Zomba. Johnston played a dual role as representative of the Crown and of the Charter Company, although he was responsible ultimately to the Foreign Office. It was a delicate arrangement, because he received £10,000 a year from Rhodes to maintain a military force of Sikhs and Africans.[1] Moreover, the Charter Company at first subsidised and later absorbed the African Lakes Company, which was the mainstay of missionary endeavour in Nyasaland, so that the missions suspected Johnston of being a mere tool of Rhodes. In sharp contrast to François Coillard in Barotseland, the Church of Scotland evangelists were from the first opposed to any infiltration from the white-supremacist south. 'A Chartered Company is not a government and never can be. To be ruled by such is to be ruled for commercial ends by absentee directors and shareholders, whose real interests are only served by tangible dividends', declared the monthly journal of the missions.[2]

It was this attitude which on May 15, 1891, forced the British government (in contradiction of Lord Salisbury's blunt refusal exactly three years earlier) to declare : 'It is hereby notified for public information that, under and by virtue of agreements with the native chiefs, and by other lawful means, the territories in Africa, hereinafter referred to as the Nyasaland Districts are under

7—Z

the protection of Her Majesty the Queen.'[3] The *London Gazette* announcement came just three months after the Command Paper extending the sphere of activity of the British South Africa Company 'over the territory under British influence north of the Zambezi and south of the territories under British influence north of the Zambezi and north of the territories of the Congo Free State and the German sphere'.[4] Johnston was well aware of the dangers of serving two masters, and commented afterwards: 'I preferred to receive no pay from the Company, so that I might not in any way compromise my position as an Imperial officer.'[5]

The boundary between Nyasaland and the Charter domain was agreed in 1891 to be the watershed between the Luangwa valley and the lake. Yet for Johnston with his handful of white officials, the boundary was of little practical significance. As the need arose, men and troops were moved without any regard for the division between Nyasaland and Rhodes's Zambezia—from fighting against the Arab slave-traders among the Yao to manning posts on the 'front line' with the Congo. The first administrative centre in what is now Zambia was set up at the end of 1890 by Captain Richard Crawshay of the Inniskilling Dragoons. He was left at Chiengi, on the north-eastern corner of Lake Mweru, by Alfred Sharpe on the way back from the abortive expedition to Msiri. Crawshay had a Union Jack, the friendship of Chief Puta of the Bwile, and little else.[6] Two years later, John Kydd and Frank Bainbridge arrived at Lake Mweru and the former ambitiously built the country's first post-office before they both died of blackwater fever. Their station on the Kalungwisi river was called 'Rhodesia', three years before the Imperial proclamation (May 3, 1895) gave this title to all territories under the British South Africa Company. In 1892, Sharpe had returned to the Luapula valley (it is not recorded whether Kazembe or Nsama asked him what had happened to the British Residents promised in their treaties) and chose the site for Fort Rosebery. This station was duly put on the maps to impress the Belgians, at a point near Johnston Falls, nearly fifty miles from the present Fort Rosebery. It was later revealed: 'Fort Rosebery, which was reported by Sir H. Johnston in May 1894 as having been fortified, has never been built, nor has any white man visited the site since Mr Sharpe selected it in 1892.'[7]

By 1897, Northern Zambezia was being rather vaguely divided into its two parts: North-Western Rhodesia, covering the exaggerated domain of Lewanika up to the Kafue, and North-Eastern Rhodesia beyond it. If it had not been for the Jameson Raid. which made Britain determined to curb the power of

Rhodes, it is likely that he would have been given as much freedom of action north of the Zambezi as he had in Southern Rhodesia. In the event, the Imperial government retained decisive rights and placed ultimate restraint in the hands of its high commissioner in Capetown.[8] Major Patrick Forbes was appointed as the administrator of the north-east regions, with his headquarters in Nyasaland and he and his successor, Robert Codrington, concentrated for the next seven years on building up the framework of white administration, wiping out the Arab slave-trade and subduing chiefs. The tactics employed for the last were succinctly explained by Johnston: 'Dissociate the personal interests of the various native chiefs and Arab sultans as far as possible; discreetly encourage their mutual rivalries (though stopping short, of course, of inciting them to civil war); bind over the more influential men to your interests by small money subsidies. . . .'[9] After a number of skirmishes and negotiations the much feared Bemba gave in more easily than expected,[10] but the south-east Ngoni put up a determined fight.

In the struggle between British power and Mpezeni's Ngoni warriors, there were several complicating and revealing elements. One of the principal of these was the presence of a German trader called Carl Wiese, who arrived in the Ngoni country about 1885 from Portuguese East Africa, and occupied much the same position in the tribe as George Westbeech did with the Barotse. Wiese settled down with his coloured Portuguese wife, Dona Romana, and because of his great friendship with Mpezeni, he was granted the right to hunt for ivory, dig for gold and start plantations.[11] His power and friendship with the Portuguese, combined with Mpezeni's refusal to grant a concession to the British South Africa Company, greatly annoyed Harry Johnston, the consul. Matters had been made even worse in April 1891, when Wiese obtained from Mpezeni a formal concession covering 10,000 square miles. The chief accepted the Portuguese flag. This created an awkward hurdle to the administration of North-Eastern Rhodesia for several years, as the 30,000 Ngoni warriors dominated the natural route westward from Nyasaland. The problem was to break Mpezeni, who became even more dubious about the advantages of British 'protection' when news came northward after 1893 of the crushing of the Matabele, who were in origins closely allied to the Ngoni. Progress towards surmounting the hurdle was made when Wiese went to London and sold out his concession to a group called the North Charterland Exploration Company—in which the British South Africa Company had a controlling interest.

Wiese then took the final step, and played on Mpezeni's

trust by accompanying a North Charterland Exploration Company expedition into Ngoni country. The leader of this expedition, Colonel Warton, carried a Portuguese flag and was introduced to the chief as Wiese's brother. It was not for a year that Mpezeni realised he had been tricked. He was then prepared to admit that his independence was gone, and asked for a British flag, but this was refused. The administration preferred to bring what it considered a dangerous abscess to a head, and then lance it. A reward of £15,000 was offered to the first prospectors to find payable gold in the North Charterland area and this naturally set several expeditions in motion. One, led by Cyril Hoste, claimed in May 1896 that it was in peril, and a small military force was sent into Mpezeni's country from Kota Kota, but the incident petered out inconclusively. Johnston 'felt the time was not yet ripe; any attack on the Angoni must be provoked by the Angoni themselves'. There seems to have been a striking similarity with the methods employed by Dr Starr Jameson against Lobengula. In 1897, the Ngoni tried to move across into Nyasaland from the Charter Company sphere, and Mpezeni wrote to Sharpe: 'I wish no war. All Cipeta was mine, and now you say it is not. Mwasi was my slave and you killed him in war.'

In December 1897 the fighting began, and the warriors were led by Nsingu, Mpezeni's son who had on several occasions been publicly humiliated by members of the administration and by white 'explorers'. When the moment came, it was ironically enough Carl Wiese who called in the troops from Nyasaland. As in Matabeleland, thousands of warriors with spears proved ineffectual against maxim-guns and seven-pounders. Villages were burnt down, and on January 25, 1898, Mpezeni's town was captured. Nsingu was tried by court-martial, found guilty, and shot at dawn in front of his lieutenants. The aged Mpezeni, who had fled into the hills, was put in prison for a time after surrendering, and later released. The Ngoni herds were taken away (they were on several occasions described as 'the loot') and by this means the British South Africa Company was able to derive a considerable profit from the 'rebellion' after covering all expenses; by 1900, the Ngoni had less than 1,250 head of cattle compared with more than 12,000 at the start of 1898. From the administrative point of view, the defeat of Mpezeni was significant because it allowed the capital of North-Eastern Rhodesia to be set up in the village of his induna Kapatamoyo; the village was renamed Fort Jameson.[12] The assertion of supremacy was given formal authority in 1900, when regulations were promulgated vesting all land in North-Eastern Rhodesia in the Chartered Company; the regulations were signed in the name of the

Crown by Commissioner Sharpe, who ten years before had helped to 'capture' the north-east for Rhodesia.

II LEWANIKA AND THE LAND

Although in the north-east the first steps towards creating a 'colonial' administration had been taken as early as 1890, Barotseland was left dormant by the Charter Company for almost a decade after Lochner had returned to Kimberley with his far-reaching concession. Inevitably, Lewanika grew restive and puzzled. The missionary Coillard had written a somewhat desperate letter to Sir Henry Loch, the high commissioner in Capetown as early as April 1892 : 'Needless to say that the situation has become a most critical one. At times we have felt little security for both our property and our persons and should this state of anarchy be suffered to continue much longer, no one can tell how long we may be yet able to hold our footing in this land.'[1] He appealed for a 'Resident representing Her Majesty's government, a gentleman of conciliatory nature, naturally kindly disposed towards the natives'. No Resident appeared, however, and Lewanika still further doubted the British ability to grant him protection when a savage raid was made on Batokaland in 1893 by the Matabele. During this raid, forty babies were strung up by their feet over a long fire, and died while the raiders sat around; men were hung upside down from trees, and a variety of other atrocities committed.[2]

It may be assumed that the Barotse learnt with relief of the crushing of the Matabele, but this did not compensate indefinitely for the neglect. Apart from occasional hunters and traders, the only white arrivals from the south were a party of prospectors led by Frederick Burnham, an American adventurer who had taken part in the Matabele war. The expedition was sponsored by Rhodes and the aim as described by Burnham was to 'look for a possible railway crossing of this great river, and with the hope that in these regions a new mineral field might be found'.[3] The effect of this visit was anything but comforting to Lewanika, because in July 1894 Coillard wrote to Dr Jameson protesting that the party had been 'bullying the natives and threatening to fight and burn down their villages'.[4] He went on to say that the 'pioneering men are looked on as mere tools to foster disturbances and bring war, so that the country may be wrested from the hands of the natives'. The Barotse relief that their Matabele enemies had been brought to the dust was by now replaced with fear that a like fate might be in store for them. The disillusionment of the missionaries was further increased by a letter written to Coillard on September 1,

1895, by John S. Moffat, who had been sent off to a remote part of Bechuanaland: 'I have been transferred to this place [Taung] to meet the exigencies of Charter Company politics—that is in plain language to get me out of the way. I am much concerned at what you tell me about the doings of white men in Barotseland. Nowadays, might is right. The Charter Company controls everybody, even the high commissioner.'[5] It was to the high commissioner that Lewanika had written just previously in a 'tone of sadness and despondency'.

Another ground for Barotse discontent was that in May 1893, Britain and Portugal had made a provisional agreement setting as the boundary of Barotseland the centre of the Zambezi river.[6] All the territory to the west was to become part of Angola, which removed from Lewanika's control a vast stretch of terrain which he had claimed, with some justification, to rule. Although relations might be strained in other ways, Rhodes and the Litunga were fully in agreement in opposing the Foreign Office's policy here. The Charter Company insisted that Barotseland extended as far as twenty degrees east (more than 150 miles beyond the Zambezi). In the later years of the decade the Charter Company sent its agents, principally Major A. St-H. Gibbons and Captain Colin Harding, to the country north and west of Lealui. The aim was to establish Lewanika's control over the Lunda, Lovale and other tribes. As has been pointed out by a leading authority,[7] there was much special pleading interpreting the results of such expeditions: Harding asserted that Chief Kakengi was 'a child of Lewanika' and that Chieftainess Nyakatore was the Litunga's blood relation,[8] thus hoping to strengthen British claims, despite the fact that the Portuguese had several forts in Lovale country and that tribal affinities had counted for almost nothing in partitioning other parts of Africa. Yet the Charter Company's efforts did not go unrewarded, because in 1903 the British and Portuguese decided to invite the King of Italy to draw the boundary. A thoroughly independent arbitrator, living in blissful ignorance of the people of the Zambezi valley, King Emmanuel took up his pen on May 30, 1905 and drew what is now the Zambia-Angola border down the line of longitude twenty-two degrees east.[9] Thus about 40,000 square miles which had seemed lost in 1893 were restored to the Barotse domain.

Meanwhile, late in 1897, Lewanika had received what he had been awaiting for more than seven years—a British Resident. The man chosen for the post was Major Robert Coryndon, a South African who had served in the Bechuanaland Border Police, fought in both Matabele wars, and acquired a name as a big game hunter. Coryndon had also been very close to Rhodes, serving for a time as his secretary and going with him to London in 1895 to face the Commons Committee investigating the Jameson Raid. Coryndon had a clear understanding of the role he must occupy in Barotseland; no control of the situation could be achieved until Lewanika's suspicions had been quietened, so he quickly wrote a letter: 'You are definitely under British protection. You gave a concession to the British South Africa Company. Afterwards you were afraid you had sold your country. Do not believe this; you have not sold your country.'[10] Yet the Resident had to contend with open opposition from the Paris Evangelical Mission, whose members were by now regretting the assistance they had given to Lochner, of whom Coillard told Jameson: 'The character of the man . . . was far from inspiring his [Lewanika's] confidence and commending the dealings of the Company whom he represented.'[11]

Although great crowds watched the arrival in Lealui of Coryndon and the six white soldiers who acted as his suite, the Charter Company possessed no administrative powers under the terms of the Lochner Concession, despite the formal extension of its authority north of the Zambezi in 1891 by the Imperial government. The Foreign Office had forced the Company into appointing Major Forbes in North-Eastern Rhodesia in 1895 and had applied pressure for the nominating of Coryndon two years later. Now it demanded a new concession in which Lewanika would grant administrative powers and which would remove the illegal trading monopoly obtained by Lochner.[12] To regularise Coryndon's position, a new concession was drawn up; it was very close in wording to the 1890 agreement, but gave the Charter administration the right to judge cases 'between white men and between white men and natives' and to 'make grants of land for farming purposes in any portion of the Batoka and Mashukulumbwe [Ila] country to white men approved by the king'.[13] Here was the first step to ceding the land. There was also a clause promising Lewanika a straight £850 a year, but nothing was mentioned about the £14,000 owing to him. To promote the signing of the new concession, headed 'King Lewanika, Paramount Chief of the Barotse Nation, to the British South Africa Company', Captain Arthur Lawley (later Lord Wenlock) was brought up from Matabeleland where he was administrator. Lawley made his headquarters on the south bank of the Zambezi, close to the Victoria Falls, and wrote afterwards: 'When the question arose as to whether the king should first call on me or *vice-versa,* they [the Barotse] were strongly opposed to his losing (as they considered it) his prestige by being the first to come and pay his respects. But on this I insisted.'[14]

After his psychological victory Lawley visited the king and discussed the new concession, but it was not signed. Perhaps matters would have gone more easily had Coillard consented to attend, but he would not. Eventually, after laboured negotiations with the Foreign Office, a modified form of concession was drawn up, and on October 17, 1900, Coryndon managed to persuade Lewanika to sign it; for good measure, the 1898 concession was signed as well. Neither Coillard nor Jalla, who had happily witnessed the Lochner concession, would sign this time and their places were taken by two Charter Company officials, Harding and Frank Worthington. It is possible to make some estimate of the manner in which the concession was obtained through the eye-witness account of Harding, who for several months had been Acting Resident while Coryndon was in South Africa. Harding wrote:

> Now although at the time this treaty was ratified at Lealui, King Lewanika declared officially that he was cognisant of its contents, on more consideration he realised that it carried him further than he meant to go, and that it contained some fresh clauses which would considerably affect not only his status and independence as Paramount Chief but also the future destiny of the Barotse kingdom.
>
> Moreover, although the treaty met with the entire approval of Major Coryndon, and to him must be accorded the credit of obtaining Lewanika's final signature to it, yet neither the Chief's nor that of his Prime Minister was affixed without some hesitation and misgiving. I would like to say here that though I was present when this Ratifying Treaty was signed and my name was appended to it as a witness to the other signatures, the full contents of the document were not divulged to me.[15]

It may be thought that since Coryndon was not even willing to show the whole document to his deputy, he may have kept it as a secret from Lewanika. Coillard wrote in a letter, 'The poor natives do not understand the situation. . . . It makes me tremble.'

From this moment on, Lewanika's power began to wane. As early as 1900, Chief Monze had declared: 'Why should I pay tribute [to Lewanika] when I am under the White Queen?'[16] The realisation that the Barotse ruler was being pushed into a corner spread quickly to subordinate tribes. Although for the purposes of maintaining its economic rights the Charter Company insisted that

Lewanika lorded all of North-Western Rhodesia, from the administrative point of view it became desirable that he should be increasingly restricted to the Barotse valley. While this process was being developed, the Litungu and his prime minister were shrewdly taken to Britain in 1902 for the coronation of Edward VII. During the visit a meeting was held with Joseph Chamberlain, the Colonial Secretary, and Harding was present on this occasion also. '... Mr Chamberlain could not and did not give any hopes that the concession which he, Lewanika, had given to the Chartered Company should be revised. . . . Lewanika left not entirely satisfied but his anxiety as towards the future was abated.'[17] Yet the abatement was short-lived, for white farmers—especially Afrikaners—were moving into North-Western Rhodesia in increasing numbers. They were given land by Coryndon in the Batoka uplands, mainly between Kalomo and Mazabuka. By 1905 the railway line from Bulawayo had advanced as far as the embryo town of Livingstone, and the Victoria Falls bridge was being thrown across the Zambezi. Between 1904 and 1909, Lewanika gradually yielded complete control of all land outside Barotseland proper, to be disposed of to settlers 'as it was from time to time required, on whatever terms the Company considered just, the Company retaining any money from such disposition of land'.[18] It is noteworthy that in these ultimate concessions, the resounding titles formerly accorded to the Litunga were removed. In the concession of 1909 he was merely called, 'Lewanika, Paramount Chief of the Barotse nation'.

There is no doubt that the Litunga and his *indunas* felt the humiliation of the administration's tightening grasp most keenly. In 1907 a meeting was held with Lord Selborne, the new high commissioner, at which Lewanika poured out his woes and appealed for direct British protection.[19] Selborne replied with a string of platitudes about various forms of government, and nothing was done. In one letter, Lewanika said: 'We are sometimes caused to feel as if we were a conquered nation, while we have made an agreement which was said to be just like an alliance between our nation and the Imperial government. When we say so, those of the British South Africa Company ask: "Do you want to be conquered?" '[20] In another letter he cried: 'Oh! that we were granted to pass directly under the government of King Edward!'[21]

A natural sequence of the condition into which Lewanika had been manoeuvred was unrest among his people. There were persistent rumours of a revolt.

In July 1907, the Secretary for Native Affairs, Worthington, warned that 'in the event of the violent death of Lewanika', all white residents were to go to the fort at Mongu; the white rifle-association was also to go there, ready for duty. Even if Lewanika died a natural death, his house was to be seized at Lealui by the Barotse Native Police, the *Ngambela* (Prime Minister) summoned and told that any disturbance would be quelled without hesitation. Then the national council would be called to elect a new paramount chief. But Lewanika did not die until 1916, by which time the resentment among certain of the *indunas* had declined into quiet acceptance.[22]

In Barotseland, as in the rest of Northern Rhodesia, three decades of Company rule produced no dramatic change or sudden upheaval. The Chartered Company kept the costs of administration to the minimum because of its financial difficulties and so could not launch anything resembling a territorial development program. White settlement was negligible and almost entirely restricted to the 'line-of-rail' between Broken Hill and Livingstone. For the Africans, these somnolent years provided few opportunities for improvement; almost the only demand upon the people was to pay tax, which drove them to migrate in search of work on the mines of Katanga or Southern Rhodesia. At home, a man's sole chance of earning money occurred if he could act as a porter to a white official on *ulendo* (safari). When Chartered divested itself—with considerable relief—of the powers of government shortly after the first world war it left as its monument one of the most neglected territories in Africa. The handsome promises made in the treaties with Lewanika and other chiefs remained unfulfilled; yet the country was to be held to its side of the bargain.

III EMBERS OF A SOCIAL SYSTEM

The inevitable consequence of white administration was a slow disintegration of the traditional African way of life. For some of the Zambian tribes the effect was gradual, so that even today they retain much of the ancient social structure. For others, such as the Ngoni whose political formation was shattered by military conquest,[1] or the Lamba whose tribal areas were swamped by white settlement, the change was overwhelming. Yet in all the tribes the new conditions quickly reduced the stature of chiefs in the eyes of their people.[2] The early administrators usually set up their *boma* close to a chief's village and demonstrated a type of relentless power which had not been seen before. The chief inherited the spirits of his ancestors and could bring rain for the crops—in him might repose the supernatural forces; he was the giver of land and the owner of ivory.[3] But in the *boma* a new variety of materialistic authority resided, which did not hesitate to impose itself even on the chief himself if in the eyes of the '*bwana mkubwa*' he seemed to be obstructionist. First and foremost, the administration brought with it the white man's law, which meant jail and sometimes beating. There were such salutory occasions as the public hanging in Kasempa in 1912 of three murderers. Chiefs, headmen and villagers were invited from as far as the Congo border to watch. 'The execution had a sobering and restraining effect on the Bakaonde for a considerable time,' said the administration.[4]

Almost as significant, however, was the first contact with a cash economy. In pre-European days, the tribe and the village were almost entirely self-sufficient and whatever might be obtained from outside was obtained by barter or war; concepts of private property were subordinate to tribal ownership in a status society. Even if tribute was paid, it was paid collectively, and a chief received and gave gifts not as an individual but on behalf of the tribe. Early in the twentieth century a hut tax was imposed by the administration, both to raise money to pay its costs and to force men to work in Southern Rhodesia, which was desperate for labour. Simultaneously with the hut tax arrived the recruiting agents. Thus the chief could not lead his young men in war, because the white men would put him, and them, in what was jovially called the 'King's Hotel'; nor could the chief pay the hut tax of his people. Even on the spiritual level, there were new pressures, for the missionaries were promoting Christianity to replace the old worship of the ancestors.[5] A man could still be proud of his tribe, but he was being made to accept compulsions beyond it.

There are, of course, conflicting opinions as to what the people lost as the new world was forced upon them. On one side, there is the portrayal of African life in pre-European days as happy, moral, courageous and free. On the other it is shown as vicious, fear-ridden and depraved. Somewhere between is the reality of Zambian society before the twentieth century, although it is hardly surprising that the first white travellers wrote in horror of a region where the Portuguese and Arab slave-trade had for decades been corrupting and brutalising African life. It is imperative to look beyond this evil and essentially non-African influence to know the natural forms of society.

Over much of the land between the Zambezi and Lake Tanganyika, the people lived by simple agriculture, in which the branches of trees (or in some tribes, the whole trees) were cut down and burnt to give the soil fertility. After three or five years, when the soil was becoming exhausted the headman would call together his advisors and suggest that the time had arrived to move elsewhere. Then young men would be sent out to select a fresh site, to which the whole village would move if the omens were favourable. The houses the people built were simple, because in a few years they would move away. Such a wandering life was possible in a region of vast empty spaces (it is estimated that the country's population has far more than trebled since the introduction of modern medicine).

African life was governed by mystery and magic and all-pervading rules of behaviour. At birth, a child would be given his 'spirit name' which was that of a relative of the same clan. By this means, the relative was reincarnated. Only when he reached the age of ten or more, would the child choose, or be given a new name; this usually described his character. All around were witches and wizards, visible and invisible, who could cause death or disasters of many kinds. In the search for witches, trial by poison was common and caused many deaths. Generally, suspects were made to swallow poison themselves, but sometimes a fowl was poisoned and if it dropped dead the witch or wizard was judged guilty, and killed.

Apart from the terrors of witchcraft, the tribes each had clearly defined bodies of laws, offences against which were taken to the court of the chief. These offences ranged from arson and assault to adultery and murder, the last two being regarded as extremely serious. Punishments were immediate and severe: executions were carried out by the spear, by burning or drowning;[6] for less serious crimes, mutilation was widely practised and a thief would be likely to lose a hand and an adulterer his eyes.[7] A persistent offender might well be banished or even sold as a slave to the Arabs or Chikunda. Sometimes a plaintiff would take an offender as a domestic slave, even though the guilty person was his neighbour. For petty theft, the headman could order payment of a fine, such as beads or grain.[8] If a man felt he had not received justice at the court of a junior chief, he had the right of appeal to a more senior ruler. But crime in African society was not as common as in many more developed societies, perhaps because of the strength of tribal taboos and the ferocity of punishment stern chiefs would mete out. Chirupula Stephenson, an administrator at the turn of the century who later settled near Mkushi with several African wives, went so far as to say that when he first arrived in the country, people never stole.[9]

Except in times of war, village life followed a slow, placid routine. Although it has been argued by some anthropologists that the men were idle and let their wives do all the work, this claim does not really stand up under close examination. To the men fell such jobs as collecting heavy firewood, hunting, fishing, honey-collecting, hut-building, carving wood, weaving, making weapons and preparing bark-cloth.[10] (The last of these was an essential and laborious task; only the Bantu Botatwe tribes wore skins and the locally-woven cotton was usually too scarce to be available to the ordinary villager.) The women and children collected kindling wood, weeded and hoed in the gardens, scared birds, watched the cattle or goats, gathered wild fruit and mushrooms, threshed corn, cooked and brewed beer. It was the women who made the clay pots, in the same way as the men smelted iron and copper.

When in the evening the people had their one meal of the day, a village would divide up into three groups to eat the millet porridge and relish. Old men would sit in one group and the young warriors in another; women and children never ate with the men and sat down around separate pots and dishes. The relish would be the stewed meat of wild or domestic animals, with nuts, mushrooms, beans, spinach and sometimes caterpillars. After the meal, the village would relax beside the fires, and hear the elders tell stories, mainly of hunting, war and magic. At a chief's court, travellers would tell of their experiences in different parts, for an important chief always had around him men who were employed as envoys to other tribes. Among the Bemba, such men were called *Ingenga*. They would bring back from their journeys calabashes, marked with symbols to record details of what they had seen.[11] Thus, when a chief's envoy reached a tribe whose people filed their teeth into points, he would mark this on his calabash. He would record the number of days' journey between one tribe or another, or one river and the next, by a line for each day.

It was through the stories of such men as the *Ingenga* that the Bemba and Lozi, at the far ends of Zambia, knew something of each other's existence and progress. Such exciting topics would be discussed far into the night beside the fires.

As today, so in pre-European times, a great deal of beer was drunk, almost any event being considered justification for celebration. (Many drinks made from wild fruit or sorghum or honey were not at all intoxicating and cannot properly be described as beer.) Apart from the usual beer made from corn, a type of honey-beer was made partly from the young of bees; it was extremely potent. Drinking always took place during important rituals, especially the initiation ceremonies of boys and girls when they reached puberty. At such ceremonies, which varied greatly from tribe to tribe, instruction in sexual and social matters was given to the initiates and often they took part in symbolic forms of intercourse.[12] After initiation, the young people were regarded as adults and became subject to the rigid rules of sexual behaviour of their tribe, whether they were married or not.

Rituals of all kinds always called for dancing and music, both so integral a part of African life. Foremost among the musical instruments was the drum, made in countless forms, but the tribes also had their specialities: among the Tonga and Ila, flutes and whistles were popular, and the Chewa played a type of violin complete with a sounding-box. Hand pianos, in which metal strips of varying lengths were attached to a wooden base, were played throughout the region.

A revealing glimpse of the past can be obtained through the games the children played, many of which resembled the games of European children. They spun tops, using whips made of dried grass. A kind of nine-pins was popular, with two rows of mealie-cobs set up on the ground about four yards apart and the contestants aiming to knock down the cobs with large tops spun across the open space.[13] With a long piece of string, or *liana,* and two pieces of gourd, African children in pre-European times would make a 'telephone' and while one child spoke into it, disguising his voice as much as possible, his friends at the other end had to guess who was speaking.[14] In an African equivalent of 'Oranges and lemons' a line of children went under the arms of two of their number, while they all sang a song: 'Lions and leopards hunting at night, lions and leopards—catch the game!' One early white traveller was astonished by the beauty and complication of 'cats' cradles' made by small girls in the villages.

Ball games were popular among all tribes, the ball being made of wild rubber collected in the forest by the boys. Among the Lozi a type of hockey was played, while the Bemba went in for their own version of rugby with a ball the size of a golf-ball. But undoubtedly the most typical pastime of all was *chisolo,* often called 'African draughts'.[15] The rules varied slightly, but basically *chisolo* involved moving pebbles around in four rows of holes in the ground The pebbles advanced according to strict rules, the aim being to capture those of an opponent till he had none left.

Some of the games of the children and rituals of the adults still survive, though in the urban areas initiation ceremonies are forgotten and guitars have replaced the *kalimbo* hand-pianos. Radios are listened to instead of the legends of the old men. The speed at which traditional customs decayed in the early twentieth century can well be illustrated by the disappearance of the Ila *isusu.* The *isusu* was the graceful spiked headdress of Ila warriors; often a yard high, it was made from a man's own hair, with that of his wife woven in. Not surprisingly, the *isusu* made a strong impression on early white arrivals and pictures of Ila warriors appeared in dozens of travel books at the end of Queen Victoria's reign. But when the Prince of Wales visited Northern Rhodesia in 1928, and wanted to see an *isusu,* not one could be found in the length of the Ila country.[16]

IV WAR IN THE BUSH

With considerable justification, historians of the 1914–18 war take little account of the military encounters along Northern Rhodesia's border with Tanganyika.[1] Such fighting as took place was sporadic and amateurish: on the Allied side, less than 500 combatants met their deaths, the majority through illness rather than gunfire. Little damage was done to property, because the adversaries rarely came across anything worth destroying.

Hostilities started with the Germans firing upon the settlement at Abercorn without effect. Four months later, they made an attack upon Fife, some 100 miles to the south-east, and this was followed by a year of inconclusive skirmishing. It was normal practice for messages to be exchanged over the telephone line linking Abercorn and Kasanga, on opposite sides of the so-called front. After one fight, which halted when the day became too hot, porters were despatched from both camps to sort out equipment which had been dropped, and bring it back to the owners. In the tall grass, rival patrols often blundered into one another along the unmarked border. What kind of war it was is summed up by the following extract from the Report of the administrator for 1916, describing an attack on Abercorn: 'After expending a large amount of machine-gun and rifle ammunition the enemy were forced to retire. We had no casualties.'

By 1916, the Allies were in a position to take the offensive in East Africa, the Germans being pressed from the north as well as the south. They were heavily outnumbered and suffered the psychological handicap of having long been cut off from their fatherland. The advance from the south was directed by Brigadier-general Edward Northey, the two columns organised in Northern Rhodesia consisting of Northern Rhodesian and British South African police and units of the South African army. The Germans were commanded by the remarkably resourceful General von Lettow Vorbeck, who decided to engage on a long, wandering campaign through Portuguese East Africa, living off the land in medieval style. He evaded his enemies without difficulty and in the closing months of 1918 had swung westward to invade Northern

Rhodesia. After capturing a deserted Kasama he moved south and was preparing to cross the Chambishi river and advance towards Broken Hill when the fighting ended in Europe. On hearing this news, he surrendered. Although there had been little bloodshed along the Northern Rhodesian border, von Lettow could look back with satisfaction to several hard-fought victories in eastern Tanganyika; that part of the campaign had cost 60,000 lives through gunfire and disease.

Of far greater significance than the actual fighting was the effect on Northern Rhodesia of the forced recruitment of porters from all districts. It has been estimated that for a large part of the war, one third of the adult African males in the country were impressed to take food and equipment to the front. Women were also employed. The carriers suffered terribly from disease, and an unknown number—at least several thousand—succumbed. Dr Michael Gelfand writes in *Northern Rhodesia in the Days of the Charter*: 'It was most unfortunate that this great contribution to the war effort by the porters should be accompanied by such huge losses, for the death-rate amongst them was higher than could possibly have been anticipated.' Gelfand goes on to point out that lack of food was 'an aggravating factor'. Because of bad weather and the lack of menfolk to raise crops, 'the majority of Africans who returned from service in the Lundazi sub-division of the East Luangwa district arrived in a pitiable state of emaciation due to starvation and dysentery'. In October 1918, an influenza epidemic swept the country, causing many more deaths; it was reported to be so serious that all forms of transport were paralysed.

There is no official record of African reactions to the experiences of the war years in which people so recently prohibited from fighting one another were forced to help white men fight white men for incomprehensible reasons. Whatever the effect on African attitudes to their rulers may have been, it is certain that the economic consequences of the war were felt for several years.

5

Colonialism and the Roots of African Nationalism

I THE DILEMMAS OF INDIRECT RULE

WITH the splendid advantage of hindsight, it is possible to identify April 1, 1924, as the day which led inexorably to the amicable granting of Zambia's independence forty years later to an African government. Had the settlers' moves for closer union with the south come to fruition in the time of Chartered administration, at least part of Northern Rhodesia would have become subject to the 'settler concepts' of political mastery and authoritarian native policy,[1] which by their nature reject any gradual and willing transference of power. It is true that in Northern Rhodesia the minority was able to make great advances towards supremacy during the era of Colonial Office administration, but however much ground that administration might have to yield, its ultimate purpose could never be surrendered.

The distinction between direct and indirect rule was fundamental. Before 1924, the Chartered Company's native commissioners did not regard it as part of their functions to build up the role of the chiefs in local administration. Lord Hailey remarked later: 'The general effect of the policy was to preserve the outward form of the indigenous systems, but to undermine the authority of the chiefs both by making them depend on the administrative officer and by taxation which obliged large numbers of men to leave their villages for considerable periods of time.'[2]

Where a chief or headman could serve some immediate purpose (such as supplying porters during the war) he was employed; otherwise he was largely ignored. With a certain justification, the native commissioners felt that in laying down the law or collecting taxes, they could do a quicker and less complicated job themselves. Many of the native commissioners had served in the army or police in South Africa or Southern Rhodesia and any suggestion that they were guiding the African to run his own affairs would have seemed ludicrous to them. With the removal of the early influence of the Imperial government in North-Eastern Rhodesia after 1911, the pattern of administration was dictated from Southern Rhodesia. Sir Francis Chaplin, administrator of both Rhodesias from 1921 to the end of Chartered rule, had his headquarters in Salisbury. John X. Merriman, the South African politician, wrote to him seeking a job in the far north for a former officer in the 10th Hussars: '. . . Newton tells me you are the autocrat of N. Rhodesia and Barotseland'.[3] It was an exact description.

At first, Colonial Office rule appeared to bring little change. The first Governor, Sir Herbert Stanley, was a South African, probably chosen by the Colonial Office because he knew the nuances of local conditions and would not provoke too drastic a transformation. During Sir Herbert's tenure of office in Livingstone (the capital was not transferred to Lusaka until 1935), the old guard of native commissioners began to fade away and new men infused with the 'Lugard Doctrine' took their places. The stage was set for the second Governor, Sir James Maxwell, who was transferred from the Gold Coast in 1927.

The theory of indirect rule in Africa was peculiarly British. In contrast, the French saw it as their duty, while developing the potential of their colonies, to strengthen the links with the metropolitan power and turn Africans into Frenchmen. The Portuguese and the Belgians had somewhat similar notions. But from before the first world war, British administrators had been feeling their way towards another conception: 'For two or three generations we can show the Negro what we are: then we shall be asked to go away. Then we shall leave the land to those it belongs to, with the feeling that they have better business friends in us.' Thus it was summed up by Sir Frederick Lugard, author of the definitive work, *The Dual Mandate in British Tropical Africa*.[4] The imperial power would stay while it could, impart what it felt was good for the indigenous people and then retire gracefully—but keeping her trade after the flag had been lowered. Implicit in this philosophy was the development of 'indirect rule', which would guide Africans towards running their own affairs. Lugard, who as a young man had fought against the Arab slavers in Nyasaland in 1888, became the doyen of British colonial administrators in Africa, retiring in 1919 as Governor General of Nigeria.[5] *The Dual Mandate* became essential reading for every ambitious cadet in an African territory, and on the west coast with its powerful chiefs it seemed logical to work through the traditional structure and hand over more and more responsibility. It was also cheaper administratively. Yet in Northern Rhodesia there were factors which made the implementation of indirect rule hazardous and difficult.

The most obvious was the presence of settlers, who were quite resolved that when power was to be handed over to anyone, they would be the ones to receive it. Then there was the weakness of tribal organisation in many areas, combined with illiteracy and poverty—offering very little to which responsibility (as interpreted by western minds) could be transferred with assurance; the development of the Copperbelt in the 1920s accentuated these conditions, by provoking a new exodus of more capable men from their home areas. Finally there was the uncertain response of the few educated Africans: they looked with disfavour on what was regarded 'as a reversion to tribal rule', complained the *Native Affairs Report* for 1931.

Yet despite all the contradictions and obstacles, indirect rule had to be implemented, as Sir James Maxwell, the second Governor, made plain to a conference of administrative officers in 1927. The following year saw the retirement of Edward S. B. Tagart, the Secretary for Native Affairs, an official of the old school who had been in Northern Rhodesia since 1901.[6] His place was taken by Moffat Thomson, a remarkable man of pronounced radical views who had first come into Central Africa as a shop assistant for the African Lakes Corporation. Although Thomson had served himself as a Chartered man for fourteen years, he was sympathetic to any development which might lead to native emancipation. Outlining the crucial Native Authority Ordinance in the Legislative Council in March 1929, he declared: 'The new Bill introduces a more advanced form of native administration, which gives to the chiefs the management of their own affairs within their tribal areas, and it is hoped it will preserve and maintain all that is good in native custom and tribal organisation.'[7] Both the Native Authority Ordinance and the Native Courts Ordinance came into force on April 1, 1930—a date which harassed district officers might in later years have considered somewhat apt. However, Thomson said optimistically in his report for 1929: 'By the end of the coming year the system of indirect rule will have been functioning for nine months and it will be possible then to report on the progress made.' If there was success 'the whole native community would be happier for the change'.

Maxwell took great care, as the new policy was initiated, to avoid rousing the fears of the white settlers. Lord Hailey was later to make the point clear: 'There are, however, many who have not realised that the virtue to which they point is not that of the system of indirect rule, but the whole political philosophy which has inspired it.'[8]

In 1929, however, the elected members of the Legislative Council did not appear acquainted with the Lugard Doctrine and Sir James in his capacity as President of the Council did not choose to enlighten them. Indeed, when the Native Courts Ordinance was debated he was at pains to liken it to legislation in South Africa; the only difference was that Northern Rhodesia was 'just beginning'. The elected members had no suspicions; in fact, they seemed rather cheerful at the prospect of tribal rulers occupying themselves in this seemingly harmless way. Leopold Moore asked jocularly whether imprisonment was a native custom: 'I have been a good many years in this country and I have never yet seen a native prison.' Only Captain T. H. Murray was a little wary. The granting of judicial powers to chiefs in Tanganyika had induced 'acts of insolence towards whites', and he hoped that nothing of the kind would result in Northern Rhodesia. The captain also offered the view that detribalism had already gone too far for the native authorities to be effective.

Within the year, Maxwell was to have considerable trouble with the settlers over 'native matters' but this was not directly connected with the new policy at home. Lord Passfield, the Labour Colonial Secretary, had declared that African interests should be paramount where there was any clash with the interests of immigrants and although this was in reference to East Africa, Moore and his colleagues scented danger. At a meeting in his office, the Governor asserted that the declaration was not really significant,[9] even if its literary style was 'irritating'. By giving their views so hotly in the newspapers, the Europeans had 'brought the discussion more prominently before the natives'.[10]

In the early 1930s, the anxieties arising from the world economic depression had pushed concern with systems of government into the background. When it was over, the partial shutdown of the Copperbelt (see chapter eight) left a deep impression on the administration. Africans who had worked for several years were thrown out of their jobs in thousands; sometimes to make way for unemployed whites. Their tribal associations weakened, they roamed, hungry and discontented, through the urban areas.

This development reinforced the belief that detribalisation must be avoided at all costs. It seemed logical to step up the policy of indirect rule, and in 1936 a new Native Authority Ordinance was introduced, which re-enacted and strengthened the policy adopted seven years earlier. The Senior Provincial Commissioner, Thomas Sandford, assured the Legislative Council that even tribes which had been weak and broken up, like the Tonga, were coming to life. 'We are really getting something that we can call useful, progressive native government.'[11] Six years later, Sandford was obliged to modify this over-statement. He told the Council in 1942: 'We have, not so very long ago, introduced the policy of government in native areas by native authorities, but that is a plant of very tender growth. I myself am inclined to date the start of that policy from the introduction of the 1936 Ordinance rather than that introduced in 1929. . . .'[12]

Anxious to nurture this tender growth, the administration was driven to extremes. The Chief Secretary, Charles Dundas, insisted that all chiefs must have safes and cheque-books. A young official called Harry Franklin protested, 'But none of my chiefs can write, sir.'[13] Then rose the difficulty of supporting the chiefs without making them appear mere tools of the government. At the Provincial Commissioners' Conference of 1938, it was proposed that chiefs' emoluments should be increased, because some of them were getting as little as £6 a year. They should be wealthy enough to maintain a personal retinue and have drummers, paddlers, *machila* carriers and perhaps dancers. But that would cost money and deny Sandford's earlier claim that 'by using native machinery of government we save ourselves a great deal of work as well as expense'. The contradictions seemed endless. In 1939, the Governor, Sir John Maybin, stressed that the chiefs 'must not be placed in the position of salaried officials, either in the eyes of government or in the eyes of the people'. At the Provincial Commissioners' Conference in 1942, the Provincial Commissioner for the Northern Province said: 'A chief is primarily a servant of government, especially so in his judicial functions.'

Another difficulty was the position of Africans who had set up non-tribal communities on native reserve land, or settled in an area under European control. As early as 1915, the East Luangwa district created by the Chartered administration, was densely populated and large tracts had been ceded to the North Charterland Exploration Company, so that it became vital to establish reserves to prevent clashes between African squatters and European settlers. An official memorandum pointed out that with the end of inter-tribal fighting 'the natives, feeling safe, began to spread in small communities all over the country. This was recognised as an evil which tended to break down tribal authority. The chiefs were unanimous in condemning it, and asserted that they had no control over their people. . . .'[14] In the early 1930s the matter came to the forefront, in connection with attempts to find an answer to the land problem. The Secretary for Native Affairs wrote in 1931: 'With the introduction of a form of indirect rule, the question of the administration of natives who reside on privately owned lands has been repeatedly brought to notice because of the difficulty to which it gives rise.'[15] Most troublesome was the way in which natives were moving on to estates, sometimes of considerable extent, which had been leased to missions. There was a strong inference that some missionaries had encouraged Africans to settle on their estates. At this time the administration harboured sombre suspicions about missionaries (especially the Methodists), believing that some mingled radical political ideas with educational instruction, and that missionary estates might become enclaves of political dissent.

Yet this dilemma was nothing when compared with the long argument over the 'industrialisation of natives'. When an African became settled in the town, he ultimately ceased to belong to his tribe and no longer fitted into the native authority system. With tens of thousands of Africans working for the mines, it might have to be admitted that indirect rule embodied certain limitations, an admission from which many consequences might stem. Government policies on education, housing—to name only two—would need immediate modification. The government began seriously to analyse its attitude to the Copperbelt Africans immediately after the May 1935 disturbances, in which six men were shot dead and more than a score injured.[16] Influences removed from tribalism had shown themselves during the troubles. The mine compounds contained rootless communities living in virtual serfdom. The Chief Secretary, Dundas, produced a memorandum referring back to a meeting held in 1933 between the former Governor, Sir Ronald Storrs, and Sir Auckland Geddes, President of Rio Tinto.[17] Geddes had said his company was then prepared to develop a settled township system for its skilled labour. Storrs had agreed that the African miners would have to be detribalised. Dundas remarked: 'It would seem that at this meeting it was clearly recognised that the compound system is bad, that detribalisation must be accepted as inevitable. It was a most radical departure from the past.' Dundas urged a stabilised labour force on the Copperbelt, although it would run counter to the wishes of the mining companies themselves, who preferred the South African pattern of compound living. He admitted the problem facing the government as whole families contracted out of the tribal system. 'Many may never go back home, or if they do they are likely to become complete misfits in the tribal society.' The ideal solution, as Dundas saw it—and broadly as Geddes had seen it—was to set up townships under government control around the mines, where the people would be 'as free as any town or village folk'.

In reply, the Governor, Sir Hubert Young, while avoiding committing himself, agreed: 'The question is the most important that has to be decided in this country.' Others in the administration were more vehement in their views. Sandford, the Senior Provincial Commissioner, opposed providing education for African children on the Copperbelt.[18] He said: 'I doubt very much whether the facilities provided in the villages are given full use; and I am certain that these native children are better off in their own villages even without education than in the mine compounds with education.' At the Provincial Commissioners' Conference in 1937, it was agreed (although the scheme was never implemented) that there should be compulsory repatriation of Africans from the Copperbelt after a maximum of two years 'to prevent detribalisation'.

In the following year, Lord Hailey wrote: 'Northern Rhodesia will provide a significant test of the question whether native authorities are able to maintain the respect and interest of a population which is subject to the powerful influence of industrial and urban life.'[19] This was, indeed, the heart of the matter, to which reference had already been made by a recently elected member of the Legislative Council, Lieut-Col. Stewart Gore-Browne. In 1936 he asked whether in the immediate future it was likely to be possible to devise some method of consulting Africans on matters which concerned them.[20] He explained that he had been addressing a gathering of Africans (a somewhat hazardous admission at that time) on the issue of a possible amalgamation of the two Rhodesias. One African in the meeting had suggested that the chiefs could speak on behalf of the people, but twenty others had immediately said: 'No, they cannot speak for us, they do not know what we are thinking, they do not know anything about it.' Gore-Browne probably had a closer understanding of the new pressures on African society than any other member of the Legislature. He had first come to Northern Rhodesia in 1911 as an officer with the Anglo-Belgian commission which had delineated the border along the watershed of the Zambezi and Congo rivers. In 1921 he returned, to settle at Shiwa Ngandu in a remote corner of Bembaland. Gore-Browne had at first run his estate around the imposing baronial-style home at Shiwa Ngandu with a feudal severity, but by the time he entered politics had acquired a remarkable foresight and sympathy with African desires.

During the late 1930s and the years of the second world war, the provincial administration clung to the whole theory of indirect rule, all the time avoiding any direct admission that a large proportion of the African population was living outside the sphere of the native authority. There was, moreover, a part of the country where the theory found its most satisfying expression. This was Barotseland, about which the administration had built up a powerful mystique. Far from the raucous, urgent Copperbelt, the 'protectorate within a protectorate' had a serene tempo all its own, notwithstanding a certain predilection for ritual murder. In this feudal atmosphere the district commissioners felt at ease and the proud *indunas* were held to be nature's gentlemen. By the end of the war the Secretary for Native Affairs was R. S. Hudson, who had started his career in Barotseland and subsequently proved his considerable abilities in the Lusaka Secretariat. In 1946, Hudson introduced in the Legislative Council a Native Authorities (Amendment) Ordinance. He described it as 'another step forward in the advance of tribal self-government' and took the opportunity to reject suggestions that the native authorities were not showing good progress.[21] Shortly afterwards, a major speech on African administration was made by Gore-Browne, by this time knighted and a nominated representative for African interests. Sir Stewart said: 'I believe we must face up to stabilised industrial labour. Our record in the country on this matter has not been particularly good. . . . Originally, the late Secretary for Native Affairs, Mr Sandford, who, to many sterling qualities, added a capacity for burying his head in the sand unequalled by any civil servant, maintained that there was no such thing as detribalised labour on the Copperbelt and that all we had to do was send the workers back to their homes at frequent intervals.'[22] Sir Stewart Gore-Browne described the official attitude as like a pendulum (with which, it should be added, he had swung himself at times). Having thought about the native authorities, he was far from happy. In the days of the Chartered administration, there had only been three well-organised tribes, and among others such as the Tonga, where they 'hardly knew what a chief was', an artificial structure had been created. Sir Stewart then returned to his arguments of ten years earlier about the need for sounding urban African opinion on matters of current importance.

Now, however, the question was much more urgent. African opinion had become decidedly less malleable and 10,000 soldiers were back from the war. When they returned to their villages these veterans of fighting in Burma and North Africa no longer rolled on their backs and clapped to greet their chiefs—instead they just cut them off a smart salute.

Hudson, the Secretary for Native Affairs, made a careful reply to Gore-Browne, in which he accepted the need for Africans to have proper opportunities to express themselves. His viewpoint, was, however, strongly traditionalist: 'There is, of course, the danger that if the native authorities do not keep abreast of the times, the more advanced elements among the African population will tend to become discontented, and, still worse, will tend to form separate political bodies instead of adopting the right course—that is, to co-operate and help strengthen the native administration.'[23] Such a move would be a 'great disservice to the African population as a whole'. Hudson made a direct appeal to Gore-Browne to use his influence to try and stop Africans from forming political parties—'which would be fatal'.

Shortly after this debate, the provincial administration began urgently to re-examine the whole local government system in the rural areas. It was an attempt to find some way of drawing the 'best and most representative elements in the African community' into the indirect rule structure, so painstakingly erected over the two previous decades. Yet time was running out. In 1948 (the year when Hudson retired from the administration), two events occurred which heralded a new era. The Northern Rhodesia African Congress was formed, and the first two African members took their places in the Legislative Council; one of these was Nelson Nalumango, who eighteen years earlier had helped to found the Livingstone Native Welfare Association.

II THE FIRST AFRICAN POLITICIANS

At a casual glance, political developments in Northern Rhodesia up to the second world war are deceptive. There appears little connection between what went on in the Advisory Council and its successor, the Legislative Council, and the gradual development of self-assertion among the mass of the population. Moreover, it is often thought that African politics were a phenomenon which suddenly burst into view in the middle 1940s. It is necessary to define what can be regarded as political in such an environment, but, remembering the absence of normal avenues of expression, it would seem reasonable to take into the reckoning any organised show of dissent against authority.

By 1924, white settler politicians had already become obsessed with two subjects which were to occupy them for several decades: Northern Rhodesia's connections with neighbouring countries—especially those to the south—and the desire to wrest executive power from the civil servants. The settlers took little heed of what the Africans thought (most would have doubted whether Africans thought about anything beyond their most immediate needs) and regarded it as no business of the black majority whether or not the country was amalgamated with Southern Rhodesia. The legislature was not to admit Africans for more than two decades, and it was not until 1938 that the first European to represent 'African interests' was nominated. But by 1930 Africans had begun to join together to discuss the state and future of the country.

One factor contributing to African awareness was the need to travel to Southern Rhodesia for work, to pay the poll-tax imposed by the administration. As early as 1909, more than 7,000 men a year were being recruited in Northern Rhodesia as labour for the south. By 1928 the figure had risen to more than 23,000.[1] One migrant, a Southern Province chief, even found his way into the Royal Navy. The recruits heard about events in South Africa, where Africans had been active in politics since before the first world war, and began to realise through seeing life in big towns like Bulawayo that white men also could be poor. Thus their migrations in search of work opened the eyes of illiterate Zambian labourers in the first quarter of the century. Even more important were the external contacts made by the embryonic African intelligentsia—teachers and evangelists who could read and write. Some of these were influenced by having worked in the south, where 'Ethiopian' churches (rejecting white guidance) had sprung up in Basutoland and elsewhere; an Ethiopian church even appeared in Barotseland as early as 1900, a breakaway from Coillard's Paris Missionary Society following a teachers' strike for more money, and it survived until 1905.[2] More pervasive, however, were the influences from Nyasaland, where the radical Church of Scotland missionaries imbued their charges with an independence of mind which was to have tremendous consequences. The Nyasas were great travellers and brought back exciting ideas; typical of the spirit of the times was the journey of Hastings Banda made in 1915, at the age of thirteen, to Southern Rhodesia and then on to the Union.[3] Educated Africans were crossing into Northern Rhodesia from Nyasaland at the turn of the century to become clerks, teachers, interpreters and evangelists. Almost the only educated local Africans were of the Lozi ruling class; several who studied in South Africa returned politically militant, notably Tawila Silumba, who became Ngambela in 1919.

After the first world war, which itself speeded up the spread of ideas among the Africans, opposition to the administration had become far more apparent. Much of this opposition was cloaked in religious guises—especially that of the wide-spread and anarchistic Watch Tower movement—but in 1923 there was a most significant development. On the country's northern border with Tanganyika, a welfare association was formed at Mwenzo and sent its rules of association to the Secretary for Native Affairs nearly 1,000 miles away in Livingstone.

The association was the idea of the four most educated Africans in the area : Donald Siwale, a Boma clerk, David Kaunda, Hezekiya Kawosa and Peter Sinkala.[4] They discussed it with Dr J. A. Chisholm, who was in charge of the mission hospital and had worked there since before the turn of the century. Dr Chisholm warned that they were 'seeking trouble for themselves by entering into politics' but did not discourage them. Siwale wrote to an Ngoni called Levi Mumba living at Ekwendeni, Nyasaland, with whom he had been at school in Livingstonia, and got from him the constitution of the North Nyasa Native Association. This was adapted for the Mwenzo Welfare Association. The wording said :

> The members thereof are to be persons of good knowledge and character. It is an open question for educated chiefs and Europeans to attend or join it as full members thereof if they choose to do so.
>
> The aim of the association is neither directly nor indirectly to subvert the authority of the government or of any lawful establishment, nor to induce the community to do so. It is rather one of the helpful means of developing the country in the hands of the two necessary connecting links—the government and the governed.
>
> It aims at making the people understand the necessity and value of order and the importance of becoming law-abiding citizens—also the necessity and value of industrious labour and in short the value of civilisation as against ignorance, laziness, disloyalty and anarchy.

In these guarded terms were expressed the first stirrings of African self-assertion. The association held regular meetings and as a result of one discussion it was agreed to protest to the local district commissioner about the rate of poll-tax. The local minister, the Rev. Jonathan Mukwasa, went to the *boma* and put the association's views. This attempt to convey what the association called the 'desires and needs of the people' was not much welcomed, but

Moffat Thomson, then in charge of the Tanganyika District, was moved to write a notably far-sighted comment:

> It must be remembered that natives who have received education at various missions in this district have reached a state where they hold communion among themselves and discuss Europeans, the government, and their own position in life. They draw comparisons of their lot with that of others whom they have met in the centres they have frequented for employment, with a result that a spirit of restlessness is being engendered. They do not consider they are receiving from life what they believe they are entitled to. This impression is much more likely to increase than diminish and it seems to me that some method will have to be adopted to enable the natives to realise their ambitions socially, politically and materially.[5]

One of Thomson's colleagues had this to say:

> The attitude of the natives has been described as satisfactory. But there are sections of the population which cannot be called happy and contented. The Welfare Association at Mwenzo and the Watch Tower movement are but manifestations, each in its own way, of the birth of a new spirit, a mental ferment caused by discontent with the present conditions of existence and a striving to better them. This is naturally one of the first results of education in all its forms, but it can only have been fostered by the unsatisfactory economic situation of the last four years. A system which drives a large proportion of taxable males hundreds of miles from their homes in order to meet their tax obligations and clothe their families is unsound.[6]

Such sympathetic attitudes towards mission-educated Africans were not usual. Much more typical was the comment of Owen Letcher, a writer and big-game hunter who had spent some time in the same north-eastern part of the country a few years earlier: 'It has been my experience that to Christianise a native is often the most effective means of turning him into an absolute rogue.... Those who teach the natives of Africa to regard the white man as his brother are dangerous maniacs.'[7]

The Nyasa-influenced Mwenzo Welfare Association had faded out by 1928 (some of its leaders left to work on the Copperbelt) but it is worth emphasising the duration of quasi-political stimulation provided by 'educated natives' from the east.[8] An illustration can be found in the 1935 disturbances on the Copperbelt, although the commissioners appointed to find the causes seemed unable to grasp what was obvious and passed almost all the blame on to the Watch Tower. Most of the clerks in the mine compound offices were Nyasas and it was accepted that there was some kind of secret communication between them; this linked all three producing mines of the time—Nkana, Mufulira and Roan. A key figure in the disturbances was Mateyo Musiska, head African clerk in the Mufulira compound. He was a Nyasa. Several African witnesses gave evidence indicating that Musiska deliberately provoked the strike, while at the same time appearing to support his compound manager, Benjamin Shaefer. When Musiska was questioned by the commission, his manner was cool to the point of insolence; one of the commissioners pointedly referred to Europeans involved in quelling the disturbances with the epithet '*bwana*', but in his reply Musika declined to take the hint and stuck to 'mister'.[9]

Nyasas were important also in the Native Welfare Associations which appeared along the line-of-rail in 1930. These associations were inspired, in addition, by the example of similar bodies in Southern Rhodesia and by the greater militancy of educated Lozis following the death of Lewanika in 1916 and the accession of his son Yeta. The associations were formed almost simultaneously in Livingstone, Mazabuka, Broken Hill and Ndola. The first-named, being in the capital, was the most active; it had to be spoken to by a government official because it tended to 'indulge in a good deal of irrelevant and rather wild talk on extraneous matters'.[10] The associations were careful not to challenge authority outright, however, and in any case a large part of their time was taken up with debating such pressing difficulties as the burial of Africans in urban areas. Yet they were unquestionably a 'detribalised force' in a swiftly changing situation. As the *Native Affairs Report* put it in 1929: 'Frequent association with natives of other territories and with increasing numbers and varying types of Europeans has brought about a change in outlook.'[11] The new influx of Europeans of an artisan class was particularly important; between 1924 and 1930, with the opening up of the Copperbelt, the white population almost tripled from 4,000 to 11,000 and the overwhelming majority of the arrivals were South Africans. Sir Charles Dundas, who came to Northern Rhodesia in 1934, summed up the character of the country at that time: '... the proximity to and trade and traffic with and through South Africa, together with the presence of South African white miners, who formed the majority of the European population, contributed a strong South African ingredient to the country.'[12] These miners, with their harsh attitudes, were a transforming factor in the situation. In earlier years almost the only whites in the country had been administrators, missionaries, farmers, aristocratic remittance men and a handful of traders—and as late as 1920 had amounted to less than one in 300 of the total population. Admittedly, the pioneers rarely hesitated to thrash a recalcitrant native and most kept a black mistress known euphemistically as the 'cook's woman'.[13] Yet the Afrikaner workman encountered under urban and industrial conditions was something different. An anonymous notice put up by a black miner at Nkana during the 1935 strike said: 'See how we suffer at work and how we are continually reviled and beaten underground.'[14]

Another influence on African attitudes was a growing knowledge of European political affairs. Those who could read studied newspapers such as the *Bulawayo Chronicle* and Leopold Moore's vociferous *Livingstone Mail,* founded as early as 1906. From these journals Africans learnt about the arguments over amalgamation with Southern Rhodesia and discovered that Europeans could disagree violently among themselves. It would be tedious to recount all the sorties in the campaign for amalgamation—a campaign which was abandoned in 1948 by the settlers' representatives when federation became the goal:[15] arguments revolved around such topics as whether Southern Rhodesia was out to snatch the north's native labour, the need for a Sinoia-Kafue rail link, the threat of Africanisation in the Northern Rhodesia civil service, and whether Nyasaland should be included; sometimes the white elected members were against amalgamation, more often (especially later on) they were for it. Yet the interminable controversy had the effect of focusing African opinion on specifically political matters.

So, too, did the newspaper reports of debates on black-white relations. As early as 1920 this subject evoked a remark by A. M. Alexander that Africans should be lifted 'a little bit above the primitive'—but not too far in case they began competing with white workers. 'To teach motor driving and so on would be wrong . . . what would become of the white children when they grew up?'[16]

The minutes of a public meeting of the Livingstone Native Welfare Association, held in April 1930, show that about 350 people attended.[17] The meeting was in the beer hall, 'by kind permission of the compound manager'. Rankin Nyirenda, in the chair, told how the first steps to form the body had been taken in 1928 and in April 1929 a petition had been sent to Sir James Maxwell, the Governor, asking for his approval; this had taken nine months to obtain. Nyirenda listed the objects of the association as: 'To build brotherhood and friendship among ourselves; to protect the native interests generally.' Most of the leaders of the association were in government employ, but this did not deter them from making some guarded but quite unmistakable criticism of the whites. Most significant was a peroration at the end of the meeting by the vice-chairman, J. E. C. Mattako: 'Some people think that since we are Africans with black skins we are only inferior creatures and that we shall never escape from that inferiority. No, that is a mistake—just let us behave ourselves like human beings and respect ourselves by co-operating with one another and we shall see a great change, and we will enjoy freedom black though we are, and even the powers that be will respect us as human beings . . . this day the association has been formed as a rope to pull the canoe of freedom little by little.'

Through frequent correspondence with Hastings Banda in America, the association's leaders knew about Marcus Aurelius Garvey, the Jamaican Negro who had formed the Universal Negro Improvement Association in New York in 1920, with the slogan 'Africa for the Africans'.[18] Two months later, the Livingstone body held another meeting and this time invited four Tonga chiefs from the Kalomo area. One of them, Musokotwani, made a speech attacking the behaviour of Europeans. There was considerable discontent among the Tonga at the time over the implementation of the Crown Lands and Native Reserves Order-in-Council (1928), which meant the removal of large numbers of tribesmen from the land adjoining the railway line between Livingstone and Broken Hill, to make way for white farmers. Musokotwani complained: 'They are chasing us from our lands where our forefathers died to lands which are strange to us.'

The report of this meeting of the association considerably alarmed the administration. The Chief Secretary, Donald Mackenzie-Kennedy, minuted to the Governor: 'I do not like it a little bit. The association must be pulled up.' Maxwell replied: 'I agree. The Secretary for Native Affairs should take action.'

Before anything could be done, the association was meeting again, to protest about racial discrimination. At that time, Africans were forbidden to walk on the pavements in the towns, and in Livingstone there had been forty-three arrests in one month for this offence. The association's treasurer, Gideon Mumana, complained that it was not even possible to look in a shop-window without being picked up. It was a situation which caused continual resentment, Nelson Nalumango describing to a subsequent meeting how he had been kicked and beaten in Broken Hill by a native constable who had caught him standing on the sidewalk. Matters reached a crisis when the new chairman of the association, Sam Mwase, sent a memorandum to the government alleging that

Africans were more severely dealt with in court than white men. Maxwell, the Governor, said that the way to treat the association was to ridicule it, and Mackenzie-Kennedy instructed the Secretary for Native Affairs, Moffat Thomson, to talk to its committee with 'the attitude of a schoolmaster towards a stupid boy in the third form'. The officials also blamed the show of defiance in Livingstone on Nyasalanders, who were accused of seeking to replace the chiefs as the leaders of the people; ever since the Chilembwe rebellion of 1915,[19] government officials had regarded 'educated Nyasa boys' as potential revolutionaries.

Although this suspicion was justified to some extent, in fact there were fourteen officials of the Livingstone Native Welfare Association in 1931, and only three were Nyasas. Much more significant is that nine of the fourteen came from the Northern Province which a generation later was to reveal itself as a breeding-place of Zambia's foremost nationalists: three of the committee came from Kawambwa, one from Kasama and one from Abercorn —and as many as four from Isoka, the district in which the Fife Native Association had been formed in 1923.

By 1932, moves were on foot for an amalgamation of all the country's welfare associations into one body. A conference was held in that year, involving the associations in Livingstone, Lusanshya, and Ndola. The organisation in Ndola was by this time more than fifty strong and holding regular meetings; it had sent a resolution to the Governor opposing any amalgamation of the Rhodesias, asserting that this would be 'greatly to the detriment of the interests and legitimate aspirations of the native population of this country'.

However, in 1933, when the first meeting of the 'United African Welfare Association of Northern Rhodesia' was held in Kafue over Rhodes and Founders' weekend, it was something of a flop. Only delegates from Lusaka, Mazabuka, and Livingstone turned up. Clements Muwamba of Lusaka was elected chairman of the meeting and made a long speech, the tenor of which was that the organisation should work to 'cement the existing friendship between the government, the settlers, and the Africans'. The new secretary of the Livingstone association, Godwin Lewanika,[20] who was later to play a prominent part in the nationalist movement, declared that Africans were protected by the justice of the authorities like 'young birds by the wings of their mothers'. He added that Africans were not yet sufficiently advanced to 'demand higher things to come to us all at once'. The only note of militancy was provided by Nelson Nalumango, who warned the meeting that the government was watching it carefully, but demanded that the united body should be allowed to stretch out its wings in the villages 'for the common good of the people'. One significant request was that the government should start a newspaper for Africans, since the country's only journal, the *Livingstone Mail*, was directed at Europeans. Such a request had been made by Africans in Livingstone six years earlier but was ignored. When the government finally launched *Mutende* (Peace) in 1936, it was not in consideration of African wishes, but as a counter-blast to Watch Tower literature.[21]

The United African Welfare Association (UAWA) was still-born, probably through being refused recognition by the authorities. Moffat Thomson, the Secretary for Native Affairs, had retreated a long way from the benevolent attitude he had shown towards the Mwenzo Welfare Association in 1923. True to the policy of indirect rule, he insisted that the welfare associations—'little else than political societies'—should not be allowed to operate in native authority areas. He was suspicious of the government clerks in the societies, accusing them of revealing confidential information at the meetings.

In 1935, with the removal of the capital nearly 300 miles north to Lusaka, the Livingstone association had become dormant and there appeared to be something of a lull in African political activity. It may be that more antagonistic attitudes by some district commissioners after the 1935 riots on the Copperbelt drove the "native intelligentsia' into its shell. By 1938 there was even concern among senior administrators at the withering of the native welfare societies. 'The old-fashioned view that anything savouring of political activity amongst natives was reprehensible can hardly be maintained,' wrote one official. Provincial commissioners had also taken note of the speech by Lord Hailey to the Royal Africa Society in 1938, in which he warned that African politics needed to be handled sympathetically or 'you will drive it into a political activity of which the first victim will be the traditional authorities themselves'. (Welfare associations had made significant appearances in Kasama rural areas and Abercorn by the middle 1930s, despite all efforts to restrict them to the line-of-rail.) Yet official attitudes were contradictory, firm hostility to African political expression being more usual. A small 'Northern Rhodesian African Congress' formed in Mazabuka by Ellison Milambo and George Kaluwa in 1937 was denied sanction by the Secretary for Native Affairs and so expired.[22]

Proof that African opinion about the future of Northern Rhodesia was crystallising came in 1938, when the Bledisloe Commission toured the territory.[23] The commission had been appointed by Britain to advise on the possibility of amalgamating the two Rhodesias and Nyasaland. This step followed a declaration by white politicians from Northern and Southern Rhodesia, after a conference at the Victoria Falls in 1936, that an early amalgamation of the two territories under a constitution conferring complete self-government would be in the interests of 'all the inhabitants'. The commission failed in the end to make any definite recommendations; but the evidence it took from Africans in the north showed that there was an overwhelming dislike of Southern Rhodesia's native policies and reinforced pass laws. The people made it plain to the commission that although many of them had to cross the Zambezi to earn money, they regarded Southern Rhodesia as a bad place to live in if one's skin was black. In this opposition to amalgamation in 1938, the Africans and the white civil servants found common ground, the latter being committed to indirect rule, whereas their Southern Rhodesian counterparts saw no value in chiefs (only starting to promote them twenty years later for political purposes).

To establish a controlled liaison between the administration and 'Africans working in the towns' (it was not to be accepted for some years that Africans were truly settled in urban areas),[24] local committees were set up just before the second world war. These were variously called native advisory councils, urban advisory committees, and urban advisory councils (UACS) at the whim of individual district commissioners (DCS), until the last became the standard title.[25] The objects of the UACS were listed as: to keep the DC in touch with African opinion; to act as a mouthpiece of the government to Africans; and to advise the DC on African welfare. Appointment to the councils was restrictive, the view of provincial commissioners (PCS) being that Africans were 'not yet ready for the elective system'. In Kitwe, for example, the Tribal Elders[26] and the Boss Boys' Committee named five members from among themselves and the DC nominated five more who he felt were representative of African opinion in the town; it is noteworthy that in 1943 the Kitwe DC nominated a young teacher called Harry Nkumbula.[27]

The process was cautiously taken further when regional councils (later provincial councils) were created, embracing both urban and rural areas; the local councils sent members to the provincial councils, who ultimately nominated representatives for the territory-wide African Representative Council. The provincial commissioner for the Western Province, H. F. Cartmel-Robinson (later Secretary for Native Affairs) signified his approval of this development by remarking that in the local councils natives had proved themselves 'capable eventually of considering problems not merely from their own selfish point of view'.

The new organisations had a certain value: under the benevolent chairmanship of provincial administration officials, members could list their grievances about racial discrimination, the lack of educational opportunities, housing conditions, and (most important of all) the intentions of the white politicians in the Legislative Council (Legco). Thus when Welensky moved in November 1943 that the Rhodesias should be amalgamated immediately,[28] with complete self-government, the Western Province and Southern Province regional councils—on which both townsmen and chiefs were represented—retaliated six months later by declaring unanimous opposition to any closer association with Southern Rhodesia. The councils were without power and since there were no political groups the proceedings rather resembled a formalised *indaba;* moreover (as Gore-Browne suggested to the chagrin of the administration) urban advisory councils were often dominated by DCs—and the UACs were the foundation of the whole edifice until they died out in 1954. Yet the provincial councils in particular had an important effect, which was never fully anticipated when the organisation was created: instead of the chiefs and other rural representatives paternally guiding urban members of the councils, the former were politically activated by the latter.* Thus, from 1943 onwards, the administration began to sponsor a system which was to undermine its hallowed doctrine of indirect rule and speed the penetration of tribal areas by modern nationalistic thinking.

Penetration was also being achieved by a resurgence of welfare associations. In 1941 a letter was sent to the DC, Isoka, asking for permission to revive the association which had existed between 1923–8 at Mwenzo mission.[29] The officials of the new organisation—Ewan Siwale, Paul Sichizya and Sidney Simpelwe—were careful to say that they intended to co-operate with the chiefs, missionaries and government 'to improve the conditions of the people'. But the PC at Kasama observed gloomily: 'I am afraid this application means the starting of an intelligentsia within the native tribal area which is foreign to the normal native structure. . . .' Sandford, the Secretary for Native Affairs, was even more downright, saying in a minute to the Governor: 'One may well ask where the native authority comes in and I hesitate to give official recognition to any

---

*** In the early postwar years, Kenneth Kaunda was on the African Provincial Council for the Western Province, which embraced a large rural area north of the Congo Pedicle as well as the Copperbelt.**

body of natives in a rural area which appears to be taking over the functions of the native authority.' However, no definite policy was agreed. The Mwenzo association flourished and others sprang to life in such remote places as Mpika, Chinsali, Luwingu and Kawambwa. Sandford himself had a considerable shock when he called on the Luwingu association in September 1943.[30] The members told him they 'had nothing to say to him' as their own representative in the Legislative Council was Lieut.-Col. Gore-Browne, the nominated member for African interests.

Sandford replied heavily that 'the Africans have a representative in the Legislative Council in the person of the Secretary for Native Affairs and he keeps in touch with Africans continuously through the provincial commissioners and native commissioners'. He also warned them to keep off politics. This droll incident had a sequel at the next meeting of the Provincial Commissioners Conference, when both Sandford and Gore-Browne were present. The latter was accused of undermining the prestige of the DCS, because the idea was getting about that he was more important than they; moreover, he was holding meetings with Africans without the DCS being present. Gore-Browne, who later revealed that the Governor, Sir E. J. Waddington, also 'put him on the carpet',[31] gave an assurance that he had no intention of undermining the provincial administration; but there was another conflict two years later when he suggested that the welfare associations were generally more vital than the officially-sponsored advisory councils. This was exactly the kind of truth the provincial commissioners were reluctant to hear, and they rejected Gore-Browne's proposal that where possible the two bodies should be merged and the officials democratically elected.

It was none the less true that the welfare associations had enlisted the support of the more educated young men, especially the teachers, and political consciousness increased as the war years advanced. In 1941, Roy Welensky, the spokesmen of the white miners and railwaymen, had formed his Labour Party, the first real political organisation Northern Rhodesia had ever known; it immediately won five seats in the Legislative Council and took a militant line on increased power for the Unofficials. African soldiers were coming home on leave from active service—although the fact that they were fighting for democracy did not give them the right to be served across the counters in shops. In 1942, a teacher called Dauti Yamba visited South Africa and returned to Luanshya—where he was secretary of the welfare association—with the novel idea of starting an African Congress.[32]

The proposal did not take root immediately, but received

new impetus when the Nyasaland Congress was formed in October 1944 and Nyasas on the Copperbelt applied to the government for permission to start branches. The secretariat reacted quite amiably to the applications and even applied to Blantyre for details of the new organisation; Congress officials sent back eight copies of the constitution with a letter couched in the most polite civil service terms.[33] Matters were taken a stage further in 1946 when Gore-Browne, his prestige at its zenith, made a tour of the Copperbelt welfare associations, attending mass meetings in all the five main towns. At Mufulira the audience numbered 1,000, in Luanshya more than 700. Everywhere the audiences pressed to know what was being done about racial discrimination and African advancement in the mines.

After the war the need for an African political party became increasingly obvious, as Welensky forced the pace towards closer association between the Rhodesias. The case for amalgamation was hammered relentlessly in the *Northern News,* a European newspaper founded by two Nchanga miners, J. C. Wykerd and George Hovelmeier.[34] The white population, though it numbered less than 25,000 as compared with an estimated 1,600,000 Africans, was clearly moving closer to a full political control, and the old Passfield doctrine of the 'paramountcy of native interests' was becoming a dead letter. In 1945, the eight elected unofficial members were supplemented by five nominated unofficials in the Legislative Council, so that for the first time the nine colonial officials were outnumbered. Although the officials kept a five-to-three majority in the Executive Council and retained all the portfolios, as recently as seven years earlier the unofficials had been in a minority in the Legco and had no seats at all in Exco. The first meeting of the African Representative Council in 1946 gathered together representatives from all over the country to discuss common problems, although Africans had few illusions about its power to change the course of events. The African Representative Council was devoid of any power to legislate and the all-white government merely 'took note' of its resolutions. A small but far more significant meeting was held in Lusaka during October the same year when a Northern Rhodesian Federation of Welfare Societies was formed. The leaders were Dauti Yamba, George Kaluwa and Godwin Lewanika, representing the powerful Kitwe African Society and at that time the most senior African clerk on Nkana Mine. The chairman of the meeting was the Rev. Edward Nightingale, a nominated Member of the Legislative Council (MLC) for African Interests. For Lewanika it was a happy moment, because he had been one of the small band who had tried to launch the United African Welfare Association of Northern Rhodesia at Kafue in 1933.

The Federation of Welfare Societies was the first step towards a national African political party, and already in the Copperbelt welfare societies the name Congress was in common use. Active in the Mufulira Welfare Society was the young Munali-educated teacher Kenneth Kaunda, who had come down to the line-of-rail from his home at Lubwa, near Chinsali. Kaunda had been born in the Bemba country, although his evangelist father was a Nyasa. Kenneth Kaunda was only twenty-three in 1947, but he had already travelled in Tanganyika and Southern Rhodesia, and was decided in his political opinions. One of his colleagues at Mufulira in 1947, John Sokoni, recalls: 'We were already nursing the Congress organisation, holding small meetings and building up support.'[35] It was with good reason that the *African Affairs Report* for 1947 remarked that the country was entering an era of 'uneasy progress in the political sphere'.

In January 1948, African attitudes hardened still further when Gore-Browne, the European in whom they reposed most trust, suddenly advocated 'responsible government' for Northern Rhodesia.[36] At that time the expression was synonymous with white rule on the Southern Rhodesia pattern and it came as a great shock that the member for African Interests in the Legislative Council, a man who had made his home among the people of the Northern Province for more than twenty-five years, should take this line. In fact, Gore-Browne had lost his patience with the stubborn attitude of the officials over the handling of government business; his motives were not anti-African but anti-civil service. As he had so often pointed out, after twenty-four years of Colonial Office trusteeship the progress in African agriculture, education, health and welfare was lamentably small. The damage was done, however, and among the people who criticised him bitterly was Kenneth Kaunda. It was a sad situation for the man who had tried his best to construct a bridge between the racial groups.

The climax of a growing African awareness that unity was essential to meet the rising political tempo came in September 1948. By this time, Zambians working as far away as Beira and Johannesburg were writing to friends on the Copperbelt to urge the formation of a national front. At Ndola, African leaders were given a £100 cheque by Indian traders, to mark the anniversary of India's freedom. There was deep suspicion of Roy Welensky's changed approach to closer associations between the Rhodesias; he had dropped amalgamation in favour of federation, which the Africans decided was merely a political wolf in sheep's clothing. In the middle of the year, Welensky had attended preliminary talks in London on federation, together with the new Governor, Sir Gilbert Rennie; despite protests from the welfare societies, two African civil servants, Safeli Chileshe and Moses Mubitana, also flew to the talks, for discussions of partnership rather than paramountcy.

In September the Federation of Welfare Societies held its annual conference at Munali School in Lusaka. It was a small meeting with barely a score of delegates, but among them were men destined to play important and often diverse roles in the coming political struggle: Godwin Lewanika Mbikusita, Mateyo Kakumbi, Dixon Konkola, Robinson Nabulyato, Isaac Mumpanshya—and a young schoolmaster from Kitwe called Simon Kapwepwe. By a certain irony the government provided food and accommodation for the delegates and the opening speech was made by the Secretary for Native Affairs, R. S. Hudson. Prayers were said by the Rev. Edward Nightingale. The temper of the conference was shown when Safeli Chileshe gave a report on the talks he had attended in London and was then condemned for having accepted an invitation. Kapwepwe, a close friend of Kenneth Kaunda since their schooldays together at Lubwe mission, was reproached by some of the other delegates for 'extremism' when he accused the government of siding with the white settlers. Two resolutions were passed, one rejecting any form of association with Southern Rhodesia and the other demanding that the government should meet an independent six-man delegation. Then, before the conference broke up, it renamed the Federation of Welfare Societies the Northern Rhodesia African Congress. The decision to create the Congress had been taken by delegates in a grass-roofed hut in Chilenje, Lusaka. Lewanika was elected president.

When the delegation met government officials, Sir Stewart Gore-Browne was present and handed round written proposals for a radical solution to the political deadlock. Sir Stewart's idea was that the country should be partitioned into 'native states' covering the rural areas, while the Copperbelt and line-of-rail should become white controlled with close ties to the south. It was not an original scheme, something of the kind having been suggested by the British South Africa Company shortly after the first world war. Kapwepwe tore up his copy of the proposals, declaring angrily: 'The country is one and is going to remain one.' Gore-Browne accepted a challenge to address a public meeting on the Copperbelt about his partition plan, but when he spoke, there was so much strong feeling that police had to intervene to keep order.

Partition thus proved to be a non-starter, but by the end of 1948 the idea of a federation had been given encouragement by

Arthur Creech-Jones, Colonial Secretary in the British Labour government. Welensky and Sir Godfrey Huggins, the Southern Rhodesia Premier, came back from London in high spirits, because at last they were making headway in Whitehall. It has recently been the pretension of Welensky that the idea of a federation never originated in the Rhodesias—thus assisting his argument that Britain was responsible for destroying what she had herself initiated. He says of his meeting with the Colonial Secretary in October 1948: 'Now I at this time was 100 per cent amalgamationist, and I did not take at all kindly to Creech-Jones's proposition that a federation would give the solution to all our problems.'[37] He then goes on to tell how later that day he went to a London hotel where Sir Godfrey Huggins was staying and persuaded him to consider the new idea. In fact, six months before, Welensky had told a public meeting in Northern Rhodesia that 'amalgamation would probably be best in the form of a federation'.[38] In June, a delegation from a group called the United Central Africa Association (formed with the encouragement of Huggins) had visited Lusaka and held talks with the elected members of the Legislative Council. Afterwards a statement was issued saying that 'the only form of closer union which was immediately practicable from the Northern Rhodesian aspect would be a federation. . . . Each country would have its own parliament, but a federal government would be established with Dominion status to which members from each individual state would be elected.'[39]

Although Creech-Jones had insisted that the federation which Welensky and Huggins had promoted must include Nyasaland, and neither of them regarded that protectorate as much of an asset, they realised that the opportunity for a decisive advance had arrived. Arrangements were put in train to call a conference of political leaders at Victoria Falls in February 1949. At the insistence of Huggins, no Africans were allowed to attend.

III LAND AND LABOUR

Between the wars the rural areas of Zambia slumbered, watched over by the DCs. Yet it was not a healthy sleep. Outside the Tonga country close to the line-of-rail, there was almost no progress in African farming, so that although the people wanted to improve their home conditions and come to terms with the modern world, they had no means of doing so. Only by migrating in search of work could a man get his hands on money to buy clothes, crockery, perhaps even a gramophone, a sewing machine, or a bicycle for himself and his family. The chronic lack of vitality throughout the vast tracts of land was inherited down the decades, so that at the present day most strenuous efforts are called for to produce a cure. During the 1920s, '30s and '40s advancement in agriculture was minimal, while the population doubled and the soils became more exhausted. Everything was against the African farmer.

Without a massive injection of capital, to make possible the use of machinery and artificial fertilisers to raise the output per acre, the great bulk of the people outside the towns was condemned to subsistence farming, growing by the *chitemene* method millet, cassava, sweet potatoes and a few more simple crops to feed themselves.[1] These were supplemented by wild fruits, mushrooms, caterpillars and such small animals as could be caught around the villages. Earlier in the century game had been abundant and this had provided protein, but as more people acquired guns the wild animals became sparse.[2] Fish was an alternative for people living near a river or a lake; villagers less fortunately placed had to barter their crops with the hawkers of dried fish travelling among the tribes on bicycles. Throughout most of the country, the tse-tse fly prevented cattle-keeping, while in any case people such as Bemba had no money with which to start herds, and no knowledge of how to care for them.

The government was faced with almost insoluble difficulties. Until the late 1930s when the copper mines began to contribute significantly to the country's revenue, there was little money to spare for improving African farming. A pathetically small Department of Agriculture concentrated on helping the few hundred white farmers, who apart from a brief tobacco boom at Fort Jameson in the late 1920s saw scant return for their ventures. As late as 1939, the department made its priorities clear in its annual report: 'The encouragement of European settlement on the land and the permanent raising of the standard of living of the indigenous population.' There was little thought until recent years of Africans producing crops for export; because of transport problems—roads being rudimentary and the country hundreds of miles from the sea—it was difficult enough for the enclaves of white farmers in Fort Jameson and Abercorn to market their tobacco and coffee profitably. Any African farm production not eaten where it was grown was sold internally and mainly consisted of maize put on the market in the Southern Province. It was estimated that in the late 1930s, cash earnings of African farmers in the whole country were about £25,000 a year, and trade goods to the same value were obtained by barter.[3] There were proposals for the development of rice and groundnuts by Africans, and experiments with cotton were made in the early 1930s, but results were negligible.

In an effort to drive the Africans to more modern methods of farming, sporadic orders were given that *chitemene* must be ended. Since no practical alternative was put in its place, and the people giving the orders had lacked understanding of soil deficiencies, the results were disastrous. In Mpika district the people for many years dated events from the famine caused by a ban placed on 'slash and burn' methods by a well-meaning DC. It is a problem which even today defies the African leaders of Zambia, although the need for concentrated, modern methods of farming have become more apparent with the sharp rise in population.

The stagnation of the rural economy produced a vicious circle. The diet available so lacked essential elements, that people had little will to advance their state. They survived, but there was no incentive or prospect for improvement. Experts said repeatedly that the Africans of Northern Rhodesia suffered from malnutrition, especially due to a shortage of vitamins and mineral salts. Major G. St-J. Orde-Browne, in his 1938 report on labour conditions,[4] pointed out: 'The African himself is aware of the shortages, as he develops a craving for the deficient elements. Meat hunger is almost universal, as is the desire for salt, while the craving for anti-scorbutics can be seen in the avidity with which a party of travelling workers will devour lemons or oranges.' The general low state of health made the people easy victims to disease, both those locally endemic and others brought in from the outside world. In 1936 the medical officer at Balovale, in the far west of the country, wrote: 'Debilitating diseases such as malaria, syphilis, gonorrhea and hookworm are rife . . . it is to be anticipated that there will be a high infant mortality rate, that sterility will be common and that the mortality from most epidemic diseases such as influenza will be high.' In the first nine months of 1942, there were 4,970 African applicants for work at Mufulira mine; only 3,271 (or 66 per cent) were passed by the doctors. At Nkana, the senior medical officer said that most of the men rejected by his staff were suffering from malnutrition.[5]

Another factor which inhibited improvement in the rural areas was the lack of able-bodied men, many of whom had travelled away from their tribal homes to find work. Shortly before the second world war, half the men were away from the Bemba country; in the Mporokoso district the proportion was estimated to be as high as two-thirds.[6] Thus the most backward areas agriculturally were left to become even worse, with old men, women and children struggling to keep the gardens going. In 1936, at least 120,000 out of the taxable male population of 288,000 were working away from their home villages. It is, of course, possible to overestimate the effect of this large-scale absenteeism; women would in any case supply most of the labour in the gardens and since Bemba men are not natural farmers they might have done little had they stayed at home;[7] yet the social depression caused by having such a large proportion of the community away made it inevitable that agriculture would at best remain static.

The division between town and country was more marked during the inter-war years than it is today. There were three gravel arterial roads—the Great North Road to the Tanganyika border, the Great East Road to Fort Jameson and Nyasaland, and the Congo Border Road through the Copperbelt—but even these were in poor condition. The only bitumen surfaces were short stretches at Lusaka and Livingstone. The country also had 5,000 miles of secondary roads, but in the words of Lord Hailey 'most of these were mere tracks'.[8] Outside the railway belt, public transport consisted of dusty open lorries on which travellers crowded with their belongings. The frequency with which fragile goods such as plates were broken by the feet of careless passengers caused endless quarrels; the need for a better transport system was a regular subject at the meetings of African welfare societies.[9] So quite apart from the cost, to make a journey from some remote district like Lundazi, Mwinilungu or Kawamba to the urban centres was a tiresome operation; most of the women and older men who could not walk so far never even attempted it. News and modern ideas filtered slowly to the tribal areas, most of it transmitted by word of mouth by miners returning home. Until the introduction of the cheap 'Saucepan Special' by Harry Franklin,[10] the Director of Information, in 1949, very few people had radios; newspapers rarely penetrated beyond the line-of-rail, because with a population which averaged only five to the square mile and was largely illiterate, distribution would have been completely uneconomic; it was not until the war years that the government publication *Mutende* achieved any wide distribution.[11]

In the urban areas, however, black and white workers were having to take up their positions in face of many new problems. The most pressing of these concerned housing conditions, social disorders created by urbanisation and the wages paid to black and white workers.

The building of good housing for Africans in towns was impeded by the official reluctance to accept the stabilisation of labour: in 1941 the government was still insisting that it could not be committed to 'the policy of establishing a permanent industrialised native population on the Copperbelt', and two years later a visiting labour expert found that he had to argue the case for stabilisation.[12] African housing generally continued to be of a poor standard until the end of the 1940s, despite the complaints of Orde-Browne in 1938. He described African housing conditions in the territory as 'discreditable' and 'deplorable', pointing to decaying, bug-ridden huts, usually of one room of only ten feet diameter for a whole family. Roofs were of tin or of thatch, sanitation poor or non-existent, and drinking-water scarce. Although admitting the high cost of improvements, Orde-Browne submitted a list of suggestions, and ended : 'At least they should enable speedy action to be taken in dealing with a situation, which, in its present condition, must reflect on the Administration of the country.'[13]

The squalid living conditions of town Africans was matched by immorality, juvenile delinquency and crime. The compound system in the mines at first made it impossible for the unskilled men to bring their wives with them from the villages, so prostitutes found ample opportunities for trade. A miner who had accommodation where he could take in a partner often preferred to have a 'town girl' rather than bring his less sophisticated tribal wife to the Copperbelt from his village. Sometimes a group of men would share one woman to cook, do the washing and divert them in turn. Generally, urbanisation produced a sharp lowering of sexual morals which was causing concern as early as 1932.[14] The children of these casual unions often turned to petty crime. Orde-Browne said : 'A disquieting feature of compounds of all kinds is the large juvenile population without occupation or control. Children and adolescents of all ages throng the vicinity, finding amusement as they can and devoid of teaching or training. In native villages this would not be the case, since almost all the tribes have very definite arrangements for training the young people according to their ideas.'[15]

The African welfare societies were anxious about the social disorder in the towns. With the help of missionaries and social workers they organised football matches, started small libraries and ran social clubs. On the mines, township welfare halls were built, homecraft classes were started for women and evening educational courses for men. Shortly before the second world war, primary schooling got into its stride and this helped to control the spread of juvenile delinquency.

Such improvements did not help, however, to remove the tensions caused by the wide gap between living standards of white and black workers. As the Africans became more sophisticated they were increasingly resentful of the fact that Europeans were paid ten or twenty times as much as they for similar work. There were many jobs to which, without the advantages of education, Africans could not aspire, but in a wide range of semi-skilled occupations a degree of competition was apparent by the middle 1930s.

In 1936, the secretary of the South African Mine Workers' Union, Charles Harris, visited the Copperbelt at the request of the white workers.[16] They were worried about the advancement of Africans, who had shown an unexpected militancy the previous year by striking, ostensibly about new tax rates (the strike was only quelled after six men had been shot dead, many more injured and scores arrested). Harris examined labour conditions on the Copperbelt, then announced his surprise that 'the native had actually encroached not only upon unskilled labour but skilled labour in this territory'. With the aim of protecting Europeans, a Northern Rhodesian Mine Workers' Union was founded; the mining companies recognised it in 1937. The union brought the industrial colour bar north of the Zambezi, drawing a sharp line between what was 'white work' and what was 'kaffir work'.

Yet attempts at job reservation never became fully effective despite the efforts of the white unionists. By 1940, lorries were being driven on one mine by Africans, on another by Europeans. The difference was that in one case the pay was £3 a month, and in the other £30.[17] The wages paid to Africans in industry, commerce and government were a constant source of tension, there being practically no increase in the national average between 1927 and 1940. Indeed, wages actually fell in the depression years and did not recover until the war. In 1928 the monthly pay for Africans on the mines was 15*s*.0*d* for surface work and 22*s*.0*d* underground.[18] Giving evidence to the commission investigating the 1935 riots, a Nkana safety-officer called Rex l'Ange (later to become Federal Minister of Works) said: 'In efficiency the natives have been improving daily and whereas at one time you had four or five boys doing one job, you now have two doing it.'[19] There was no correlation between efficiency and reward, however: the commissioners were told that of 5,829 workers at Nkana, only 800 were paid more than 30*s*.0*d* a month, and 2,300 were receiving below 20*s*.0*d*.[20]

In 1940 the starting rate was 12*s*.6*d* on surface and 22*s*.0*d* below, despite an increase in the rate of poll-tax; the average European wage was more than £40 a month.[21] Matters reached a climax early in 1940 when European miners at Nkana and Mufulira struck for increases and better conditions. On March 27 the strike was settled after government intervention, the workers being in the main granted their demands. A day later, Africans on the same mines struck for more money;[22] in all, 15,000 came out—reputedly encouraged by some of the Europeans. Anonymous notices had been posted up near the Nkana compound office during the white stoppage. One of these said :

> My friends, young men of the Mine, I have words to tell you. You know how the Europeans left their work on a matter of increased wages : I ask you, therefore, what will you do if the Europeans receive an increase in wages? I ask you, will you see them resuming their work unless they receive an increase? Certainly not, Sir. I am very angry about this. See what we did in 1935 without any result. Also at Luanshya some of our friends died and nothing was done for us because in fact we are their slaves. So if the Europeans receive an increase by leaving their work then we should cease working too. We should not fight or cause disturbances because if we do, they will bring many machine-guns and aeroplanes. In this matter we are in God's care—he really loves us. Look at the police—they are like Europeans here at Nkana. We should beat them. We are like slaves because of the police. If you fail to do this you are only women. You have defiled your mothers. If you think they will kill you—not at all. They are only human beings like ourselves. Indeed it would be a good thing if they gave us an increase. All would be well.

The notice was signed cryptically *Katwishi Chowa* (=I don't know the name).[23]

After six days of the African strike, 3,000 men tried to attack 130 blacklegs while they were drawing their pay. Police used tear-gas, then when the disturbances became more serious opened fire. Seventeen men were killed and sixty-five wounded; the miners went back to work. But the strike was not without effect, for by August 1942 the average wages of Africans were 35*s*.6*d* surface and 52*s*.11*d* underground.[24] These advances proved to be more apparent than real, however, because acute shortages during the war put up the prices of all basic commodities by between 50 per cent and 100 per cent.[25] In 1943, a South African labour expert produced a report at government request on African living-conditions on the Copperbelt. The expert, E. Lynn Saffery, estimated that the poverty datum line for a family with two children was an income of £6.11*s*.7*d*—and then showed that with rations, free housing and other sources of income, the average mine family was only getting £4.14*s*.7*d*. In secondary industry the income was as low as £2.5*s*.10*d*. Saffery stressed the opinion of medical authorities that malnutrition was widespread. His report was printed but never published,[26] such copies as were supplied to senior government officials being marked 'Strictly confidential'. One mine manager who saw the report passed it off by saying: 'According to Saffery all my workers are dead—they haven't got a living wage.'[27]

Until the 1940s no organisation existed specifically to protect the interests of African workers, apart from an ineffectual Native Industrial Labour Advisory Board, whose membership was entirely white; nor was there, until 1940, a Labour Department. When the Forster Commission investigated the causes of the 1940 riots on the Copperbelt, the desirability of an African trade union was discussed. The commission decided, however: 'All the weight of evidence produced before us was to the effect that African mine employees do not demand trade union organisation and are not ripe for it.' Instead, the commission proposed an extension of the 'elder' system by which men chosen from each tribal group working on the mine formed a body to speak for their colleagues.[28] In 1942, 'boss boys' committees' were also set up—boss boy being the official description for a man in charge of a gang. One of the complaints raised by the Roan Antelope boss boys' committee in 1943 makes droll reading: 'If a man is assaulted by a European he goes at once to the nearest official to complain, either shift boss or mine captain. He is thereupon assaulted again for complaining.'[29]

It is perhaps because of the peculiar state of race relations in Northern Rhodesia that tentative moves by some of the white miners to bring Africans into the existing Mine Workers' Union met with no success. Dave Welensky, brother of Roy, and vice president of the union, took a strongly segregationist view and insisted that he did not want to help in organising black workers. Roy Welensky, for his part, long opposed in the Legislative Council any idea of an African trade union movement. Not until 1946 did it become clear that a non-European labour organisation was inevitable: the African workers, both in the mines and in commerce, were demanding trade unions; many Nyasas working in Northern Rhodesia pointed to the power that had been wielded in South Africa by the non-white Industrial and Commercial Workers' Union, founded by a Nyasaland Tonga, Clements Kadalie.[30]

In their demands the Africans now had the support of missionaries and welfare workers (one of whom was sacked in Kitwe in 1946 for telling the African Society that only trade unions could force employers to pay higher wages).[31] Roy Welensky had also changed his attitude and with Sir Stewart Gore-Browne held discussions on Northern Rhodesia's labour problems during a visit to the Colonial Office in London. In 1947 an experienced trade-unionist, William M. Comrie, was sent out to the Copperbelt as a labour officer and quickly began laying the foundations of an

African labour movement.[32] As Comrie began to attract attention, the president of the European Mine Workers' Union (a self-styled communist called Brian Goodwin) again suggested that it would be better for Africans to demonstrate 'solidarity' with the white miners. But the European union had forfeited respect by boycotting the Dalgleish Commission appointed in October 1947 to investigate the possibilities of African advancement in the mines:* the union's objection to the commission had been that its British trade union chairman, Andrew Dalgleish, was too pro-African.[33] Dalgleish, a prominent member of the British TUC, had visited Northern Rhodesia eight years before, when he was a member of the Forster Commission.

In February 1948, the first branch of the African Mine Workers' Union was formed at Nkana. Its chairman was Lawrence Katilungu, a Bemba clerk who had worked in the mines since 1936. His defeated rival for the position was Godwin Mbikusita (Lewanika) who later in the year was to be elected president of the Northern Rhodesia African Congress. By the end of 1948, unions were operating in all the mining centres, and by March 1949 these had merged to form what was soon to become the strongest African trade union south of the equator. Although it was constantly urged by authorities to keep out of politics, it was inevitable that the African Mineworkers' Union was to become a potent force in the nationalist struggle. The union branches became focal points for the discussion of political grievances and many union officials were simultaneously leaders of Congress.

IV EDUCATION: THE TWO STREAMS

The Northern Rhodesia government assumed formal responsibility for education in the territory in 1925. It inherited from the Chartered Company the supervision of the Barotse National School (founded in 1906), a small school in the native location at Livingstone, and rudimentary facilities for children of the white settler community. Outside the government's direct control were some 2,000 mission schools, with a nominal enrolment estimated at 89,000 and an attendance half to two-thirds that number. The Native Schools Proclamation (No. 28 of 1921) exerted a modest control over the registration and inspection of 'secular' mission schools, and the quality of their African teachers. Except that the Paris Missionary Society received from the Barotse Trust Fund an

* See p. 170.

annual grant of £185, no subsidies to missionary societies for educational work had been made.

To administer this structure, two government departments were established, one for the education of the Europeans, the other, a sub-department of the Native Affairs, for Africans. Twice, in the mid '30s and late '40s, proposals to merge the two departments were considered but shelved. The supporters of each system feared that the other would be favoured financially by government if they combined. The dual system of education thus continued until the eve of independence. When amalgamation took place in January 1964, the European community had achieved education generally comparable in scope and quality to other western systems. African education was, however—despite much extension and improvement—flawed in ways that were crucially important.

The task facing the new Department of European Education at its establishment in 1925 was of no great size. It was estimated that 300 of the 900 European children of school age were not in school, but the inspector of schools reported in 1925 that it would require less than £1,500 from government revenue to achieve seven years' free, compulsory education for all white children.

The reluctance of so large a proportion of the European community to put their children to school was due largely to their own ignorance and poverty. The influence of the European upon the African 'both as leader and example' made the acting director, J. B. Clark, declare that illiterate 'poor whites' needed special attention. Exhortation, correspondence courses, and school boarding hostels failed to overcome parental indifference, but the changed social conditions created by the booming mine townships were more successful. By 1933 the number of school-age European children not receiving education had fallen to thirty-six out of a total of 1,314, and it was possible to introduce legislation for compulsory education in 1941. After laboured arguments as to whether Northern Rhodesia was healthy for white adolescents, an adequate secondary school system was created in the post-war years, although many parents still preferred to send their children to boarding schools in the south.

The European education system had its difficulties, but they were minute compared with those of the African Education Department. When the government took over African education in 1925, the most urgent tasks were to raise the standard of teaching in mission schools and to devise a satisfactory basis for paying grants. To achieve both ends, grants were related to the number of acceptably trained teachers employed by a missionary society. This had the effect of forcing the larger missions to establish teacher-training centres and recruit qualified educationists from abroad to run them. The department examined the candidates at the standard-four level and awarded conditional certificates, pending satisfactory performance at an inspection. The department also laid down a curriculum for aided schools.

These were the first steps to apply order to the medley of mission schools, whose primary aim was to produce teacher-evangelists; most of the teachers were themselves barely literate.

Under the direction of a former native commissioner, G. C. Latham, within five years the department established its authority over secular education, examined its first trained teachers—281 out of 524 passed the first three annual examinations between 1928–30; achieved the passing of the Native Schools (Amendment) Ordinance 1927, for the registration and control of schools, and raised the amount of government funds spent on African education from £348 in 1924–25 to £15,284 in 1930–31. Comparatively, this was an explosion of activity after twenty-five years of the Chartered Company's neglect, but the 1931–4 depression caused cuts in the grants to missions and most capital development stopped. Some attention continued to be given to the training of teachers, however: in 1932 five candidates from Lubwa passed the lower middle-school teachers' examination, based on standard-six work; Lubwa was the mission near Chinsali where Kenneth Kaunda grew up.

By 1936, when the depression ended, the aided mission schools of the territory had enrolled 23,300 children, of whom perhaps three-quarters attended throughout the year. There was also a remarkable increase in the number of unaided 'bush schools', which in 1936 enrolled 83,000 pupils. All but a few of these schools were educationally worthless. Three-quarters of the ostensible enrolment took place in the Eastern Province, where the competitive zeal of the White Fathers and Dutch Reformed Church Missions assumed this curious form, in sharp contrast to their constructive work in other areas.

Other developments were of more importance. Central village schools, often situated at a chief's village, and drawing pupils from the surrounding country, were an innovation of the Livingstonia Mission in 1933, and became popular from 1935 onwards, especially in the Northern and Southern Provinces. By comparison with the small village schools, they were economical and efficient.

The Northern Province also pioneered with local school committees, which, it was hoped, would interest the newly-created native authorities in the education of their people and village improvement. By 1934 these were operating in Barotseland and the Southern Province. Financial responsibility of a sort was accorded these committees for the first time in 1936 when D. S. Miller, the provincial superintendent of native education at Kasama, gave them authority to collect tuition fees and spend the money on books and equipment. In 1936 the system was improved by the creation at Chinsali and Broken Hill of district advisory committees.

During the depression years many teachers left the profession for better-paid jobs at the line-of-rail—a process hastened by a general cut in teachers' salaries because of 'enforced economies' in 1935. The following year a new salary scale was devised for introduction in 1937; this, it was hoped, would help stem the out-flow from the profession to clerical jobs on the Copperbelt. Instead of a scale increasing from 15*s.* to 30*s.* a month over eight years for elementary teachers, a new scale provided for 17*s.*6*d* increasing to 40*s.* over ten years. The range over ten years for lower middle-school teachers was from 25*s.* to 47*s.*6*d.*

If education in the rural areas made no great strides during the depression, the same was doubly true of the industrial areas, particularly the Copperbelt. Latham's early reports, from 1926 onwards, called attention to the almost total lack of education for the growing child population on the mines; the mine companies themselves were extremely reluctant to take any responsibility. The first properly planned and supervised school on the Copperbelt was therefore begun by the government at Ndola only in 1931. The 1933 census revealed a child population of 3,760 in the three main urban centres of the Copperbelt, of whom only 250 were in daily attendance at school. 'The problem of these industrialised natives becomes more pressing each year' reported P. S. Tregear, the local superintendent of native education. The 1935 Copperbelt disturbances were regarded as a hint of what was in store if more was not done quickly for the welfare of urban Africans. In 1937, when the territory's revenue had begun again to increase, a five-year educational program for the Copperbelt was approved by government and its implementation began the next year, following the arrival of a new director of native education, C. J. Tyndale-Biscoe.

The government's partner in the new scheme was the recently-formed team of the United Missions in the Copperbelt, while the mining companies displayed an awakened interest. The only real bar to the success of the project appeared to be the shortage of teachers. Unexpected difficulties lay ahead, however—the most important being the apparent impossibility of estimating correctly the number of school-age children. In 1938 the number on the Copperbelt was shown as 4,500, the following year this was revised to 6,000 and by 1944 the number was thought to be at least 13,000. The government's reluctance to adopt a clear policy of labour stabilisation and fruitless attempts over many years to enforce repatriation of children to the rural areas led the educational planners into grave underestimation of the accommodation required, and to delay the creation of facilities for some children to go to the limit of the primary school course, if not beyond. The difficulties were compounded by the shortage of builders and a severe reduction of building programs in the early war years. The five-year expansion program on the Copperbelt, due for completion in 1941, was only achieved by 1944, and gave facilities then for 7,000—about half the number of children thought to be of school age. In Broken Hill and Livingstone, where (as in Ndola and Kitwe) compulsory education regulations were in force, the schools enrolled 2,500 and 1,500 children respectively, which was fairly close to the estimated school-age populations. In Lusaka, however, only about one third of the 1,500-2,000 children were in school.

Government expediture on African education, which stood at £28,680 in 1937 (when revenues first significantly increased after the depression), soon more than doubled, to £98,000.[1] School enrolments increased proportionately from 42,283 (in government and aided schools) in 1939 to 93,505 in 1943. Remarkable though this expansion had been, considering the uncertainties of the war years and the curtailment of mission funds from Europe, the system which had developed was characterised by extreme waste and imbalance. Over half the children enrolled were in the first class of school. In 1942, out of 86,300 on the roll, 47,500 were in sub-standard A, 3,000 in standard three, and less than 500 in standard six. In the entire territory there were thirty-five secondary school students.

Before he left Northern Rhodesia in 1944, Tyndale-Biscoe sounded 'a note of caution', warning that before further additions were made there should be a period of consolidation. His successor, R. J. Mason, endorsed this view and immediately set about translating it into practice. Initial enrolments, which reached a peak of 68,000 in 1946, were thereafter deliberately curtailed, while the intake to succeeding classes was improved. Nevertheless, in 1948, out of a total enrolment in government and aided schools of 134,400, 59,000 were in sub-standard A and only 1,700 in standard six. Of the 370 post-primary students, 130 were preparing for academic secondary school courses. The smallness of the last figure is partly explained by the need for moderately well-educated teachers; many more primary school graduates were taken on for teacher-training by the government and missions than entered secondary schools. Between 1937 and 1946 the number of African teachers of all grades employed or subsidised financially by the government rose from 593 to 3,550.

Industrial and manual training had been a feature of African education from the days before government assumed responsibility. Agriculture and handiwork classes were considered essential if Africans were not to lose tribal links or start thinking that work with the hands was degrading. In the old Barotse National School, industrial training received pride of place; in the new system of education on the Copperbelt it was considered especially important. In 1943 a special school was opened at Mwekera near Ndola to provide a one-year manual training course after standard four, for boys going to the upper school course. When the school closed down in 1946, mainly because the site was malarious, the extra year of manual training was consolidated with the upper school course. This system was generally opposed by Africans and became the subject of a protest by the African Representative Council at its first meeting in 1946. On the advice of the African Education Advisory Board, however, the system was maintained.

Trades training was provided at Munali Trades School (which later became Hodgson Technical College); but the enrolment was only seventy in 1948. Though 'apprenticeship' training in various crafts had been given in several institutions under the Employment of Natives Ordinance, when the country's first apprenticeship legislation was passed in 1943 it specifically excluded Africans—thus making it impossible for an African to become a qualified journeyman in the only way which would give him an equality of status with white artisans; the technical qualifications then available to him, most admittedly below 'artisan' standard, became automatically inferior. The entrance examination for apprentices, which was laid down in the Ordinance as form two, was in any case beyond all but a handful of Africans at the time the law was made.

V CHALLENGES TO THE CHARTERED COMPANY

The agreement by which the administration of Northern Rhodesia was taken over by the Colonial Office in April 1924, greatly strengthened the British South Africa Company's legal hold on its mineral rights. Despite an appeal to London by white settlers, and an ignored recommendation by the Buxton Commission that a decision by the Privy Council was desirable, the Company was confirmed in its position. Winston Churchill, as Colonial Secretary, had accepted the Buxton Commission's recommendations and had taken steps for the mineral rights to be investigated by the Privy Council's judicial committee. The Company appeared to prevaricate. In October 1922 the Coalition administration to which Churchill then belonged was removed from office. A close friend of senior Chartered officials, William Ormsby-Gore, became parliamentary Under-Secretary for the Colonies and the Devonshire Agreement (named after the new Colonial Secretary) was signed on October 1, 1923; it specifically confirmed the mineral rights. In the mid-20s, this all seemed of comparatively minor importance: revenue from mining was negligible and exploration had not yet given any clear proof that vast sulphide ore-bodies lay beneath the Copperbelt's low-grade oxides. Not until 1931 did Nkana and Roan begin producing, and the slump that followed blurred for some years the realisation that Chartered had unwittingly struck a remarkable bargain when it retired from the labour of administering its vast northern domain.

In the early '30's, the settlers were much too concerned with the country's economic straits and with the amalgamation controversy to care much about their Aunt Sally of yesteryear. Only in Barotseland was the smouldering resentment against Chartered still alive. The Paramount Chief, Yeta, took advantage of his farewell message to Sir Herbert Stanley, the retiring Governor, in 1927 to say: 'The British South Africa Company administered this territory for a considerable length of time, and yet no benefit, advancement nor good was there for the natives.'[1] In 1921 and 1923, Yeta had sent vigorous petitions to London, demanding that Chartered should relinquish its land and mineral rights. In 1930, Yeta again protested to the government: 'The British South Africa Company has not carried out the obligations imposed on it by the terms of the concessions granted to it, and it is my wish that it should be compelled to do so.'[2] The officials in Livingstone reprimanded him for dragging up dead issues.

Interest in the mineral rights rose among Europeans in the country shortly before the second world war, as the Copperbelt got into its stride and the mining companies began to pay royalties on a handsome scale. Southern Rhodesia had bought out Chartered's rights in 1933 for £2,000,000 and in the Lusaka Legislative Council Sir Leopold Moore argued that Britain could have done the same thing for Northern Rhodesia in 1924 much more cheaply: 'We could have had the mineral rights of the Chartered Company for £250,000, but the Imperial treasury was pretty well empty.'[3] Moore made this claim during an important attack on the Chartered's mineral rights by elected members in December 1938. This attack had been encouraged by the recently-published observations of two very diverse personalities. One was J. E. "Chirupula" Stephenson—who had first come to the country as a Chartered employee in 1899. Stephenson was a man of some learning and in 1937 published an autobiography called *Chirupula's Tale*.[4] He vehemently challenged the British South Africa Company's rights and was particularly scathing about the concessions obtained by Joseph Thomson in 1890, in an area where Stephenson had personally run up the Union Jack less than a decade later. Ammunition of a different kind was provided by Sir Alan Pim, in his official report on the financial and economic position of the country.[5] Sir Alan's masterly survey, which ranged from staff problems in the secretariat to the condition of African beer halls, pointed out that the 1923 agreement was a 'remarkably good one' for Chartered. The Company's mining revenue had risen from £12,781 in 1925 to £300,000 in 1937, which was nearly half the total Northern Rhodesia government income from the mines. Sir Alan also mentioned Yeta's appeal to Britain in 1917, in which the Paramount Chief had claimed that the Company's rights were obtained in its capacity as the government—the inference being that without the responsibilities of administration it must also abandon its rights. In a series of lectures at Oxford, Sir Alan reiterated: 'Even allowing for the great fluctuations in the copper market, the financial position should make it possible to count on resources adequate to a large expansion in the essential services of health, education and agriculture, but for the fact that the British South Africa Company receives the whole of the mineral royalties paid in Northern Rhodesia, while the British government receives half the income tax on all companies domiciled in the United Kingdom.... The territory has a great deal of leeway to make up both in public works and in the social services.'[6]

Sir Hubert Young had already approached the British South Africa Company President, Sir Dougal Malcolm, without success,[7] and in August 1937 had sent a long dispatch to London expressing profound doubts about the mineral rights. The Governor argued that in 1900 Lewanika's kingdom was defined as only reaching the lower Kafue in the east (which did not include the Copperbelt) and that the 'certificates of claim' issued by Johnston in 1893 did not embrace the Copperbelt either. However, Sir Hubert speedily came into conflict with William Ormsby-Gore, who by this time had advanced to becoming Colonial Secretary. Ormsby-Gore, who was related by marriage to Sir Dougal Malcolm, replied to the Governor: 'I wish at the outset to make it clear in the most explicit manner that I am not prepared to re-open the question of the title of the British South Africa Company to the ownership of the minerals throughout Northern Rhodesia.' He then proceeded to admit that there was a 'conflict of evidence' about tribal boundaries but said any investigation would be 'entirely unprofitable'. In 1938, both Sir Hubert and Ormsby-Gore left their current posts, but a dispatch for publication came from Malcolm MacDonald, the Colonial Secretary, in March 1939, rejecting outright any challenge to Chartered's mineral rights.[8] The British Attorney General, Sir Donald Somervell, and the Solicitor General, Sir Terence O'Connor, were agreed that the rights were valid : 'Apart from the legal aspect . . . from the point of good faith the Crown would not be justified in challenging the Company's title.' Yet MacDonald's dispatch was far from satisfactory, since it did not even consider whether the concessions obtained in 1890 were tenable under African customary law, which it had become Colonial Office policy to treat with great respect. Nor did it face up to the crucial fact that North-Western Rhodesia had been enlarged in 1905 to embrace the mineralised region—although a singular admission was made : 'It is worth observing that unless Lewanika's jurisdiction were treated as running over the whole area covered by the (1905) order, there is no suggested right to make a basis for this Order.' Never had it been seriously maintained before that Barotse rule extended as far as Mkushi.

Perhaps the only sentence in MacDonald's dispatch which met with general agreement in Lusaka was that which said the relationship between the Crown and the British South Africa Company was 'a peculiar one'. But while the unofficials were winding themselves up for another onslaught in the Legislative Council, the second world war broke out and mineral rights were temporarily forgotten. No heed was given to the findings of the MacDonell Commission (which in 1941 excised the Balovale District from Barotseland)[9], although this still further weakened the Chartered case by deflating to reality the size of the Lozi kingdom. It was only at the end of the war that serious attention was once more paid to the royalty question, as money became urgently needed for a £13,000,000 Development Plan. By now the member for Broken Hill, Roy Welensky, had asserted his dominance of the Legislative Council and as a self-confessed socialist it was natural for him to take over from Gore-Browne, who had remarked gloomily in 1946 : 'We are saddled with these royalties and for the moment we must leave it at that.'[10] Although Chartered was by now extracting over £400,000 a year, and the administration had been corresponding for six years with the Colonial Office, no headway was being made. When they visited London after the War, the engine-driver and the Old Harrovian had talked around the problem with the British government, which then toyed with the idea of offering the British South Africa Company £10,000,000 compensation, but changed its mind.[11]

Irritated by the continual indecision, Welensky asked at the end of 1947 whether anything had been done 'on the question of the expropriation or purchase of the royalties claimed to be held by the British South Africa Company'.[12] He was given no answer. In January 1948 he said: 'If we do not get a reply by March, then it is my intention to move a vote of no confidence in this government. I have no other weapon, unless I go to the people and stir them up to make out-and-out trouble.'[13] Throughout the year he kept up his bombardment, which reached a climax when he proposed a 50 per cent tax on the royalties, which had by now soared to £2,000,000 annually with the rise in copper prices. In March 1949, the Officials walked out of the Council when a vote was taken on Welensky's motion that the time was opportune to impose a special royalties tax. One of the two African members, Nelson Nalumango, voted against the motion, because as a Barotse he felt it necessary to defend the *status quo;* all the other unofficials supported Welensky, although with qualms about the size of the foe they were tackling.

Until that moment, the Chartered Company had done almost nothing to defend its case. It was understandably loath to engage in public discussion of the history of the mineral rights and had preferred to keep piling up royalties behind the barricade of Malcolm MacDonald's 1939 dispatch. However, Sir Dougal Malcolm now decided that the moment had come for a counter-attack and with considerable acumen he chose Southern Rhodesia as the place from which to launch it. Addressing the National Affairs Association in Salisbury on April 14, 1949, Sir Dougal used precisely the argument that Chartered was to employ again so effectively sixteen years later: if the royalties were challenged, then the City of London would not invest in Rhodesia. The City was only too keen to 'assist' Rhodesia, but because of what seemed a 'violent turn to the left', investors were having second thoughts. He quoted a letter from the Chairman of Cable and Wireless Ltd. which had (by some lucky coincidence) been sent to him just before the meeting. The letter described Welensky's suggestion of taxing royalties as 'dastardly', and went on: 'Where would the African be today if it were not for the pioneers who took all the risks, such as the British South Africa Company?' Such words could scarcely have been more fitting if Sir Dougal had composed them himself; he did not mention that Cable and Wireless was a prominent shareholder in Chartered. The audience was warned against consoling itself with any idea that what might be done in the north was no concern of Southern Rhodesia—the City of London did not differentiate between the two Rhodesias. 'What happens there affects you here,' said Sir Dougal—an arrow which struck home doubly hard in view of the growing prospect of federation. In his impressive peroration the Chartered president invoked God, the King, and British honesty, while roundly condemning Roy Welensky. Next day, large numbers of leaflets containing the speech were distributed.

A week later, a courier arrived in Lusaka from Salisbury. He was a Mr Porter, director of a commercial firm in which Chartered had a controlling interest. Porter approached Geoffrey Beckett, Welensky's closest ally in the Legislative Council, and said that Sir Dougal Malcolm was anxious to open talks.[14] From then on, events moved at a remarkable speed. Welensky and Beckett went secretly to Bulawayo and had a discussion lasting several hours with Sir Dougal and Sir Ellis Robins, local director of the British South Africa Company. The next month, discussions were transferred to London, under the chairmanship of Creech-Jones, the Colonial Secretary. On August 10, agreement was announced. This guaranteed the Company 'undisturbed enjoyment' of the mineral rights until October 1, 1986, and ruled that during that time there should be no special rate, tax or duty imposed on the royalties.[15] If at any time before the date of transfer the British government should take steps to relinquish responsibility for the government of Northern Rhodesia, it should 'in so far as it is possible to do so' secure that the new government would be bound to observe the provisions of the agreement. Any dispute would be referred to the Privy Council.

Welensky had thus completely abandoned his argument that the mineral rights were invalid and that royalties should simply be expropriated. The terms did not rest on the legality of the rights, but merely served to limit them to thirty-six years and at the same time assured Northern Rhodesia of one-fifth of the revenue. Nor had compensation been chosen as the solution, because Chartered demanded £20,000,000 to £40,000,000. Welensky's agreement was hailed as a stupendous victory, because its terms gave the territory greatly increased revenue from the royalties. However, time was to prove that the Company had again done extremely well.

Sir Ellis Robins, who had attended the secret meeting in Bulawayo in 1949, later became Lord Robins, President of the British South Africa Company. As late as 1961 he reiterated his confidence in the 'wise and courageous leadership' of Sir Roy.

6

Federation—Genesis and Exodus

I THE IRRESISTIBLE PROGRESS

SIR GODFREY HUGGINS, Prime Minister of Southern Rhodesia, dominated the two-day conference of white politicians at Victoria Falls in February 1949. He talked of partnership in the proposed federation of the Rhodesias and Nyasaland, but left no doubts in the minds of Northern Rhodesia delegates about how he felt it should be implemented. He was quoted : 'For the time being the natives must be ruled by a benevolent aristocracy. . . . The history of the world suggests that there is *prima facie* evidence that there is something wrong with the Bantu branch of the family.'[1] Roy Welensky was subdued at the conference, and was later reproached by Europeans in the north for having let Sir Godfrey dictate terms, when in reality the latter was an anxious suitor. An editorial in Lusaka's *Central African Post* remarked : 'It is our money that Southern Rhodesia is after. Does anyone believe for a moment that she would have the slightest desire to federate with us if we had no very profitable copper mines?'[2] The Southern Rhodesian economy was expanding rapidly in the post-war years, but was overstrained and needed additional revenue to carry it through to the time when secondary industries would achieve profitability.

The conference was completely unofficial, and in the secretariat at Lusaka the senior civil servants decided to maintain an attitude of guarded neutrality. District commissioners were being badgered by Africans for information, and in turn asked the Secretary for Native Affairs what they should say. After discussions between the Secretary for Native Affairs and the Chief Secretary, a circular letter was sent to all *bomas* advising that Africans should be told that before any decision was taken about federation it would be voted upon by the provincial councils and the African Representative Council.[3] The inference (which was misleading) appeared to be that such voting would influence the course of events. However, African opinion was already crystallising, because of Welensky's remarks at the opening of the new Legislative Council in November 1948. The white elected members had achieved parity with the officials and the Governor had yielded his position as President to a Speaker. Welensky, addressing the Speaker, had said: 'Your appointment . . . indicates to us the gradual transfer of power from Downing Street to the people of this country.'[4]

There were few doubts that he was thinking mainly of the 32,000 white people and not the 1,600,000 unenfranchised Africans. Welensky had gone on to talk of the political future, stressing that he was still as much as ever a believer in the amalgamation of the Rhodesias, but had abandoned it because of African opposition. 'I hope the government will use its influence—I do not want you to influence Africans in favour of federation, let them judge it on its merits.'

In numerous statements since that period, Welensky has argued that federation was torpedoed by the antagonism of Northern Rhodesia's white civil servants.[5] In fact, the civil servants were eager to promote racial harmony and were trying to wean Africans from the controversial doctrine of paramountcy. Addressing the African Representative Council in 1948, the Secretary for Native Affairs (Hudson) said: 'The development of Northern Rhodesia is based on a genuine partnership between Europeans and Africans. . . . The present and future interests of Northern Rhodesia can only be served by a policy of whole-hearted co-operation between the different sections of the community, based on the real interests of both sections.'[6] Hudson's reference to partnership is illuminating, since it was to become the catchword of federation; its use in connection with race relations in Central Africa was not new, however—Sir Stewart Gore-Browne had employed it as early as 1935 in an article for the *Journal of the Royal African Society*.[7]

Everything revolved, of course, around the interpretation of 'genuine partnership', as Hudson carefully phrased it. The Federationists have argued that the Africans never really wanted it, but were intent on political domination. There is no question that Africans regarded themselves as in a state of tutelage, which ultimately would bring them to a condition where they could run their own affairs. But they retained, in those early post-war years, a deep faith in the British government, and its representatives in the colonial administrations. Although race relations in Northern Rhodesia were much more strained by 1948 than they had been a decade earlier,[8] Africans were anxious to avoid appearing un-co-operative. Thus in January 1949, the Secretary-General of Congress, Robinson Nabulyato, wrote to the Chief Secretary to ask whether Africans would be allowed to attend the Victoria Falls conference : 'We are scared of the European threats and we must know our position before we decide whether for or against the federation issue.'[9] Nabulyato urged that the African delegation, if allowed to attend, should be accompanied by the Secretary for Native Affairs. This proposal came to nothing, as did the appeal by Nelson Nalumango, one of the two African MLCs, for a conference between Africans of the Central African territories to consider their attitude.[10]

The gulf widened as news of the attitude adopted by Sir Godfrey Huggins became common knowledge. Gore-Browne held meetings throughout the country to sound opinion. He said he had not made up his own mind; but his audience had made up theirs. At Chingola a meeting lasted for more than five hours and ended in unanimous rejection of federation.[11] When the Colonial Secretary, Arthur Creech-Jones, visited the territory in April he was presented with a memorandum by the African Mineworkers Union (which by now had 11,500 members) vehemently opposing federation. Creech-Jones tried to calm African suspicions by saying, before returning to London : 'Permanent white settlement needs to be controlled. Because Northern Rhodesia is a protectorate, the Africans have been granted certain inherent rights and therefore in agricultural developments there are certain definite restrictions as far as Europeans are concerned.' He went on to stress that the whites would have a permanent place in Northern Rhodesia, but his outline of British policy was infuriating to Welensky, who retorted : 'If the British government wants to implement it, it will have to bring troops to this country to carry it out. . . . I will never accept that Northern Rhodesia is to be an African state.'[12] This utterance served to harden even further the attitude of the junior partners.

An elaborate statement of case was meanwhile being prepared in the North London suburb of Brondesbury Park. Dr Hastings Banda, who had not seen his Nyasa homeland for more than thirty years, had gathered around him a group of African students who were anxious about the settlers' intentions. One of these was Harry Nkumbula, the teacher who (with Gore-Browne's sponsorship) had gone first to Makerere College in Uganda and later to the London School of Economics. The group decided that Banda and Nkumbula should write a memorandum for submission to parliamentarians in Britain and to senior officials in Central

Africa. Earlier, Nkumbula had written a letter to the Northern Rhodesia Governor, Sir Gilbert Rennie, who had shown it to the Executive Council: Roy Welensky and his three supporters in the council had been angry that a student on a government scholarship (even a student aged thirty-two) should demonstrate such temerity.[13] This second dissertation was to cause even more annoyance. Banda and Nkumbula went to great lengths to show how incompatible were the policies of Southern Rhodesia and the two northern protectorates; in the former, 'any African who is not demonstrably servile and obsequious is classed as cheeky or impertinent'. The whites in Southern Rhodesia 'regarded themselves as superior beings'. The two African spokesmen heaped praise on the British government, which they said treated Africans as 'human beings with a right to a dignified and refined existence'. The memorandum, twenty-five pages long, declared eloquently: 'Our boys had fought and died in Abyssinia, in the desert and the swamps and jungles of Burma, for the same king, in defence of the same right to justice, and the same empire and Commonwealth.' Federation would only be acceptable if there was universal franchise in all three territories; there must also be the right of secession if at any time the majority of the people of the territory regarded membership of the federation as 'incompatible with their full political, social and economic progress'. The writers ended by calling for an immediate union between Northern Rhodesia and Nyasaland, because some tribes were split by the boundary and both were under the United Kingdom. An 'organic union' would be of 'political, economic and social advantage'. When the memorandum arrived in Lusaka in the middle of 1949, there was concern in the secretariat, but a suggestion that Nkumbula's scholarship should be withdrawn was vetoed, in case this should provoke questions in the House of Commons.

At the end of the year, Welensky and his colleagues in the Legislative Council decided to throw down the gauntlet, because in London opposition was mounting—the Churches and radical political groups growing notably dubious. Welensky, fresh from his apparent triumph over the Chartered mineral royalties, moved that 'in the opinion of this House, the time is opportune for His Majesty's government to take the lead in creating the Central African State'.[14] The result of this initiative was to create an even bigger rift between the elected and official members of the government. After a full debate, the officials declined to vote (an action which had been agreed in advance with the Governor). This might seem an entirely justified action, for as the Colonial Annual Report for 1949 pointed out, African opposition to federation had throughout the year 'increased and become more vocal'; moreover, the British government had by no means committed itself to federation, so that an 'aye' vote by the civil servants would have tied London to an emphatic and unqualified acceptance even before a federal constitution had been evolved. Welensky was deeply wounded by the official show of neutrality. He has called it 'as near a death-blow as our campaign suffered'.[15] The civil servants, as he rightly points out, were then widely trusted by the Africans, who therefore took the walk-out from the chamber as a condemnation of federation. Sir Roy never considers whether he might not have shown more discernment to press his case privately, rather than attempt a public and premature trial of strength.

The debate revealed the attacking mood of Welensky's followers and the uncertainty of the small nucleus of Africans and nominated members. Welensky concentrated upon the economic benefits of federation, and said the suspicion of the settlers' motives was deeply resented. 'Political rights, after all, mean very little to a man with an empty stomach. If we are genuinely concerned about the Africans, let us give them economic development and political rights can come later.' E. W. Sergeant, a railwayman, asked whether anyone in the British government had 'read the Boston Tea Party' and said he wondered if history was going to repeat itself—'because I can see that coming'. Rex Lange,* a miners' spokesman, stressed the need for a 'strong and virile nation' in Central Africa, adding that 'the European is mentally superior to the indigenous race'. A member of the so-called inferior race, the Rev. Henry Kasokolo, said: 'I want to stress my own personal opinion that what we are looking for is a Northern Rhodesia where all races will live happily together, with equal opportunities to share in all the resources of the country, as equals, with full citizenship rights. We hate anything in this country which suggests the subordination of one race to another.' But, complained Kasokolo, the way the Victoria Falls conference was conducted had caused marked distrust. This fact was also enlarged upon by Sir Stewart Gore-Browne.

Throughout most of 1950, the Huggins-Welensky campaign for federation at the earliest possible moment was largely halted, because of political conditions in Britain. At the February general election, the 'austerity' program of the Labour Party had been weighed in the scales of public opinion and the 1945 landslide majority of 186 was cut to eight. Creech-Jones, the Colonial Secretary, lost his seat and was replaced by James Griffiths, whose

---

*** He later spelt his name L'Ange.**

knowledge of African affairs was minimal. The hectic battle in the Commons and speculation about how long Clement Attlee would cling on before going to the country again diverted attention from the appeals of 160,000 white settlers 5,000 miles away. In the Central Africa arena, however, the opposing forces were consolidating their positions. Argus newspapers in both Rhodesias (the *Northern News* had now been sold by Welensky to this South African combine) were tireless in its advocacy; the Africans had no journal to speak for them. The federationists were also now receiving the backing of big business through the pressure group called the United Central Africa Association, which was very active in London. Prominent in the group was the British South Africa Company, which after the royalties *détente* in 1949 had acquired a warm regard for Welensky and sympathy for his politics; support also came from Rhodesian Selection Trust and the Anglo-American Corporation, who between them owned the Copperbelt. (All three of these groups were subsequently to give financial aid to the United Federal Party,[16] Anglo-American and Rhodesian Selection Trust withdrawing in July 1959 and Chartered continuing its subvention until 1962.) During 1950 this high-powered advocacy of Central African federation began to penetrate the City of London, a development which was to bear fruit when the Conservatives took office in 1952.

Africans were, rather naturally, unaware of how the tide was beginning to run against them and in Northern Rhodesia the organising of African opinion was impeded by weakness in the leadership of the African Congress. Godwin Lewanika still retained the presidency of the party and the suspicion with which he was regarded by many members (especially the Bemba) resulted in apathy. A rudimentary organisation was being developed in the rural areas, however, by younger followers. The case of Kenneth Kaunda was typical: in 1949 he had thrown up his job as a boarding master at the Mufulira primary school, resigned his seat on the provincial council, and returned to Chinsali to try his luck at farming—an occupation in which one of his elder brothers was already engaged. In March 1950, Kaunda converted the local African Welfare Association into a Congress branch and was elected the secretary. Leaving the farm to the care of his wife Betty, he toured the surrounding villages on his bicycle, playing his guitar to draw an audience and then singing political songs of his own invention.

Towards the end of 1950, Griffiths accepted a proposal by Sir Godfrey Huggins which had been hanging fire for some months, and announced that he was arranging a conference between the senior civil servants of all three Central African territories to draw up a draft federal constitution. This was a decisive move, for although Griffiths insisted that the conference would commit nobody, the calling together by Britain of senior civil servants only convinced the Africans that their views had been ignored. It was equally decisive that the chairman of the conference was George Baxter, a prominent Commonwealth Relations Office official who was an ardent federationist.[17]

On the instructions of Huggins (who was still talking about amalgamation) the Southern Rhodesian delegation pressed for the closest possible association. Those from the two protectorates were much more cautious. After talking for three weeks, the officials drew up their proposals, asserting: 'The solution that we recommend for adoption is that of a true federal structure.'[18] The fundamental dilemma which had faced the conference was how to relate the 'native policy' of Southern Rhodesia with the trusteeship principles by which Nyasaland and to a lesser extent Northern Rhodesia were governed. The answer, as the officials saw it, was to retain native affairs as the responsibility of each territory, and also to insert safeguards into the federal structure.[19] Therefore, it was proposed to have a Federal Minister for African Interests and an African Affairs Board, whose members would include the three Secretaries for Native Affairs. The Board would be able to compel the Governor General to withhold consent from any discriminatory legislation until the British government had considered it. Since Britain had held the power (albeit dormant for twenty-five years) to veto discriminatory laws in Southern Rhodesia, it might have been expected that Huggins and his cabinet would accept the federal 'safeguards' as similar window-dressing. Instead Sir Godfrey rejected the proposed Minister for African Interests as 'the cuckoo in the nest'; Patrick Fletcher, Minister for Native Affairs in Southern Rhodesia, said that 'African opinion did not count'. Fletcher was annoyed because the Secretary of State for Commonwealth Relations, Patrick Gordon Walker, had been touring Central Africa and heard repeatedly from Southern Rhodesian natives, including chiefs, that they would only favour federation if the north's policies could be incorporated into their own country. The habit of Labour Party leaders of consulting the majority profoundly irritated Southern Rhodesians: Huggins believed it only confused and frightened the Africans.

With the publication of the official recommendations in mid-June 1951, and the announcement that a political conference would be held in September at the Victoria Falls to consider it, the tempo of public interest rose. In Britain, papers such as *The*

Times, Manchester Guardian and the *Observer* began to editorialise on the difficulties caused by African fears. Dr Hastings Banda distributed printed copies of an amended version of the memorandum he and Harry Nkumbula had prepared two years before. Nkumbula was by this time back in Northern Rhodesia—in disgrace with the authorities because he had not passed his examinations at London University through too much political activity with the Fabians. He was making a precarious living by travelling to Beira to collect seashells, which he then sold to tribesmen in the Southern Province. Leaders of the African Congress asked Nkumbula to address them at a meeting at Kabwata, Lusaka, and his fiery remarks sent a thrill through the audience.[20] Nkumbula had turned down angrily a job offered him as a government clerk and in July 1951 was easily elected president of Congress; the previous incumbent, Godwin Lewanika, was yielding to pro-Federation pressures from Barotseland and left soon after to take a course in Moral Re-Armament at Caux, Switzerland. Under Nkumbula's dynamic leadership the African Congress (into whose title the word National was inserted) quickly spread its influence throughout the land from its Chilenje headquarters in Lusaka. Provincial and district officials were appointed, chiefs were approached for support, and fund-raising conducted on a big scale; a close understanding was also built up with the African Mineworkers Union, which by 1951 had enrolled more than 20,000 members.

The second Victoria Falls conference opened under the chairmanship of Sir John Kennedy, Southern Rhodesia's Governor—to a background of antagonistic noises. Congress supporters carrying anti-federation posters appeared near the Victoria Falls Bridge, and protest meetings were held in many towns. In his campaigning, Nkumbula was helped by two white Congressmen, Commander Thomas Fox-Pitt, a former PC, and Simon Zukas, a young radical. In spite of Huggins's reluctance, Northern Rhodesia and Nyasaland each had several Africans at the talks. Although Griffiths fondly regarded this as a hopeful sign, the delegates were all opposed to federation (which had now become enough of a probability to be written with a capital F). The voicing of Southern Rhodesia's native opinion was entrusted to Patrick Fletcher. The conference was inconclusive, for while it was sitting came the news that Attlee had decided on a general election in Britain; this not surprisingly diverted the attentions of Griffiths and Gordon Walker, and delighted Huggins, who knew that his policies were much more in tune with those of the likely victors, the Conservatives. Even Welensky, who by now had stopped calling himself a socialist, and had disbanded his own Labour Party, was realising that he had more in common with British patricians such as Lord Salisbury.

To the dismay of Nkumbula and his followers, the Conservatives won by eighteen seats, and Oliver Lyttelton (later Lord Chandos) became Colonial Secretary. While not opposed to West African independence, Lyttelton was in favour of a slower approach in those parts of Africa where whites were an important element. He quickly announced in the Commons that the new government was fully in favour of Federation, whether or not Africans supported it. Lord Salisbury, now Privy Seal, put across the same message to the House of Lords. The Labour Party protested at this roughshod approach, but were in no strong position to complain, since by their own weakness they had abetted the progress of the white settlers. Huggins warmly praised Lyttelton's attitude as 'more realistic' and flew off to London for talks.[21] He said publicly that he intended to have the safeguards for Africans removed. Early in 1952, the Governors of Northern Rhodesia and Nyasaland were called to London to discuss the mechanics of setting up Federation with the least delay. Huggins there performed the feat of winning over Sir Gilbert Rennie, the Northern Rhodesia Governor (who was to become in 1954 the Federation's first High Commissioner in London).

In March 1952, there was a Commons debate in which the Labour Party once more attacked Lyttelton's approach, but the Tories won through with a small majority when the division was called. The Federationists had now finally decided Africans were impossibly antagonistic to the federal idea, but would have to be coerced. Welensky was to make this policy clear when he said that if Africans did not 'come in' they would suffer the same fate as the Red Indians—a remark which gave black politicians ample scope for suggesting that an extermination campaign was being prepared. In both northern territories, the anti-Federation pressure was stepped up, while the Africans of Southern Rhodesia remained in general more subdued and fatalistic. Nkumbula had called a big Congress assembly in Lusaka at which seventy chiefs were present, and it was decided to set up a supreme action council, four of the nine members being trade unionists.[22] In the fight against Federation, this body was empowered to start action that would 'paralyse the country', including the calling of a general strike on the Copperbelt and the railways. In the event this action council proved futile, but its creation engendered an entirely new relationship between the African National Congress (ANC) and government; previously the Secretary for Native Affairs, R. P. Bush, had genially attended Congress meetings, but now it became policy for the government to fight the party right down the line. Nkumbula was warned that the authorities would not hesitate to 'use their powers'.[23] An opportunity to prove this new policy came when Simon Zukas began to make dangerously provocative speeches. Zukas was the son of a Lithuanian trader on the Copperbelt; he had graduated in civil engineering at Capetown University in 1950, where he was alleged to have acquired left-wing leanings, and had then returned north to work for Ndola municipality. In Mufulira on February 16, 1952, he told a rally: 'You people are Christians and think that reason is more powerful than force. That is wrong.' Shortly afterwards he was arrested and special branch men found in his office desk a memorandum headed *Ten Points for the Revolution.* After several months in Livingstone jail, Zukas was deported to London.

In his own account of the Federal campaign, Welensky accused the Churches in Britain of whipping up opposition. This charge he particularly aimed at the Church of Scotland, and it was in Edinburgh that one of the most significant anti-Federation meetings took place. It was organised by the World Church Group,[24] an inter-denominational organisation on whose executive there sat a Tanganyikan student at Edinburgh University, named Julius Nyerere. The meeting was attended by 1,200 people, who listened to speeches by Dr Hastings Banda, the Rev. Kenneth Mackenzie, a missionary who had worked in both protectorates of the proposed Federation, and a Labour Party expert on colonial affairs, John Hatch. On the platform sat Sir Gordon Lethem, a former Colonial Governor, the Bishop of Edinburgh, a professor, and leaders of the Church of Scotland. At the end of the meeting a resolution was unanimously passed rejecting any closer association of the Central African territories 'without the free consent of the African peoples'.

Such demonstrations crashed in vain, however, against the determination of Oliver Lyttelton. A further conference was opened in April in London to work out firm details of a federal structure. When the results were released,[25] it was seen that Huggins had achieved his aim of removing the cuckoo from the nest—there was to be no Federal Minister for African Interests; in addition, the Secretaries for Native Affairs were no longer to be on the African Affairs Board, which would draw its membership from the Federal Assembly only. Five Africans from Northern Rhodesia and Nyasaland flew to London for the conference, but showed their attitude by boycotting it and sending a letter to *The Times* which ended: 'We appeal to the electors of the United Kingdom, who are responsible for our welfare, to protect us from the machinations of the European minority among us, and not to be deceived by their plots . . .'[26] The Northern Rhodesian signatories were Pascale Sokota, MLC, A. K. Walubita, and Gabriel Musumbulwa (later to join the United Federal Party and become a Northern Rhodesia government minister). Two Southern Rhodesia Africans did not boycott the conference: they were Joshua Nkomo and Jasper Savanhu. Although Nkomo and Savanhu made it plain that they wanted a clear definition of the word 'partnership' before they could support Federation, their presence at the conference undoubtedly helped the settlers, apart from earning them considerable unpopularity among their own race. On the other hand, the boycott by the Northern Rhodesian and Nyasaland delegates was pointed to by Federationists as proof that Africans were unreasonable and wanted 'Gold Coast government'; they were just not interested in partnership.

Once again it came back to what might be meant by the word. In Northern Rhodesia, the government made an attempt to reach a definition and the African Representative Council was asked to consider a draft put forward by the Secretary for Native Affairs. Nothing came of this till July 1953, when the African Representative Council drew up a seven-point statement on 'principles of inter-racial policy'.[27] The meeting refused to use the word partnership, because of the 'general unpopularity it has gained' and instead gave its definition of equality. The first two points of the statement were crucial.

1. The ultimate political objective for the people of Northern Rhodesia is self-government within the British Commonwealth, based on a truly democratic franchise.
2. No race must ever be in the position to dominate the other for its own selfish interests. The only way for this to be done is for each to have equal power in the Legislative and Executive Councils.

The rest of the statement proposed safeguards to protect the racial groups and to ensure that there would be 'equality of opportunity'—an obvious reference to the widespread racial discrimination, much of it entrenched by law. The African Representative Council closely reflected the views of Congress at this time (for example, the African Representative Council committee chairman, Mateyo Kakumbi, was also the general treasurer of Congress) and it might be thought that the statement showed moderation in a country where Africans outnumbered all others by approximately fifty to one. However, when a delegation from the African Representative Council went to meet the government the following week, it was in for a disappointment. Sir Gilbert Rennie and his most senior officials were waiting together with Sir Roy Welensky and several other MLCs. The talks lasted for three days and ended in complete disagreement over the phrase 'a truly democratic franchise', which Sir Roy argued might be misconstrued.[28] The Governor supported him in this. The Governor also warned the African delegates that he would not support their demands for parity in the legislature, even though they explained that they only wanted parity with the elected Europeans, so that when the Officials were taken into account they would still be racially outnumbered.

Representation in Northern Rhodesia's Legislative Council remained, however, of minor importance when compared with the struggle still raging around Federation. In mid-1952 the British government had published its Draft Federal Scheme, and followed this up in January 1953 with another White Paper;[29] it was obvious that the British cabinet was set on launching Federation within a matter of months. The last serious hurdle was cleared when Huggins won a fairly narrow victory in a referendum among Southern Rhodesia's white voters, many of whom would rather have gone in with South Africa. The British Premier, Winston Churchill, sent Sir Godfrey a glowing message of congratulations.[30]

The pace of events tended to spread a mood of resignation among many of Federation's former opponents in Britain: it would be sensible to make the best of things. This mood was well expressed by the Archbishop of Canterbury in the House of Lords debate in April 1953. He said: 'I cannot think that, whether Federation is accepted or rejected, any of us can be without grave doubts and anxiety for a good long time to come to know how in fact it will work out.'[31] The Archbishop added: 'Under Federation there will be a direct association between all the Africans of Nyasaland, Northern Rhodesia and Southern Rhodesia, and if you do like to put it so, the Africans of Northern Rhodesia and Nyasaland are coming to the aid of their brethren in Southern Rhodesia.' It was a warming prospect of the meek inheriting the earth, but hardly how the white politicians in Central Africa saw matters. The Southern Rhodesia Minister of Native Affairs, Patrick Fletcher, declared: 'If we fail to secure Federation, it will be regarded as a triumphant victory for a handful of irresponsible African politicians who are working against the best interests of the ignorant masses of their people.'[32] Welensky told an audience in Southern Rhodesia: 'We have no intention of handing over Federation to anyone.'[33]

At this time, Welensky was strenuously campaigning to overcome doubts about Federation among the large Afrikaner community in both Rhodesias. He was helped by being partly of Boer stock himself and had an invaluable spokesman in Guy Van Eeden, a right-wing member of the Federal Party who had been born in Fort Jameson but was imbued with the genuine *platteland* spirit. Thus it was slightly droll when Sir Dougal Malcolm, President of the British South Africa Company, published a statement in London saying: 'Having regard to the extent to which infiltration into Northern Rhodesia of Afrikaners from the Union is proceeding, can anyone feel sure that in a few years the anomalous powers of the elected members will be in hands as wise and sympathetic with the Africans as are those of Mr Welensky and his friends?'[34]

When a final debate was held in Northern Rhodesia's Legislative Council in April 1953, Federation won overwhelming support. The only people to vote against it were the two Congressmen, Yamba and Sokota, and the nominated members for African Interests, the Rev. E. G. Nightingale and John Moffat. The latter, who had replaced Gore-Browne, was a former DC from a distinguished missionary family. In his speech, Moffat appealed: 'This is the time, above all others, for us as Europeans to justify our claims to the right of leadership, and to prove our belief in British principles of justice and fair dealing by declaring in the clearest terms our intentions regarding the Africans among whom we live.'[35]

Such appeals carried little weight, because the whites now felt confident that they had the measure of African opposition. In March 1953, Harry Nkumbula had called a massive conference of chiefs and party officials in Lusaka. He had prepared the ground well, it appeared, winning widespread agreement from the tribal rulers that Federation must be resisted at all costs. Three months earlier he had distributed a manifesto stating the Congress case and accusing Europeans of 'laughing and sneering' at proposals for a multi-racial democracy. At the conference Nkumbula burned in front of delegates seven copies of the British government's White Paper on Federation and declared: 'Both the delegates' conference and the supreme action council have decided that should Federation be imposed against the opposition of the Africans, measures would be taken to paralyse the industries of this country.... The union leaders have at these meetings put it in express terms that their unions are behind the African National Congress.'[36] Nkumbula also warned that the chiefs had decided to adopt a policy of non-co-operation with the government. The result of the conference was the calling of 'two days of national prayer' during which no Africans would go to work. It was hinted that this would only be the start of a nation-wide campaign.

Immediately Nkumbula's plans were known, the government took strong counter-measures. All daily-paid Africans in the civil service were told that they would be summarily dismissed if they obeyed Nkumbula's orders. Similar warnings were given by the mining companies and other big employers. In the event, African courage generally failed and the proposed days of 'national prayer' were a fiasco. Only in Lusaka did Congress achieve as much as fifty per cent support. On the Copperbelt work went on as usual, apart from at Mufulira, where four-fifths of the men stayed out. Nkumbula furiously criticised Lawrence Katilunga, the miners' leader, of having stabbed him in the back, but the damage was done. Amid the humiliating shambles, little was achieved to restore the shattered prestige of Congress by the release of a petition signed by 120 chiefs,[37] who included Chitimukulu,[38] Paramount of the Bemba, and Mpezeni, Paramount of the Ngoni. The petition was sent to both Houses of Parliament in London, and said: 'The Europeans are trying to bring us under the same domination as our brother Africans in Southern Rhodesia and South Africa. We cannot accept this for our children and beg you to help us so that we shall never have to turn for help to anyone else, but only to God and to you our Queen.' A petition was also sent to the secretary-general of the United Nations, appealing for a hearing before the International Court of Justice. When a group of chiefs from Northern Rhodesia and Nyasaland flew to London and asked for an audience with the Queen, their request was rejected on the advice of the Colonial Secretary.

The African opposition was, however, not entirely in vain, although its effect would not become apparent for some years. The repeated appeals to Britain as the protecting power by the people of Northern Rhodesia and Nyasaland brought several assurances that their political advance would not be slowed by Federation. Changes were made in the draft of the Federal constitution: Northern Rhodesia and Nyasaland were promised in its preamble that they should continue 'under the special protection of Her Majesty, to enjoy separate governments for so long as their respective peoples so desire, those governments remaining responsible (subject to the ultimate authority of Her Majesty's government in the United Kingdom) for, in particular, the control of land in those territories, and for the local territorial and political advancement of the peoples thereof. . . .' This categorical promise to the protectorates was reinforced by a clause in the Federal constitution which ruled that any changes in the balance of Federal and territorial responsibilities would need approval from Britain, the Federal Assembly and each of the three territorial legislatures. Sir Godfrey Huggins had much wanted the police and judiciary to be under Federal control, but had been baulked; the constitution would now make it most difficult for such a crucial change to be made at some later date.

In July the Royal Assent was given to the legislation which would authorise the promulgation of the Federal Constitution by Order in Council. The Labour and Liberal Parties had fought a rearguard action in Parliament against the inevitable, being outvoted again and again. Clement Attlee conceded defeat and said that it now behoved everyone to try and make Federation work 'to the best of our ability'.

There was a sequel to the failure of the Congress 'national prayer'. In August, 400 delegates met in a Lusaka beer hall. The mood was one of bitter despair, for Federation was to come into operation on October 23 : the four years of oppostion had achieved nothing. When it came to the election of senior officials, only Nkumbula kept his place. For the rest, the delegates demanded a clean sweep; it was a moment for the young militants. There were two nominations for the key position of secretary-general, and because feeling was so intense among the delegates, nobody would trust anyone else to count the votes.[39] Nkumbula turned to a local journalist, Frank Barton, and asked him to act as returning officer. The voting papers were put in a hat, and it became clear who would be the winner by the time Barton was half-way through the count. He recalls : 'When I pointed to the character with the bright eyes and a tattered pair of shorts, there was a big roar of delight.' The choice was Kenneth Kaunda.

II THE PROUD YEARS

In his study of the workings of federal forms of government, Dr K. C. Wheare has said that the difficulties encountered by the Central African Federation were not caused by its structure, but by the fact that it was a union at all, and that Africans objected to the placing of control in European hands : 'As a result, the political history of the Federation was concerned with the struggle for power between African nationalists and Europeans, and provided little material for the normal workings of a federal system.' This would have appeared to many observers too harsh a verdict in the first five years, 1953-8. The racial discord was indeed increasing, but was generally submerged in the flood of optimism engendered by material progress. Events were seeming to prove the dictum of Sir Roy Welensky and others that political problems would lose themselves if the Federation's economy was kept moving forward. Fortune smiled and the figures could not be gainsaid. The net domestic output of the Federation had soared from £265 million in 1953 to £369 million three years later.[2] This was in the main due to the heady rise in world copper prices, which meant that until 1956 the Copperbelt alone contributed more than a quarter of the net domestic output.[3] Although copper prices had begun their long descent by 1956, so that in 1958 Northern Rhodesia's mines were only providing an eighth of the total, the initial buoyancy had a lasting psychological effect. Wages and salaries went up from £144 million in 1954 to £186 million in 1956, and £223 million in 1958.[4] As will be seen, there was a distinction in the way this increase was distributed, but the voters (who were white) had every reason to be satisfied with their lot. The allure of Central Africa for white settlers was proved by the net immigration figures: 1954, 5,000; 1955, 11,000; 1956, 18,000.

With plenty of money around and investment coming in at a promising rate, the Federationists could add to the credit side the supremacy achieved by the Federal Party itself. In the thirty-five-member Federal Parliament, the party held twenty-six seats; any objections from the six Africans and three members representing African interests could easily be brushed aside. In February 1954, the Federal Party captured ten of the twelve elected places in an enlarged Northern Rhodesia Legislative Council. Although there had been no referendum in Northern Rhodesia, as Sir Roy Welensky had once promised there would be, the results showed that whites, at least, had endorsed Federation's creation. With the departure of Sir Roy to become Federal Minister of Transport and Communications, the political leadership was bestowed upon John Roberts, a farmer who represented Broken Hill. This had long been Sir Roy's own constituency and he continued to represent it in the Federal House. The two men were very close.

Under the Federal constitution, powers were divided between the central and territorial governments, in a manner which strongly suggested that it was the former which cared for white interests. European education and agriculture 'went Federal', while African education and agriculture stayed under territorial control. Other subjects on the Federal list included defence, taxation, posts and immigration. At first it did not seem to worry the Federal government that law and order remained territorial responsibilities, since there was constant liaison between the individual special branch organisations and the Federal Intelligence and Security Bureau in Salisbury.[5]

The dominance of the Federation's affairs exerted by Southern Rhodesia in the early years would be difficult to exaggerate. The Prime Minister until November 1956 was Lord Malvern (formerly Sir Godfrey Huggins) who had been the doyen of Southern Rhodesian politicians since long before the war. His six-man cabinet consisted of four Southern Rhodesians, one member from Northern Rhodesia and one from Nyasaland. It came as little surprise, therefore, when it was announced early in 1954 that Salisbury, also the Southern Rhodesia capital, would become the Federal capital. It is common practice (Canberra being an example) to avoid choosing a territorial or state capital for a federation as well. Sir Roy Welensky had himself advocated the choice of some 'neutral' town before the Central African Federation was created and six years later the Monckton Commission was to point out how African antagonism had been intensified by the selection of Salisbury.[6] In fact, a select committee had first suggested that the capital could best be sited in Northern Rhodesia, but retreated under the remonstrances of the Federal cabinet.

Salisbury grew at astonishing speed as major commercial and industrial organisations, such as the Northern Rhodesia copper companies, moved their headquarters to the seat of power. New hotels were opened up and did remarkable business. In Lusaka the luxurious Ridgeway Hotel, built at a cost of £200,000 in 1951 by the mining groups and the British South Africa Company, stood forlorn and almost empty; it was to make a loss of £300,000 during Federation. Although the figures did not become available until years later, Southern Rhodesia was also receiving marked preference in the allocation of Federal revenue.

In Northern Rhodesia the operations of the Federal government were at first completely unchallenged by the civil servants. There was a certain relief that Sir Roy Welensky was no longer present to harass them in debates; during his final session in the Northern Legislative Council he had taken the opportunity to reiterate: 'My elected colleagues and I resent the determination exhibited at all times by the Colonial Office to maintain the tightest possible grip on this country.'[7] There was also the fact that support of Federation was now official policy, as expressed in the promise of Sir Gilbert Rennie to the Governor-General, Lord Llewellin, and the Federal government: Northern Rhodesia would 'co-operate whole-heartedly with them in making the new arrangements work—and work well'.[8] Finally the Federation was the product of the British Conservative administration, with which through class background the civil servants would tend to sympathise.

The first severe jolt to the general mood of acquiescence was provided early in 1955, by the Federal government's unilateral decision to build the £90 million Kariba Dam, disregarding an agreement signed eighteen months earlier by Sir Godfrey Huggins (on behalf of Southern Rhodesia) and Sir Gilbert Rennie (on behalf of Northern Rhodesia) that the Federal government would first construct a dam on the Kafue river within Northern Rhodesia. The manner in which the Federal cabinet took this step well illustrated their cavalier attitude to Northern Rhodesia; there was no prior consultation with the Northern Rhodesia government, whose Chief Secretary, A. T. Williams, later disclosed that his first knowledge of the decision was from a newspaper shown him by a friend.[9] The Federal government's choice of Kariba, despite the agreement of September 3, 1953, and the fact that Northern Rhodesia had already spent more than £500,000 on preparatory work for the Kafue scheme, was additionally significant: a huge prestige symbol of Federation was called for, and a dam which would tame the Zambezi and create the biggest man-made lake in the world amply fitted this requirement. Lord Malvern told the Federal Assembly: 'Its size and all that sort of thing makes such a popular appeal and it will be an excellent advertisement for the whole Federal area.'[10] From the Salisbury point of view, Kariba also had the advantage of not being exclusively in Northern Rhodesia—the power station is on the Southern Rhodesian bank of the Zambezi. Events have clearly shown that Kariba was too big for Central Africa, because it has never been possible to take up even its full first stage output of 700 megawatts; nor did Kariba have any irrigation potential like that of the Kafue scheme. Although the Federal government defended itself in 1955 by saying that data on Kafue was incomplete, it was to turn out that Kariba was even more vulnerable in this regard: a large area of weak rock was discovered on the south bank, and in 1962 the dam had to be hurriedly underpinned and buttressed.

Both Northern Rhodesia mining groups had been in favour of the Kafue scheme, for which the Anglo-American Corporation had been consultants; John H. Lascelles, a senior director of Rhodesian Selection Trust, was on the Federal Hydro-Electric Board. With the announcement that the Northern Rhodesia project had been abandoned, Lascelles immediately resigned from the Board and issued a statement attacking Lord Malvern's decision on technical grounds.[11]. The Federal Premier reacted to the by calling the leaders of the mining companies to his office in Salisbury and telling them that if they refused to support Kariba he would place an export tax of £50 a ton on copper.[12] With output running at nearly 400,000 tons a year, this was a £20 million threat, and it worked.

Among the white Northern Rhodesian public, the announcement provoked an outcry, especially in Lusaka, which would have been the closest big town to the Kafue Dam. At a meeting attended by 1,300 people there were demands that the territory should secede from the Federation immediately;[13] the Mayor of Lusaka sent a petition to the Queen. In the Legislative Council a long emotional debate was held. In a devastating speech, Harry Franklin, one of the members for African interests, declared: 'Amongst the people of this country this Kariba decision has become symbolic. . . . The country feels that if a solemn agreement can be curtly dismissed, that if the powerful Southern Rhodesian element in the Federal Parliament can secure such an action, then there is great cause to worry over the future of Northern Rhodesia.' For the Federal Party members, the debate constituted an acute dilemma. In a nervous contribution, John Roberts supported the motion expressing 'disappointment and disquiet', but insisted that he did not intend to show any disloyalty to Federation or his leaders in the Federal Party. He ended by asking the House and the country to 'close our ranks, to re-hoist our somewhat tattered flag and give impetus towards strengthening the Federation. . . .' An attempt to support Kariba earned Rodney Malcolmson (Federal Party) the epithet 'party hack' from John Gaunt. Lewin Tucker, who was also a director of Rhodesian Selection Trust, and represented the mining town of Mufulira, said: 'Any further arguments about this decision, unless very carefully handled, could only go towards destroying confidence in our Federation.'

There was a short but prophetic speech by Robinson Nabulyato, whose own home was in the Southern Province, near the site of Kariba. He asked the Secretary for Native Affairs what method it was intended to use to move from the Zambezi valley the 40,000 Africans who would have to leave their traditional homes as the waters rose. More than three years later, when police were trying to force Chief Chipepo's people to move to higher ground, fighting broke out. The police were attacked with spears and when they opened fire eight tribesmen were killed and thirty-four wounded.

A person who said little during the 1955 furore over Kariba was Sir Roy Welensky. Like John Roberts, he was in an awkward position, because on December 7, 1951, he had declared: 'The best bet for this country is to spend every penny it can now afford on the development of the Kafue hydro-electric project.'[14] In his own account of the Federal era he does not mention the consequences of the switch to Kariba. Yet it sowed the seeds of dissent in the minds of many Europeans who had until then supported Federation. It was decisive for 'liberals' who had already become unhappy about lack of progress in the racial sphere. Dr. Alexander Scott, who owned the *Central African Post* in Lusaka and sat in the Federal Assembly as an independent, said in August 1955 that he was 'disillusioned' and from then on turned to the most bitter condemnation of the way Federation was being implemented.

Even more significant was the hostility towards the Federal government that the affair had engendered in such senior officials of the Northern Rhodesia government as the Financial Secretary, Ralph Nicholson; alongside him was ranged Harry Franklin, who in 1955 joined the Executive Council with the portfolio of Education and Social Services. The new Governor, Sir Arthur Benson, maintained a position of neutrality until late in 1955, when he too began to turn sharply against the powers in Salisbury. (After a term as Chief Secretary in Nigeria, Benson had returned to Northern Rhodesia where, before Federation, he had served on the Central African Council, which ran various common services; he had in 1951 helped to draft the first Federal scheme, which advocated a Minister for African Interests—the 'cuckoo' which Malvern had subsequently removed from the nest.) In his address to the Legislative Council in July 1955, Sir Arthur went out of his way to applaud the improved consultation between Salisbury and Lusaka. Soon, however, he discovered that the Federal government was going behind his back to the Colonial Secretary (Lennox-Boyd) by using the Secretary for Commonwealth Relations (Lord Home) through whom to make their representations; there were sixteen such interventions in one year.[15]

In mid 1956, Benson wrote a dispatch to Lennox-Boyd, in which he accused the Federal government of trying to crush the territorial governments and create an amalgamated dominion. Such a policy could be contrary to the spirit of the preamble to the Federal constitution. Benson's dispatch, which only spelt out in detail Malvern's broad intentions, was passed by Lennox-Boyd to Lord Home at the Commonwealth Relations Office. Home sent a copy of the dispatch straight to the Federal government in Salisbury.

In the middle of 1956, Malvern had gone to London for a Commonwealth Prime Ministers' Conference, and while there had pressed the British government to grant a higher status for the Federation. He made no headway, but news of these overtures leaked out, and when Malvern returned to Salisbury, he had to give an account of his activities to the Federal Assembly.[16] Malvern put forward the proposition that it was possible for the Federation to advance to full independence in the matters over which it had control, while still leaving the northern territories in protectorate status. This was attacked as being both unworkable and contrary to the constitution: Malvern became involved in a long argument with Sir John Moffat about the interpretation of the Federal constitution, Moffat coming off distinctly better. Guy Van Eeden argued that the Prime Minister had merely roused African suspicions to no good purpose, and claimed that the only way to achieve dominion status was to completely partition the country into white and black states; this was the old scheme for amalgamating the Northern Rhodesia line-of-rail and Copperbelt with Southern Rhodesia. Vexed by the all-round criticism, Malvern made an attempt to regain the initiative by declaring: 'We have complete control of our own Defence Force. I only hope we shall not have to use it as the North American colonies had to use theirs, because we are dealing with a stupid government in the United Kingdom . . . our job is to consolidate our position economically, to advance our people as we do, and when we are strong enough we do not care, because nobody can stop us doing what we like.' (Applause.)

In November 1956, Welensky took over as Federal Premier, and immediately increased the pressure for an amendment to the Federal constitution, for giving more power to the white-controlled legislatures in Northern Rhodesia and Nyasaland, and greater Federal control of external affairs. Sir Roy also wanted a declaration that Britain would never legislate for the Federation without its request. All these changes were designed to loosen the ties with the Colonial Office, against which Welensky had fought so relentlessly until 1953. He told Lennox-Boyd that the Africans 'prefer to aim for black rule and hope they will experience this, which they regard as the apotheosis of Colonial Office policy'.[17] To prevent the apotheosis becoming reality, the Africans would have to 'get used to the idea' that a break-up of the Federation was utterly impossible and that secession of any territory would never even be considered. Steps must be taken to 'hammer home' these points to every African. Behind this aggression, there was a revealing hint of uncertainty.

Lennox-Boyd accepted Welensky's proposals for increased Federal power, in return for an assurance that the latter was not after amalgamation. Their joint condemnation of amalgamation (and secession) was embodied in a public statement.[18] However, the extent to which the Federal Party was intent on increasing the authority of the central government had been shown by a brief debate in the Northern Rhodesia Legislative Council shortly before Sir Roy went to London to discuss his demands with the Colonial Secretary. John Gaunt (Dominion Party) moved that a Federal Police Force should be set up, as provided for in the Federal constitution.[19] The motion was opposed by the Federal Party leader, John Roberts, on the ground that under the constitution the force could only be used at the request of the territorial governments, and it might therefore be a useless expense. But he added that he and most members of the Federal Party would like to see the constitution amended, to create one police force 'throughout the Federation'.

The high-water mark of Federal power was reached between the beginning of 1958 and the first quarter of 1959. Opposing forces were assembling for a decisive onslaught, but throughout these fifteen months Welensky and his subordinates were able to register several political successes. In Southern Rhodesia the dangerously liberal premier, Garfield Todd, was ousted from power in February 1958 and his United Rhodesia Party was absorbed by the Federal Party—which took the title United Federal Party throughout the Federation. Sir Edgar Whitehead became premier and Todd was also compelled to leave the cabinet in April 1958. Sir Roy Welensky declared: 'We already have a right-wing party, and it is only proper that there should be a home for the leftists, who feel that the UFP is not moving fast enough for them. The UFP is a centre party. . . .'[20] The final obliteration of Todd came at the Southern Rhodesia general election in June when despite the growing momentum of the extremist Dominion Party and Sir Edgar Whitehead's marked lack of personal magnetism, the UFP was able to slip home with a seventeen-thirteen majority. Todd could not even retain his own seat at Shabani.

In the Federal Assembly, major changes to the UFP's advantage were produced through the enlargement of membership from thirty-five to fifty-nine by the Constitutional Amendment Act and the simultaneous evisceration of the African Affairs Board. This Board was under the chairmanship of Sir John Moffat, who had been nominated to the Federal Assembly from Northern Rhodesia in 1954, and it bitterly opposed the changes as being discriminatory. Sir John pointed out that the new House would have less true African representation than the former, because forty-four members would be white and of the twelve Africans eight would be returned by predominately white electorates.[21] The only Africans who would in any sense speak for their own race would be the four chosen by 'electoral colleges' in the Northern Rhodesia and Nyasaland protectorates—in the case of Northern Rhodesia by the African Representative Council. Moreover, the members of the Board would be selected by the African members of the Assembly, and the three Europeans representing Africans—a group in which the eight 'moderate' Africans would have a majority.

The Federal government defended its proposals by claiming that it was pursuing the goal of non-racialism, notwithstanding a two-tier franchise which would prevent all but a tiny minority of the Africans getting on the 'general roll' which alone elected forty-four out of fifty-nine MPs. It professed liberal motives in giving the white electors a vote in the choice of African candidates.[22] However, since it was estimated by the Federal government itself that general roll voters would outnumber special roll voters by 37,000 to 21,000 in Northern Rhodesia, it was clear that the elected Africans could only be—in the common parlance of the period—'stooges'.

To anyone who was prepared to sit down for an hour and study the whole scheme, it was obvious that the Federal government was intent on an arithmetical confidence trick of astounding size. White control of the Federation was about to be entrenched. Sir Roy Welensky has revealed that even Lord Home was doubtful whether he could accept it, but was talked round at a meeting in Salisbury.

In his turn, Home was able to persuade the British government, who overruled the objections of the African Affairs Board (Sir John Moffat subsequently resigned); and when the changes were debated in the Commons there was a comfortable victory for the Tories—who in 1955 had increased their parliamentary majority to fifty-nine. Sir Roy cabled his gratitude to Lord Home, saying that he was sure that they had found a solution 'which we can safely leave to historians to place in its proper perspective'. The Federal general election was held in November 1958, with an almost total boycott by Africans, who since they saw they had been given no chance to affect the result, had not bothered to go on the roll. In Northern Rhodesia, the two elected Africans were Godwin Lewanika, the one-time Congress president who had joined the UFP after a talk with Sir Roy, and Justin Simukonda, another former Congressman. Overall, the UFP took forty-six out of the fifty-nine seats, and in the minds of its leaders the party now became virtually synonymous with the government.

In Northern Rhodesia itself, the Federationists were after an even more important prize : complete control of the legislature by the elected members, which would be tantamount to self-government. Elections were due in March 1959, and negotiations had been in progress since the end of 1957 on the form of the new constitution. Although the Federal government was not strictly entitled to become involved, Sir Roy Welensky applied all possible pressure publicly and in private through Lord Home.[23] The UFP was demanding that among other things there should be an elected Chief Minister, to be selected from the majority party. But Welensky ran up against the obdurate views of the Governor, Benson, who was at this time receiving a larger share of support from Lennox-Boyd. It had apparently become obvious to the British government that it was no longer practical politics to hand over control to a white minority amounting to barely two per cent of the total population; on the west coast, Ghana was already independent.

The constitution which emerged for Northern Rhodesia was complicated to a degree and satisfied nobody. In March 1959 it gave the UFP thirteen of the twenty elected seats, but when six officials and two nominated unofficials were counted in, the party had just failed to obtain an overall majority in the Legislative Council. From this moment on, the tide began to recede.

III THE MEANING OF DISCRIMINATION

Although Federationists might blame African opposition to white rule on 'agitators' and 'mischief-makers', yet the driving force of African nationalism was everywhere provided by racial discrimination; political control was seen as the only alternative to humiliation.

In the years on each side of 1953 the African spokesmen devoted far more time to protesting against discrimination than they did to campaigning for new constitutions. Immediately the Federal Assembly met, the Northern Rhodesian representative Dauti Yamba moved that 'equal treatment be accorded immediately to all races in public places and that such action be enforced by legislation to be passed by the Federal Assembly'.[1] His speech, and that of his seconder, Wellington Chirwa, was greeted with sarcastic interruptions by white members. V. N. Joyce, a white back-bencher representing Mufulira spoke for the majority of the Assembly when he dismissed the motion as 'futile and insincere'. Lord Malvern declared that white women could not be expected to stand in queues with African mothers bearing dirty babies. He was prepared to admit that Africans had contributed their labour to the development of Central Africa, but Europeans must be given full credit for their achievements.

Yamba's motion was a protest against a condition which had not significantly changed since the post-war years—and which was to continue with only minor improvements until 1961. In the middle 1950s, Africans could not enter a theatre or a cinema in Northern Rhodesia; they could not eat in an airport restaurant, even though they were waiting to board a plane; they were not able to go to churches in the European areas without being the object of angry glances from the white worshippers; hotels and cafés were closed to them and in the grocery stores they had to wait their turn until all Europeans were served.

Shortly after Yamba was rejected in the Federal Assembly, John Moffat achieved what appeared like success in Lusaka's Legislative Council. Despite last-minute attempts by the officials to stop him from doing so, he put forward a motion which condemned discrimination in all its forms and called for a policy which would 'remove from each race the fear that the other might dominate for its own racial benefit'.[2] With a memorable speech Moffat overwhelmed his opponents in the Council and his motion was carried easily. At the time, what became known as the 'Moffat Resolutions' were regarded as a landmark. Yet their true value was small, and their impressive sentiments failed to produce action. In later years, Moffat's inability to win African support for his middle-of-the-road Liberal Party could in part be traced to the refusal of the Northern Rhodesian government to implement his resolutions, even though he was in no way to blame.

The next round came in March 1955, when Pascale Sokota moved in the Legislative Council that the Trades and Business Ordinance should be amended so that it would be an offence for any person to practise racial discrimination in places licensed to serve the public.[3] In the end, the Council accepted an amendment from the Chief Secretary that a committee should be appointed to study the extent of racial discrimination and to make recommendations.

After more than eighteen months, when the committee had reported what everyone already knew, a Race Relations (Advisory and Conciliation) Bill was introduced into the Legislative Council and passed after long and tortuous arguments which produced a number of weakening amendments.[4] The result of the Bill was to create a central race relations board and local committees which could hear complaints. There was general agreement that legislation to ban discrimination was impossible, but results of the Bill were negligible.

In the struggle to break the colour bar, another move was made in July 1959 by Sir John Moffat—now knighted and back in the Legislative Council as leader of the Liberal Party—after three unrewarding years in the Federal Assembly. He proposed that legislation be brought in if necessary to end discrimination by the start of 1960. This was rejected by both the officials and the UFP[5]. The Chief Secretary, Martin Wray, said that the government would not be 'frightened' by Moffat into taking such action. The government was frightened, however, two months later, by an incident in Chingola. Sir Francis Ibiam, a Privy Councillor and chairman of Ibadan University's governing council, crossed into Northern Rhodesia by car from Elisabethville on his way to a religious convention at Mindolo, Kitwe. In Chingola he stopped for a cup of tea and was ejected by the café proprietor. In an attempt to answer the resultant international furore, Northern Rhodesia's administrative secretary, Humphrey Jones, said: 'Such unfortunate incidents as that at Chingola can only cause great damage to the name of Northern Rhodesia . . . they bring nearer the day when the government will be forced to legislate.'[6] Even Sir Roy Welensky (himself a Privy Councillor) felt constrained to apologise to the Prime Minister of Nigeria and said: 'Our business should be to set an example as to how to behave in a civilised manner to civilised people.'

By this time, Africans were starting to challenge directly the 'café bar' with sit-in demonstrations; the owners were retaliating with inflated prices: in one Copperbelt café an African was asked £5 for a cup of tea. Finally, the government accepted a select committee's report that legislation was inevitable. At the start of September 1960, all cafés and cinemas were forced to admit Africans, and there was a minimum of difficulty.[7]

The discrimination in public places was complemented by the barriers between workers of different races. During the earliest years of white occupation in Northern Rhodesia, Africans generally lacked the education and skills to compete with Europeans. By the post-war years, however, the gulf of capability was beginning to narrow in manual and clerical fields, notwithstanding the legislation which made it impossible for an African to become apprenticed to any trade. The *Dalgleish Report** in 1948 advocated the opening of numerous work categories in the copper mines to Africans. But this was completely rejected by the powerful European mineworkers' union on the grounds that Africans would have to be paid the 'rate for the job' and that there could be no fragmentation. A stalemate ensued, with mounting African frustration. Following a three-week strike in 1952, due to the rejection of a demand by Africans for a rise of 2*s*.8*d* a shift, C. W. Guillebaud was appointed as arbitrator. He awarded substantially more than the companies had offered, although only about half of what the Africans had demanded. In his report, Guillebaud remarked on the barriers against African advancement and said that 'the fundamental issues which led to the appointment of the Dalgleish Commission remain unsolved and throughout this arbitration I have been conscious of them hanging like a dark cloud in the background'.[8] Early in 1954, advancement talks began between the companies and the unions, but ended in dead-

* See chapter 5. p. 134

lock after four months. A visit to the Copperbelt by Sir Will Lawther, secretary-treasurer of the Miners' International Federation, produced a conference between African and European miners' leaders under his chairmanship, but no tangible progress.

In August 1954, a Board of Enquiry headed by Sir John Forster was appointed to study the colour bar in the mines and platitudinously decided that the European attitude would, 'if persisted in, bar the Africans' advancement for ever'. James Young, who had been a member of the Dalgleish Commission and subsequently became an official of the International Confederation of Free Trade Unions, remarked that the *Forster Report* was no advance at all on the recommendations of six years before: 'If the report had been acted upon when it was presented the problems would now be well on the way to a solution.'[10] Eventually, under pressure from the mining companies, the European union yielded various 'white jobs' to the Africans, but its mood was reflected by a strike of 1,000 white miners at Mufulira, in April 1956, immediately the first 'advanced' Africans went on shift underground as pipe-layers. Matters only gradually improved after Ben Peterson, the vociferous secretary-general of the European union, returned to South Africa in 1958.

The promotion of a few hundred Africans out of 35,000 did not, however, do much to end the two-level wage structure on the Copperbelt. In the first place, an African who took over a European job was paid on an average a quarter of his predecessor's salary; even when the job was fragmented the Africans concerned received less than what had been received by one European.[11] Secondly, the average African wage continued to be approximately one-tenth of the European. The average earnings of employees in the copper mines during the years 1953–60 were as follows:[12]

	Europeans	*Africans*
1953	£1,782	£124
1954	£1,734	£123
1955	£1,943	£134
1956	£2,295	£166
1957	£1,910	£189
1958	£1,699	£200
1959	£1,868	£218
1960	£2,160	£258

Over the period, African wages had more than doubled; the European wages increased by only a quarter. Yet in absolute terms the wage gap had grown wider during the years, from £1,658 to £1,902.

Of their respective races, the African and European miners were always Zambia's money-earning élite; no other industry paid its employees so much. Yet where the scales were lower, the differential was the same—even in government, whose African employees were mainly below the poverty datum line during the years of Federation.[13] In 1954, the annual average wage of Africans in Northern Rhodesia was £79; by 1960 this had risen to £131. For Europeans the corresponding figures were £1,233 and £1,512. Asians and coloureds occupied a precarious position between the two, their average earnings being £417 in 1954 and £573 in 1960.[14]

The urge to discriminate against Africans in money matters made its appearance at every level. When the first two Africans were appointed to the Legislative Council in 1948, the *Central African Post* strongly criticised the white elected members for voting them equal salaries. Roy Welensky was accused by the newspaper of pandering to African opinion; Europeans should be paid an attendance fee of £3.3*s*. a day, and Africans 15*s*.0*d*.[15] In 1952, the *Follows Report* on civil service salaries recommended that African graduates should be paid three-fifths of the amount paid to similarly-qualified Europeans. John Mwanakatwe and Job Mwemba, two graduates teaching at Munali secondary school, protested in a private circular: 'It is now over fifty years since the Europeans came to live with us here in Northern Rhodesia; and during these years the theory has been held that Africans do not deserve high wages because they are not highly educated and their standard of living is low. That argument is probably true, but we do not believe that an African graduate can be said to be living at a standard lower than that of an average European. . . . What makes the difference that people holding the same qualifications, doing the same job, are paid differently? We are baffled and finally are constrained to think that it is nothing but colour.'[16] In 1958, Mwanakatwe was appointed principal of Kasama secondary school and considerable publicity was given to the fact that he was the first African placed on the full education officer scale.[17]

Discrimination in the field of education extended much further than the salaries paid to teachers. Expenditure by the Federal government on European education worked out at more than £103 a child, while the figure for African education in Northern Rhodesia was £9 per child.[18] Although the Education Department increased its total spending on African education from £1.6 million in 1955 to £3.9 million in 1961, the main objective was to give as many children as possible four years in primary school. From standard two onwards there was an ever-increasing 'fall-way' as less and less children could be accommodated in the higher standards. In 1958 there was only one African school in Northern Rhodesia which could provide a full secondary course to university entrance level; the total enrolment in all African secondary schools (mainly restricted to two 'junior' years) was little more than 1,000.[19] One half of the African children of school age could get into class in the first place, and less than .5 per cent of those could ever hope to go beyond primary level. The consequences of this situation were spotlighted in 1964, when Education Minister John Mwanakatwe disclosed that Zambia was moving into independence with only 960 Africans of school certificate standard in a total population of more than 3.5 million.

IV THE AFRICAN REVIVAL

The failure of the Congress campaign to stop the imposition of Federation had a lowering effect on African morale for several years. Without a clear objective the mass movement lost momentum and began to disintegrate. After the ineffectual 'days of prayer' Congress was flooded with complaints from men who had lost their jobs. What did the organisation propose to do for them now? At a meeting in Lusaka, President Harry Nkumbula told these unfortunates that their only course was to go home to their villages and take up farming.[1] The black majority was temporarily on the defensive and Sir Roy Welensky seemed justified in asserting that Federation would 'consolidate and strengthen' the position of the Europeans.[2] In a search for some way out of this dilemma, Nkumbula toyed for a while with the idea of partition. At the end of April 1953, Sir Stewart Gore-Browne had emerged from retirement to urge this solution at a Lusaka assembly; in supporting him Nkumbula declared that partition 'offered the only hope of Africans' ever attaining any measure of self-government'. Amid cheers from the floor, this attitude was attacked by two delegates from the Southern Rhodesia Congress and Sir Stewart returned disappointed to Shiwa Ngandu, having apparently played 'the last political card of his career—that frayed old joker partition'.[3]

Later, Congress decided to co-operate in the first Federal elections, to ensure that the African voice could be heard in the Salisbury Assembly. On November 30, 1954, Nkumbula and Kaunda wrote to the Governor-General, Lord Llewellin in protest at the Northern Rhodesia Governor's refusal to allow the African Representative Council to choose its quota of two Federal MPS from outside its own ranks. Their complaint was ignored, and from then on Congress steadfastly boycotted the Federal Assembly.

To overcome its frustration, the hard-core of Congress turned to specific local issues. There was a campaign in the Luapula Province against fishing regulations; four chiefs who had sided with Congress were deposed.[4] In the extreme south of the country, in the Gwembe valley, there was defiance of the DC after Congress had begun to organise in Chief Simamba's area and its officials had been arrested. Kaunda wrote angrily to the Secretary for Native Affairs, that the troubles were due to 'maladministration' and that Congress should not be blamed.[5] This was one of the first of many trials of strength between government and the nationalists for the allegiance of the chiefs. Rennie, the Governor, had warned that 'all chiefs must realise where their true interests lie and that no good can come to them or their people by following the bad advice of misguided men'.[6] Throughout the final decade of Colonial Office rule the war to subdue African politics in the rural areas never abated: DCs would encourage chiefs to harass the 'evil men' and when Paramount Chief Chitimukulu banned Congress from his area in 1958, the Governor presented him with a chiming clock.[7]

Chiefs who supported Congress were branded as 'unsound' and official recognition was transferred to someone more amenable. These appointees would often lack the vital *vandalilo* (spiritual power) and the deposed ruler would still continue to receive gifts from his subjects.[8] The deposition of chiefs during the struggle was a constant source of distress to the African people, and in June 1955 Dauti Yamba moved in the African Representative Council that the procedure should be reviewed and that public consent be obtained before the government acted. Yamba's motion was put to the vote, and the Council supported it 26–0.[9]

If the government found that a tribal ruler was pro-Congress but was too powerful to subdue, efforts were made to prevent the news becoming generally known. In the Eastern Province, for example, when in November 1958 the Chewa Paramount Chief Undi went to London to protest at the new Northern Rhodesian constitution on behalf of Congress, on the orders of the PC all mention of Undi's journey was excluded from the official newspaper for the area, *Nkhani za kum'mawa* (News of the East).

Occasionally Congress far over-reached itself in its efforts to exert control of the rural areas. An instance was when it promoted a campaign in the Southern Province during 1957–8 to prevent farmers from having their herds inoculated against trypanosomiasis (sleeping sickness).[10] All the veterinary services were boycotted. The government reacted by throwing cordons round the areas and waiting. Eventually the farmers realised they had been duped, and appealed to the veterinary department to send in its inoculation teams to save their remaining cattle. The price of this struggle was more than 6,000 head of cattle, worth more than £70,000.

While the perpetual cold war in the bush received little publicity, Congress demonstrations against the colour bar in urban areas attracted more attention. The boycott was used on shops where Africans were discriminated against. Before Congress was formed, Kenneth Kaunda had staged a demonstration at Mufulira by walking into a chemist's shop and demanding service across the counter, with a group of his school pupils in attendance.[11]

Now boycotts and other demonstrations were organised on a concerted pattern. The first Congress demonstrations had begun in Broken Hill in May 1953 when Dixon Konkola, a leading Congressman and trade unionist, led a group of supporters into the European section of the post-office and demanded in vain to be served.[12]

Although the boycotts were generally ineffectual, Congress decided on an all-out campaign in the months at the beginning of 1956. The secretary-general, Kaunda, said that it was decided that the colour-bar must be broken and that prices must be reduced. In Lusaka, pickets were placed before all shops on the Congress blacklist, and business was brought almost to a standstill, for weeks on end. The boycotts spread to Broken Hill and the Copperbelt, but after numerous cases of assault and intimidation Kaunda had to warn that any pickets found guilty of hooliganism would be expelled from the party. European reaction was intense, the *Central African Post* demanding that the portfolio for Law and Order should be handed over by the Chief Secretary to an elected MLC.[13] 'Only then will the European settler population feel they can meet Congress on something like equal terms. . . . It is inconceivable that such a boycott would be allowed to go on in Southern Rhodesia'. Although Nkumbula stepped in to call off the boycott in Lusaka after three weeks, it went on sporadically elsewhere until June. Under Federal Party pressure, the government brought a test case in Mufulira against several senior Congress officials, charging them with conspiracy.[14] The party employed Leslie Blackwell, QC, a former South African judge and MP, to defend the men and they were acquitted.

The vexation caused by the boycott campaign provoked a series of motions in the Legislative Council. One of these was brought by a UFP representative, William Rendall, calling for a government investigation into Congress and an assurance that the party would not be allowed to 'subvert peace and good order'.[15] Two others brought by the right-wing Independent, John Gaunt, sought stronger legislation to control boycotting and picketing.[16] The African members all argued that if there were no colour bar, the Congress campaign would be eliminated, precisely the point made earlier, outside the House, by Kaunda.

The boycott movement had helped Congress survive a period of weakness, when the officials were often reduced to extremes of poverty. 'Sometimes Kaunda and I would make a meal off one tomato—it was all we had to eat', recalls Wellington Sikalumbi, who was treasurer at the party's Lusaka headquarters. A slow resurgence had begun in 1955, a development which was in some measure helped by the authorities when they jailed Nkumbula and Kaunda for two months for possessing prohibited literature. The sentence drew attention to the party and surrounded its leaders with an aura of martyrdom. On the day of their arrests, Simon Kapwepwe arrived back in Lusaka from four years in India on a Congress scholarship, and took over the presidential chair. He sent to all branches telegrams declaring: 'This is the beginning of freedom!'[17] Kapwepwe was the son of the Boma head messenger at Chinsali; he and Kaunda had been at school together and the pair had later kept in close contact, both entering politics on the Copperbelt in the forties. Kapwepwe was a militant and with his natural powers of oratory and flamboyance had already been recognised as a leader—especially by his own Bemba tribe.* The charge against Kaunda and Nkumbula concerned a publication called *Africa and the Colonial World,* sent to Congress by the British Labour MP Fenner Brockway, as well as magazines produced by the American Committee on Africa in New York, and various unsolicited communist journals. In Fort Jameson a few weeks later, two senior Congress officials were jailed for six months for the same offence.[18]

While Kaunda and Nkumbula were in Lusaka's Central Prison, Kapwepwe set the fashion of wearing black armbands as a sign of mourning, and also designed a distinctive black shirt which was adopted as a uniform by some Congress enthusiasts. With his restless energies and strong following from among his own Bemba people, Kapwepwe became almost overnight a rallying force in the nationalist movement—so much so that Nkumbula became disturbed and wrote to him from prison: 'Please don't destroy my Congress.'[19] To the return of Kapwepwe in January 1955 can be

---

* See Chapter 5, p. 125.

traced the origins of the dissension within the leadership which was to split Congress in 1958. In 1956, Kapwepwe was elected the treasurer-general of Congress and received support in his radicalism from Munukayambwa Sipalo, who had also studied in India and been secretary-general of the Africa Bureau there.

This new dynamism was not immediately apparent, however. The 1955 annual report of the African Affairs department reported that 'post-Federation fears and uncertainties had diminished'; the PC for the North-West Province was able to record that Africans under his supervision were 'genial and pacific people who see no reason to go out of their way to make trouble or to encourage trouble-makers'. Even in the volatile Northern Province, main attention was devoted to the phenomenon of the prophetess Lenshina, whose Lumpa religious cult drew 6,000 pilgrims during the year: 'The charnel-house of surrendered bones and horns and other witchcraft paraphernalia at Lenshina's village represents a far greater reality to the average African than the windy talk of politicians who seem sometimes to forget the real problems of the people.'

Although in the middle of 1955 Nkumbula had revealingly insisted that 'the fight against Federation is still on',[20] the first serious show of African defiance after 1953 had no overt connection with political affairs. This was the series of strikes and disturbances on the Copperbelt which culminated in the declaration of a State of Emergency on September 11, 1956, and the arrest of the sixty leaders, many of them Congress officials as well as trade unionists. The source of the disorders was the announcement by the mining companies in March 1955 that they would recognise the 'white-collar' Mines African Staff Association.[21] This was followed by the companies' insistence that the majority of Africans taking 'advanced' jobs must leave the African union and go on to monthly pay. Coming immediately after an eight-week shutdown of the mines by a wage-claim strike of 30,000 African miners, these moves were seen as an attempt to destroy the union leadership, although the companies offered most of the union officials affected daily-paid jobs at no loss of money. The union felt it was being deliberately challenged by the removal from its ranks of the African élite. At a meeting attended by Lawrence Katilungu, the AMWU President, in June 1956, Nkumbula remarked: 'It looks at the moment—and I have checked this up—as if they are trying to undermine the union leadership. They are taking all the intelligent and well-informed young miners into the Salaried Staff Association.' Suspicions were increased by the fact that the president of the association was Godwin Lewanika, a Federationist.

The AMWU President, Katilungu, was an astute organiser and held that nationalisation of the mining industry was the only means of providing industrial peace—an opinion which was not calculated to endear him to the Anglo American Corporation and Rhodesian Selection Trust.[22] He was, however, far more moderate than many of his lieutenants, so that when matters came to a head in the middle of 1956 he yielded the initiative to the union's head-strong secretary-general, Matthew de Luxe Nkoloma. With policy out of his control, Katilungu found it preferable to stay in the background. He was absent from the Copperbelt when the first strike at Kitwe began on June 20 and was also away when a series of 'rolling strikes' was set in motion at the end of July. These rolling strikes lasted from two to five days and stopped production at each of the Copperbelt mines in turn as well as at Broken Hill. Nkoloma next declared a ban on all overtime. Katilungu vanished to attend a meeting of the Southern Rhodesia Joint Industrial Council and refused to return until the Emergency had been declared and almost the entire membership of his union's supreme council had been removed to places of detention; in the round-up, troops with armoured cars were used and police reinforcements were brought in from Nyasaland and Southern Rhodesia.[23]

Katilungu ordered his members back to work on September 18, and all the branches obeyed him within a few days. In his appearances before the Commission of Enquiry headed by Sir Patrick Branigan, Katilungu put up a brilliant defence of his union and frequently won verbal duels with counsel representing the mining companies, but his behaviour during the strikes marked the beginning of his descent from a position of authority in the Northern Rhodesia labour movement.

The lifting of the Emergency at the end of 1956 did not produce any lasting return to normalcy in Northern Rhodesia. In fact, the next few months were to produce an upsurge in African feeling, for between them the British and Federal governments provided the Congress with the material it needed to rally African support. Early in 1957, the Colonial Secretary, Alan Lennox-Boyd, paid a visit to the protectorate and despite a meeting with the African Representative Council during which he was told of that body's rejection of Federation, he stuck firmly to his belief in the policies of Sir Roy Welensky. 'My own support of the Federation is unshaken . . . there will be no whittling away and no question of secession.'[24] Next came the news that there would be a conference in 1960 to consider advancing the Federation to dominion status within the Commonwealth.[25] Finally, there was the Constitution Amendment Bill, which in the middle of the year made the long term intentions of Welensky completely plain. As the *African Affairs Report* for 1957 put it: 'Politically the line-of-rail and Copperbelt areas had a difficult year, with strongly adverse reactions to the amendment of the Federal Constitution and the enactment of the Federal franchise law. . . . In certain rural areas attempts were made to undermine the authority of the chiefs and native authorities and to breed an atmosphere of unrest and opposition to authority in general.' This verdict was to be reiterated in 1959 by the *Ridley Report*: 'They (the African leaders) had not seen the partnership policy implemented and had become distrustful of European politicians, particularly since the Constitution Amendment Act (No. 16 of 1957) had been passed through the Federal Legislature, in their view affecting an alteration in the Federal Constitution before the date due in 1960.'[26]

In May 1957, Nkumbula and Kaunda flew to London at the invitation of the Labour Party to attend a conference on Commonwealth affairs. The previous year they had both been asked to attend the Asian Socialist Conference in Bombay but the Federal government had rejected their application for exit visas; for Kaunda, this was his first journey outside Africa.[27] The two men took advantage of the trip to argue the case against Federation, although they found scant understanding of Central Africa among most MPs, whether Labour or Conservative. Kaunda has remarked: 'The people whom I met in England who were interested in Africa were very kind and polite and sympathetic, but like my European liberal friends in Rhodesia, they were political babes in the wood.'[28] Yet his ideas were much matured and broadened by the trip. The Congressmen asked for an interview with Lennox-Boyd, who had refused to see Nkumbula when the latter was in Britain eighteen months previously; eventually Kaunda was able to meet Lord Perth, the Minister of State at the Colonial Office, but the interview was quite unfruitful.[29] By this time (September 1957) Nkumbula had flown home, while his secretary-general stayed on to take a course in party organisation. The London journey was significant for the nationalist movement in Zambia, because during it Kaunda and Nkumbula grew more antagonistic towards each other, the younger man coming to believe that Nkumbula was not devoting enough of his energies to the political struggle. Disapproval of Nkumbula's leadership was also spreading to Africans in London, and a law student called Mainza Chona urged Kaunda to take over the leadership as soon as he returned home.[30] Kaunda was unwilling to unseat Nkumbula and thought instead of retiring from politics completely and going back to farming at Chinsali.

While Kaunda was still away in Britain during November

1957, there were important developments in Lusaka. An African summit meeting was held to decide on Federation-wide policy for the forthcoming elections. Nkumbula and T. D. T. Banda, the president of the Nyasaland Congress, agreed on a complete boycott; but Joshua Nkomo, leader of the newly-formed Southern Rhodesia Congress, chose a more 'moderate' course, in the hope of influencing the course of Federation from inside the Assembly.[31] At the territorial level, the local UFP men (with the astute legal guidance of the Federal Law Minister, Julian Greenfield) were putting forward their suggestions for the new Northern Rhodesia constitution.[32] In the Legislative Council the Secretary for Native Affairs, D. B. (later Sir Douglas) Hall made a most emphatic statement on the political future : 'The Federation is a fact, it has come to stay, it is not going to change, and it is the duty of us all to make it succeed in the best possible way.'[33] Hall was supported by the Chief Secretary, E. D. (now Sir Evelyn) Hone : 'Federation is part of the government's policy and as such it is up to every officer of the government loyally to help its course in every possible way . . . the correct way to realise African aspirations and indeed the aspirations of all people living in the Federation is through a legitimate political movement and not through strong-arm methods and thuggery.'

With the most senior civil servants making uncompromising statements and time running out, it was inevitable that African fears would disturb Nkumbula's free-wheeling leadership of Congress. The first open sign was Nkumbula's dismissal of Sipalo, his own private secretary; Nkumbula claimed that Sipalo had been 'fomenting trouble'; the latter retaliated by calling the Congress president a 'tin-pot dictator'.[34] It fell to the *African Times,* a progressive but short-lived newspaper launched by Dr Alexander Scott, to publicise the unpopularity of Nkumbula. When Kaunda returned from Britain in December it carried a front-page picture of him with the headline 'Man of the Moment'.[35] The following week, it declaimed of him : 'Already the second most important African in the country, the chances are that even if he remains No. 2 man he will become the power behind the throne of Congress.' Nkumbula was worried at the rising tide of feeling and sought extra control of the party to safeguard his position, including the right to select his own senior officials. Elias Mtepuka, the *African Times* editor (who was to die a few weeks later from a blood infection), said that the new powers Nkumbula was seeking 'looked like dictatorship'. Extra confusion was added to the dispute by Jonathan Chivungu, the Congress leader on the Copperbelt, and a rising trade-unionist, when he demanded that Nkumbula's ally Lawrence Katilungu should be expelled from the nationalist organisation for having joined the multi-racial Constitution Party.[36] Finally, under pressure from Nkumbula, Kaunda restored some semblance of unity by issuing a statement in mid-January: 'I feel that I cannot step into Nkumbula's shoes. I am very happy to serve my people as Secretary of Congress for as long as they want me, but lack of qualities I know to be necessary for a national president make my blood run cold at the suggestion I am heir apparent and about to take over.'[37]

Shortly afterwards, the two men went to Government House to present Sir Arthur Benson with the Congress proposals on the constitution. The same day, Kaunda received a letter from a mysterious organisation calling itself the 'Union for the Eastern Kingdom'.[38] It threatened to kill him, warning: 'You are weak and hopelessly slow to bring about the African objective—self-government.' The writer of the letter was never identified but it was generally accepted that he was one of the Congress dissidents, offering Kaunda the hint that he should break with Nkumbula before it was too late.

By this time, Congress had recovered its pre-Federation strength, despite dissensions at the top, and could boast of more than 400 branches throughout the country. It contained, however, the seeds of dangerous indiscipline, many of its more recent recruits being bitter men who had lost their jobs in the recession caused by a fall in copper prices.[39] An alarming amount of lawlessness, for which Congress inevitably took the blame, occurred in the country, including attempts to derail trains and sporadic outbreaks of arson. On the other hand, the Africans accused the police of harshness and provocation. Kaunda said in a circular to all branches: 'We implore all our officers to stress more and more to all our people to remain non-violent. We must deny government a chance for mowing down our people. It has happened before on the Copperbelt and it can happen again on a larger scale if we give them a chance.'[40] Shortly afterwards he said: 'If I were to call for bloodshed and violence—even though I know I would be locked up within the hour—the crowd would roar its lungs out and that would sign a campaign that would set us on the road Kenya has followed.'[41] However, there were disturbances at Ndola during April 1958 in which police opened fire and one man was shot dead; a majority of those jailed for taking part in the riot belonged to the Congress 'action group'.[42]

In May 1958, Kaunda went to Dar es Salaam to attend a World Assembly of Youth conference and from there flew to India at the invitation of the Council for Cultural Relations; at least some of the Congress executive, including Nkumbula himself, appeared uncertain where their secretary-general had gone—some thinking he was in London. Nkumbula took advantage of Kaunda's prolonged absence to dismiss numbers of provincial officials whom he suspected of disloyalty, thus making the impending split even more inevitable. Then he went away to London himself. Fostering rebellion all this time was the treasurer-general, Kapwepwe, who was accommodating the sacked Munukayumbwa Sipalo at his house. Both Kapwepwe and Sipalo had a keen personal dislike of Nkumbula and suspected his friendship with Harry Franklin, who held the portfolio of Education and Social Services in the government. They were secretly corresponding with 'extremists' such as Justin Chimba and Reuben Kamanga, and by the time Kaunda returned home in August 1958 the foundations of a breakaway movement were well laid.

The last quarter of the year was a time of particular excitement for the Europeans of the Federation, because of both the Federal election campaign and a two-month strike by the European Mineworkers' Union. The latter was only ended by the Governor's intervention.[43] In a barn-storming election campaign, Sir Roy Welensky went on record as saying: 'I have never been afraid of the black man and I see no reason to fear him in future.'[44] He also declared that adult suffrage was 'rubbish and completely unsuitable for Africa'.[45] The UFP's success was hailed by the *Northern News* as 'a vote of confidence in the partnership policy' and a sign that Federation wanted its racial affairs settled at the pace devised by the UFP.[46] A weekly journal called the *African Eagle,* subsidised by the mining companies, also proclaimed its pleasure at Sir Roy's victory, adding censoriously: 'There are still, no doubt, a few die-hard nationalists who think the only course open to Nyasaland and Northern Rhodesia is their dismemberment from the yoke of Federation.'[47] This was a remarkable understatement, seeing that four months before, Dr Hastings Banda had returned to Nyasaland and was everywhere being hailed by his people.

The moment of division in the Northern Rhodesia Congress received comparatively little attention. The *Northern News* reported that at an emergency meeting in Lusaka, Nkumbula had resigned and had been re-elected amid scenes of jubilation; women had danced in the assembly hall.[48] 'It is understood that Mr Kapwepwe and Mr Kaunda and their supporters have formed a new congress—the Zambezi African National Congress—and held a private meeting.' (Zambezi ANC was the interim title of the breakaway party, 'Zambia' being coined later by Kapwepwe.) The immediate reasons for the split were not explained, although Kaunda has since stated that the immediate issue was Nkumbula's wavering over the draft Northern Rhodesia constitution, disclosed in Lennox-Boyd's White Paper during September;[49] a six-man subcommittee from the Congress executive had been appointed, with Nkumbula's approval, to compile an analysis, which when it appeared was an outright rejection of the proposals. Nkumbula burnt the White Paper publicly, in the same way as he had burnt the Federation White Paper five years before. Shortly afterwards, however, Nkumbula came forward with the idea that Congress should fight the election in alliance with Franklin's Constitution Party, which was a protegé of the Capricorn Africa Society; the crisis came when Nkumbula propounded his alliance scheme to the Congress executives and Kapwepwe produced an identical version from his pocket which he alleged had been distributed to Constitution Party officials by Franklin. Nkumbula's account is that there was no real division on policy, it having been secretly agreed that Congress would in fact contest the elections—with himself, Kaunda, Kapwepwe and five others fighting the eight 'African' seats; he blamed the split on the ambition of Kapwepwe.

The inaugural meeting of the Zambia African National Congress (ZANC) was at Broken Hill on Sunday, October 26, and at a mass meeting afterwards more than 1,000 ANC members handed in their party cards and joined the new body.[50] Kaunda was unanimously elected president, Kapwepwe treasurer-general and 'Munu' Sipalo re-emerged to become secretary-general. The leaders of the Zambia African National Congress were penniless, Kaunda and Kapwepwe having on the day of their election only 2*s* 0*d* to buy mealie-meal for their families. But behind them were a high proportion of the young radicals of the nationalist movement, although all officials belonging to Nkumbula's own Bantu Botatwe tribal group stayed with him, together with some others such as Solomon Kalulu and Titus Mukupo.

Within a matter of weeks ZANC had won widespread allegiance from Congress branches in the north, from much of the Copperbelt and parts of the Eastern Province. The *African Affairs Report* of 1958 says of the Northern Province: 'When the Zambia African National Congress was founded almost all the adherents of ANC turned over to Zambia and ANC virtually ceased to exist in the province.' The strength of the new organisation was not apparent, however, to the European public, the *Northern News* remarking in a brief editorial that it was doubtful whether Kaunda would have much success: 'The average African, who has given his allegiance to Mr Nkumbula for the last half-dozen years will not be easy to convince that he must swap horses in midstream—and will not understand the situation well enough anyway.'[51]

Early in December both Nkumbula and Kaunda were invited to Accra for the first All-African People's Conference.[52] Well-wishers there tried to make them sink their differences. Dr Banda, George

Padmore and the Rev. Michael Scott were all concerned in these efforts, which culminated in a meeting with Dr Nkrumah. But any hopes of a reconciliation were wishful thinking, because at home the rival parties had already publicised, in the absence of their leaders, sharply conflicting attitudes to the forthcoming elections. On behalf of ZANC, Sipalo had put out a pamphlet saying that no African should take a seat in the new legislature.[53] He alleged that in the urban areas the government intended to have 'two stooges' elected, while in the rural areas the fact that candidates needed the nomination of two-thirds of the chiefs made the election a nomination : 'All our chiefs are government nominees and therefore civil servants, and the government definitely knows what it wants—the weak-kneed politicians of the old African Representative Council, the old school of yesmen.'

On behalf of Congress the new secretary-general, Titus Mukupo, told Africans to register for the elections : 'I do not think that in this particular case a boycott would produce the best answer.'[54]

When Nkumbula returned from Ghana on Christmas Eve it was announced that he and Kaunda, together with the Northern Rhodesian trade unionist, Gordon Chindele, had signed an agreement 'stressing our mutual interests and pledging that we would work together for the common cause'.[55] Chindele said : 'Dr Nkrumah advised us to bury the hatchet.' Sipalo issued an angry denial, telling Nkumbula to keep quiet and leave the political job to 'more determined people'. The uncertainty in the Zambia ranks was dispelled when Kaunda flew home in the middle of January, after taking a course at the Ghana University College. He declared that he and Nkumbula had agreed on co-operation to destroy Federation, but no more;[56] ZANC would oppose the Northern Rhodesia elections, for the franchise was worse than that granted for the Federal elections. The split in the nationalist front was absolute and the two organisations were committed to a trial of strength in which Nkumbula found himself aligned, for the first time in his career, with the government.

V ACCRA AND AFTER

The year 1959 was a watershed. From then on, until its demise, the Federation was almost continuously in a state of strife and emergency. The Federationists were put on the defensive and dissolution became only a question of timing and method. Sir Roy Welensky blamed the African resurgence on the Afro-Asian bloc and the communists, tracing the growth of a conspiracy against 'civilised standards' to the Bandung Conference of 1955 and the Cairo gathering of December 1957; came the climax in the All-African People's Conference at Accra in December 1958—'It was, in fact, a good hot bath of nationalistic fervour and a meeting of extremists. . . .'[1] Central African newspapers reported the Accra conference cursorily (almost the only public reaction being the announcement by a certain David Blackman in Southern Rhodesia that he was forming a white Congress) but it was given close attention in high circles.[2] Copies of resolutions passed at the AAPC were distributed from Salisbury to the territorial governments and these tended to confirm Sir Roy's earlier prophecy that the tide of black nationalism was running faster and only concerted action could stem it. Note was taken of the resolution which called for a 'final assault upon the denial of freedom, liberty and final human rights to the people of Africa', and of the AAPC's guarded support for people who were obliged to 'retaliate' when they were subjugated by violent means.

Thus the AAPC provoked a new note of anxiety in the utterances of Federation's protagonists. In Lusaka, John Roberts lost his former reserve and said that the UFP was 'very much in favour of establishing a Federal Police Force'.[3] In London, the Chartered Company director, Harry Grenfell, addressing the conservative Royal Africa Society,[4] pointed to the Accra conference as proof that 'nationalism' was in the ascendant; in Central Africa the authorities had a duty to act in good time before 'the poison has infected the body politic'. Sir Roy asserted that the AAPC had inspired the Nyasaland disturbances: 'Now we face the most critical period in the life of the Federation as we approach the time in 1960 when we may properly pursue our determination to gain full membership of the Commonwealth.'[5]

The Accra conference certainly exhilarated the Central Africans among the 300 delegates. Kenneth Kaunda mounted the rostrum and shouted 'Freedom! Freedom! Freedom!' It also produced a new unity of purpose between the nationalist leaders—the exception being Harry Nkumbula, who felt he had been slighted and made a bitter attack on Dr Banda after his return to Northern Rhodesia.[6] Yet events were set on a collision course well before the end of 1958; any hope of an accommodation between Welensky and the Africans had vanished with the failure of his belated 'meet the people' tours through the northern territories; Nyasaland was beyond restraint after the return of Dr Banda in July 1958; Southern Rhodesia's rural areas were in a turmoil over the Land Husbandry Act; attempts to derail trains in Northern Rhodesia were answered by a State of Emergency along the line-of-rail, sabotage or attempted sabotage being punishable by death.[7]

The Africans were determined to come to grips with Welensky before the Federal review conference. When Dr Banda was declared a prohibited immigrant in Northern Rhodesia at the start of 1959, Simon Kapwepwe commented: 'This action has spread fear and alarm among the Africans. If we, as protected people, are treated like this, what will happen when Europeans get independence in 1960?'[8] 'Munu' Sipalo told a Zambia rally at Chingola: 'We must have self-government and a democratic constitution now in Northern Rhodesia. We must get it before 1960 or face the prospect of Dominion status. . . .'[9]

There has been speculation about how much the Federal government forced the territorial governments into the 'big sweep' of February-March 1959, by which 2,000 Africans were arrested throughout Central Africa. Under the Federal constitution, Sir Roy could not move troops without a request from the territorial governors, and when British socialists subsequently accused him of having dictated the round-up, he threatened to sue them if they repeated these charges without parliamentary privilege. Harry Franklin has said cautiously: 'There seemed to be a clearly concerted move, perhaps approved by the British government, certainly by the territorial and Federal governments, to administer a sharp lesson to African nationalism following the Accra conference.'[10]

In fact, Welensky called a meeting of his defence chiefs as early as January 17 to discuss the troubled situation in Nyasaland and later in the month he detailed a senior Royal Rhodesian Air Force officer to investigate conditions in the protectorate and send him a secret memorandum.[11] The Governor of Nyasaland, Sir Robert Armitage, was a mild man who had gone through rather unnerving experiences with the terrorists in Cyprus, his previous posting; Welensky considered that Dr Banda was being given too much rope. However, Armitage had sufficient spirit to resent being dictated to and when Sir Roy suggested a meeting in mid-February he turned down the offer. In Northern Rhodesia, Sir Arthur Benson (with whom the Federal government was scarcely on speaking terms) was resolved to handle affairs in his own way. The *Northern News* accurately reflected Federal government opinion when it said: 'There is a feeling that the disorders which break out from time to time in this country and Nyasaland would be discouraged by firmer handling.'[12] It was not until February 20 that Sir Roy was able to muster a meeting with the two northern Governors, as well as the Premier of Southern Rhodesia. Sir Edgar

Whitehead, and the Governor-General, Lord Dalhousie.[13] Events then moved swiftly: Emergencies were declared in Southern Rhodesia and Nyasaland on February 26, and March 3, respectively, and the Zambia leaders were arrested in Northern Rhodesia on March 11. Although Sir Roy could not direct events personally, it is significant that Whitehead (a member of his own UFP) acted first, although Southern Rhodesia was the least disturbed of the three territories.

Governor Benson had originally intended to limit his action to the arrest of Kaunda and Sipalo 'not later than February 23';[14] the likelihood of this was known to the Zambia leaders at least a week earlier, and on February 16 the *Northern News* said of Kaunda: 'This leader of Zambia is both threatening government and challenging its authority with an audacity equal to Dr Banda at his worst. The country dare not let it continue.' That Sir Arthur delayed until March 11 is probably because Sipalo and Kaunda went off to the Eastern Province towards the end of February, for a secret meeting with Nyasaland Congress officials near Fort Manning; it was not easy to apprehend them until they had come back to Lusaka.

The primary reason for the liquidation of ZANC was its opposition to the territorial elections. The organisation had made clear by December that it wanted all Africans to boycott the voting. Sipalo opened the campaign in Broken Hill by saying that anyone who ignored the order would be 'punished'.[15] Zambia's first national council assembly in Lusaka, over Christmas 1958, had reiterated the plans for a boycott. Throughout January and February, party officials told rallies that pickets would be out for the general election on March 20, and that there might be trouble. Zambia's campaign was so effective that despite a most forceful registration drive by the government and Nkumbula's Congress, only a quarter of the estimated African voters were enrolled.

The Zambia African National Congress was in a militant and somewhat desperate mood in the weeks before it was proscribed and its officials made statements which could well be regarded as inflammatory. One used on several occasions exhorted Africans to 'hate anything white on two legs'. Wilson Chakulya, the Broken Hill district chairman of the party, was charged in March for using this expression.[16] Yet the official enquiry into the activities of ZANC failed to produce a single instance of violence attributable to the party before March 11. The party's constitution stated that its intentions were to 'work relentlessly by non-violence for the attainment of self-government and national independence'. Shortly before his arrest, Kaunda had made a public statement calling on members to remain non-violent and to keep away from the polling booths.

Although the Governor was naturally anxious that a general election a few weeks before his retirement (and under a constitution which he had strongly defended against inroads by the Federal government) should go off quietly, other reasons for his determination to ban ZANC can also be identified. In the Northern Province, for which Sir Arthur had a deep affection, the ill-fated £2 million development scheme financed by the Rhodesian Selection Trust was in full spate. District commissioners had been ordered to devote all their energies to the plan, which the Governor hoped would be a monument to his term in the country. Zambia officials headed by Robert Makasa, the regional president —later to become Resident Minister for the Northern Province— were considered determined to frustrate the various projects. Next, Benson was a keen believer in the role of the chiefs and saw the nationalist politicians as the greatest threat to their position. Finally, ZANC had scarcely endeared itself to Sir Arthur by calling him: 'cruel, imperialistic, inhuman, Satanic and brutal'.[17]

In banning ZANC, the Governor called its leaders 'racketeers' who had instituted a reign of terror, had practised witchcraft and threatened to kill or mutilate women and children. He compared the party with 'Murder Incorporated' in the United States. But unlike the authorities in the other two Federal territories, the Northern Rhodesia government did not declare a State of Emergency: in the first place, to have done so would have entailed the postponement of the general election, and secondly under the amended Emergency Powers Ordinance the Governor was able to detain people without trial, to forestall actions which might lead to an Emergency. More than fifty men were arrested, including Kaunda, Kapwepwe, Kamanga, Sipalo, Chimba, Dingiswayo Banda, Alexander Zulu, and Sikota Wina; the last was a political journalist who edited the *African Life,* a magazine which was published in Ndola and promoted the Zambia cause. The policy of the government was to detain the African leaders at places as remote as possible from their tribal homes, so that they should not influence local people. Thus Kapwepwe, a Bemba, was sent to Barotseland, while Sikota Wina, a Barotse, was detained in Bemba country. Kaunda was flown to Kabompo and Sipalo to Feira; subsequently these two were jailed for nine months each on political charges, a consummation which Benson had all along desired.

The banning of ZANC was immediately followed by a campaign of 'protest' violence which lasted for two months. Shop windows were smashed in Lusaka, cars were damaged and there were numerous acts of petty arson; two attempts were made to burn down the rest-house for African Legislative Council members in Lusaka. The only incident in which people were hurt was at Chilubi Island, at the north end of Lake Bangweulu in the Northern Province. During riots there, four Africans were shot dead after the DC and his assistant had been wounded with spears; ninety people were jailed.

Police informers had told the government that ZANC possessed a 'shadow executive' which would take over when the known leaders were arrested, and Kaunda had hinted that the party might 'go underground'.[18] Although some tentative plans to this end had been drawn up, the police were able to catch almost the entire leadership on March 11, so that African political activity was reduced to a minimum until late in 1959 when the principal 'agitators' re-emerged from the detention camps and jails. Writing to a cousin from the lonely Luwingu *boma* in June 1959, Sikota Wina quoted a poem by Boris Pasternak:

I am lost like a beast in an enclosure;
Somewhere are people, freedom and light;
Behind me is the voice of pursuit
And there is no way out. . . .

When the new Legislative Council met for the first time in April, there was general approval for the Governor's actions, although Sir John Moffat and Harry Franklin hinted at the need to appreciate the extent of African grievances and to remove them. The satisfaction of the UFP at the curbing of African nationalism was marred, however, by its failure to win any measure of non-white support at the polls. The UFP received only six per cent of the African votes; the two UFP Africans returned were elected by white votes in the 'reserved' constituencies.[19] Nkumbula won an easy victory against Robinson Nabulyato in the Southern Province, where tribal loyalties had maintained the power of Congress after the split with ZANC. The only other Congress candidate, John Banda, was beaten in the Eastern Province by Alfred Gondwe of Moffat's Central Africa Party.

The first signs of a revival of ZANC under another name came in June, when two new parties made their appearance—the African National Independence Party and the United National Freedom Party.[20] These quickly merged to form the United National Independence Party (UNIP) under the leadership of Paul Kalichini, the vice president of ZANC, who had been released in June. At the same time there was new dissension in Congress which produced a breakaway by the Bemba secretary-general Titus Mukupo, along with

Solomon Kalulu and Mainza Chona, Northern Rhodesia's first African barrister.[21] For several confused months there were two Congress organisations, but on October 26 Chona announced that his faction had combined with UNIP. Chona was appointed interim president with Frank Chitimbala (a former detainee) as secretary-general. By the end of November UNIP had become sufficiently established for the Governor to agree to meet a five-man delegation. The delegation warned that the party would boycott the Monckton Commission which was being assembled at the time by the British government.

In January 1960, first Kaunda and then Sipalo came out of prison; Kapwepwe had been released shortly before from detention at Mongu. At the end of January, UNIP's interim officials stood down and the trio which had led ZANC were elected to precisely the same positions that they had occupied in the banned party.

During the nine-month breathing space, the Northern Rhodesia government had been resolutely building up its coercive powers, a process which culminated in the Preservation of Public Security Ordinance.[22] This piece of legislation, which Moffat described as 'outrageous' and even the right-wing *Central African Post* branded as 'obnoxious to all right-thinking people', gave the Governor almost unlimited authority for the arrest and detention of people without trial and for the running of the country in times of emergency; it was passed through the Legislative Council in the same week as Kaunda was elected president of UNIP.

There were other developments in January 1960, however: Harold Macmillan made his 'wind of change' speech in Capetown at the end of his African tour, and the Monckton Commission was on its way to Central Africa.

7

The Creation of Zambia

I MONCKTON AND THE SECESSION STORM

THE point at which the British Conservative government decided that the Federation was unlikely to survive intact is debatable. Many seeds of doubt were sown by the events of March 1959, the Labour and Liberal parties joining with the Church of Scotland and much of the national press to demand a sharp re-appraisal by Britain of what it had created in Central Africa. As Lord Home put it,[1] he could not remember a situation which had 'caused so much interest and concern' in Britain. In the columns of *The Times,* Lord Salisbury, Field Marshal Sir Claude Auchinleck, Lord Robins, Miss Margery Perham and others debated possible courses of action. Sir Edgar Whitehead's Preventive Detention Bill was condemned in Southern Rhodesia by the Churches, the Bar, the Central Africa Party and the University College, thus revealing important divisions in the 'white front';[2] in July 1959 the Federal Chief Justice, Sir Robert Tredgold (who later resigned) added to suspicions that repression of the African majority was being taken to extremes when he protested at inroads being made into basic principles of common law.

In July, just as the publicity given to the March disturbances and arrests was dying down, another thunderbolt hit Federation. It was a thunderbolt of the Conservatives' own making—the report of a commission, let by Mr Justice Devlin,[3] which had enquired into the Nyasaland disturbances and their causes. The commission's statements that the protectorate was a 'police state' and that African opposition to Federation was almost universal were indictments which could not but relate to the Rhodesias as well. The *Devlin Report* came almost simultaneously with the Hola revelations,[4] so that the Colonial Secretary, Lennox-Boyd, was brought perilously close to resigning; Governor Armitage of Nyasaland was in a like predicament. The Conservatives declined to accept the main findings of the report.

The *Devlin Report* encouraged the view that the Federation might be better off without Nyasaland; after all, Welensky and Huggins had only accepted the protectorate in return for British agreement to political association between the Rhodesias. Yet however much the Federationists might wish that they had never got Nyasaland in the first place (and despite the fact that it cost £5 millions a year to support) its secession could not now be contemplated, for this would make the African nationalists in Northern Rhodesia impossible to contain. For this reason, Welensky was insistent in the final months of 1959 that the advisory commission being set up to survey Federation before the Review Conference should have clearly defined terms of reference. If the advisory commission was allowed to consider the possibility of any territory opting out, Federation was on the road to disintegration. He also stood on the widely held view that Britain had no legal power to change unilaterally the Federal structure.[5] Welensky has told how when Lord Home visited Salisbury in March 1959 to persuade him to accept the idea of the advisory commission, the difficulty of retaining Nyasaland was even then discussed.[6] With misgivings, the Federal government agreed to the commission, accepting the assurances of Macmillan that the terms of reference were safe and precise. The British Premier declared that the aim was to advance the northern protectorates to full self-government so that they would stand 'entirely on their own feet as components of the Federation'.[7] Welensky was much relieved (and the Africans cast down) when the Conservatives were returned to power that October with an increased majority. Lennox-Boyd became a viscount and was replaced as Colonial Secretary by Iain Macleod, a pragmatist on the liberal wing of his party, to whom Africa was virgin ground.

In his efforts to keep faith with Welensky and to persuade the Labour Party to fill three places on the commission, Macmillan became noticeably ambiguous during the last two months of 1959 about the limits of the terms of reference. He could not, however, go far enough to satisfy Hugh Gaitskell, the Labour leader, so that the commission found itself in the unhappy condition of being condemned by both the British opposition and the Federation's eight million Africans before it even started work. The African boycott, which was enforced in the northern territories (frequently with intimidation and even witchcraft) was scarcely surprising in view of the final composition of the commission.[8] Nineteen of the twenty-six members were white, several of the Central African representatives were known Federationists, and even some of the British element appeared unsympathetic to the African cause; Elspeth Huxley, for example, had written in 1959: 'In none of these (Central African) countries does one meet more than a small handful of politicians, and a very small handful at that, with mental grip and ability. Their lieutenants, however amiable, seem steeped in ignorance and conceit.'[9] The five Africans were either, like Lawrence Katilungu of Northern Rhodesia, politically suspect, or insignificant like Chief Sigola of Southern Rhodesia. It was the Monckton Commission's appearance of being weighted towards the white settlers, and the refusal of people like Kenneth Kaunda or Hastings Banda to even talk to it which was to make its report even more disastrous for the Federal government.

The commission formed, Macmillan flew off to Africa, on a tour which took him through Nigeria, Ghana, the Federation and South Africa. It was in Capetown on February 3, 1960, that he said: 'The most striking of all the impressions I have formed since I left London a month ago is of the strength of this African national consciousness. . . . The wind of change is blowing through the continent. . . . Our national policies must take account of it.' Macmillan spoke three days after the end of the All-African Peoples' Conference in Tunis;[10] Tanganyika had been given an African majority; Nigeria was near independence; a Kenya constitutional conference was being held in London; 1960 was 'Africa Year'.

When he visited Lusaka, Macmillan saw the leaders of all the Northern Rhodesian political parties, including Nkumbula and Kaunda. The latter, who had only been out of prison for ten days, was just starting to hold a press conference to complain that the British premier had ignored him when he received a telephone call inviting him to Government House for an interview. The two nationalists repeated to Macmillan that they would not meet the Monckton Commission and that they were unalterably opposed to Federation. The African public reinforced this message by waving at every vantage point placards bearing such sentiments as 'To hell with Welensky'.

The same placards were displayed a few weeks later when the Monckton Commission arrived to begin hearing evidence; one bore the observation: 'You cannot kill Federation—it is already dead.' Strenuous attempts by white liberals to persuade the black politicians to put their case were unavailing and Kaunda angrily denied a report that he had told Sir John Moffat, when the latter had visited him in prison, that he might speak for UNIP.[11] Even

Monckton's probably calculated indiscretion to one of the Northern Rhodesian Africans on the commission, that 'not even the Angel Gabriel' would dictate his terms of reference, was insufficient to break the boycott—although the remark quickly reached the ears of the nationalists. Yet in the rural areas, where the DCs scoured the villages for witnesses, some Africans did give their views. Memoranda in bizarre but graphic English were presented, the hostility to Federation being so constant that commissioners such as A. E. P. Robinson (later Sir Albert, Federal High Commissioner in London) came to the conclusion that the nationalists were intimidating Africans into giving evidence as well as into not giving it.

European witnesses fell mainly into two groups. The spokesmen of the UFP, such as John Roberts and Rodney Malcolmson, argued that there had been great economic advances since 1953 and that the improvement of services such as posts, roads and health were in marked contrast to pre-Federal standards. They also asserted (notwithstanding the results of the elections a year earlier) that there were many moderate Africans who really supported Federation but suffered acutely from intimidation; to support this contention they were able to produce men like Gabriel Musumbulwa, Minister of African Education, who articulately supported partnership and Sir Roy Welensky. The much smaller number of white liberals argued principally from the unrest in the country. A most influential witness was Moffat, whose Cassandra-like warnings throughout the 1950s were now seen to have been amply justified. Moffat said emphatically that as a political association, Federation had no future, but it should not be entirely dismembered; there was a powerful case for retaining some kind of a common services organisation. Sir Stewart Gore-Browne, living in retirement at Shiwa Ngandu, showed that he had done considerable rethinking since 1953 by advocating a common voters' roll and an African majority government in Nothern Rhodesia: even though Whitehead had warned that Southern Rhodesia would secede if the northern territories were given 'Gold Coast governments', this was a risk that must be taken.

Quite apart from receiving the great weight of violently conflicting evidence (that for Northern Rhodesia alone was to cover nearly 600 folio pages of fine print) the commission was in the awkward position of trying to paint a portrait of a subject which refused to sit still.[12] During the nine months of the commission's existence, Dr Banda was released in Nyasaland and a constitutional conference held by Macleod promised Nyasaland an African majority; Welensky argued that this alone 'made nonsense of the commission's work'. In Southern Rhodesia, there was preparation for a new constitution, in a tense situation following serious rioting which police and 2,000 troops only suppressed with the loss of several lives; Garfield Todd, whose increasing radicalism made him detested by almost all of his own race, demanded that Britain should send in troops.

In Northern Rhodesia, the African pressure for immediate self-government reached uncontrollable proportions; although the Governor assured the Legislative Council that there were no plans to alter the constitution, and no negotiations would take place until after the Federal Review Conference, seven weeks later he was holding 'exploratory' talks with political leaders.[13] At the Federal level, it was decided to spend more than £3 million in the next financial year on enlarging and re-equipping the armed forces, including the creation of an all-white infantry regiment.[14] The Commissioners also had to contend with the knowledge that relations between the British and Federal governments were fast deteriorating so that their Federal liaison officer, A. D. (now Sir Athol) Evans, was regarded coldly by some of the British members.

The Federal government's anxious mood during the time of the Monkton Commission was indicated by its switch to an aggressive and costly propaganda campaign in Britain. Until early 1960, external publicity had been low-powered, restricted to such ventures as commissioning a retired brigadier to write a subsidised eulogy of the Federation.[15] But in March, Welensky announced that plans were in train to employ public relations consultants to 'sell' Federation in Britain;[16] by a certain irony, the organisation selected was Voice and Vision, a Colman, Prentice and Varley subsidiary which had considerably helped Macmillan to win the 1959 general election. The engaging of Voice and Vision was quickly followed by the appearance of large advertisements in British newspapers defending the Federation's record. Much other publicity material was put out, and parties of MPS were flown to Central Africa for conducted tours. Sir Roy personally contributed to this campaign with TV appearances in which his man-of-the-people charm made a considerable impression on the British public.

The Federation's publicity campaign was swamped, however, when the *Monckton Report* was released in October 1960. The report declared that in the northern territories the opposition to Federation was 'widespread, sincere and of long standing. It is almost pathological.'[17] There had been failure to demonstrate the reality of racial partnership and discrimination still existed. Federation in its present form could only be maintained by force, which was unthinkable, and since the existing structure had become so identified with white domination, the very name should be changed. The majority of the Commission thought that there should be racial parity in the Federal Assembly and an African majority in Northern Rhodesia. The report was full of warnings that events in Africa were moving like an avalanche, and 'those who merely cling to their familiar positions will be swept away'. Crucial, however, was the Commission's decision that the British government retain unfettered power to 'make provision for the future of the Federation in any manner they may think fit'—and this included the right to let any territory secede. The release of the *Report* had been preceded by bitter exchanges in private between Welensky and the British government.[18] Writing to his friend Lord Home, the Federal Premier said despondently: 'We have now come to a parting of the ways.' In Salisbury Assembly, he accused Britain of dishonouring its undertakings and announced that he and his colleagues completely rejected the secession proposals.[19] Welensky realised that the *Monckton Report* had imposed the death sentence on Federation. 'It only remained to discover, in sorrow and pain, when and how judgment would be executed.'

II THE ADVANCE OF THE UNITED NATIONAL INDEPENDENCE PARTY

After the first national conference of the UNIP at the end of January 1960, its leaders were faced with a variety of urgent problems in their efforts to construct an effective organisation. One was that although the party had almost total control of the Northern and Luapula Provinces, and a large following on the Copperbelt, it was by no means territory-wide. The Ila-Tonge-Lenje group of the Southern and Central Provinces were unwavering in their support of the ANC, while the Eastern Province was almost equally divided between the two movements. The Litunga (Paramount Chief) of Barotseland, Sir Mwanawina Lewanika, would not allow any political party to set up branches in his 'protectorate within a protectorate' and in the backward, thinly-populated North-Western Province the political temperature was low. European and Asian following was negligible. The United National Independence Party's biggest advantage was that it had a magnetic appeal to the more educated elements in the African community—the clerks and teachers; quite apart from a very keen feeling of grievance in this group about salaries and social conditions, it saw in dynamic, toga-wearing leaders like Kaunda and Kapwepwe the embodiment of Pan-Africanism.

Yet this support was not enough. The party also had to

convince the chiefs that African nationalism would not reduce them to insignificance. The government had always been at pains to put the chiefs on their guard against 'agitators' and many of the tribal rulers were profoundly suspicious of outsiders of any colour; they regarded branch officials (some of whom were unquestionably of poor calibre) as intent on usurping their own authority. To demonstrate their loyalty to the chiefs, the UNIP leaders always included in their constitutional proposals a House of Chiefs with wide powers; thus in February 1959, the Zambia ANC advocated that such a body should have powers to check all legislation.[1] In May 1960, secretary-general Sipalo sent a circular letter to the 700 chiefs in the country, appealing for support for UNIP and promising 'happiness under freedom'. When Kapwepwe went to Ghana in July to attend the Republic celebrations he wrote from Accra to several of Northern Rhodesia's most influential chiefs (including the Litunga) to reassure them about conditions in an independent African state, and brought home a photograph of himself shaking hands with the Asantehene.[2]

Yet the problem of building up a nation-wide following and overcoming the suspicions of the chiefs were small in early 1960 compared with the need to establish discipline and avoid violence. It was a heavy responsibility for Kaunda, the UNIP leader, because Northern Rhodesia was by now living on a ridge of tension. The day he came out of prison he issued a statement which referred to non-violence four times and urged the African people to be 'calm and patient'.[3] In contrast, the party's welcoming address read to him the following afternoon did not mention non-violence at all, but laid emphasis upon the need to be 'tough', to fight and die for the country.[4] During a tour of the Western and Central Provinces during late January, and mid-February, Kaunda addressed twenty meetings—at all of which he condemned lawlessness, while at the same time speaking fervently about freedom and self-government. When the first issue of the *Central African Mail,* a weekly paper launched to support the nationalist cause, appeared at the end of February, its front-page headline read 'Kaunda is Firm—No Violence'.[5] Kaunda's difficulty in keeping events under control was increased by the party slogan 'Independence by October!' which had been coined while he was still in prison. It was a wildly impracticable target and created a dangerous mood of excitement, yet for Kaunda to have rejected it outright would have carried the risk of being scorned by more headstrong party officials.

The pent-up mood of the country was reflected in a series of disturbances in schools during March. Five large education centres had to close, affecting more than 1,000 students. In the

Luapula Province there were outbreaks of arson and all UNIP meetings were banned; on the Copperbelt petrol bombs were thrown, obstructions put on railway lines, and more than forty cars stoned during April and May; there were frequent clashes between police and crowds. The party denied responsibility for the troubles, arguing that when a national movement existed and was struggling for political power, it could not be held to blame for the behaviour of hooligans upon its fringes; the government was able to show, however, that eighty-four UNIP officials had been jailed within five months for a variety of offences. Kaunda later said that he realised there was a 'terrible danger' of some of the young extreme elements in UNIP getting out of control.

The government, meanwhile, had prepared thoroughly for a trial of strength. The expenditure on the police force had risen from £1.5 millions in 1955 to £3.5 millions in 1960; between 1958 and 1960 its manpower advanced from 4,200 to 5,600. Special attention was paid to the improvement of the Mobile Unit, a striking force designed for putting down riots. Twenty-eight detention camps, each capable of holding 200 men, were built around the country. To keep a close check on the intentions of the nationalists a network of informers was developed, some very highly placed in UNIP. The poverty of the party at this time was of considerable help to the Special Branch.

Disorders reached a climax early in May when a young white woman was stopped in her car near Ndola and fatally burned in a petrol attack; her children were injured. The murder occurred just after local UNIP officials had called a public meeting in defiance of a police ban. The police attempted to encircle the crowd, and more than a hundred arrests were made. The attack on the car took place a few hours later. The 'Burton Murder', as it became called after the name of the victim, resulted in the banning of UNIP on the Copperbelt and caused a profound worsening of race relations in the country. It gave impetus to the formation of white 'vigilante' groups and was to be a significant factor in the general election more than two years later.[6]

While the violence was intensifying, most of the UNIP leadership was out of the country. Early in April, Kaunda had flown to America to attend the Africa Freedom Day rally and make a lecture tour; secretary-general Sipalo and Justin Chimba, a provincial president, were in Ghana for the Positive Action conference; four other senior officials, including Frank Chitambala, the deputy secretary-general, had been jailed for sedition. Kaunda returned to Lusaka in mid June, after a prolonged tour of Europe and Africa which ended suddenly when he was deported from Kenya at one hour's notice.[7] During his travels he had seen Macleod in London, thus taking up an invitation made when the Colonial Secretary had visited Northern Rhodesia at the end of March. Macleod warned the UNIP leader that violence must be halted; moreover, there was not the slightest prospect of self-government being granted by October.[8] Kaunda fully realised the truth of this, but it was to take all his political skill to persuade his followers, in a year during which Nigeria, a dozen French colonies and the Belgian Congo were achieving independence. At the first public meeting he addressed after his return there were shouts from the crowd of 3,000: 'Independence by October—no change!'[9] The tension was lowered in August when Sir Evelyn Hone, who had been appointed Governor in 1959, began holding private discussions with political leaders; it became evident that some advance was being made and acts of violence noticeably decreased. At the UNIP annual conference early in September, Kaunda was able to combine realism with oratory: if it was found that the Governor was 'merely adopting delaying tactics', party members would be told to take positive action of a non-violent kind.[10] Thus the momentum was kept up and the reward came three weeks later when on September 28 Macleod announced that constitutional changes were planned for Northern Rhodesia; a conference would be held in December, concurrently with the Federal Review.[11]

The announcement was a landmark in Zambian history. For the first time, African pressure had scored a political victory over the settler population, because only a few months earlier the UFP leader, John Roberts, had been insisting that the Lennox-Boyd constitution—which had only been in force for eighteen months—would run its full course until the end of 1963.[12] From the constitution just granted to Nyasaland guaranteeing an African majority, it could be inferred that Northern Rhodesia was also heading for a transference of power; as the *Central African Mail* unsympathetically commented, this marked for Roberts the 'twilight of a political career'. The announcement also consolidated Kaunda's leadership of UNIP and strengthened his party *vis-à-vis* the African National Congress, which was expecting to make capital out of the failure of the 'Independence by October' slogan. Finally, it cut the ground from beneath the middle-of-the-road forces led by Sir John Moffat, who was on the point of abandoning his Central African Party alliance with Garfield Todd to form a purely Northern Rhodesian Liberal Party; Moffat now lost for ever many Africans who had been impressed by his trenchant attacks on Federation and feared to align themselves with UNIP in case it was banned like its precursor.

Macleod had clearly been influenced in his decision by the *Monckton Report,* which had been available at high government level since the first week of September.[13] The Africans had no grounds for expecting any help from the report, but when it was released on October 11 it recommended that a new constitution for Northern Rhodesia should be put into effect without waiting for a full revision of the Federal structure. The constitution should be comparable with that given to Nyasaland. Suddenly, UNIP's demands for an assembly of approximately sixty members, of whom three-quarters should be Africans, looked much less fanciful.

The Federal Review Conference at Lancaster House, London, was fruitless, except in so far as it demonstrated to the British government the complete lack of common ground between the nationalists and the Federationists. After a week of set speeches and walk-outs by the African delegates, the conference was adjourned by Duncan Sandys, the Secretary for Commonwealth Relations, with a formal and never fulfilled declaration that it would be reconvened after new constitutions had been devised for the two Rhodesias.[14] The shift in the British government's position can be seen when this is compared with Macleod's statement of seven months earlier that a conference on Northern Rhodesia's constitution must await the outcome of the Federal review.[15] Another pointer was the appearance in two influential London journals (the *Economist* and *Observer*) of 'inspired' articles suggesting that Northern Rhodesia and Nyasaland might be better federated with East Africa; the articles appeared a fortnight after Macleod had held talks with Julius Nyerere, then Chief Minister of Tanganyika. After the abandonment of the main conference, two brief gatherings of the Northern Rhodesian delegates were held, under Macleod's chairmanship, to discuss the new constitution. It immediately became apparent that there was no hope of an accommodation between the ruling UFP on one side and the UNIP-Congress delegates on the other. In private, the Colonial Secretary told Kaunda and several other members of his party that he intended to give Northern Rhodesia a scheme similar to Nyasaland's.[16]

The London conferences achieved none of their overt aims, and additionally marked the failure of Welensky's efforts to produce an African counter-balance to the nationalists; despite a powerful campaign by Voice and Vision to put forward men like Lewanika and Musumbulwa as the spokesmen of 'moderate' opinion, the British press and public (and the Colonial Secretary) were not convinced; instead, Kaunda—who had been in jail at the start of the year—attracted most of the attention, with even the senior Congress representatives, Nkumbula and Lawrence Katilungu, being forced into the background. Equally important was the division created between the Northern Rhodesia Officials and the UFP. Under the guidance of the Chief Secretary, Martin Wray, there had for eighteen months been a close liaison between the elected and civil service Ministers; Wray was not present at the London talks, his place being taken by the Minister of Finance, Ralph Nicholson. During discussions of the franchise qualifications for a new constitution, Nicholson argued that income should not be the deciding factor, because the total European income worked out at £580 a head annually, and that of Africans at £24 a head.[17] This statement was loudly applauded by the UNIP and Congress delegates, while the UFP group sat in silence.

The reopening of the conference at Lancaster House at the end of January was preceded by a series of heated exchanges between the Federal and British governments. The draft constitution worked out by Macleod was intolerable to Welensky: 'It will drive Southern Rhodesia out of the Federation . . . feeling is running high', he warned Macmillan.[18] Sir Roy, who had put up almost no fight over Nyasaland's constitution the previous August, was privately reconciled to the secession of the poorer of the two northern protectorates, but was determined to hold Northern Rhodesia at all costs. Africans ought to have no doubts 'which the white man will choose and what he will fight for,' said the Federal premier. Roberts, the UFP leader in Northern Rhodesia, was even more explicit: 'We shall fight with every means at our disposal.'[19] After Welensky and several members of his cabinet had flown to Lusaka, Roberts announced that he and the other UFP delegates would boycott the London talks; the extremist Dominion Party took a similar line.[20] However, when the Governor and the other delegates had already set off, Sandys arrived in Central Africa and suggested that Roberts should go to London with Julian Greenfield, the devoted and subtle Federal Minister of Law. Roberts accepted this proposal and the two men flew to London at short notice; a few days later they were followed by Athol Evans, the permanent secretary to the Ministry of Home Affairs, and one of Welensky's closest advisers.

As the constitutional talks got under way, an unprecedented pressure campaign developed in both Central Africa and Britain. Greenfield and Evans, with the aid of Lord Salisbury, canvassed right-wing support at Westminster, while Roberts made a bitter attack on Macleod when he addressed the Conservative backbenchers; Roberts took his stand on the 'principles of the 1958 constitution' (a constitution which the UFP had condemned when it was introduced) and sixty-five MPS signed a motion tabled in the

Commons which criticised the Colonial Secretary.[21] An editorial in *The Times* entitled 'No Going Back' urged Macleod not to give way[22]; it concluded: 'For the British Government, the path of wisdom in this era of revolutionary changes in Africa lies in going ahead, coolly and inflexibly, with measures to recognise that the Africans in Northern Rhodesia are a vast majority of its population and that the time has gone when they could be kept at arm's length.'

What was happening on the surface in London was a small indication of the struggle taking place behind the scenes. Harry Franklin, who was a Liberal Party delegate, has said that the conference was 'a mere cover for a major battle. . . . We could almost hear the heavy artillery of the British and Federal governments thundering through the park from Whitehall. But we never knew which way the battle was going and that was hard to bear.'[23]

Only much later did it become possible to piece together a full record of events during the first three weeks of February 1961. During that time Welensky hovered on the very brink of a *coup d'état*.

It was clear at the opening of the month that the Federal government contemplated extreme measures in an effort to stop the granting of an African majority constitution, and that much of the white population was ready to play its part. On February 6 the leaders of the 5,000 European mineworkers on the Copperbelt announced that a general strike would be called if the constitution was 'unfavourable';[24] white workers in Southern Rhodesia declared themselves willing to take similar action. At a meeting in Salisbury, the leader of the Federal Fighting Force, Colin Cunningham, warned that there would be 'civil war' in Northern Rhodesia if Macleod imposed a constitution. On February 7, the *Central African Mail* appeared with a front-page story headlined 'Can Welensky Do It?'. It claimed there were growing fears that the Federal premier might seize independence: 'This would be a completely illegal action, presenting a challenge which Britain could not ignore.' The article then went on to discuss a possible call-up of the Federal army and suggested that if this happened, Britain might fly in troops from outside. In fact, Britain had already taken precautionary moves in this direction, because troop carriers had been moved from Aden to Nairobi, where there was a big military base. Welensky had received information about this, and confirmed his suspicions by sending a Royal Rhodesian Air Force Canberra to Kenya on a reconnaissance mission.[25]

It was decided in Salisbury that if the British attempted an 'invasion' of Northern Rhodesia, runways would be blocked and the RAF Britannias and Comets shot up as they came in to land. On February 8, Welensky had a telephone conversation with Greenfield in London and said that if Macleod tabled unacceptable proposals he would recall parliament and 'do something else I can't talk to you about on the phone'. In the midst of these cloak and dagger moves, Kaunda issued in London a statement (prepared for him by another member of the UNIP delegation) in which he said that should Britain yield to the Federal government and refuse to concede an African majority, trouble would break out which by contrast 'would make Mau-Mau look like a child's picnic'. Kaunda was immediately rebuked by Macleod and put out another statement expressing his belief in non-violence and saying that he had been trying to make Britain realise the urgency of an 'appalling situation'.[26]

On February 12, after receiving a cable from Macmillan setting out new and still completely unacceptable constitutional proposals, Welensky called up the two battalions of white territorials in Northern Rhodesia.[27] By law, mobilisation could only be ordered at the request of the Governor, but Welensky took this action on his own initiative and then told the Acting Governor, Martin Wray, that he had done so. The Governor, Sir Evelyn Hone, was in London for the Constitutional conference; when he heard about the call-up he 'certainly did not like the move'. Wray tried to explain it away by saying that Patrice Lumumba, the former Congolese premier, had escaped from captivity in Katanga and might try to cross the border.

The territorials carried out 'show of strength' manoeuvres through African townships on the Copperbelt; the acting president of UNIP, Solomon Kalulu, ordered party members to remain calm, asserting that African morale was stronger than FN rifles* : 'If they seek to take away your life, peacefully show them the nearest part of your heart. . . Life is not worth living under such high-handed military intimidation.'[28] On February 17, Macleod dissolved the London conference and said that he would reveal his constitutional proposals in a White Paper four days later.

On February 21, Welensky called up four battalions of territorials in Southern Rhodesia and announced that he was reconvening the Federal Assembly. It was known in Lusaka government circles that he had plans to arrest the Governor and the Judiciary; a list of 'anti-Federation Europeans' who should also be detained by the troops was drawn up by the UFP. Welensky made

* FN rifles = the standard title of a type of high-velocity rifle. It derives from Fabrique Nationale—a Belgian arms factory—and was standard NATO equipment.

a bitter speech on the radio, attacking the British government and claiming that whatever might happen was not his responsibility; he repeated this warning privately to the British High Commissioner in Salisbury, M. R. Metcalf.[29] The following day, on Sir Roy's orders, all five UFP Ministers in the Northern Rhodesia government handed in their resignations.

It now appeared that the moment for a unilateral declaration of independence had arrived. Welensky had, a few days earlier, challenged the British government about the possibility of military intervention from outside, and had been assured that this would not take place.[30] Approximately 7,000 white troops, including regulars, were standing by. Yet in the three crucial days of February 22-5 he did not act. All other considerations apart, he lacked the military force to carry off a unilateral declaration successfully. The expansion of the Federal defence force announced in July still largely only existed on paper; the regular army was based on four African battalions with white officers; the ranks could certainly not be relied upon and many of the officers might refuse to abandon their oath of allegiance to the Queen. There was also a powerful Northern Rhodesia police force to be weighed; it was more than 5,000 strong, and although a third of the officers were either South African or Rhodesian, and so might sympathise with the Federal government, the 4,000 African constables certainly would not. In a vast area of Central Africa, with a population of 8,000,000, the white territorials were just not enough. The most decisive factor of all was that Sir Edgar Whitehead, the Southern Rhodesia premier, refused to allow any of his four battalions of territorials to be moved north of the Zambezi, for fear of leaving his own country without sufficient security forces.

Sir Roy retreated from the precipice and his speech when the Federal Assembly met at the end of the month was an anti-climax.[31] He said that he only had a mandate to seek independence for the Federation by constitutional means: 'I have no mandate to go beyond that. . . .' He might have to call a general election to seek approval for 'whatever line I intended to take'. What the line might be, he did not specify. Even the rushing through of a Defence Amendment Bill to allow the Federal government to call up all white men between the ages of eighteen and fifty could not conceal that the 'Boston Tea Party' had only been a fleeting dream.

As the unused territorials were stood down, the Africans of Northern Rhodesia realised that matters had gone their way. The UFP Ministers, led by Roberts, had gone into opposition and the government was being run by a patched-together coalition of Liberals and Officials. The Macleod scheme was for a legislature of forty-five members, of which fifteen would be elected by mainly white voters, fifteen by Africans and fifteen by both rolls together. The restricted franchise would put on to the upper roll about 25,000 Europeans, 3,000 Africans and 2,000 Asians—while the lower roll would admit about 70,000 Africans. All this was only barely tolerable to the nationalists, because it was clear that the British government intended that most of the fifteen national seats should go to the Liberals;[32] to qualify in the national seats, candidates would have to win a prescribed percentage of votes from both rolls—a condition which favoured a 'middle' party. However, it was most likely that the constitution would produce an anti-Federation majority, so that both Kaunda and Nkumbula hinted that their parties would accept what was being offered.

As work went on in the following three months to fill in the details of the constitution, it became clear that the Federal government had not given up the struggle. The constitution was one in which a few minor variations concerning the national seats could entirely change the balance. In the middle of March, Welensky flew to London for a Commonwealth Prime Ministers' conference and took the opportunity to strengthen support for his case among Conservative back-benchers and to appeal directly to Macmillan. On March 20 the two premiers issued a statement in which they said that while there had been nothing in the nature of negotiations, a valuable exchange of views had taken place. 'The United Kingdom government confirmed that they are prepared to consider any proposals, within the framework of the White Paper. . . .'[33] Due regard would be paid to suggestions put forward by the Federal government. A week later in the Commons, Gaitskell questioned Macmillan about the implications of this statement and received an indefinite reply. In an editorial, the *Central African Mail* referred to a declaration by a previous Colonial Secretary, Oliver Lyttelton, that the Federal government would have no power to accelerate or retard the political advancement of Africans in the Northern territories—'no power to interfere with the territorial governments in this matter'.[34] The newspaper wondered whether the guarantee was being honoured.

As the weeks went by, suspicions increased. The Governor was under great strain as he went through the motions of holding private talks with political leaders. Moffat warned that if the draft constitution was altered there would be chaos. In the middle of June, Macleod was on the point of announcing the final scheme when Welensky sent Greenfield and Evans to London with instructions to influence the percentage basis for the fifteen national seats at all costs.[35] For four days they applied relentless pressure to

Macleod; the British government also knew that Welensky was threatening to come to Britain and create a public controversy which might well split the Conservative Party down the middle; at this point at least one-third of the Conservatives were opposed to the 'Macleod line' on Africa, many of them having been persuaded during tours of the Federation organised by the British South Africa Company and Voice and Vision. Powerful help was given to this movement by Lord Robins, the president of Chartered, and Lord Salisbury, father-figure of the Tory right; in February, Salisbury had branded Macleod with memorable effect, 'too clever by half'.[36] In the last stage of the constitution-making at Westminster, both the Governor and Moffat went to Britain. The latter repeated his warnings that if any concessions were made to the Federal government, serious trouble must follow. On the Copperbelt, Kaunda had already told a mass rally that he was prepared to launch a 'master plan' to paralyse the country.[37] He hinted that if he could not succeed, he might resign and hand over to others who would 'speak the language the British would understand'. The UNIP leader then also flew off to London, but was completely unable to penetrate the Colonial office smoke-screen behind which Greenfield and Evans were operating.

On July 26 Macleod presented his scheme to the Commons;[38] ostensibly, the details were the 'recommendations of the Governor' and the Colonial Secretary praised 'the statesmanlike way' in which Sir Evelyn had discharged his responsibilities, a compliment which was small reward for bearing the burden of obloquy which was to follow. There was little variation from the proposals of February 21, except as regards the national seats, but here the changes were crucial. Candidates would be required to obtain 12½ per cent or 400 votes (whichever is the less) of the votes cast by both races. In the national seats, there would never be more than 3,000 votes cast by whites, so to qualify an African candidate would need 12½ per cent (about 375 votes) which would be an insurmountable hurdle. On the other hand, there would be a total of at least 10,000 African votes in each national constituency, so that European candidates would only need 400 votes—which was four per cent.[39] There were numerous other details which made the constitution the most mystifying ever imposed on a British dependency, but they were all insignificant when set against the qualifying percentage rule.

James Callaghan, the Labour Party spokesman on Colonial affairs in the Commons, described the constitution as a 'tissue of nonsense that would scarcely stand up to a single election'.[40] The voters would need a slide rule. Jo Grimond, the Liberal leader, remarked that in Britain electoral reform had always been rejected because it would be too difficult for the voters to comprehend, yet Britain nonetheless felt it right to offer the 'three-fifteens' scheme to people who were reputedly not yet ready for universal franchise. In Central Africa, Welensky now described the constitution as a 'reasonably workable instrument.' A few days later, speaking at Bulawayo, he was more precise : 'I believe that if the Federal Party handles its cards well, it could emerge from any election with a substantial majority. You have only to look at the press reports of the reactions of the African nationalists here to see the extent to which they are opposed to this constitution, and you can ask yourselves the obvious question, why?'[41] Sir Roy's satisfaction at his success made him casual about revealing the role he had played between February and June. He spoke of the representations his government had made to Britain. The advance press release of his speech to the Federal Assembly included the phrase : 'the agreement we have reached with the British government', this was later modified to 'the settlement of the Nothern Rhodesia constitution'. Feeling that he had regained the initiative in his struggle with Macmillan, Sir Roy also began pressing for the re-convening of the Federal Review Conference.

Among the 'cards' which the UFP was holding in readiness in Northern Rhodesia was one ultimately played in October 1962. Throughout the first half of 1961, overtures were made to the African National Congress; a number of secret discussions were held between the leaders of the two parties, with Malcolmson prominent on behalf of the UFP. Negotiations became easier when Lawrence Katilungu took over Congress leadership from Nkumbula, who had gone to prison for a serious driving offence.[42] The UFP theory was that if it could not collect 400 African votes on its own, the Congress could supply them, and in return receive enough white votes, so the two parties could sweep the national seats. Even if the alliance was temporary, the UFP would emerge with a majority.

The sequel of the June conference was never in doubt. The Governor made an unhappy speech to the Legislative Council in which he commented on the calm which had existed while the constitutional talks were in progress.[43] Now 'the security forces at our disposal are well prepared to deal with any trouble from whatever source it may come'. He asked the political parties to 'accept the rough with the smooth'. It was an appeal which fell on deaf ears because Kaunda immediately denounced the British government's 'betrayal'. Africans should save up their money for what lay ahead, he declared. The *Central African Mail* shouted across two pages 'A Constitution like a pit latrine', explaining pungently that the more you dug into it the more it stank.[44] The *Northern News*, which supported the UFP, commented that UNIP's disappointment was understandable after what it had been led to believe the constitution would provide: 'Federal government intervention produced last-minute adjustments which make an African majority unlikely.'

Feelings were further exacerbated when Kaunda, returning from a brief trip to West Africa, was searched at Salisbury airport by Federal immigration officers and had a brief-case seized; the incident gave the impression that the nationalists were being humiliated deliberately, after being defeated.[45] In the Legislative Council, Hugh Stanley (UFP) referred contemptuously to UNIP officials as the 'scum of the earth'.[46] The African counter-attack was not long delayed, the 4,000 delegates assembled at UNIP's annual conference near Broken Hill on July 10 giving Kaunda emergency powers to put his master-plan into action. Kaunda said: 'If the British government goes ahead and forces this constitution through, UNIP and all its supporters will boycott the elections. But we shall not let the constitution survive.'[47]

The Africans received powerful support from the Churches. In the middle of July the Christian Council of Northern Rhodesia, representing all non-Catholic denominations, sent a delegation led by the Anglican Bishop, the Rt. Rev. O. Greene-Wilkinson, to see the Governor.[48] They were told that the constitution was 'irrevocable', and a similar answer was given to the delegation sent by the Catholic Bishops' Conference. The government refused to call a meeting of the Chiefs' Council in Lusaka to discuss the constitution, realising that the council would probably demonstrate further opposition; however, Chief Mapanza, Secretary of the Council, outflanked official policy by publicly condemning the Colonial Secretary's decision.[49] Finally, there was the dilemma of the Liberals, who considered resigning from ministerial office. Moffat, Franklin, and Gondwe all attacked the constitution in the Legislative Council, although as members of the government they should have accepted it. The Liberals stayed on only because of an appeal from the Governor, who asked them not to impose on him the 'final indignity' of having to call back the UFP to form another government.

The first disorders came in the middle of July, with beer-hall boycotts and crude attempts at sabotage by the UNIP Youth League on the Copperbelt.[50] In the Luapula Province, several bridges were destroyed. Early in August, sabotage developed with an attempt to blow up a bridge on the Ndola-Kitwe road, with the cutting down of telephone wires and outbreaks of arson on government property.

Police reservists and troops were put on the alert to guard installations. Meanwhile, Kaunda went on a 3,000-mile tour of the northern areas during which he made repeated appeals for non-violence. The people interpreted this in their own way, avoiding physical assaults but launching a widespread campaign to bring the country to a standstill. Within a week, almost the whole area beyond the Congo Pedicle was in a state of insurrection. Thousands of trees were cut down to block roads, bridges were burnt and government buildings such as schools and transport workshops were destroyed. The people deserted their villages and marched chanting UNIP slogans, in bands of up to 1,000 strong, through the bush. The government responded to this challenge by moving in all the riot police it could spare from other areas, followed by troops and spotter planes. UNIP was banned in the Northern and Luapula provinces. This meant that even if Kaunda was able, or willing, to halt 'positive action' he would not be allowed to address members of his party, which officially had ceased to exist in the troubled areas.

As clashes between security forces and the people intensified, with small administrative outposts often cut off for several days at a time, Kaunda flew to London. He said there was nothing he could do, except to try to persuade the British government to alter the constitution. Mainza Chona, who had recently replaced Sipalo as UNIP secretary-general, said in Lusaka: 'If only the British government would make small amendments, the country would progress peacefully.'[51] But the struggle dragged on and although the administration tried to reduce casualties by attaching civilian officers to all armed patrols, the toll mounted; official reports listed nineteen dead, while UNIP claimed that the figure was higher because many casualties had been carried away into the bush.[52] There were more than 3,000 arrests, and 2,600 men and women were jailed, some being sentenced to long terms of imprisonment.

A significant feature of the disorders was that the 'insurgents', as the official communiqués described them, never attacked Europeans except in clashes with the security forces, although they had every chance to kill isolated farmers and groups of unarmed missionaries.

While the Governor insisted that there could be no negotiation under duress, the Christian Council of Northern Rhodesia tried to call a round-table conference of political leaders; the scheme collapsed when first the UFP and then UNIP refused to take part. The initiative would have to come from London. The start of September saw both Moffat and Kaunda making approaches to the British government for an urgent reappraisal of the constitution.

They were not without allies, the Labour Party pressing for implementation of the *Monckton Report* recommendations on Northern Rhodesia and many Conservatives coming to a growing awareness of what the rules for the national seats implied.

On September 7, press reports hinted that Macleod was having second thoughts. On September 9, Welensky was told that the British government intended to issue a statement saying that when violence stopped it would be willing to hear proposals within the framework of the White Paper which 'might offer the prospect of general agreement'.[53] Despite the Federal government's vehement opposition, the statement was released on September 13.[54] For the third time in a year, Britain had given way to pressures—twice from Africans and once from Europeans—concerning Northern Rhodesia's political future.

III THE FATEFUL ELECTION

In September 1961 the British government announced it was reopening discussions on the Northern Rhodesia constitution. Less than three months after Macleod's avowed final decision, an African uprising had undone the utmost efforts of the Federal government to retain what it considered to be 'responsible government'. It was now clear how naïve was the idea that Macmillan's 'wind of change' policy had been inspired by any coherent set of new principles rather than by a purely pragmatic acceptance that nationalism was irresistible. After the departure of the old-style 'imperialists' such as Chandos, Lennox-Boyd and Salisbury in 1959, Britain was only motivated by a desire for disengagement. The liquidation of the African empire was carried out on an *ad hoc* basis, the colonial peoples themselves making the timetable. When Britain had to choose between the nicely-balanced opposing forces in Central Africa, it wavered unhappily.

The announcement of September 13 enraged and baffled the Federationists. After the setbacks inflicted upon them by the Nyasaland conference and the *Monckton Report,* they had believed in June that at last there was a chance to hold the line. If only the UFP could get back to power in Northern Rhodesia, a strong internal policy might make it possible to contain the situation for another five years; it was felt that during this period the dynamic of Pan-Africanism must fade away. In the Federal Assembly on September 14, Welensky expressed the settlers' mood when he said: 'When the signs first appeared I was hesitant to believe that the British government could contemplate a retreat in the face of violence—after all, we have had numerous assurances from the Secretary of State that violence does not pay.' He compared the decision with the 'tradition of Munich'.

During the debate, R. L. Moffat argued that it was futile to fight 'a rearguard action for European supremacy' and blamed all that had happened since June on the Federal government, for having driven the British government into accepting changes which would benefit the UFP. Moffat painstakingly led the Assembly through the details of the national seats to prove his contention. In reply, Welensky asserted that he himself had 'objected very strongly' to the June constitution—although he would not be drawn into arguing about the crucial qualifying percentages. An aspect never touched upon was the widely-held view that Macleod was re-opening talks through a belated realisation that he had been out-witted by Greenfield and Evans during the days of June 23-6. During July Macleod had vehemently assured leading British journalists that the constitution would still produce an African majority and that his critics (including Kaunda) had misunderstood it.[1]

If Britain had not understood what it was doing, this was an excuse which could scarcely be made public. The government could only say that it wanted to produce 'something like parity between the races' and that it was trying again to find a solution 'acceptable to all'.[2] The UFP in Northern Rhodesia reacted to generalities of this kind by declaring that Britain was 'succumbing to blackmail through violence'.[3] The important Luanshya branch proposed that the Federal government should appoint a Resident Minister to Northern Rhodesia to show its 'determination to resist any adverse changes in the constitution';[4] a large part of the Federal army must be kept in the territory; 'phase four' of the Luanshya plan included a token general strike and a refusal to pay Crown rents or any territorial surcharge on income tax. Another plan of operations called for an 'all-out campaign' against the Northern Rhodesia government,[5] from which the Federal government should withdraw recognition. Control should be exercised over the use of the railway by colonial civil servants, a Federal police force should be created, and the thirty-forty age group should be called up for military training. (A copy of these proposals was acquired by a white journalist at Lusaka, and a photostat sent to London; the photostat was passed to James Callaghan, who produced it dramatically in the Commons.)[6] Julian Greenfield, the Law Minister, had attended a Broken Hill conference, and said that 'hard action by unconstitutional means would inevitably be necessary'.[7]

Apart from the organising of a petition, little came of this belligerence. Instead, the UFP was steered to the task of building up African support, its leaders believing that many people were disgusted with the recent UNIP violence and it would therefore be a good moment to enlarge the 'moderate' camp. This drive was combined with the 'Build a Nation' (BAN) campaign, which had been started by Sir Edgar Whitehead in Southern Rhodesia. It was also complemented by the Federal Information Department's energetic publicity service, built around the pamphlet *Fact,* for which a phenomenal readership was claimed. However, the search for African membership achieved scant success, progress being hampered by BAN's shortage of funds in Northern Rhodesia and its obvious links with the UFP (some organisers going so far as to put their party insignia on BAN publicity material). There was also the Northern Rhodesia government's long-standing refusal to handle contentious Federal publications.

As well as soliciting African support on its own account, the UFP showed increasing sympathy for the ANC during the second half of 1961. Lawrence Katilungu, who was widely admired by Europeans for his intelligence and moderation, was put forward as an African nationalist with whom it was possible to co-operate; Sir Albert Robinson, the Federal High Commissioner, propounded the same view to political, and business circles in London—a sensible but genuinely 'African' alternative to UNIP existed and it deserved encouragement.[8] The ANC's reputation was further enhanced by its decision not to boycott the June constitution but to adopt what it called an attitude of 'positive-negation'. Any idea of a UFP-ANC alliance was kept in the background, although the ANC national secretary, Job Michello, issued a distinctly equivocal statement about the constitution in August containing the threat: 'Should the Europeans become greedy and try to get a lion's share, the African voters are in a very strong position to paralyse the National seats....'[9]

On behalf of UNIP, Chona remarked that it looked as though Congress was likely to co-operate with the UFP. Patrick Wall, a leading right-wing protagonist of Federation, told the Commons: 'The African National Congress under Mr Lawrence Katilungu—a man of far more political experience and negotiating ability than Mr Kaunda—is gaining in power. He represents perhaps Africans in the higher income group and in certain tribal groupings.' What was definite was that ANC saw in the banning of UNIP in the north an ideal opportunity to develop a following in an area which had been virtually closed to it since the breakaway of Zambia in October 1958. Katilungu was himself a Bemba and a distant relative of the Paramount Chief Chitimukulu; with the cautious assistance of the provincial administration he made a number of tours in the disturbed areas to set up branches in Kasama, Abercorn and elsewhere. He sought the aid of chiefs who were known to be upset by the campaign of violence and made strong attacks on Kaunda and Kapwepwe. These tactics resulted in great enmity between the two nationalist parties, for whereas Kaunda and Nkumbula had been able to form a united front during the Lancaster House conference in February 1961, Katilungu was now viewed as little different from Godwin Lewanika and Justin Simukonda, the UFP Africans in the Federal Assembly. The similarity became more marked when Katilungu established close ties with Moise Tshombe, as much admired at that time by the UFP as he was anathema to the Pan-Africanists. In return for a promise from Katilungu to advocate the acceptance of an independent Katanga, Tshombe agreed to augment the funds which ANC was already receiving by way of Elisabethville from certain British financial interests.

Although UNIP's 'positive action' against the June constitution certainly increased European antagonism towards the party, it in no way lessened African support. On the contrary, Macleod's decision to 'think again' once more demonstrated that the party's aggression had reaped a reward. By the end of 1961 UNIP was winning over more and more of the intelligentsia, who now saw it was unmistakeably the party of the future. On paper, UNIP had suffered a severe setback by the jailing of hundreds of party officials and activists, but when the various bans on the party were lifted by the Governor in November, the territory-wide organisation was seen to be as strong as ever. There was a well-defined chain of command running down from the central committee through the twenty-four regions to the local branches; the women's brigade and the youth brigade, working in conjunction with the branches, were also directed from the Lusaka headquarters. UNIP boasted of representatives in Tanganyika, the United Arab Republic, Britain, the United States and elsewhere. Foremost among these representatives was Arthur Wina,[10] member of a well-known Lozi family who combined postgraduate study at the University of California with publishing a UNIP broadsheet which was sent to sympathisers throughout the United States. The extent of the UNIP organisation, both internally and externally, combined with the youth and inexperience of some key officials, made it inevitable that orders sometimes became misinterpreted and statements issued which embarrassed the party leadership. A memorandum presented to the Belgrade Conference of Non-Aligned Nations in September 1961 attracted widespread condemnation when it alleged : 'It is hard to escape the conclusion that a well-planned genocide operation is being conducted on the three million innocent and unarmed Africans of Northern Rhodesia by the European settlers of the country with the paternal sanction of the British government.' The memorandum had been signed by Reuben Kamanga, deputy president of the party, former secretary-general Sipalo, and the UNIP London representative, M. Kamalondo. It became the subject of a debate in the Legislative Council, but Kaunda's strength was shown when he issued a statement rejecting the 'genocide' charge as untrue and apologising to the British government.

While Northern Rhodesia waited for the British government to move towards altering the constitution, UNIP repeated its calls for a 'clear African majority'. At the first meeting of the party's national council since the Mulungushi Conference it was demanded that a full and formal conference should be called by Britain. A five-man delegation was sent to Government House early in November for preliminary talks and when the new Colonial Secretary visited Lusaka shortly afterwards it was grudgingly accepted that nothing more than changes in the national seat percentages would be forthcoming. Reginald Maudling was non-commital, refusing even to say publicly that the constitution would be altered at all. He was clearly impressed, however, by the unanimity of African opinion. A delegation of chiefs led by two paramounts, Undi and Mpezeni, with senior chief Chikwanda and chiefs Ikelenge and Mapanza, called for African majorities in both legislative and executive councils. The ANC delegation led by Mr Mungoni Liso, the new acting president, made similar proposals.[11]

Maudling returned to London with the realisation that he would have to impose changes, and said that he would make an announcement 'on or about January 14'. In a reference to Welensky he stressed that the final decision was with the British government. UNIP ordered its followers to be patient, but ready to act if necessary. 'An imposition is far better than a swindle' it observed philosophically. The wait was longer than the Colonial Secretary had forecast. Once again a furious backstage struggle was going on between the Federal and British governments.[12] At the end of February Sir Roy gave an interview to the *Daily Express* in which he said, among other things: 'The Federation is mine, and I am prepared to fight, to go the whole hog if necessary.'[13] He then took a plane to London. The British cabinet met and argued at length over what should be done, Lord Home coming down firmly on the side of the Federal government.

When Maudling announced his decision to the Commons on February 28, he had done no more than alter the qualifying percentage in the national seats from $12\frac{1}{2}$ to 10 per cent and remove the 'or 400 votes' clause. This appeared to create a situation where instead of the UFP having a chance of winning the seats, now nobody could win them. After a five-hour meeting, the UNIP national committee decided to accept Maudling's ruling, narrowly deciding that it would be better to fight an election rather than start another round of 'positive action'. The UFP in Northern Rhodesia also accepted the changes, Roberts saying bleakly that he was still hopeful of gaining a majority. Reaction from the Federal government, was, however, far more vehement. Addressing the Federal Assembly, Welensky accused the British government of evasion and discourtesy; he was determined to halt 'the erosion' of the Federation.[14] He felt that the best thing for the future might be to divide up Northern Rhodesia into three parts—a remarkable attempt to revive the old 'partition plan'. He then went ahead with plans to call a Federal general election, to seek a mandate from the voters.

This election was held in April, and although the UFP emerged with fifty-four out of fifty-nine seats, there was a general air of unreality. Forty of the seats were uncontested, the Africans imposing a total boycott and the new right-wing grouping in Southern Rhodesia, the Rhodesia Front, declining to become involved because it was preparing for the colony's impending general election (which it subsequently won). In the balloting, Welensky only gained a positive mandate from less than 20,000 people out of the Federation's total population of eight millions. With the Federal election concluded, attention was concentrated upon the registration campaign and delimitation of constituencies in Northern Rhodesia. To bring the country to the polls before the start of the rainy season in November, haste was essential. The constitution imposed a severe test on the Delimitation Commission, and the registering officers had to enrol nearly twenty times as many voters as had been enfranchised by the 1959 constitution. The preparations were imperilled for some weeks by violent clashes on the Copperbelt between UNIP and ANC—in one incident at Ndola six people were killed[15]—but when the disorders had subsided an energetic registration campaign was mounted. Political parties co-operated with the government in helping potential voters to obtain recognition that they fulfilled the qualification (on the lower roll, voters had to be literate in English—or in certain circumstances merely in the vernacular—earn £120 a year or own immovable property worth £250). When the final registration figures were announced, 92,000 people—almost all Africans—were listed on the lower roll and 37,000—about two-thirds European—on the upper.

Electioneering began seriously at the end of August after

the Delimitation Commission had issued its report.[16] It was obvious from the start that the campaign would be hard and racialistic, but it was not until the middle of September (six weeks from voting day on October 30) that it became clear just how relentlessly the UFP was preparing to fight. Alfred Adams, the party's senior organiser, paid a series of visits to Lusaka from Salisbury, and at meetings of the divisional executive an overall strategy was conceived. In a sentence, this was to denigrate UNIP as vicious and the Liberals as futile; ANC was to be another matter. Welensky had set the pattern in a speech to UFP supporters in the Lusaka Showgrounds on September 1, not speaking of ANC once during a long condemnation of the other opponents.

It was soon to become plain just how close was the friendship between Roberts and Nkumbula, but initially the rumours of any election alliance were all centred on the Liberals and UNIP. On the UNIP side, some senior officials were tempted by the hope of improving their chances in the national seats through receiving Liberal votes. There was a strong current of opinion inside UNIP that the party should fight entirely alone and thus unequivocally demonstrate the extent of its following; if the Liberals wanted to help the progressive movement, then they should disband themselves and unite with UNIP, Sikota Wina declared at a Bancroft rally.[17] This was a proposition which was unacceptable to Moffat who still believed (as did the British government) that moderation was a rallying-call.

In an effort to reassert its independence, after its flirtation with UNIP, the Liberal Party was obliged to move further to the right; one of its election slogans was 'A vote for UNIP may be a vote for extremism'.

The United National Independence Party planned its campaign on daring lines, Kaunda in particular arguing that it was imperative to go all out for the support of Europeans and Asians.[18] The party's recognisable non-African support was small, being limited to radicals like the lawyer James Skinner and the missionary Merfyn Temple; prominent also were an Asian businessman, T. L. Desai, and the redoubtable Sir Stewart Gore-Browne, who had declared his allegiance to UNIP early in 1961.[19] However, some of the central committee believed there was a considerable reservoir of European goodwill to be tapped, and at one stage Kaunda even said that he would contest a national seat to demonstrate his faith in 'non-racialism'. So the party decided to spend at least half its financial resources on appealing to Europeans, especially on the Copperbelt where four of the seven double-member national constituencies would be decided. To this end, a

20,000 word party manifesto, explaining UNIP, was widely distributed.[20]

UNIP knew that its greatest hurdle would be to present itself to the Europeans as an organisation mature and responsible enough to be considered as a future government. The *Northern News* spoke for the bulk of non-Africans when it contrasted the record of the UFP with that of the nationalists.[21] It asked pointedly whether the achievements of the past were to be cast aside 'for the gamble that men who have never sat in a parliament, and whose party has a past record of violence and a present record of intimidation, can do better'. Kaunda protested that the newspaper was carrying out a ruthless war of 'cheap and intentional propaganda' against UNIP: 'It has done everything to paint my party as a party of devils and wrong-doers.'[22]

In the pursuit of respectability in European eyes, UNIP weighted its list of candidates with 'new men'—members of the African intelligentsia who had comparatively recently come out in its support. The team was impressive, including graduates who had held senior positions in the civil service—Elijah Mudenda, Arthur Wina, John Mwanakatwe and Mubiana Nalilungwe; there was one of the country's handful of African doctors, Dr Mushekwa Nalumango; the Rev. Isaac Mumpanshya and a Barotse princess, Makwae Nakatindi. The white candidates also bore little resemblance to terrorists, including Gore-Browne, Temple, Skinner, John Anderson, a farmer born in South Africa, and Andrew Sardanis, a leading Copperbelt businessman. Although the most senior party officials were standing, there was some grumbling inside the party from other 'old guard' officials who felt they had been brushed aside to make way for the newcomers who had never suffered jail and poverty in the cause. Sipalo, whose reputation alarmed many Europeans, stayed out of the country as the campaign was fought.

Kaunda worked eighteen hours a day during September and October, to win over the non-Africans, talking to them in school halls, cinemas and at cocktail parties. His message was 'let's look to the future and unite'. Wherever possible, white and black UNIP candidates campaigned together, to project the multi-racial image. Yet even the more sympathetic Europeans mainly took the line that they might vote for UNIP 'next time', after they had seen how the party behaved in the Legislative Council; for the moment, they were not going to leap into the unknown.

And the sympathisers were few. Most of the Europeans might understand the complexities of the constitution even less than did the Africans voters,[23] but they were quite emphatic that they must vote for Welensky and the UFP (the two being almost synonymous). The extent to which the white voters were entrenched was to be shown in one of Lusaka's constituencies on the upper roll where the UFP executive put forward Musumbulwa, a former Minister to be sure of having him returned. The local UFP branch had proposed its chairman, A. O. R. Mitchley, but gave way after a public squabble; although Musumbulwa did little campaigning, the UFP label enabled him to crush all his four white opponents by collecting 1,200 of the 1,800 votes. One of these opponents, Mrs Rina Allard (Liberal), remarked despairingly when the result was announced: 'They would have voted for a cow.'

The UFP played on white fears with ever-growing intensity as October 30 came nearer.[24] Expertly-produced campaign leaflets campaigned on one theme: UNIP was a party of criminals, who in the words of Welensky wanted to replace the security of Federation with 'some unholy alliance dreamed up by Pan-Africanism'. A European who voted for UNIP was a traitor, a Copperbelt audience was told by Sir Donald Macintyre, Federal Finance Minister. With its own future and that of Federation at stake, the UFP fought in a manner it had never contemplated before. Much of the propaganda material published was printed in Southern Rhodesia, and some of it was put out in the name of Dixon Konkola, a one-time ANC leader who in the previous April's 'phoney election' had entered the Federal Assembly on the strength of twenty-two votes. Konkola styled himself the President of the 'Central African People's Union', a party which did not exist.

One particularly effective leaflet was entitled 'You have been warned' and contained a list of all the most damaging incidents which could be laid at UNIP's door, including the murder of Mrs Lillian Burton in 1960 and Sipalo's statement in 1958 that Africans should hate everything white which had two legs. In the fervour of the campaign, the influential *Northern News* committed itself fully to the UFP. On election eve it appeared with an editorial which recalled Sir Arthur Benson's 1959 comparison of ZANC with 'Murder Incorporated'.[25] UNIP was a gamble which there was no need to take, for although the UFP had made mistakes, it had brought progress and defended democracy: 'No one can prove that Mr Kaunda is not sincere, and equally no one can prove that he is.' In the press, UNIP had no counter, although it brought out its own election newspaper; at that time, the *Central African Mail* had an insignificant European readership. At a meeting in Lusaka, the UNIP president broke down before an audience of 15,000, describing how his efforts to achieve unity of purpose with the Europeans had failed and been treated with contempt. Despite help from Sweden and America, and the donations from its members, the party had also run short of money.

While the UFP was condemning one nationalist party, it was at the same time building up another. Congress was promoted as a 'moderate' organisation and non-violent ally; Nkumbula (who had reassumed the ANC presidency after ending his prison sentence) was given every kind of help, including a white 'election adviser', Roy Horrell, who had previously served with the UFP in Southern Rhodesia. On the Copperbelt the two parties combined to form the United Anti-UNIP Movement (UAU), which recruited bodyguards for ANC members and skirmished with UNIP's Youth Brigade. The bodyguards were paid £2 a week out of UFP funds. The co-operation went much deeper than this, however, for it became obvious on nomination day that there was an arrangement to divide up the national seats. Although the plan did not work out precisely in all constituencies, in most an ANC man was teamed up with a UFP man. Here was the deal hinted at as early as August 1961 : each party would supply the other with the votes it needed in order to qualify. The scheme was denied until a fortnight before October 30, so that ANC members would not have much time to grow disillusioned about having to cast their votes for the Federationists, against whom their leader Nkumbula had fought for more than a decade. The results were to show how effective the alliance had been, with the voters of both parties obediently following the orders given on thousands of leaflets which listed only the names of the candidates and not their parties; the leaflets were the work of yet another UFP front organisation.

In Barotseland, where two lower roll constituencies were at stake, the UFP set up the Barotse National Party (BNP). This, it was hoped, would receive the blessing of the Litunga and support of traditionalists against the two UNIP candidates, Arthur Wina and Mubiana Nalilungwe. The BNP was supplied with money, vehicles and a white publicity relations officer from Salisbury; Godwin Lewanika was active in its support and there was a general feeling that UNIP would have a difficult task in the 'feudal backwater' of Barotseland.

As the results of the voting came in, three main facts were apparent : the polarisation of the races was much more absolute than anyone had expected, no party had won a clear majority of seats, and the Liberals had been obliterated. On the African lower roll, UNIP gained 78 per cent of the votes and 12 seats, while ANC had 21 per cent of the votes and 3 seats. On the upper roll, where almost four-fifths were white and the rest higher-income Africans, the UFP had obtained 70 per cent of the votes and 13 seats, while

UNIP collected 20 per cent and 1 seat (in a rural constituency with a predominance of African voters).

In the national constituencies, four UFP-ANC candidates were successful, giving both parties two more members. On the other hand, the UNIP candidates in the national seats were utterly crushed, obtaining almost all of the African votes and a handful of European votes. For example, in the Chambeshi constituency, Gore-Browne collected 11,264 African votes and 55 European votes; his running-mate, Matthew Mwendapole, scored 11,286 and 69. This was a measure of the racial gulf. The Liberals lost their deposits in 28 of the 30 constituencies that they contested and immediately disbanded.

So on November 3, with all the results in, the state of the parties was UFP 15, ANC 5, and UNIP 14 (including the special Asian-Eurafrican seat). In the by-elections held soon afterwards in an effort to fill some more of the national seats, the 'pact' worked again to raise the UFP total to 16 and the ANC to 7. The country waited tensely to see what would happen. Would the UFP and ANC unite to form a government? If so, what would be the reply from UNIP now that it had proved at the polls its overwhelming following among the African people?

IV THE AFRICAN COALITION

Throughout November 1962, a trial of strength went on between UNIP and the UFP for the allegiance of ANC. A local newspaper summed up the situation in a cartoon which portrayed Nkumbula dressed as a bride with both Kaunda and John Roberts kneeling beside him as suitors. The ANC, occupying the position which the Colonial Office intended to provide for the Liberal Party, savoured its bargaining power for as long as it could, putting the price of its favours high. The situation was not without irony, but was also extremely dangerous for the country. If the UFP could manage to transform the pre-election alliance into something more permanent and thus return to power after an interval of almost two years, a vista of discord would be opened up.

The handicap which faced the UFP was that on fundamental issues it and ANC had nothing in common. By its very name, the UFP was committed to Federation, which since Nyasaland had been given the right of secession was already on the verge of disintegration. Further, the ANC would not abandon its slogan, 'One man, one vote'. In expressing his hopes for a coalition, Roberts suggested that he and Nkumbula could 'reserve their positions'.[1] Where the parties did agree, it was over personalities rather than policy, both condemning Kaunda and Hastings Banda but praising Tshombe. On the other hand, UNIP and ANC had complete identity of object. Unia Mwila, UNIP's director of elections, burst into verse in full-page advertisements during November; his final stanza proclaiming:

UNIP and ANC
Stop and look
Our common enemy
The lion, the snake, UFP must die![2]

The chiefs exerted their influence at a meeting in Lusaka by appealing to the two nationalist parties to re-unite, but were answered with a statement by Nkumbula that ANC would remain unaligned until after the by-elections on December 10.[3] In fact, Nkumbula had already decided to form a coalition with UNIP, but maintained his national seat alliance with the UFP in the hope of gaining more seats and thus improving his bargaining position. The hope was justified. After a joint meeting in London with R. A. Butler, who had been given overall responsibility for Central African affairs, the two leaders returned to Lusaka to tell the Governor that they were ready to take office. Despite his party's inferiority, in terms of both votes and seats, Nkumbula was able to wrest from Kuanda an agreement that six ministries should be equally divided. The UNIP leader's attitude was that the constitution had been proved unworkable and would have to be changed within months; the absolute priority was to have an anti-Federation government in office, however high the price in political pride.

Creating the coalition was not without its snags. The constitution ruled that at least two ministers must be Europeans and between them the nationalists had only two white MLCs—both in Congress. One of these two, Frank Stubbs, had repeatedly said that he would not have any connection with a UNIP government; only at the last moment did he yield in the 'interests of the country'. Another complication was a last-ditch stand by the election adviser, Horrell, who tried to persuade a section of ANC to disown the coalition but was ultimately disowned himself.[4] On December 15 the government was announced, the ministers being Kaunda, Kapwepwe, Kamanga, Nkumbula, Stubbs and C. E. Cousins, and four civil servants. At parliamentary-secretary level, UNIP brought in three of its graduates—Mudenda, Mwanakatwe, and Arthur Wina.

The year of the coalition was marred by constant inter-parliamentary squabbles. Sharing the responsibilities of government did nothing to re-unite the nationalist front. Because no other method would have worked, each minister had a parliamentary secretary of his own party. Nkumbula repeatedly threatened to resign and at first there were rumours that he might once again join up with Roberts.[5] The strains which the situation created were shown by a petrol-bomb attack on Sipalo. He was gravely burned, but survived; his attackers were never discovered.

In May there were attempts to form a merger between ANC and UNIP during Kaunda's absence in the United States to receive an Honorary Doctorate of Laws at Fordham University and to meet U Thant. But when Nkumbula announced that he had been having talks with some senior UNIP officials, this was hotly denied, and the negotiations petered out.[6] By the middle of the year, Nkumbula was even having trouble holding his own party together, a faction led by Job Michello, parliamentary secretary to the Ministry of Lands and Natural Resources, ultimately breaking away to form the People's Democratic Congress (PDC). First hint that the split was not limited to comparatively junior officials on the Copperbelt came when Nkumbula told a rally in Kitwe that Michello was threatening to depose him. He also asserted that the rebels were about to receive funds from 'UFP sources in London', who were angry because ANC had combined with UNIP. Michello replied that Nkumbula should be suspended from the ANC leadership for failing to agree to a 'drastic reorganisation to cut out dead wood'; he also complained that ANC youth-wing members were trying to intimidate him. The real dilemma within ANC was, however how it should cope with its mountain of debts. At a meeting of the national assembly, Michello dramatically took fourteen writs from his pocket and waved them at the delegates. The rebels formed the PDC after their failure to oust Nkumbula from his presidency, amid a furore about the future of Zambia. It became known that ANC officials were in contact with Frederic Bennett, a Conservative MP who had been an adviser on regionalism to the Kenya African Democratic Union.[7] Bennett was about to fly to Lusaka from Salisbury when a Northern Rhodesia newspaper reproduced a letter he had written. The letter outlined the 'regional' policy, stressing that each region must keep control of its police force: 'What we need above all is not constitutional safeguards which can be thwarted by ruthless men by unconstitutional means, but a constitution which in itself has to survive, whatever the "national" leadership, because the state is of such a loose federal or regional structure that the power to assume overall dictatorship does not exist.' This proposition alarmed UNIP, which saw that such a 'Tshombiste' construction would allow the Southern Province, where ANC was entrenched, virtually to secede. Both Nkumbula and Michello accused one another of being 'regionalists' and Bennett cancelled his visit. He explained that ANC had approached him for help and that he had agreed to give it without any remuneration, in his private capacity as a lawyer.

Renewed fears that the coalition might collapse followed the formation of the PDC. For some weeks the two white ANC ministers, Stubbs and Cousins (to the latter Michello was parliamentary secretary) hovered over the idea of resigning from ANC; with Michello and several members of the National Progress Party (as the UFP was later to be named) they could then form a new parliamentary group. The danger for UNIP receded as a result of appeals by the Governor to Stubbs and Cousins, and the failure of Michello to find funds to launch the PDC nationally. During August he had led a delegation (which included the enigmatic Horrell) to see Tshombe in Spain at the same time as a representative of ANC; this so perplexed the exiled Congolese leader that he gave money to neither.[8]

The rivalry and instability among the politicians was reflected among the people, constant fighting taking place in the Copperbelt towns during the first half of 1963. In the first six months there were 1,133 political crimes, compared with less than 300 in the same period of 1962. Except in Mufulira, ANC was weak on the Copperbelt, and its outnumbered followers had an anxious time; intimidation by youths was rife; many of these youths were unemployed and acted brutally in the name of UNIP to slake their boredom. Of about 50,000 jobless on the Copperbelt, half were adolescents for whom there were no places in schools and no opportunities in the mines. They lived off relatives in the traditional African manner, hung around bars, sometimes smoked *dagga* (Indian hemp) and looked for trouble in the townships after dark. After a string of murders, the climax came in Nchanga mine township when seven men were murdered with spears and axes; 100 were injured. A commission of enquiry led by a judge and including members of both governing parties was appointed.[9] When it reported in August, the commission identified a number of chronic causes of unrest, stressing unemployment and lack of education. Of the immediate reasons, it pointed out: 'The present political frustration was described in one memorandum as generating a sense of anti-climax and loss of direction, owing to the virtual attainment of the principal political objectives and thus contributing to a psychological restiveness.... Several witnesses expressed regret at the indecisive outcome of the 1962 general election and considered that a coalition government was unsatisfactory at this stage of the territory's constitutional development... the opinion was also expressed that there was disappointment that the coming into power of a nationalist government had not resulted in immediate and widespread benefits to the mass of the people.' The principal recommendation of the commission was that there should be a new constitution as soon as possible and that the general election date should be announced quickly.

This was exactly in tune with UNIP's thinking. Kaunda had repeatedly condemned the coalition, saying that nothing could be done with a 'three-legged' government—UNIP, ANC and the civil servants. He had pressed for an election before the end of 1963, whereas Nkumbula and Roberts not unnaturally wanted to delay the moment of decision until May 1964. It was obvious that the British government would, after the fiasco of the oversubtle Macleod-Maudling constitution, move on to a formula which would enfranchise the great mass of the Zambian people; with UNIP's record in October 1962, the outcome was inevitable. Early in September the Governor announced that the general election would be held in January and that the registration of voters was to begin immediately, the registration campaign being designed to divert the frustration to which the Copperbelt commission had drawn attention. When registration ended in October more than 1,000,000 Africans had been enrolled, compared with less than 100,000 in the previous year and 7,000 in 1959—reflecting the pace of political advance from a restrictive franchise to universal adult suffrage. This trend was also reflected in the size of the legislature: 20 elected members in 1959, 45 in 1962 and 75 in 1964. For the sake of speed, Kaunda had agreed to the maintainance of ten seats for Europeans in the 75.

The country prepared for another general election in a mood much changed from that of twelve months earlier. Principally, this was because 1963 was the year in which Federation was dissolved—in an atmosphere of curious lethargy. After all the anguish of 1958-62, the contestants had perhaps run out of nervous energy.

Indeed, Federation died with a whimper. Just before the start of the year R. A. Butler had defied the protestations of Welensky and told the Commons that the British government accepted the right of Nyasaland to secede.[10] As the Federationists had always known, Northern Rhodesia must now go the same way and in February its Legislative Council passed, after a six-day debate, a 'secession now' motion proposed by Nkumbula and seconded by Kaunda.[11]

There were signs that the Conservatives would have liked to delay the final reckoning on Federation until after another British general election, when they might be in a stronger position to deal with any revolt by right-wing backbenchers; alternatively, should the Labour Party win it would then have to bear the obloquy. In a typically guarded statement, Butler told the Commons that his aim was to 'secure an acceptable form of association between the two Rhodesias';[12] this implied close economic links, for which there was great pressure in the City from Southern Rhodesian financial interests. Denis Healey, then Labour Party spokesman on colonial affairs, advised Butler to 'stop dithering' and admit that the Federation was dead. In Lusaka, Kaunda said: 'We have made it perfectly clear that we will not accept the imposition of any association. What links are made must be an expression of the people's desire.'

When the Northern Rhodesian delegation reached London, it was aggressive: there would be no talks on long term policy until Butler announced that the country had the same right of secession as Nyasaland. Welensky was also in London and tried to make a last stand. But he was alone, for the UFP had been ousted from power in all three territories of the Federation. His only weapon was the now blunted accusation that Britain had dishonoured her solemn pledges to support the Federation rather than tear it apart. He went so far as to quote the confidential minutes of the conference in 1953 which designed the Federal constitution. Butler issued a White Paper which confirmed rather than denied Welensky's contention.[13] However, *realpolitik* had become more important than promises, and on March 29 the British government conceded the Northern Rhodesian demands.

All that remained were the timing and mechanics of dissolution and these were arranged by a drab conference at the Victoria Falls in which Butler skilfully diverted all contentious issues to committees of civil servants. Dr Banda boycotted the conference and the Northern Rhodesians found no opportunity to cross swords with anyone.[14]

The end of the Federation provoked an urgent re-appraisal in the minds of Europeans in Northern Rhodesia. In the business community especially, it was seen to be necessary to reach an understanding with UNIP, which was obviously going to achieve absolute power during 1964. By March there was an open retreat from the UFP, which shortly afterwards contracted out of the struggle for political power by renaming itself the National Progress Party and announcing that it would follow a 'convergent course' with the nationalist government. There was also a distinct evaporation of white sympathy with ANC, which no longer found itself able to obtain credit from commercial interests. Kaunda and Kapwepwe, who had so long been the victims of vilification, became honoured guests and after-dinner speakers. Welensky's former paper, the

Northern News, also discovered new perspectives. The only crucial subject at issue was how close an economic relationship could be maintained with the south, because many companies were established on both sides of the Zambezi. The expiring Federal government, which after the middle of 1963 identified itself more and more with Southern Rhodesian interests, mounted a persuasive campaign for a 'Rhodesian common market' and J. A. Clark, the Federal Minister of Commerce and Industry, addressed Northern Rhodesian businessmen in a series of closed meetings. A White Paper presented to the Federal Assembly in June affirmed : 'Indeed, it is imperative that no effort should be spared on the part of every single person to secure the greatest measure of economic association and the lasting benefits which must flow therefrom to each territory and their respective peoples.'[15] For more general consumption, a booklet was put out with the title *How Grim is My Future?* The common market scheme foundered, however, on the Northern Rhodesian belief that the territory had suffered financially from Federation and should now treat all its neighbours on their merits; it was officially stated that there had been a net loss of revenue of approximately £10 million a year since 1953 and that Southern Rhodesia had been the main beneficiary—a claim that had first been made by the *Central African Mail* in 1960.[16]

Thus when the country went into the election campaign in December 1963, the issues were clearer than they had ever been before. Could Zambia (as it was generally becoming known) be welded into a truly non-racial state? That UNIP must form the next government was never in doubt, because it could not fail to capture at least 50 of the 65 lower-roll seats. Interest centred on the showing ANC would make in its Southern Province stronghold and the way Europeans would vote in the 10 reserved seats.

Congress went into the campaign in dire straits, being almost entirely without funds and enduring several important defections—the most important being that of its director of elections, John Banda, who flew secretly out of the country and left behind him a letter revealing that Nkumbula had told him the ANC would be 'lucky if it won seven seats'. At this, such enthusiasm as the party's officials had been able to muster sank to nothing. Just before nomination day, Nkumbula announced a reunion with Michello, but many of the PDC candidates refused to accept this and so in a number of constituencies ANC-PDC candidates found themselves competing against PDC men as well as UNIP.

The UNIP list was a delicately constructed balance between the leadership and 'intellectuals' and the middle-level officials. The latter had to feature prominently in the Assembly to avoid the dangers of disaffection in the rural branches. On the reserved roll, UNIP produced a formidable team, including Sir John Moffat, who had been invited to stand by Kaunda, C. E. Cousins, the former ANC Minister who had crossed over to UNIP, Richard Sampson, ex-mayor of Lusaka, and William Rendall, a former UFP member of the Federal Assembly. The ten also included A. O. R. Mitchley, a lawyer—whose brother, H. E. Mitchley, another lawyer, was standing for the NPP. The NPP fielded politicians whose experience dated back to the middle 1950s, including Roberts, Malcolmson, Burney and Stanley.

The elections were overshadowed by events in East Africa, where a series of army mutinies broke out on the eve of polling. The shock was considerable, for President Nyerere was regarded by Europeans as the 'ideal nationalist', the man upon whom Kaunda had modelled himself. Thus any chance which UNIP might have had of capturing some of the reserved seats vanished. But nonetheless, the party was able to show that it had received more than one third of the European vote and almost all the Asian vote, compared with only one thirtieth of the two together in October 1962.[17] Moffat was beaten by Burney by 121 votes in a poll of 2,363; Cousins and Sampson came equally close to success. The NPP's most emphatic victories were in the Copperbelt towns—a sign of the conservatism among miners of South African origin.

On the main roll, UNIP was unopposed in 24 seats and won 31 others, leaving the ANC with 10. But sobering figures came out of the polling for Kaunda. He had made no inroads at all into the Southern Province; if anything, ANC support was stronger than ever there, with several of the UNIP candidates forfeiting their deposits. Congress was also able to take the Mwinilunga constituency along the Katanga border, although it narrowly lost Mufulira on the Copperbelt—where a few weeks previously it had swept the municipal elections. In the Northern and Luapula Provinces, UNIP had crushing victories wherever ANC stood—and managed to win throughout the Eastern Province, although ANC demonstrated that it still had a significant following there. Overall, Congress had received slightly less than a third of the 826,237 votes cast, despite its poverty and lack of leadership. Even assuming that UNIP would have won easily in the 24 uncontested seats, ANC still had the following of about a fifth of the electorate.

Yet this fact was swamped in the pleasure of the appointment of Zambia's first all-African cabinet, with Kaunda as premier, at the end of January 1964.

V THE REPUBLIC OF ZAMBIA

Kenneth Kaunda became the first Prime Minister on January 23, 1964. His thirteen-man cabinet welded together all the elements in UNIP, and this skill was equally demonstrated in the appointment of parliamentary secretaries. His life-long friend, Kapwepwe, was given the key ministry of Home Affairs and the party's deputy president, Reuben Kamanga, became Minister of Transport and Communications and Deputy Premier. In four ministries the obvious choices were made: Arthur Wina (Finance); Mwanakatwe (Education); Mudenda (Agriculture) and Chona—who had narrowly captured the Livingstone seat—became Minister of Justice. Sikota Wina became Minister of Health, and Solomon Kalulu, UNIP's national chairman, took the portfolio of Land and Works. Sipalo returned to the front as Minister of Natural Resources and the leader of the UNIP Youth League, Dingiswayo Banda, was given the vital subjects of Housing and Social Development. The three other ministers were Mundia (Local Government), Zulu (Commerce and Industry) and Justin Chimba (Labour and Mines). It was very much a cabinet which had been tried in the fires of nationalism, for more than half the ministers had served prison sentences or detention for their political beliefs.[1]

In the Legislative Assembly the new government quickly made an impressive showing. Kaunda had ordered that hard work must be the rule and business was conducted with few of the heady speeches that had marked the achievement of power by nationalists in other African countries. In one sense, the length of the struggle for independence had not been without its rewards, because the Zambians had learned from the errors of people who had trod the path before them. As Kaunda said: 'The pent-up emotions of seventy years of colonialism have to be worked off and it must be understood that the restoration of human dignity is more than a rattling of tea-cups. Yet we are young and invigorated by our sense of purpose.'[2] It was certainly true that the first Zambian cabinet was youthful—its average age was 36. At 39, Kaunda was the youngest Premier in the Commonwealth.

The route by which the country should become the independent Republic of Zambia was already charted. Kaunda had set his sights on independence on October 24, 1964, because it was United Nations Day and also marked the seventh anniversary of the founding of the short-lived Zambia African National Congress. He also sought a constitution which would have an executive President at its head. Britain raised no objections to these proposals and the independence conference was convened in London at the start of May. Representatives of the three political parties attended, general agreement being reached between them on the structure of the republic's constitution. The conference lasted a fortnight and was completed amid expressions of goodwill on all sides. The outline of the constitution is given in Appendix I.

In the three months before the independence celebrations the cabinet was much occupied with two most dissimilar subjects. One was a series of violent clashes between security forces and the followers of Alice Lenshina (Regina) Mulenga, whose Lumpa Church had wide support in the Chinsali, Lundazi, Kasama and Isoka districts.[3] Inevitably, the 'Lenshina troubles', as they became called, attracted world-wide attention and in some measure damaged the image of Zambia's calm and stability.

There had been tension for many months in Chinsali district, where the Lumpa sect had its headquarters at Sione (Zion) village. The origins of this tension are held to be obscure, but they certainly had much to do with attempts by local officials of UNIP to dragoon the sect members into joining a political party and registering as voters.[4] Family feuds also played their part in increasing ill-will. Repeated attempts were made during 1963 by senior UNIP officials from Lusaka to smooth out dissension. Both Kenneth Kaunda and Simon Kapwepwe, who had grown up in Chinsali district, held meetings with Alice Lenshina; Kaunda was particularly concerned to achieve a peaceful settlement, because his mother had been close to the Lumpa sect, and his elder brother Robert was for several years one of Alice's senior 'deacons'. However, spasmodic outbreaks continued. Typical was an affray at a Lumpa prayer-meeting on December 22, 1963, in which a young girl was shot dead with a muzzle-loader. Four men sentenced to death for her murder heard their appeals rejected in the Lusaka High Court on July 31, 1964, at the height of the disturbances.[5]

A serious situation developed in the first half of 1964, when the Lumpa followers began to build stockaded villages from which they harassed surrounding areas. Platoons of the Mobile Unit were drafted to Chinsali; troops followed in July after a white police officer was speared to death when he tried to enter a stockaded village.

Two army battalions were occupied in pursuing 5,000 'hard-core' members of the sect, whose feelings had by this time mounted to one of desperate fanaticism. On July 30, the security forces surrounded Sione and after being attacked fought their way into the church; 74 people died and 40 were wounded. As a reprisal, the Lumpa followers attacked Lundazi township, over-running it, capturing the police station and killing 150 persons before fleeing at dawn. Senga tribesmen wiped out the Lumpa village of Paishuko; there were 46 victims. Although Alice Lenshina herself surrendered on August 11,[6] and was placed in indefinite detention in Mumbwa prison near Lusaka, elements of the sect continued to hide in the Luangwa valley until the end of 1964. Some fled as far as the Congo. In all, the Lenshina troubles cost at least 700 lives; this official estimate was conservative.

A second subject which dominated other events in July-October 1964 was the struggle to regain control of Zambia's mineral rights, held by the British South Africa Company. This reached its climax only a matter of weeks before the date of independence, although it had been apparent for at least two years that an African government would not accept the continued diversion of copper royalties to Chartered. Over the years up to 1963, the company had received more than £160 million gross, £82 million net.

Since 1960, the royalties had been worth more than £6 million net annually, and in an interview given when he became prime minister in January 1964, Kenneth Kaunda described the Chartered position as 'the saddest economic arrangement ever made in this country'.

After the middle of 1963, when the Victoria Falls Conference had made the dissolution of the Federation a certainty, the company had begun approaches to discover what terms the Northern Rhodesia government would concede for taking over the mineral rights.[7] The company simultaneously tried to make itself less unpopular with the African nationalists by assuming a more progressive attitude. Scholarships were offered to students and a loan of £2 million at five per cent interest was made to the Northern Rhodesia government for housing; the late Lord Robins, a warm admirer of Sir Roy Welensky, was replaced as president of the British South Africa Company by a far milder personality, Mr P. V. Emrys-Evans, and a former governor of Uganda, Sir Frederick Crawford, succeeded Lord Malvern as resident director in Salisbury.

Although the African ministers in the 1963 coalition government were resentful of the power exercised by Chartered over the country's natural resources, they had little detailed knowledge of the origins of that power. Questions in the old African Representative Council and in the Legislative Council had always been turned aside by the colonial office administrators with flat statements that the mineral rights were unassailable. Attempts by historians to gain access to documents on the original concessions were always subtly hindered. Consequently, the African ministers accepted assurances that 'buying out' Chartered would cost about £50 million. It did not seem too bad, since under the 1950 agreement the company seemed likely to receive rather more than £130 million by the time the agreement expired in 1986, assuming the 1963 level of royalty payments was maintained. In October 1963, serious negotiations were begun in London at the offices of the territorial government's financial advisers, Warburg and Company. The British government sent an observer to the talks.

Through the financial advisers, the Northern Rhodesia Finance Minister, Mr Trevor Gardner, told Chartered that if they would transfer the mineral rights he would offer 22½ equal tax-free annual payments covering the years up to 1986. These payments would total rather more than £50 million, and be paid in sterling in London free of tax. Even at a discounted 3.6 per cent per annum, the proposal was worth £35 million. But the company hesitated, asking that Britain should guarantee the payments—a demand that was refused. Mr Harry Oppenheimer, who was on the Board of Chartered, then came forward with a scheme by which his own Anglo-American Corporation and Rhodesian Selection Trust should guarantee the payments. Still Chartered was uncertain and the chance slipped away for ever.

After January 1964, when Northern Rhodesia was self-governing, attitudes hardened. Mr Arthur Wina, the new Finance Minister, studied documents which made him decide that the Chartered case was so weak that the amount of compensation should be much lower, if any was justified at all. He retained the services of Maxwell Stamp Associates, a British firm of economic consultants, and a team of lawyers, historians and economists were employed to write a complete history of the mineral rights; they had access to archives which had previously been kept out of reach by the colonial administration.

While the history was being compiled, widespread attention began to be directed to Chartered's position in the future Zambia. Financial journalists in London speculated with fair accuracy that the company was willing to settle for £50 million. In Lusaka, Kenneth Kaunda, the premier, described these speculations as 'blackmail'. He added: 'It must, in fact, never be forgotten that the circumstances under which the British South Africa Company acquired these royalties—and the historical background to this question—places the royalties in Northern Rhodesia outside the normal commercial or industrial activity existing anywhere in the world today.'[8]

By the time of the May independence conference in London, the Zambian cabinet had resolved to avoid any negotiations until it had all the facts at its disposal. These facts would then be published as a White Paper immediately before the negotiations, as a 'softening up' barrage. An astute use of public relations was also swinging much of the British press over to the view that Chartered had done uncommonly well out of the royalties, and should accept whatever it was offered with a good grace. The company, on its part, was becoming alarmed at the uncompromising attitude in Lusaka, and was pressing harder for a settlement.

On May 4, a meeting was held at the offices in London of Warburg and Company. Present were Kenneth Kaunda, Harry Oppenheimer and the representatives of both RST and Chartered. Before any proposals could be made, the premier said that he could not agree to talks until after the Independence conference. The British government then wrote into the Order in Council which created the Zambian constitution a clause protecting the mineral rights, and there the matter rested for two months. Kaunda had said that talks would be held in Lusaka in June, but the company waited in vain for an invitation.[9]

On August 20, Arthur Wina, Zambia's Finance Minister, told the Lusaka parliament that research had now established 'grave doubts' about the legality of the mineral rights.[10] 'All our advice so far indicates that to the extent that the claim is valid at all it derives from legislative and administrative acts of Her Majesty's Government and not from any treaty of concession which would ever have stood up to examination in a court of law.' With only two months to go to Independence, this statement marked out the arena in which the final clash was to take place. From now on, Zambia would pass to Britain the task of finding a solution. If compensation was to be paid, it was Britain which would shoulder the burden. This concept had little appeal for the Conservative administration, harassed enough by a crumbling economic situation and a general election campaign.

Arthur Wina stepped up the pressure on September 11 by asking if he could be received in London for decisive talks. Two dispatches asserted that the British government was entirely to blame for allowing Chartered to receive royalties 'to which it was not legally entitled'. An ultimate warning was added: if there was no settlement before October 24, Zambia would take steps to appropriate the royalties without compensation of any kind. Emrys-Evans, the British South Africa president, was provoked into replying that leading counsel had assured the company that its rights were unassailable; he appealed for 'justice and fair compensation in accordance with fundamental rights which are internationally recognised'.[11]

On September 21, as talks began in London, the government in Lusaka issued its White Paper,[12] a hotly-phrased indictment of British 'deceptions' concerning the royalties for more than four decades. Wina told Lord Dilhorne, the Lord Chancellor, that his delegation was not prepared to meet the Chartered representatives; that was a matter for the British government. However, as a 'show of goodwill', Northern Rhodesia would give Britain £2 million to pass on to the company; not without a certain justification, Lord Dilhorne described this sum as 'derisory'. For its part, the company asked for £15 million. Lord Dilhorne moved between the contending parties, hoping to narrow the gap between them to something which the British Treasury might be persuaded to bridge. He was unsuccessful and the talks expired on September 29. Immediately a Bill was introduced into the Lusaka parliament by Kenneth Kaunda to hold a referendum to alter the constitution so that the mineral rights could be acquired. The company publicly branded the White Paper as 'no more than a propaganda document designed to justify barefaced expropriation'. Arthur Wina distributed a letter to Chartered shareholders saying: 'You have our sympathy and we ask for yours: for the action which we are compelled to take is hurtful and unpleasant. We hope it will not result in permanent harm to the relations between Zambia and Britain.'[13]

A week later, the company lowered its compensation demand to £8 million, and appealed to Northern Rhodesia (which would become the Republic of Zambia in little over a fortnight) for a settlement. The reply was a polite suggestion that this appeal should be addressed to London. The battle had now become a rout. It was pointedly disclosed in Lusaka that machinery for the post-independence referendum was already being put into motion. On October 15, the British general election returned the Labour Party, far less sympathetic to a company like Chartered than the Conservatives had been.

In the last few days before October 24, it had become tacitly understood by all concerned that the company would receive £4 million—£2 million each from Britain and Zambia. Emrys-Evans was officially advised to fly to Lusaka for the Independence celebrations, which were being attended by Arthur Bottomley, the new Secretary of State for Commonwealth Relations. Discussions between the two were held behind a tea-tent at the state garden party on October 23, and in the evening the British South Africa president was called to Government House.[14] There he was given eleven minutes to decide to take the £4 million, even though the British half might be liable to tax. (This was because the Zambian ministers refused to accept the £2 million as a gift and then pass it on to

Chartered, because this would cut across their insistence on Britain's exclusive responsibility.) Emrys-Evans acquiesced and journalists at the Independence Stadium near Lusaka were given the news in an impromptu press conference behind the stand from which guests from forty countries were watching tribal dancing. Three hours later the Zambian flag was raised.

On December 14, 1964, the company formally signed away its mineral rights, with effect from Independence Day, and early in 1965 vacated its offices opposite the Ministry of Finance in Lusaka. It was perhaps fitting that in the final ten months, January-October 1964, the Chartered receipts from royalties were £8.5 million net, a record level.

Despite fears that the forceful method of acquiring the mineral rights might have damaged Zambia's reputation in international business circles, there was no indication of this when President Kaunda made an extensive tour of Europe and America immediately after the Independence celebrations. It was generally recognised that the British South Africa Company was a 'special case' and Kaunda made a point of repeating his promise that Zambia had no intention of nationalising the copper mines. During the tour, he had talks with the heads of the British and United States governments and attended the United Nations with Simon Kapwepwe, who had been made foreign minister in an extensive Cabinet reshuffle at the time of Independence. While Kaunda and Kapwepwe visited western capitals, Mainza Chona, the minister of Home Affairs, and Nalumino Mundia, the minister of Commerce and Industry, went to the Soviet Union and Belgrade.

Zambia adopted a position of careful non-alignment after independence. Diplomats were sent to Moscow as well as Washington; on the basis of populations, Communist China was recognised instead of Taiwan, and West Germany rather than East Germany. As a sign of the new republic's dedication to Pan-Africanism, six diplomatic posts were established on the African continent, in Accra, Lagos, Leopoldville, Cairo, Addis Ababa and Dar es Salaam. The president summed up his attitude: 'It has been my privilege to be chairman of the Pan-African Freedom Movement for East, Central and Southern Africa (PAFMECSA). I look forward to ever closer ties with our neighbours in Tanzania, Malawi and the Congo, and to the fullest participation of Zambia in the councils of the continent. . . . I believe that Africa has a unique place in determining the future of world affairs as long as it keeps clear of power blocs.'[15] Within six weeks of independence, Zambia had to declare itself on the international furore over the Belgian-American landings at Stanleyville to rescue white hostages. Despite a general dislike in Zambia of Moise Tshombe (who had been kept away from the Independence celebrations) Kaunda and Kapwepwe were restrained in their comments and worked behind the scenes to avoid a serious breakdown of relations between the United States and the members of the Organisation for African Unity.

Zambia's role in the political advance of Southern Africa is both vital and delicate. For historical reasons the country is dependent upon Rhodesia and South Africa for outlets through which to export its copper and has always bought the bulk of its imports from these countries. In 1964, out of world imports totalling approximately £70 million, Zambia bought goods worth £15 million from South Africa and £28 million from Rhodesia.[16] Although there was a need to tread warily until new lines of communication (such as the Tanzania rail link) could be established and other sources of supply developed, the Zambian government made no secret of its distaste for this enforced relationship. In December 1964 it was announced that there would be no trade agreement with Rhodesia and at the beginning of 1965 notice was given that the tariff concessions granted to South Africa by the former Federal government would lapse after the obligatory twelve months' notice. Contacts between the Zambian and Rhodesian governments were reduced to a minimum as their policies steadily diverged and there was speculation about the future of such organisations as Central African Airways, Rhodesia Railways and the Kariba hydro-electric scheme, which the two countries administered jointly.

After independence, Lusaka replaced Dar es Salaam as the headquarters for more than a dozen 'liberation movements'. The president warned them that he was not prepared to see Zambia used as a base for military action, but was prepared to give every help in the training of refugees for administrative and technical posts in their own countries. The dangers of intrigue and espionage if 'freedom fighters' congregated in the capital was obvious; strict security precautions were taken. With funds supplied by international groups, an agricultural training centre and secondary school for refugees was started early in 1965 at Mkushi, 150 miles north of Lusaka.

Another danger to the orderly progress of the country to which the government addressed itself soon after independence was the chaotic state of the labour movement. As early as 1960 African trade unions had become the subject of serious internal strife, with the powerful African Mineworkers Union pitted against the new leadership of the United Trade Union Congress following the overthrow of Katilungu in 1961. Matters had been exacerbated in 1962 when United National Independence Party stopped a general strike by the African mineworkers over a pay claim. The United National Independence Party's action was prompted by fears that the strike would disrupt the October general election. Throughout 1963, John Chisata, the union president, found himself in a precarious position, frequently coming under attack from both UNIP officials and his trade union rivals, although he was at the same time a member of the UNIP group in the Legislative Council. After further dissension which threatened to have serious repercussions inside the government itself, Justin Chimba, the Minister of Labour and Mines, ordered Chisata and two other prominent trade-unionists, Jonathan Chivunga and Wilson Chakulya, to give up all connection with the labour movement. When this had been done, a completely new executive of the UTUC was appointed at a meeting chaired by Kapwepwe. By this time, the UTUC had broken its former connection with the International Confederation of Free Trade Unions (ICFTU) and moved closer to the All-African Trade Union Federation (AATUF).

However, other factions appeared and struggles for control of the UTUC became more tortured than ever. In December, the Trade Unions and Trade Disputes (Amendment) Bill passed through parliament, but not without a heated debate between the government and opposition. The Bill enforced the policy of one union for each industry, gave the Minister of Labour and Mines power to veto appointments to office in the Zambia Trade Union Congress, strengthened control of trade union finances, and made the acceptance of funds from outside the country by any trade unionist subject to ministerial approval. It became apparent that in line with the UN/ECA/FAO report's call[17] for wage restraint, the Zambian trade unions would be impelled to devote themselves more to seeking 'fringe benefits' for their members than to pressing for 'European' wages and salaries.

As Zambia began its first full year of independence in 1965, the details of a £35 million transitional capital development plan to last until mid-1966 were announced. President Kaunda described the plan in a New Year message as 'designed to ensure a prosperous future'. It emphasised the strength of Zambia's economy. During 1964, Zambia had a visible trade balance of more than £89 million and manufacturing output rose by 13½ per cent. Mineral output was worth nearly £150 million. Plans were made for a £27.5 million government building program, which was expected to give work to 40,000 more people and so cut urban unemployment by more than half.[18]

Great changes came over social conditions in the first six

months following independence. The last vestiges of racial discrimination were swept away and insults to a person on account of his race or tribe were made a criminal offence.[12] European control of municipal councils was ended and by the beginning of 1965 most towns had African mayors. In the civil service, what was described as 'Zambianisation' had started with the appointment of Africans to senior administrative posts. Through the lack of trained local people, it was clear that non-Zambian technicians would be needed in many sectors for at least two decades, yet the government demonstrated its resolve to overcome the costly dependence on ex-patriates. For 1965, £6 million was set aside for education and nine new secondary schools were opened as the year began; the University of Zambia, designed ultimately to accommodate 5,000 students, was planned to open early in 1966.

The first sentence of the UN/ECA/FAO report released in December 1964 had said: 'The great majority of the people in Zambia are poor, under-educated (if not illiterate) and unhealthy.' But its new leaders were striving to raise the country on to a plane of well-being from which it would be able to take a conspicuous role in the progress of the African continent.

VI THE INTEGRATION OF BAROTSELAND

A delicate problem which faced the Zambian government when it came into power was the complete absorption of Barotseland into an independent state. Historically, the Lozi people had a strong claim to special treatment, but the nationalists had long made it plain that they intended to bring the Litunga (Paramount Chief) down to the same level as other traditional rulers such as Chitimukulu, Mpezeni and Undi. The process by which this was achieved was carried through with some reluctance by the British government and it is likely that the Litunga would have retained far more privileges for his 'protectorate within a protectorate' if he had been more personally popular in Barotseland and had avoided allowing himself to become a pawn in the struggle over Federation.

The source of Barotseland's special position was the Lewanika Treaty of 1900, in which the Paramount Chief was referred to as a king and the British South Africa Company severely limited its own rights in 'Barotseland proper'. When Lord Selborne refused in 1907 to grant Lewanika's request for the protectorate to be entirely removed from Northern Rhodesia and given the same status as Bechuanaland, he nevertheless assured Lewanika that his domain was in direct relationship with the

British Crown and that the Chartered Company was only an 'Instrument'.[1]

Thus the elevation of Barotseland was founded on the need of Rhodes for a concession to secure territory and mineral rights, and in return he and the Imperial power were prepared to concede much in the name of the Queen; afterwards it was important to treat Lewanika and his successor, Yeta, with a sufficient deference to prevent any too noisy repudiation of the terms of the 1900 treaty.

This policy of deference was perpetuated by the Colonial Office administration after 1924. Although the formal sway of the Barotse ruler was much reduced—the limits of Barotseland at no point reaching even to the Kafue river—the excising of Balovale from the protectorate took several years of portentous argument, including repeated meetings between the Governor and the Paramount Chief;[2] the agreement was sealed with a large cash payment. Such respect for the pride of any other tribal ruler in the country would have been improbable.

The *Bledisloe Report* (1938) had pointed out the treaty obligations of the Crown towards Barotseland, and when the Federation was imposed in 1953 these were recognised in the Federal constitution. The Paramount Chief had been persuaded to accept Federation by the Governor, Sir Gilbert Rennie, who had told him that it was 'the Queen's Federation'. This appeal was overwhelming, because the mystique of Barotseland's direct links with the Queen had been fortified over decades in conversations between the Paramount Chief and the administrators.[3] As a reward for this approval, changes were made which appeared to further enhance Barotseland's status.

The PC in Mongu was re-named the resident commissioner, thus underlining the fact that Barotseland was not a province like any other in Northern Rhodesia; if a DC became for some reason *persona non grata* with the Barotse Royal Family, he was always removed. In this old-world atmosphere the hierarchy of the Lozis grew more powerful, with *indunas* related to the ruler in control of the numerous sub-tribes within the Barotse borders.

On three occasions between 1945 and 1950 the British government had given assurances that 'no constitutional changes affecting Barotseland would be made without full consultation with, and the prior consent of, the Paramount Chief'. A similar assurance was given by the Colonial Secretary, Lennox-Boyd, in 1958. In 1959, the Paramount Chief was knighted, the first (and last) non-European in Central Africa to receive this honour. However, Sir Mwanawina Lewanika was not deceived into imagining that his position was impregnable and that the political struggle in Central Africa could be kept outside his borders indefinitely. When the Governor, Sir Evelyn Hone went to his winter capital, Limalunga, in May 1959, to present him with the insignia of knighthood, Sir Mwanawina took the opportunity to say: 'We are quite confident that in spite of the European settlers' clamour for dominion status and responsible government, Her Majesty's government will continue to safeguard and preserve its treaty obligations to the Barotse nation and will not be persuaded to hand us over to independent settler governments in the Federation.'[4] Two months earlier, the former Administrative Secretary to the Barotse native government, K. Mulonda, had been elected to the Legislative Council and wasted no time in pressing home the fact that he spoke on behalf of the Paramount Chief and had been allowed to represent Barotseland only on condition that no law passed by the legislature could be allowed to apply in the protectorate if it clashed with any agreements or treaties.[5] Mulonda showed strong pro-nationalist sympathies, however, introducing motions that called for an African majority and the break-up of the Federation.

Paradoxically, the reduction of Mulonda's influence could be traced to the rise of the nationalists in Northern Rhodesia; among their leaders were several educated and iconoclastic Lozis, such as Sipalo, Mundia and the Wina brothers. In the endless intriguing (seasoned on occasion with ritual murder) which had always gone on around the Barotse establishment, there was ample opportunity for the politicians to encourage disaffection. One fertile soil for the seeds of revolt was the alleged murder of the son of the previous ruler; another was a complex dispute in the 1940s, which had produced the dismissal of Ngambela (prime minister) Wina, father of the two nationalists; a third was the charge that Sir Mwanawina was trying to bestow favours on his son SiiSii, against the wishes of the people.[6] Under this new pressure, the Paramount Chief turned more and more to his relative, Godwin (Mbikusita) Lewanika, who by this time had risen to be a junior minister in the Federal government. Lewanika's argument was that Barotseland must secede completely from Northern Rhodesia while time remained. This was a return to the ideas at the start of the century, but although it had great romantic appeal it ignored several realities: the country was land-locked and poverty-stricken, needing help from Northern Rhodesia of around £250,000 a year merely to keep it on a 'care and maintenance' basis. The colonial administration's refusal to allow the use of forced labour to clear the drainage canals on the Barotse Plain had caused increased flooding, smaller crops and recurrent famine among a rising population; without the unlikely discovery of minerals, Barotseland would have to live on charity from somewhere for ever. However, upon Lewanika's advice, Sir Mwanawina decided to make his stand, and the first indication came in the Legislative Council in November 1960 when the *Monckton Report* was being debated. Burney (UFP) was attacking the principle of secession and suggested that the Paramount Chief of the Barotse might say he did not want to stay in a separate Northern Rhodesia. The Chief Secretary, Wray, interjected : 'He has said that already.'[7]

It was perhaps the most calamitous interjection ever made in the Legislative Council. Newspapers and politicians seized on it, and although Wray tried to withdraw it later, the damage was done. In Lusaka a meeting of the Barotse National Society, to which most urban Lozis belonged, ended in uproar after a row between Nalumino Mundia and Franklin, who had attended because his constituency covered Barotseland.[8] A new organisation, the Barotse Anti-Secession Movement (BASMO) was formed under the umbrella of UNIP and began to agitate against Sir Mwanawina both in the protectorate and along the line-of-rail. If anything, this served to confirm Godwin Lewanika's claim that the nationalists could not be negotiated with. When a strongly traditionalist Barotse delegation went to London in April 1961 it repeated the demands for secession; the Ngambela Imasiku told the Colonial Secretary, Iain Macleod, that the Paramount Chief, the Barotse native government and the people were unanimous in demanding a separate state. Macleod rejected this demand, but gave reassurances that Britain recognised the protectorate's special status and as a sop agreed that Sir Mwanawina should in future officially be known by the honorific title 'Litunga'.[9]

As the struggle over Federation became more intense, Barotseland began to assume a new role. In Salisbury it became apparent that the Litunga could be used against the nationalists, if his full support could be fully obtained. Thus in February 1962 a bold *coup* was attempted when Duncan Sandys, the Secretary of State for Commonwealth Relations, was visiting the Federation. He was invited by Godwin Lewanika to make a trip to Barotseland and flew down secretly from Salisbury in a Royal Rhodesian Air Force plane.[10] This was done over the head of the Governor and the Colonial Secretary, Macleod. While he was there, Sandys was given a document signed by the Litunga and his most senior advisers, calling for a separate Barotseland 'within the Federation'. Godwin Lewanika had foreshadowed this development during a speech in London three weeks earlier when he suggested that

Northern Rhodesia could become a 'federation within a federation'. The trip by Sandys created an uproar and civil servants from Lusaka flew hurriedly to Barotseland to restore the indeterminate *status quo*. The effect was to further isolate the Litunga and to make UNIP's victory in Barotseland easier in October 1962.

The next round came when it was announced that the Federation would be dissolved in 1963. Once again the Litunga and his *indunas* pressed for secession—a demand which Godwin Lewanika had already been making in London to Butler.[11] However, UNIP had just won all twenty-five elected seats in the Barotse National Council and dominated the coalition government, so that it was in a much stronger position to influence the British government.

With the assistance of lawyers from Salisbury, the Barotse native government produced a memorandum for submission to Butler which put forward a new line:[12] there was no question of Barotseland seceding from Northern Rhodesia, but only of reinstatement, because it had existed as a well-defined state long before Northern Rhodesia had done so. The Litunga's lawyers then went on to define the historic boundaries of the Barotse state—extending them right up to the Kafue river from its source to the confluence with the Zambezi. This included, incidentally, the two biggest Anglo American mines of Kitwe and Nchanga. The memorandum asserted that Northern Rhodesia was a 'new state' and Britain could not transfer her rights and obligations in Barotseland to her any more than she could to Germany, Portugal or Belgium.

The dispute was pressing, because the next elections would give Northern Rhodesia complete self-government as a prelude to Zambian independence. The elections could not be held in Barotseland as well as the rest of the territory unless the Litunga agreed. In September a conference was held at the Victoria Falls under the chairmanship of Sir Colville Deverell, sent out by the British government. Little was acheived, the *indunas* arguing again and again from Britain's many promises and the long associations between the monarchs of the imperial power and the protectorate. But agreement to the holding of the election was extracted and in January 1964 UNIP was able once again to prove its popular support in the protectorate.

The inevitable solution was reached in April 1964, when provisional agreement was signed in Lusaka. It was ratified in London after the Zambia independence talks—although not without some strained feelings because the British government had wanted to invite the Litunga to take part in the conference; the nationalists, afraid that Sir Mwanawina might create a last-minute obstacle, successfully defied this proposal. The agreement terminated all obligations between the British government and Barotseland and ruled that Britain would cease to retain any responsibility for the protectorate.[13] The last ties of the 'special relationship' had been cut and Barotseland was irrevocably part of Zambia. The Litunga retained certain traditional powers over land, and little else. Under 'financial responsibility' the agreement promised that Barotseland would be treated 'fairly and equitably in relation to other parts of the Republic'. With the Barotses powerfully represented in the Zambia cabinet it was sure to be the case; the feudal backwater was expected to see more development during the next decade than in the whole colonial era.

It appeared in November 1964 that the final step had been taken for the complete integration of Barotseland when Hastings Noyoo, a member of UNIP, was elected by the National Council to be the new Ngambela. The post had been vacant since the previous incumbent, Siyubo, had been forced by political pressure to resign early in the year. However, the Litunga showed reluctance to accept Ngambela Noyoo despite visits to Barotseland by several government leaders, including the Vice-President Kamanga. The installation of the Ngambela with the traditional ceremonies (which included total immersion in the Zambezi) was postponed on the ground that the moon was in the wrong position. Only after Sikota Wina, Minister of Local Government, had warned Sir Mwanawina that the central government was preparing to rule Barotseland by decree did the installation take place on December 19, 1964.

Then in March, 1965, the new relationship was underlined when President Kaunda and almost his entire cabinet went to Lealui for the annual *kuomboka* cermony, in which the Litunga moves to his winter capital at Limulunga. In colonial days, Governors had often attended the cermony. Relations between the President and the tribal ruler appeared cordial and much stress was laid upon the aid Barotseland would receive from Zambia's transitional development plan.

VII ZAMBIA'S EDUCATIONAL NEEDS

In the Zambia of 1965, the shortage of educated and trained personnel, particularly for posts in the civil service, and in quasi-government operations, reached near-crisis proportions. The causes were clearly to be seen in educational policy during the two previous decades and in the very short period during which expenditure on educational services had come anywhere near the task of providing a feasible minimum standard. The initial aim of the government was to provide four years of primary education for as many school-children as possible. Although by 1963 this goal had still not been fully achieved, education did nonetheless account for a gradual increasing proportion of public expenditure.[1]

During the period 1947–56 a ten-year plan for African education was put into effect. The plan was stated to be complete two years ahead of schedule. Its main objectives were 'to consolidate and improve the lower primary school system, to expand and improve the upper primary school system, to develop secondary education on sound lines, to initiate technical education and community development and adult education schemes, to increase the supply of well-trained teachers, to expand and improve the education of girls and adult women, and to develop the system of community service camps and character-building generally.' This was the statement of the triennial survey of the Department of African Education for 1955–7.

It also identified the main object, which was to 'ensure that as many children as possible not only started but completed the four-year lower primary course, which, in the immediate post-war years, was considered to be a minimum course of education necessary for permanent literacy and maximum social adjustment.' In 1946, 11,645 children had completed the course, stated to be eighty per cent of those taking it.

With the advent of Federation, responsibility for European education had passed to Federal government from January 1954. African Education was made subject to a fresh plan in 1955 with the avowed aim of achieving 'universal full primary education . . . in both rural and urban areas'. This plan was thwarted by the fall in prices of copper and in government revenue. But so far as the Copperbelt and Broken Hill areas were concerned, the two copper groups (by creating the Northern Rhodesia Educational Trust) permitted educational expansion to continue to the point where nearly all children received education up to standard four, and ensured that upper primary and secondary schools were more plentiful than elsewhere.

By 1963 the situation had been reached where most African children were probably getting a minimum of four years schooling. It is impossible to be precise, because it was in 1963 that the first serious census of the African population was held. This showed that the African population was around 3.5 million—some 40 per cent higher than had been estimated; more than 50 per cent were under 21 years of age. Following the census the urgent need to again expand primary school facilities came into focus. Far more serious however were three other aspects of the educational system :

1. The system is tapered to such an extent that numbers completing more than six years of education are relatively negligible; secondary, technical and university facilities cannot be fully utilised because of lack of pupils with adequate preparation.
2. The great bulk of the adult population remains illiterate or semi-literate.
3. Illiteracy among women is vastly greater than among men.

A crash program was vital and inevitable, and as Education Minister John Mwanakatwe pointed out in March 1965, Zambia's expansion in this field would be virtually unparalleled in Africa. Nevertheless the highly qualified finished product would not emerge until the 1970s. The past omissions of the educational system had given rise to a manpower problem of imponderable dimensions. When it became apparent in the middle of 1965 that development and administration were endangered, urgent attempts were made to attract skilled Europeans to the country on two-year contracts.

8

The Copperbelt

I THE ANCIENT MINERS

IT is not known for how many centuries the people of Zambia have mined and smelted copper. At the settlement of Ngombe Ilede near Kariba, copper crosses and tools for making wire and ornaments have been found, dating from the first millennium; the crosses came either from the mines of Lomagundi district in what is now Southern Rhodesia, or from the Lualaba region. Within Zambia itself, mining certainly dates back to the beginning of the nineteenth century and archaeological work is likely to prove it began much earlier.

The Portuguese half-castes, Baptista and José, noted that in 1802 in Katanga, 'natives dig the copper; in the midst of this country is where they make the bars.'[1] Several years earlier the Lacerda expedition to Mwata Kazembe had seen copper bars being exchanged for cloth in the Luapula Valley and since Kazembe controlled the Congo-Kafue watershed, there is no doubt that the metal came from that area. When the slight clues are exhausted, it is necessary to fall back on generalisations, such as that by Dr J. Austen Bancroft, a distinguished geologist: 'The approximate date in the dim and mysterious African past when the earliest of their workings for copper were exploited is not known, but it seems reasonable to believe that, for many centuries before they had seen Europeans, Africans were engaged in searching for copper deposits and in the opening up of their best finds to shallow depths.'[2]

The biggest pre-European mining area in Zambia was at Kansanshi, 100 miles west of the modern Copperbelt, where digging for malachite 'greenstone' covered an area five miles across. When Kansanshi was 'discovered' at the turn of the century by George

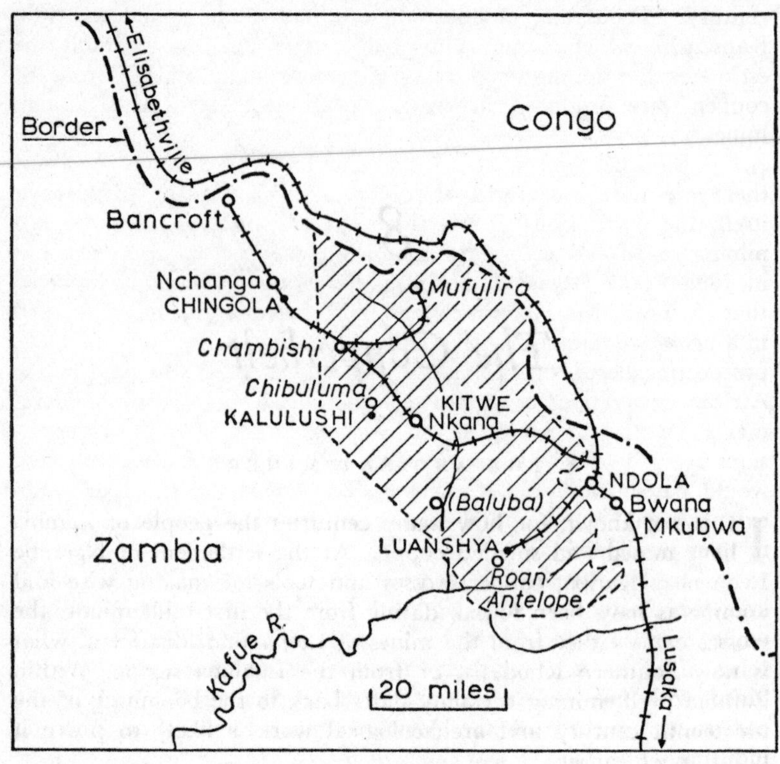

3. *The Copperbelt*

Mines belonging to the Anglo-American group Nchanga
Mines belonging to the Roan Selection Trust group *Chibuluma*
Defunct or dormant mines (Baluba)
Townships CHINGOLA
Shaded area is that of the original Nkana concession

Grey's expedition, there was amazement among the white prospectors at the size of the shafts and trenches on and around Kansanshi Hill.[3] For this reason, it was often argued that the Africans had not worked the mine on their own initiative, but under the whips of Arab slave-traders. Yet William White, who visited Kansanshi in 1901, recalls that 'there were even large trees growing out of some of the shafts and diggings, indicating that they had been worked possibly 100 years or more before'.[4] Quite apart from the evidence of early Portuguese travellers, White's statement indicates that the remarkable excavations at Kansanshi pre-dated the incursions of the Arabs or Yeke in the middle of the nineteenth century. 'Thousands of tons' of ore had been excavated from Kansanshi, which is not improbable after bearing in mind the estimates by mining engineers that more than 100,000 tons of copper were produced in pre-European days from the Katanga mines.[5]

Elsewhere, in parts of the country where outcrops occur, there are numerous signs of 'old workings'. On the Copperbelt itself, the convulsions of the slave trade appear to have brought mining to an end before the first white prospectors appeared, but in 1898 Frank Lewis of the Northern Copper Company reported that in the Kafue Hook 'some of the mines are still being worked in a primitive manner by the natives'.[6] In the 1920s, when intensive prospecting began on the Copperbelt, close regard was paid to the African excavations as guides to mineralisation. Dr Bancroft comments: 'Today many of the old workings are such shallow depressions overgrown with trees and other vegetation that the uninitiated would pay no attention to them, while others are so superficially extensive that one wonders how many individuals were employed in their development.'[7]

In recent years, old men have been found with some residual knowledge of copper smelting, and they have been put on display while exercising their craft. They are no more than a curiosity, relics of a past age, yet their memories of childhood can be combined with eye-witness accounts from earlier in this century to construct a picture of the African copper mining and smelting industry.[8] The mining was done in the dry season (April-October) when there was time to spare from farming. Before the work began, the tribal ruler prayed to the spirits of former chiefs: 'You have preceded us; it is you who have opened the inside of the mountain for your children; grant us the favour of finding treasure there.' Then with the spiritual adviser and the master-smelter (the 'copper eater'), the chief would lead the miners and their families to the outcrop. There, the men would start digging with their picks, either extending a mine worked in previous years or starting a new one where the malachite or azurite was visible on the surface. The main shafts might go down as far as 100 feet and were timbered if they looked like falling in. Crosscuts of up to 60 feet were driven off from the main shaft, following the seams of ore.

Straw was burnt to provide light underground, and if a section of the ore body rock was too hard to break with picks it was cracked by making a fire on it. Most of the workers down the mine were women, who passed the baskets of ore and waste rock to the surface while standing on ladders. Sometimes ore was hauled to the surface in bark buckets on long ropes. At the surface, ore was hand-sorted by women and children, and usually washed in a near-by river before being taken to be smelted. The smelter (*umu-fushi*) was the master craftsman, whose knowledge was surrounded by mystery and taboos; he might not, for instance, have intercourse with his wife the night before smelting, otherwise the metal would fail to harden.[9] After a good supply of malachite had been prepared and smelting was about to begin, an area was cleared near a stream or river. The secrets of smelting were usually passed down the tribe in one clan, and much ritual was associated with the work.

The first task was the cutting of wood of the common mubanga tree (*Afrormosia angolensis*). The hard and close-textured mubanga was chosen because of its excellent charcoal. With due ceremony the wood was burnt and after three days the charcoal was ready. Then in the open space by a stream, the smelter bathed his hands and face in a concoction of bark made by a local witch-doctor, and was ready to begin. He would select spaces about a yard square on the ground for the furnaces, and in the centre of each space make a shallow hole to receive the molten metal. On the open ground the smelter next spread a layer of charcoal and then carefully piled up dry wood to a height of two or three feet. The furnace was made around this pile, from anthill earth propped up with sticks. Building the furnaces was regarded as secret work so was done by the smelter alone.

Into the bottom of each furnace were inserted *tuyères* (blast pipes) made of clay pierced with iron rods. Through the pipes were pushed tubes of green wood, and on to the tubes were fixed hand bellows made of antelope skin.

When all was ready, the people gathered around, prayers were said and the spiritual counsellor performed his ritual with bark and herbs. Then the fires were lit. As the flames shot out, the malachite charge was poured in, the pieces being no bigger than a man's thumb. In each furnace as much as 100 lb. of ore was piled up, to produce perhaps 30 lb. of metal. As the men worked the bellows, crouching naked around the hot furnaces, people would sing. Soon the flames coming from the top of the furnaces changed colour, first to green, then gold. After an hour or more, the copper would start to run, either into the hollows in the furnace centres, or out through air-holes, depending on the type of furnace.

At a signal from the 'copper-eater', young men went forward and broke open the furnaces, pushing aside clay and ashes to lay bare the molten metal. This was a moment of supreme excitement for the onlookers. 'It is a manifestation of the power of the spirits of the mountain, evoked by their chief, that touch the stones and draw from them that precious liquid, the water of copper.'[10] When the copper solidified it was taken back to the village and next day broken up for refining in other furnaces set under the trees. A refining furnace had within it the bottom part of an earthenware pot which served as a crucible. The metal was fused with charcoal and when the pot was full of molten metal the furnace was demolished. Close to the furnace stood the moulds, made of ant-hill clay or of soapstone (*steatite*). His hands protected by wet rags, the metallurgist would pick up the pot of molten metal and fill up the moulds. The malachite won from the hills of Zambia had been painstakingly translated into metal of high purity. 'Both intelligence and skill were displayed by those who evolved their methods of smelting', commented Dr Bancroft.

The African smelters cast their output into two main forms, bars and crosses. The bars were passed to the smiths for turning into ornaments, wire, bullets and hoes. The crosses were used as currency throughout Central Africa and varied in size from 3 ft long and 100 lb., to 1 ft long and about 20 lb. weight. For the biggest crosses a beautiful girl could be bought. A man was worth less. For their labours, the smelters and miners each received a fifth of the output. The rest went to the village headman and the chief.

II THE ELUSIVE ORE-BODIES

One hundred years ago, the world's annual production of copper was less than 100,000 tons. Fifty years later it reached 1,000,000 tons and today it is more than 4,000,000 tons.[1] Although the existence of copper north of the Zambezi was known in 1890 when the British South Africa Company began its penetration of the region, this was only interesting in so far as it might indicate the presence of more desirable minerals. The goldfields of Matabeleland had proved disappointing and Northern Zambezia was looked to to restore the Chartered Company's waning fortunes. Cecil Rhodes was also anxious that gold should be found along the route of his projected railway to Lake Tanganyika, so that the line could help to produce profits as it moved forward.[2]

It was for these reasons that Rhodesia Concessions Ltd, which was closely linked to the Chartered Company (and incidentally had the author Rider Haggard on its board) sent two prospectors into the Muchinga Mountains from Nyasaland in 1895;[3] David Livingstone's much quoted remark that there was gold in the Muchingas had started a trail which was to prove false and expensive. In 1897 another gold-seeking expedition was sent to the Muchingas under the leadership of Frank Smitheman: finding nothing, it moved west to the Irumi Mountains near Mkushi and built Fort Elwes as its headquarters. The gold remained illusory. One of the prospectors was William Selkirk, who years later became managing director of Roan Antelope and vice chairman of Selection Trust; he died in 1961. Selkirk with others of the party journeyed down to Bulawayo in 1899 (missing the Copperbelt area completely) and afterwards declared : 'The Katanga will be tapped for its gold and copper.'[4]

Although he could not have known it, African produced copper had earlier been exported to Angola not for itself, but for its gold content.

Further expeditions were sent from the south into Northern Zambezia around the turn of the century by Robert Williams' Tanganyika Concessions and by a group of companies controlled by Edmund Davis, the financier, which were ultimately consolidated as the Rhodesian Copper Company.[5] With instructions from Davis, two prospectors called Frank Lewis and Orlando Baragwanath pegged five mines in the Kafue Hook before 1900, and also located an outcrop on the site of the present Nchanga mine.[6] They also reached the vicinity of Kansanshi. As a result of their prospecting in the Hook, Lewis and Baragwanath started work on two copper occurrences given the names Silver King and Sable Antelope; in the Silver King, at 52ft, a pocket of ore averaging 48 per cent metal was located, although the promise was not sustained. Both of these mines were short-lived, the Sable Antelope finally closing down during the First World war; yet they have the remote distinction of being the first copper properties developed by Europeans in Northern Rhodesia. It is worth mentioning that that in the area there were seventy 'ancient workings', one of the pits being 40 ft deep and 50 ft across.[7]

By 1900, Rhodes and his associates were somewhat reluctantly being forced to the conclusion that another Witwatersrand was not likely to be found north of the Zambezi and that they should concentrate their efforts on locating base metals. They were encouraged in this reappraisal by a rise in prices; copper had gone up to nearly £77 a ton in 1899, a climb of 25 per cent in two years.[8] In 1901, Davis sent an experienced mining engineer, Thomas Davey, an Australian like himself, northwards to direct the operations of Lewis and Baragwanath; using the mines at the Hook as a base, Davey went eastward at the start of 1902 to look for 'certain old workings' he had been told about. It was the height of the rains, and Davey's guide became lost. In their wanderings Davey noticed a steep hill which aroused his curiosity. He climbed up in the dusk and quickly realised that it was heavily mineralised.

This was the discovery of the Broken Hill lead mine, which Davey named after a major property he had known in Australia.[9] By 1906, Broken Hill was starting operations and had become the railhead for the route from the south. Thus it was zinc and not gold which offered justification for continuing the railway across the Zambezi, and but for Davey's discovery in 1902 the line would probably have been routed through the prospects operated by Lewis and Baragwanath near Mumbwa.

Among the large corps of prospectors responsible to the Rhodesia Copper Company were William Collier and Jock Donohoe, who in 1902 pegged the surface indications of Roan Antelope mine, an incident which has become a legend in the history of the Copperbelt.[10]

After being thwarted in his enquiries for 'native workings' by Chiwala, a Swahili slave-dealer who had settled in Lamba country,[11] Collier noticed the tell-tale green copper stain on a rock where he had shot a buck.

Roan Antelope was further pegged by a prospector called Poingdestre in 1904, but no development took place for another twenty years. Of more immediate interest to the early copper exploiters was Bwana Mkubwa (near Ndola) which was shown to Collier and Donohoe by a trader named Robert Wright in 1902.[12] Bwana Mkubwa had been the scene of very extensive African mining. There were two parallel excavations, one nearly half a mile long and 160 ft deep in one place. Vast amounts of high-grade ore had been excavated at Bwana Mkubwa and smelted beside a nearby *dambo*.

All the copper prospecting so far described had been done on the initiative of Edmund Davis. The Tanganyika Concessions Company controlled by Robert Williams was active meanwhile along the Kafue-Congo watershed and farther north in Katanga itself. In 1899, Williams sent George Grey (later killed by a lion in Kenya) to the headwaters of the Kafue to search for copper deposits and gold.[13] Grey travelled through Kaondeland and ten miles from the Rhodesian-Congo border made contact with a minor chief called Kapiji Mpanga, who showed him the Kansanshi mine.[14] Kapiji Mpanga, who was still living thirty years ago at the age of about eighty, told Grey that his people collected malachite from Kansanshi and smelted it, but quite obviously the Kaonde were not the ones who had made the great excavations there. Kansanshi was to have a tantalising career for the next sixty years, its development coming to a sudden halt in October 1957 because of flooding.[15] Yet it was Northern Rhodesia's biggest copper mine in the first decade of this century and by 1910 more than 1,500 tons of copper extracted from comparatively rich oxide ores had been exported. Kansanshi was, moreover, important as the headquarters from which the Tanganyika Concessions Company prospectors made their copper discoveries in Katanga under an agreement between Robert Williams and King Leopold. These discoveries were, indirectly, the salvation of the financially desperate British South Africa Company. Without the early development of Katanga's fabulous oxide deposits, the link-up between the Rhodesian railway and the Belgian Congo would never have taken place and the Chartered Company must have gone into liquidation.[16] Perhaps fittingly, the Company was rescued through its monopoly of rail traffic to a mineralised region where its agents had been narrowly forestalled in the previous decade.

By 1905, the term 'Copper Belt' was already in use to describe the mineral occurrences of Northern Rhodesia,[17] yet interest was beginning to evaporate. The price of copper fell, because of mass production in America of copper from porphyry, or 'disseminated deposit' mines, on a scale never contemplated before.[18] This technique involved excavating vast tonnages of ground, generally by block caving or opencast methods, instead of following high-grade veins in the time-honoured way.

By 1906 the United States was turning out most of the world's copper needs. Katanga's unparalleled oxides, despite difficulties of treatment, remained viable in the face of this new development, but the lower-grade Northern Rhodesian occurrences, far from the centre of fabrication, quickly proved uneconomic. The vast sulphide ore-bodies of the Copperbelt had not at this time been identified, so that the flotation methods invented in 1911 for treating sulphides found no immediate application in Central Africa.

By 1914, serious copper production in the country had come to an end. Kansanshi closed down after producing 2,500 tons of metal, and the mines in the Hook became ineffectual small-workings. At Bwana Mkubwa, production began in 1913 and stopped a year later, then was renewed unprofitably for a further two years.[19] The discovery of the Nkana outcrop in 1910 by a native commissioner named Moffat Thomson aroused no interest whatsoever,[20] and William Collier's claims at Roan Antelope were almost entirely forgotten. The railway kept busy, moving machinery and coal from the Wankie Colliery to the Katanga mines and bringing out concentrates to Beira (the Lobito Bay line linking Katanga to the Atlantic through Angola was not opened until 1931). But the only Northern Rhodesian mine which looked at all promising was Broken Hill. This produced 14,700 tons of lead by the end of the first world war.

Then, within the next four years, interest in the Zambian copper deposits began to revive. On June 8, 1922, the British South Africa Company issued Government Notice No. 73. This closed to prospecting and pegging an area of 1,800 square miles along the Congo border to the north-west of Ndola. The area was to become known as the 'Nkana Concession' and its boundaries embraced Nkana, Mufulira, Roan Antelope, Chibuluma and Chambeshi.

III PROSPECTORS AND FINANCIERS

Throughout the years 1910–20 there was a consistent pessimism in the annual reports of the Department of Mines in Livingstone.[1] The country as a whole was in a lack-lustre condition epitomised by a remark in the Department of Mines Report for 1914: this said that 12,500 tons of copper matte had been taken to the railway station from Sable Antelope—'after lying at the mine for some years'. During the years 1914–18, the 1,500 Europeans in the country were devoting their attention to the slightly comic-opera war with the Germans in Tanganyika, either by serving at the ill-defined front or by growing food for the troops. In 1921, the Secretary for Mines was still devoting most of his report to minor gold prospects in the Petauke-Fort Jameson area, and complaining: 'I regret that I am unable to report any increasing activity in mining during the past year and until the conditions of the Law and Prospecting Licence are modified and made more attractive it is unlikely that any development will take place.' Behind this statement was a growing realisation that mineral resources would never be exploited if the country was left open to small-time searching and pegging. Yet to grant exclusive concessions to big companies, who could devote vast sums to exploratory work, meant facing the charge of 'locking up the country for monopolies'.

In 1922, the problem was again raised in the Department of Mines Report, by the Acting-Secretary; he was Moffat Thomson, who twelve years earlier had been shown the Nkana outcrop by the local chief. Thomson pointed out that because of the lack of mining development there were no jobs for the African population, which was in a desperate plight because of poor harvests. Men were offering to work for seven shillings a month—a bargain for prospecting companies, if they were given the right inducements to come in.

In fact, they were coming. Not surprisingly, the newcomers were Americans, because the United States had in the first two decades of the century asserted technical and financial supremacy in the world of copper.[2] The initiative came from consulting engineer Chester Beatty, who although he had taken out British citizenship in 1913, was still closely connected with leading American mining corporations. Associated with him was Preston K. Horner, who in 1912 had become Director-General of Union Minière in the Congo.[3] In 1920, a company called Selection Trust (formed some years earlier by Beatty) bought an interest in the dormant Bwana Mkubwa mine, which Horner argued had great potential. Late in 1921, another company called Copper Ventures was floated with a capital of £5,000. The primary intention at that time was to treat the oxide ores at Bwana by a new process which Copper Ventures had bought and which later proved a failure. Horner had also suggested, however, a wider investigation of copper deposits in Northern Rhodesia.[4]

As a step in this direction, Copper Ventures obtained an option on claims at Nkana. Since 1918, a miner called William Lee had been digging at Nkana on two blocks he had bought for £100 from Eli and Harry Susman of Livingstone.[5] In 1920 Lee sold out to Colonel James Donaldson and Edward Sievwright in Johannesburg, and kept working on the prospect for them. The way in which Copper Ventures obtained its crucial option on Nkana has been variously described.

One account is that a Mr J. H. Curle, hearing that Donaldson and Sievwright wanted to sell, obtained the option and passed it on to Minerals Separation Corporation in America, who passed it to Minerals Separation, London, who passed it to Copper Ventures.[6] Another version is that Gordon James, an English engineer and big game hunter, was recovering from sleeping sickness in Broken Hill hospital and heard the miner William Lee telling his wife in the next cubicle how promising the Nkana claims looked. Taking this hint, James acquired the option on behalf of Beatty, after reluctantly agreeing that should the option be exercised, the price would be £35,000.[7] Whatever the facts, by early 1922, Copper Ventures had a firm basis for expanding their activities in Northern Rhodesia and so began negotiating with the British South Africa Company for a major concession.

In December 1922, Copper Ventures were granted exclusive rights in an area entitled the Rhodesian Congo Border Concession, which covered 50,000 square miles running from nearly 100 miles east of Broken Hill to the Angola boundary. It also obtained prospecting rights in the Nkana Concession, which covered 1,800 square miles and embraced the sites of three of today's major producers—Nkana, Roan Antelope and Mufulira.[8] Before the end of the year, Chester Beatty had hired from Union

Minière a distinguished American mining engineer, Raymond Brooks, to be general manager for Copper Ventures in Northern Rhodesia.[9] The moment which was to transform the territory was at hand.

In an area where sleeping sickness and malaria were endemic, Brooks was faced with a pioneering task into which he flung himself with tremendous energy.[10] At first he operated from a marquee near the Ndola boma, and picked his prospectors by the simple expedient of asking them to identify mineral specimens.

After organising his labour force, Brooks developed the road system on the Copperbelt, set up a headquarters in Nkana and started a drilling program there. By modern standards his methods were primitive, but they produced results. The prospectors were sent out in pairs, each with a gang of twenty Africans, one of whom pushed a measuring wheel, equipped with a bicycle cyclometer.[11] Every week the prospecting teams sent back maps and reports and samples to headquarters. Another fruitful method of finding outcrops was equipping local villagers with four-pound hammers and telling them to knock lumps off any rocks they could find. Brooks offered a prize of £5 to anyone who brought in specimens showing copper staining.

Within nine months, Brooks was able to report the discovery of a large oxide ore-body at Nchanga, destined to become the second richest copper mine in the world.[12] The ore-body was uncovered in October 1923 by driving a trench through a swamp, and the man in charge of the work was the same William Collier who had pegged the Roan Antelope outcrop twenty-one years before. In June of the same year, two other prospectors had found copper outcrops which were to become Mufulira, now the vast Rhodesian Selection Trust* property. The outcrop of Bancroft was also found early in 1924.[13] However, before Brooks was able to prove the value of these and several other discoveries, difficulties began to arise in London. Chester Beatty and his associates were finding the vast operations in progress too expensive to carry.[14] Efforts to induce other mining organisations, particularly the big American corporations, to put up money met with little success.

On February 26, 1924, Copper Ventures sold its rights in the Nkana Concession to the Bwana Mkubwa Mining Company for £60,000, and 517,000 fully paid shares of five shillings each.[15] This was to prove a costly deal, because Copper Ventures and ultimately Rhodesian Selection Trust thereby lost its chance of owning the whole Copperbelt. Twelve days before the deal, Sir

---

* Renamed in 1965, Roan Selection Trust.

Ernest Oppenheimer's Anglo American Corporation of South Africa had bought 100,000 Bwana Mkubwa shares; the impending struggle for control was casting its shadow before. Holding a central position in the financial manoeuvres was Sir Edmund Davis, 'father figure' of Rhodesian mining, who twenty-four years earlier had developed the Broken Hill mine and Wankie Colliery.[16] Davis was by this time in his seventies, but his mind was as subtle and devious as ever.

There have been considerable differences of emphasis in later interpretations of the financial dealings between the two principal Copperbelt groups. Bradley, writing on behalf of Rhodesian Selection Trust,[17] has declared that Beatty introduced Edmund Davis to Oppenheimer to assist him 'on the technical side of the operations' of the Rhodesian Congo Border Concessions and that Beatty had 'recommended' Davis to acquire the Nkana Concession. Bradley also asserted that 'so far as Mr Beatty's enterprises on the Copperbelt were concerned, there has never been any struggle for control between the British and the American interests'. This version has lately been flatly contradicted by Sir Theodore Gregory, in his definitive account of Oppenheimer's career.[18] Gregory makes it plain that there was, in fact, a sometimes frantic tug-of-war between those who wanted the Copperbelt to remain an 'Imperial sphere' and the opposing 'pro-American' group.

Had Beatty been able to hold out a little longer, until the Copperbelt ore-bodies had been proved beyond doubt, American financial interests would have gained control of the whole of the Copperbelt. Raymond Brooks, born in Chicago and educated at Princeton, later drily remarked: 'None of the three major American mining groups sent engineers to report on what was being done in Northern Rhodesia. They showed no curiosity or interest whatever, even though one of them had been invited to subscribe to the exploration undertaking in 1924 and had been informally and accurately advised about progress and expectations as developments proceeded. This has long been one of the enigmas of the copper mining business. . . . One prominent American mining company did send representatives to London in 1928 to try to secure control of the Nchanga Mine, but it was too late.'[19]

By the latter part of 1924, the Anglo American Corporation's consulting engineer, Carl Davis (somewhat ironically, also an American) was closely examining progress in Northern Rhodesia. As a result Oppenheimer increased his interests during the following year. Anglo American Corporation became involved in the Broken Hill mine, the Rhodesian Congo Border Concession

Limited, and other concession companies as well as Bwana Mkubwa.[20] Equally significant, the Anglo American Corporation had insisted that as a condition of participation in these ventures it should be appointed consulting engineers, and later in 1926 opened a lavish headquarters in Broken Hill for the whole country. Thus it was able to know of all new mineral discoveries and drilling disclosures.

Meanwhile, Chester Beatty had liquidated Copper Ventures and was in the slightly odd position of having to buy his way back into the Nkana Concession, which he had sold to Edmund Davis in February 1924. In February 1925 the Northern Rhodesia Company was registered and acquired numerous old claims, primarily those at Roan Antelope.[21] In September, Beatty's Selection Trust took over these claims and formed a company with a capital of £200,000 to develop them. Oppenheimer was offered, and accepted a twenty-four per cent 'ground floor' share in this new company.[22] The immediate result was development at the Roan, where Russell J. Parker, another American geologist with experience in the Congo, had by the end of 1925 established the great potential of the underlying sulphide ore-body.[23] In April 1926, a director of Selection Trust arrived at the site to decide on a drilling program; by 1928 this had established the existence of 40,000,000 tons of ore averaging three-and-a-half per cent copper. The director was William Selkirk, who nearly thirty years before had journeyed through Northern Rhodesia with a gold-seeking expedition. In June 1927, Roan Antelope Copper Mines Limited was formed with a capital of £600,000.

By this time, Chester Beatty's pioneering general manager, Raymond Brooks, had resigned and returned to America in a cloud of disagreement. There were several reasons for this and it is difficult not to sympathise with Brooks, although he was undoubtedly an individualist who was truculent when specialists from London offered him advice. After Beatty had sold his rights in the Nkana claims to the Bwana Mkubwa Mining Company (and thus ultimately to Oppenheimer), Brooks moved his headquarters westward into Rhodesian Congo Border Concession territory and concentrated, with William Collier, on the exploration of Nchanga's ore-bodies.[24] They drilled a series of holes which ultimately proved the existence of rich sulphide-oxide deposits between 575-650 ft. It is typical of Brooks that he had continued drilling despite orders from Chester Beatty's consulting engineer, Preston Horner, that he should stop at 480 ft. Yet this drilling was the first proof that sulphides of commercial grade existed at depth in Northern Rhodesia.

Another source of trouble was the head-on clash between

Brooks and the incoming Anglo American Corporation of South Africa Ltd. who despised his 'primitive' prospecting and wanted more scientific methods instituted in the concession areas.[25] Brooks was infuriated when in 1926 two planes were sent from London without warning to make an aerial survey; he had to call on the government to help him find labour for building the airstrips and the unexpected cost of these operations caused hard feeling between himself and his superiors.[26] In fact, all the evidence suggests that Chester Beatty, who was financially pressed throughout 1925–6, agreed in return for financial aid from Oppenheimer that Brooks should be pushed into a position where his pride would make him quit.

The following extract from Brooks's own account of his last months as the general manager of Rhodesian Congo Border Concessions Ltd shows how strained relations had become: '. . . in May 1926, just thirty-six months after the first prospecting parties were sent out into a roadless, mapless and practically unknown country, we received the most unusual cable of that entire period. It closed with the classical phrase: "We must have several developed mines by the end of the year." '[27]

There was another, absurdly petty, incident which resulted in Brooks falling out with the autocratic William Selkirk, who was on the board of Rhodesian Selection Trust Ltd. Selkirk had come out to examine Roan Antelope prospects in April 1926 and Brooks took him on a tour of Nchanga and other prospects. A picnic lunch had been prepared and in advance Selkirk had let it be known that he liked cucumber sandwiches. Brooks had tried to find a cucumber, but failed, and when the lunch was unwrapped Selkirk was enraged. The Rhodesian Selection Trust directors were advised by cable that Brooks was not up to his job.[28]

A highly efficient Canadian geologist, Dr J. A. Bancroft, was chosen by Oppenheimer to take over prospecting in 1927 and it is typical of the feuding between the rival organisations that neither Brooks nor Bancroft ever had a good word to say for each other.[29] The latter derided his predecessor, asserting he had proved nothing about the geological formations of the Copperbelt. Brooks defended himself: 'The principal copper occurrences must have been found by the earlier system of prospecting, because no important new discoveries or undertakings have been announced since.'[30]

Most of the principal characters in the opening-up of the Copperbelt—Ernest Oppenheimer, Edmund Davis, Carl Davis, Horner, Selkirk, Brooks, Bancroft—are now dead. Chester Beatty alone survives today (1965). Brooks did not return to southern

Africa until 1947, when he discovered the important copper deposits near Sinoia, Southern Rhodesia. He spent his last years on a small copper prospect near Mumbwa, where Northern Rhodesia's first mines were discovered. In August 1960 he died, impoverished and forgotten, in Lusaka hospital at the age of 80.

IV YEARS OF TRANSFORMATION

During 1928 the financial structure of the rival Copperbelt groups crystallised. In that year, both Rhodesian Selection Trust Ltd. and Rhodesian Anglo-American Ltd. were set up.[1] Although there was interlocking between the groups, hostility at board level was considerable, and has been by no means absent in more recent times. Rhodesian Selection Trust was powerfully supported by the American Metal Company Ltd. (predecessor of American Metal Climax Inc.), which had acquired an interest in Roan Antelope by 1927: two-thirds of the first Rhodesian Selection Trust Board were Americans and it is clear that Chester Beatty would have been obliged to merge his Northern Rhodesian interests with those of Ernest Oppenheimer but for the availability of transatlantic funds with the rise in base metal prices during the late '20s. Rhodesian Anglo-American also had American support, but in this case from the Newmont Mining Corporation with which Oppenheimer had for some years been associated, yet the Johannesburg mining interests and the British South Africa Company retained effective control. There is some irony in the fact that, despite the much-paraded rivalry between 'Imperial' and American interests, most of the opposing financiers were of German extraction.

Exploitation of the deep sulphide deposits was a massive undertaking and the 1927-30 build-up on the Copperbelt transformed Northern Rhodesia from a stagnant backwater to an exhilarating land of promise. Forgotten was the declaration in 1924 by the Governor, Sir Herbert Stanley: 'I will base no part of our program for the development of Northern Rhodesia on the doubtful possibility of finding mineral deposits of importance.'[2] By 1927 the annual Report of the Department of Mines was saying: 'The concession companies have become the real pioneers of industry in the country and have been working under the control of the Anglo-American Corporation. . . . Not only is it a great mark of confidence in the mineral future of the country, but the presence of that staff is a very considerable asset.' At long last, the forecast of the Duke of Abercorn to shareholders of the British South Africa Company in 1902 seemed to be coming true: 'So I think that there can no longer be room for doubt that in the north we shall shortly see mineral production upon a very large scale.'

Millions were poured in to bring the mines into production. A race developed between Nkana (Anglo-American) and Roan (Rhodesian Selection Trust) to be the first to export copper. Development was also in progress at Chambeshi, Mufulira, and Nchanga. In 1927, work was restarted at Kansanshi, which had been dormant for thirteen years. The only mine actually producing copper at this period was Bwana Mkubwa, which had been reopened in 1926. Yet the two 'veteran properties' were the failures: at Kansanshi work was impeded by flooding and at Bwana the opencast methods employed proved completely uneconomic, although 22,000 long tons of copper were extracted in the years 1926-31.[3]

The Copperbelt began to pulsate with activity as the bush was cleared for townships around the first headgears. Black and white recruits streamed to the new El Dorado to be housed in camps and 'compounds'. In 1924, there had been 1,300 Africans employed on the Copperbelt; by 1928 this figure rose to 16,000 and by 1930 to 30,000.

Until the development of the Copperbelt there was little scope for employment in Northern Rhodesia. More than 20,000 local people had crossed the Zambezi to take jobs in Southern Rhodesia, and another 10,000 went to work in the Katanga mines of the Union Minière.[4] Now there appeared a brighter prospect for young men in the northern part of the country, and a high percentage of the men taken on at Nkana and Roan belonged to the Bemba, Bisa and related tribes. (The consequences of this for the rural areas is discussed elsewhere.) Many of the senior African employees also came from Nyasaland. Some of these Nyasas had useful experience of mining in South Africa, and others took clerical jobs, for which Northern Rhodesians were not available because of the British South Africa Company's attitude towards 'native education' during its years of administration up to 1924.

In 1925, labourers were paid approximately 10*s*. a month for surface work and 15*s*. underground; the contract was for six months and at the end of that time a man was sent home with a blanket and a supply of food to eat on the way to his village. By 1930 the wages had approximately doubled—'a noticeable development' having taken place in the average skills of African miners.[5] Europeans had to be lured to the Copperbelt in the early days with high wages, because of the very real dangers of malaria and sleeping-sickness. A semi-skilled man could command £30 a month or more—an abnormal rate by South African standards at that time. Although by 1930 the companies had obliterated the risks to health,

Europeans retained a wage structure which was destined to create an economic and social dilemma for the whole country until the 1960s.

The soaring price of copper and the leap in world consumption in 1928 produced unbounded optimism in Northern Rhodesia. United States consumption of the metal rose by nearly a fifth and production by a tenth; America was at that time producing almost half of world output and it appeared that supply could not keep pace with demand. Consequently in the space of a year, the price of copper soared from 12.92 cents per lb. to 24 cents per lb. and to ensure some measure of stability was pegged by general agreement in April 1929 at 18 cents (equivalent to £75 a ton).

The mood of the time is reflected in the increases in the capital of Rhodesian Anglo-American. In December 1928 the initial capital was £2,500,000. This was increased in October 1929 to £3,500,000; in June 1930 to £5,000,000, and in January 1931 to £6,500,000.[6] European immigration into Northern Rhodesia, mainly from South Africa, was at an unprecedented level as the mines demanded more and more employees. In 1924 the non-African population of the country had been a mere 4,000, less than double what it was before the first world war. By 1928 it was up to 7,400 and at the start of 1931 reached 13,800.[7]

Then came the effects of the slump, just as Roan Antelope and Nkana mines were going into production. Roan had narrowly won the race, but it seemed at the time a futile victory. Copper fell to less than five cents per lb. during 1932 and the desperate producers, holding vast stocks for which there was no market, agreed on a 73 per cent cut-back in output. On the Copperbelt, black and white employees were dismissed wholesale, generally with twenty-four hours' notice. In 1930 there had been nearly 22,000 African miners and by 1932 there were 5,500. The figures for Europeans went down from 3,300 to less than 1,000. Work at Kansanshi, Bwana Mkubwa, Chambeshi Nchanga and Mufulira was halted; mine offices were padlocked, furniture abandoned in the houses and grass grew in the streets. At Mufulira, destined thirty years later to become the richest underground copper mine in the world, the workings were allowed to flood in January 1932. Nchanga, whose output in 1963 had a value of more than £40,000,000, was put in the charge of 'two Europeans and thirty natives'; one of the Europeans was William Collier, discoverer of Roan Antelope in 1902. Restricted production was maintained at the Roan and Nkana, but at the former a shut-down was only avoided through the backing of the American Metal Company, which agreed to pay for the concentrate as soon as it was on rail in Northern Rhodesia.

A cable was sent from the mine immediately a consignment was in the waggons and by this means it proved possible to meet the wages bill.[8]

Although the white population was not to reach its 1931 level until the early years of the second world war, the cautious return to expansion had begun by 1935, when the Rhokana Corporation Ltd. was able to pay its first dividend of 2*s*.6*d*. The London price for blister copper had risen to £32 a long ton in 1935 (£38 in 1936) as against the lowest ebb of £26 in July 1932. Production costs of Northern Rhodesian copper were at that time approximately £26 delivered to European ports, so a narrow margin of profit had reappeared by 1935.

By the end of 1935, both Nkana and Roan Antelope were producing at the rate of 50,000 long tons a year, the former mine having already opened an electrolytic refinery so that less than half of its output was in the form of blister. The Roan was also smelting concentrates from Mufulira, which had been dewatered late in 1933 but which did not bring its own smelter into operation until the beginning of 1937. The sinking of new incline shafts began in 1937 at Nchanga, which had been dormant for six years, and Nchanga Consolidated Copper Mines Ltd. was formed with an initial capital of £5,000,000. At this point the ingrained jealousy between Oppenheimer and Beatty once more made itself apparent.[9] The Anglo-American Board felt acutely its loss of prestige because the combined output of the Rhodesian Selection Trust mines was, at the start of the second world war, more than half as much again as that of Anglo-American—140,000 long tons to 92,000.

However, such matters were reduced to insignificance by the needs of the Allied war machine and during the years 1939-45 output was boosted to the utmost on the Copperbelt. Combined production reached more than 250,000 long tons in 1943—a mere ten years after only two mines had been working with skeleton staffs and others had been abandoned. The wear and tear on surface plant during the war years, with new equipment almost unobtainable, was considerable and it was not surprising that output should fall back to 182,000 tons in 1946. Nevertheless, Northern Rhodesia had now established itself as one of the world's major copper producers and the two decades of pioneering were over.

From 1950 onwards a steady advance in production was recorded, with the two younger mines, Nchanga and Mufulira, both overtaking the original producers in their respective groups by 1955. By 1959, the Copperbelt was responsible for more than one-seventh of the total production of the non-communist world: 594,000 out of 3,359,000 short tons, second only to the output of the United

States. In that year, the figures for the four major mines were as follows: Nchanga, 192,000; Mufulira, 118,000; Rhokana, 109,000; and Roan Antelope, 107,000. (By 1964, the first two had gone still further ahead).[10] The rapid advance of the Copperbelt is indicated by Anglo-American's profit after taxation of £17,692,000 in 1963, compared with a mere £390,500 in 1940.

During the '50s, two new mines were exploited—Bancroft and Chibuluma. The former was a Rhodesian Anglo-American property, named after the well-known geologist who had been connected with the Copperbelt since 1927. Although the mine has known ore reserves of more than 100 million tons—the bulk of which averages more than four per cent copper—Bancroft has been experiencing much difficulty through water, drainage being in the order of 40 million gallons a day—more than double that of other Copperbelt mines with much higher production. Bancroft has the potential to become a major producer. Yet it has still to prove its profitability; operations were suspended in 1958-9 when the world price of copper fell to less than £200. Chibuluma is a smaller property with ore reserves of 10 million tons and an output of approximately 20,000 tons of metal annually. In 1963, work began on stripping the overburden at Chambishi, where a large sulphide-oxide ore-body is being exploited by opencast methods similar to those at Nchanga. After being the headquarters of Rhodesia Selection Trust on the Copperbelt until 1929, Chambishi was then abandoned in favour of Mufulira and only a few broken walls remained as evidence of the original enterprise when development was renewed after thirty years.

The reliance of Zambia on its copper (which gives it on a *per capita* basis the highest exportable value of any African country) makes the world selling price of the metal of great significance. Between 1955 and 1960 the price showed alarming fluctuations, reaching £420 a ton in March 1956 and slumping to £181 at the end of the following year. These variations not only seriously affected the revenues of the country, but also shocked the producers themselves, since prices above £300 make copper vulnerable to substitutes such as aluminium. In the early '60s, concerted efforts were made to stabilise the price at about £230 a ton, by a voluntary cut-back in output and by the abandonment of London Metal Exchange quotations when demand temporarily outstripped supply at the start of 1964.[11]

Despite the volatile nature of the metal market, Sir Ronald Prain, Chairman of Rhodesian (now Roan) Selection Trust Ltd., expressed confidence in 1963 as follows: 'The published reserves of copper in Northern Rhodesia at present considered economic represent about the same proportion of total world reserves as do the oil reserves of Kuwait. When one considers that not all reserves are published, and that many more are as yet undiscovered, one is left with the feeling that there can be few countries with such a heritage of future wealth. During its short life the industry has produced copper to the extent of about 8½ million tons with a historical value of about £1,400 millions—or, at today's prices, a value of about £2,000 millions.'[12]

V OWNERSHIP OF THE COPPERBELT

The chart, Appendix III, sets out in simplified form the ownership of the Copperbelt's producing mines, which have an output in the region of 700,000 short tons annually.

It is impossible to show on a two-dimensional diagram all the companies involved, either as share-holders or through the numerous prospecting, service and sales companies in each group, or companies owned jointly by both groups. Moreover, the picture is liable to constant change—for example the takeover in May 1964 of the struggling Bancroft mine by the most profitable Nchanga.

The Anglo-American group is the larger in terms of copper production and it also has considerable holdings in some of the RST group mines. The group also controls the Broken Hill lead and zinc mines and Wankie Colliery, and is associated with brewing and other industrial companies. It has two defunct mines, Bwana Mkubwa and Kansanshi. Zambian Anglo-American itself is controlled by the Anglo-American Corporation of South Africa Ltd. and its management reflects a certain amount of integration with its South African parent—it is in no sense either English or American.

The largest shareholder in Roan Selection Trust Ltd. with 46.1 per cent, is American Metal Climax Inc. (AMAX), but there is no executive linkage. Selection Trust itself, having traded its Rhodesian copper holdings for American Metal shares during the slump of the thirties, now only has a financial interest in Roan Selection Trust through AMAX, but it does provide some consulting services for the Roan Selection Trust group.

The British South Africa Company, which until October 1964 held the mineral rights and received variable royalties, depending on the London Metal Exchange price of copper, had substantial shareholdings in several of the companies shown in the chart, particularly those of the Anglo-American group. To complicate the picture, the Anglo-American group had shares in the

British South Africa Company now merged into Chartered Consolidated. Rio Tinto is another international concern, with minority holdings in some of the mines. When interlocking directorates are taken into account, the associations of the Copperbelt companies are remarkably widespread in world mining.

The investment in the industry is estimated at around £300 million, although the value of the fixed assets in the companies' balance sheets amounts to much less than this. Table 6 gives an idea of the comparative size of the mines with:

(a) the productive capacity in short tons, including extensions in hand.
(b) the total number of employees.
(c) ore reserves, and
(d) grade.
(e) gross profit from sales of copper in the year ended 1963 (not a good year)—i.e. profits before tax or provision for replacement.

Net dividends after tax and distributed to companies not in the table, or to individuals, totalled about £12 millions, while the British South Africa Company obtained another £6 million net from royalties. Dividends paid by the mining companies in the period June 1954 to June 1964 totalled £259 million, including internal payments between companies.

VI PROSPECTS FOR THE FUTURE

The future of the Copperbelt came under examination early in 1964 by an economic mission provided by the United Nations. This body conducted a study of the whole economy designed to form the basis for a general development plan. Its recommendations on policy towards the mining companies and the copper industry give likely pointers to the shape of things to come.

The report examines the prospective world market. While noting the threat posed by aluminium, it points to a United Nations analysis of world demand for copper (E/CN/13/49) and accepts its estimates that from 1959 to 1970 world copper consumption would increase by about four per cent annually. In view of this expanding market, the mission questions whether published development plans of the copper companies will maintain Zambia's current share of world production. Why an established share should necessarily be maintained in a world market subject to the entry of new producer countries is not closely argued. However, with a continuing share of fifteen per cent of the estimated world market (given the four per cent annual rise in consumption and a copper price averaging about £240 a ton) exports of approximately 800,000 tons annually would be just adequate to produce the foreign exchange earnings required to finance the economic development plan.

From the thesis that copper production in Zambia represents a reducing portion of world supplies and also because of the unique role of copper in the economy, the report suggests that government must have a more decisive say in the policy of the copper producing companies—an attitude which has been confirmed by President Kaunda and his cabinet. From 1960 to 1962 output actually fell, due to a voluntary scheme to restrict supplies. Some other world producers did not conform. The mission suspected that an unfairly heavy part of the burden fell upon Zambia, precisely because of the producers' freedom to manoeuvre unrestricted by government pressure.

Too much should not be made of this argument; if the 1962 production figures, country by country, are compared with either the 1953–7 average or with 1958 production, the Zambia mining groups do well by comparison with other major producing companies; possibly, the mission's choice of a basic year for comparison was not wholly unrelated to the thesis that it wished to prove.

To enable legislation to at least be intelligible and beneficial rather than the reverse, the UN mission recommends that the Mines Department of the government should be built up far beyond its present establishment and that a separate Ministry be established with an exceptional salary scale. Government should fully participate in all aspects of the development of the country's mineral wealth. Steps to this end were taken in 1965, when a Ministry of Mines was created. In May it was announced, after long expectation of a new taxation-royalties formula, that the old formula would be retained and that mines operating at a loss could appeal to the government for financial concessions. An appeal was immediately made on behalf of Bancroft, which had lost £1.5 million in 1964–5.

The mining groups will be assured of tenure for at least the medium term. No longer will they be treated as a separate kingdom within the realm. They will increasingly have to accustom themselves to government interference in staffing, distribution policy, the international disposition of funds and in the planning of new development. It does not follow that relations will become strained, there being encouraging signs in 1964 of a satisfactory working relationship between the companies and the nationalist government.

The greatest problems may well arise not over copper

development and marketing policies but rather over policy for wages and the numbers employed. For it is likely that to increase foreign exchange earnings, the mechanisation of the mines will be pushed at an increased pace; government, having a preoccupation with the level of employment—especially high wage employment such as the mines provide—will be likely to find itself in a predicament when disputes arise.

VII GEOLOGY OF THE COPPERBELT

A mineralised arc 400 miles long runs from Broken Hill north-west to Kipushi in Katanga.[1] It is in this field that the Copperbelt minerals lie, the deposits having a geological history going back more than 600 million years. It has been established that at the earliest time the lowlands of the region were covered by sea invading from the south-west, minerals were washed down from the mountains and deposited along the edge of the sea. Sediments now known as the Lower Roan group were laid upon these deposits and later action by the sea added dolomites and limestones which became the Upper Roan series.

Between the two glacial periods (the second approximately 250 million years ago), the surface of the earth buckled and the positions of the mineral deposits were changed. The strata became deeply tilted and as wind and rain wore down the surface of the land, certain outcrops were exposed. For one period, deep sand of the Kalahari type covered what is now the Copperbelt, then it was blown away and a layer of *laterite* took its place. Rain leached out much of the copper in the upper levels of the ore-bodies and washed them down the rivers, so that sulphide indications on the surface were removed. Left on the surface were oxides, such as malachite—the clues to the deep sulphide ores below the dolomitic rocks. The sulphide ores are disseminated (scattered through shaley rocks) in the Lower Roan formation. The shale varies in thickness from 20 to 150 ft in width.

The Nchanga mine is exceptional in the geology of the Copperbelt;[2] at other mines the primary copper sulphide minerals (chalcopyrite, bornite and chalcocite) account for the bulk of the ore, going down at least 3,000 ft below surface. At Nchanga, secondary minerals such as malachite, and azurite have also been deposited to form 'enriched ore'.

9

Economic History of Zambia

ZAMBIA had virtually no economic history prior to 1924 and very little before 1946. There were political factors of great future economic significance, many concerned with copper and the companies controlling its developments. But also relevant was the attitude of the Imperial government and its definition of responsibilities towards colonial territories. Nevertheless there remains a void in the economic and social development of the country.

The outcome of this delay in the basic development of Zambia was to produce an extreme imbalance in the economy, which was remarked as early as 1938 by the *Pim Report* already referred to,[1] and more recently by the Rural Economic Development Working Party (1960).[2] It was described in detail by the draft report of the Economic Survey Mission (UN/ECA/FAO), 1964. This lack of balance exists not only between European and African, between urban and rural areas, but between mining development and development of other sectors of the economy. It represents sectors, geographical and social, in which money is spent and not spent. In Zambia a variety of areas and institutions related to a small proportion of the population has more or less monopolised private enterprise expenditure, and until recently government expenditure has been concentrated on the same areas.

The paradox can be understood partly by relating it to the ethos of the times; before 1924, Zambia was about as economically significant as Bechuanaland. It was a protectorate controlled by a colonial power which was no longer imperialist in ambition and yet had no concept of government's role in stimulating economic growth. Zambia was less developed than many other British controlled territories which had even less potential at the time. The overriding reasons for this were geographical. Landlocked in the centre of a continent, Zambia has even now grave problems of communication; in the context of the first quarter of the twentieth century this meant that the countries with a seaboard developed first. Most colonial territories in Africa were created by inland penetration from the nearest seaboard; thus even the innermost parts had direct access to the sea without crossing a frontier. The pattern of communications in Africa, especially rail communication, developed from the coast, directly inland. Zambia, by contrast, was opened up from South Africa; consequently her line of communication was attenuated and costly. The relatively high cost of getting out raw materials undoubtedly hindered their development, and for a long time Zambia did nothing to exploit the wealth dormant in the soil. When the major source of Zambia's wealth was discovered its development required capital far beyond local resources. Similar circumstances had existed in Katanga where rich copper ores from which the metal could readily be extracted were discovered and exploited some two decades earlier. When financial backing became available to the Rhodesian Copperbelt the ensuing boom was shortly eclipsed in the backwash of the most severe cyclical depression that the world has yet known. Notwithstanding these delays and obstacles, copper has been and is the basis of the country's economic history.

A significant primary source of income is agriculture. A minor source is timber extraction, which has provided foreign exchange for some fifty years. The other major source of income is government. Whilst a non-trading government normally has little income that is not acquired by taxation, it is within its powers to control its own income by levying tax or by borrowing and then to create additional taxable income, through the medium of public expenditure. Government is also one dynamic element whose role in the mid-1960s was actively to push the economy along the direction thought best for it. Since the war, the expansion of the extension services for agriculture and regulation or stimulation of the economy in other spheres, have clearly shown government's acceptance of some responsibility for the level of activity within the economy. However, for most of the period prior to 1939 it had been the dominant preoccupation of government to preserve law and order and balance budgets. Underspending of estimates was widespread and seems frequently to have been encouraged; more often than not deflation was the keynote of monetary policy.

It is desirable to sketch briefly the progress of the country's economy sector by sector, up to the second world war. The first observation of any continuing relevance is the fact that while political control of the territory remained in London, Zambia was divorced from the most likely sources of economic motivation. There were several reasons: in the first place colonisation, as far as it applied to Northern Rhodesia, had been effected only with reluctance by the British government. Furthermore government, especially colonial government, existed to govern, not to stimulate growth. A second factor related to the first is, as we have seen, that Rhodesia was never a point of first entry to Africa. It was one of the most remote and inaccessible of many British colonies in Africa. Had it been the sole colony of a European country, like the Belgian Congo, it might have received more attention. The majority of Zambia's industries with international connections came first to South Africa or Southern Rhodesia and only later established themselves in the north.

Agriculture

Farming and the development of commercial agriculture were made possible by the railway. Rather by chance this was constructed from Livingstone, via Lusaka and Broken Hill through possibly the largest area of high agricultural potential in the territory. The early European farmers settled in widely scattered areas from Abercorn in the extreme north to the Fort Jameson area in the east and in a number of individual localities now no longer farmed, as well as along the line-of-rail. Beef cattle and maize farming have been by far the most consistent of all activities, but numerous other crops were attempted from time to time, among them sisal and other fibre crops; cotton showed promise several times in particular areas, only to succumb eventually to the combination of falling world prices and the difficulties of pest control. In Abercorn district, coffee-growing succeeded for a time until in 1937 there were twelve estates with 404 acres under coffee. But with the war, estates were abandoned and crops uprooted to avoid disease. Most noteworthy of farming centres off the line-of-rail has been Fort Jameson. Here, apart from cattle and maize, virginia tobacco has been grown since before 1914. Indeed, the area has experienced tobacco growing booms. In 1926-7 the crop advanced to 2¾ million lb. and reached 3¼ million lb. in the following year before falling to 1.15 million lb. by 1935-6. Following the second world war another boom in virginia tobacco growing took place; registered growers in the area rose to 219 in the early 1950s but again prices proved erratic and the exceptional costs of growing what is in effect an industrial crop in a remote part of the country again reduced the crop to negligible proportions.

The better farmed line-of-rail area became established between 1910-23. Of many crops tried, until relatively recently, maize has been the most successful. Until the Copperbelt opened up, farmers were as dependent on exports to the Belgian Congo as they were upon the internal market. The *Pim Report* noted that by 1936-7 deliveries of European grown maize amounted to about 321,000 bags, of which 119,000 were sold internally, 158,000 were exported and 44,000 remained on hand at the end of the year. African farmers delivered 234,000 bags, of which slightly over one third remained on hand. It was therefore already clear that the country could produce maize in excess of the domestic needs—but this applied to a country whose population was mostly not within the cash economy. Almost from the beginning of its development, the authorities recognised that the economy was too dependent on a single commodity, not least because this commodity provided, directly and indirectly, overwhelmingly the major source of government revenue. Nevertheless progress in diversification was slow: the acreage under commercially grown maize increased only from 42,000 in 1937-8 to 49,000 by 1946-7 and virginia tobacco from 4,245 to 6,500. Of subsistence agriculture little is known in quantitative terms, though it is evident from the increasing production for sale by African farmers that maize was replacing millet. So a factor of economic significance during this period was the entry of a number of African cultivators to the cash economy.

Mining

Copper-mining is dealt with elsewhere. From the economic development of the territory it has been noted that without minerals it is doubtful whether substantial development would have taken place; the railway line, which arrived at Broken Hill in 1906 and Ndola a few years later, represented a considerable hostage to fortune by the Chartered Company. The economic justification was initially shown by benefit to the territory's development generally rather than by profits to the railway operators, for the first major development in traffic, stimulated by the copper mines, was not to come until the late 1920s. From that time onwards the economy had the primary source of income that was to dominate its development. In fact, it should be possible to demonstrate that the level of economic activity of all kinds in the country was and is very closely related to the world price of copper.

Population

There are human pre-conditions for every form of economic growth. In Zambia, economic progress was delayed by the late arrival of Europeans in any significant numbers, to provide examples of a way of life which might be imitated with possible advantage.

Then even when they did come the very few fields in which Europeans took any active part at all (principally mining and government)—meant that the ordinary people remained far longer out of contact with the modern world than Africans in more accessible regions. The result has been that change when it came, had to be a more accelerated process than elsewhere in Africa.

Changes in the very structure of society became necessary. Of great significance among Zambian institutions in need of change are the various systems of land tenure, the super-democratic attitude towards economic institutions whereby so much consultation is required that efficiency is crippled, and the liabilities of tribal clan and family kinship.

Although the traditional African 'social security' system has undoubtedly been a major stabilising factor hitherto, it acts as a drag upon the economically successful and as a disincentive to individual effort. However desirable the implications of equality of wealth, that social arrangement increases the difficulties of the embryo African entrepreneur who has to compete with entrepreneurs of other races unhampered by similar egalitarian institutions; moreover in the long run it is an obstacle to the accumulation of personal savings so necessary for investment made in private enterprise.

Before 1939 there was no pressure upon land or revenues by the country's population. Censuses of the European population were made in 1911, 1921 and 1931 but no complete census of Africans was ever carried out. The following figures of Africans are therefore only estimates, as are those for Europeans in 1935. They are extracted from the *Pim Report* :

Year	Europeans	Africans	Proportion of Africans to one European
1911	1,497	821,063	548
1921	3,634	979,701	270
1931	13,846	1,372,235	99
1935	9,913	1,366,425	138

Natural Resources

Up to 1939 the national exploitation of Zambia's natural resources was little known, save in so far as copper and other base metals were concerned. Early in the period game was plentiful, and only in more recent years has government appeared to be aware of game as an expendable natural resource.

One of the principal non-mining industries was sawmilling. In 1936 Zambezi sawmills employed 100 Europeans and 3,700 Africans, but the *Pim Report* noted : 'Exploitation has been entirely uncontrolled, without any working plan or attempt to secure a rotation.' Around the copper mines, government received no direct income from the exploitation of forests, which was carried out 'in a haphazard and unsystematic way through contractors'.

Government

All through the pre-1939 period the economic role of government was essentially minor. The British South Africa Company had, understandably, seen no role for itself beyond maintenance of law and order and financing the minimum pre-conditions for development of minerals. Colonial government had different theoretical aspirations and recognised some responsibility to advance the peoples of the territory. Nevertheless, there was no concept of a timetable for advancement; the primary task was still to govern and there could be no question of the country's living beyond its means. Admittedly government did not aim to pay dividends so any surplus from taxation could be used for education, encouragement of agricultural development through teaching better methods by 'extension services', communications and so on. But it was mandatory that the territory should finance its own economic growth. Table 1 (see Appendix) shows the sharp cuts in recurrent expenditure enforced by the fall in revenue in 1932-3. This was nearly 30 per cent less than in 1931-2 and being some 24 per cent down on estimated revenue the government experienced a major deficit in its budget. This shortfall was anticipated in April 1932 and a finance commission was appointed to report on reduction of expenditure and increase of revenue. The outcome was dramatic; the European departmental establishment was reduced from 685 in 1932 to 516 in 1934; deflation was reinforced by a levy on official salaries and by changes in taxation. In the meantime the protectorate's capital was transferred from Livingstone to Lusaka with the attendant extraordinary capital expenditure. It was only possible to achieve this by dint of assistance from the Beit Trustees* and the Colonial Development Fund. Budgetary policy was fixed when the Governor was informed by the Secretary of State that his budget should balance by 1935. Primary product producers were particularly hard hit by the slump. In the circumstances these draconian methods of restoring the balance were to be expected and corresponded with the approach adopted in most parts of the world.

Reductions in total expenditure (ten per cent lower in 1934 than in 1931–2) mask the full effect, since the 1934 figure of £694,416 includes increases in excess of £100,000 in the items 'Charges on account of Public Debt' and 'Pensions and gratuities'

* An educational trust fund derived from bequests of Sir Alfred Beit, a contemporary of Rhodes.

which represent in great part external payments. The cuts had the most disastrous effect in the department of agriculture which did not recover for a decade. The *Pim Report* wrote that although the department of agriculture had done 'valuable work in relation to such crops as coffee and tobacco it cannot be said that it has made any substantial contribution up to the present to the solution of the problems of native agriculture'. The wholesale reduction effected was based on a short-sighted view of the requirements of the country. Out of an establishment of 23 in June 1932 only five were left by December 31, 1933.

The void in the territory's economy is fully attributable to the actual part played by government. An infrastructure of communications and of public services had to be built up before development could take place. All developments were started by imported skills and other countries were better adapted to compete successfully for the limited supply of staff available. Moreover, the country had to build itself up from its own resources—from income generated internally. With the recovery in copper prices and production and the consequent increase in income and revenue, government was able to spend more. In 1938 revenue exceeded £1.5 millions and £270,000 was put to reserve. From that time onward there were to be no further recessions either in copper prices or in revenue until the 1957–9 period, a twenty-year era of income stability that culminated in the 1956 copper boom.

THE YEARS UP TO FEDERATION: 1939-53

During the immediate pre-war years the Northern Rhodesian economy appeared to be in equilibrium both internally and externally. Capital was no longer the limiting factor in promoting private investment; the greatest needs were for entrepreneurs, whether agricultural or industrial, and for a domestic market to sustain production at economic levels.

One can now discern that the pattern which followed might have been custom-designed to create an unbalanced economy. This was the outcome of the 1939-45 war. Large scale wars create increased demand for raw materials and this one was no exception. The copper mines had an unlimited market at an assured price (up to £66 per ton) which enabled them to expand production to the limits of their capacity. Revenues were buoyant for all—mines, mine employees and government alike. Copper and, to a lesser extent, zinc and lead from the Broken Hill mine provided the principal economic *raison d'être* for the country; it followed that development of services, communications and commerce would be concentrated upon the already advanced metal producing sectors of the economy.

The 1939–45 war had other effects. It brought about or at least hastened the process of decolonising territories ruled by the nations of western Europe. Although the tempo of political evolution had changed, the outlook of the rulers had not. The time was most inopportune for any drive to restore the economic balance between different sectors of the economy—rather the reverse, the job of the government was to keep the peace and allow copper to be produced. A depleted staff had no time to concentrate on plans to develop the economy.

Even had government staff been available there was an additional bottleneck in supply of capital equipment—a shortage that lasted until about 1950. Equipment for transport, road-making, agriculture and industry was exceedingly scarce; even the mines found it impossible to re-equip adequately, which is why production fell immediately after the war. Amid the absence of so many pre-conditions of economic growth, the dearth of entrepreneurs was possibly the most decisive, and the war years were no time for immigration. And still the government showed little sign of becoming the dynamic motive force needed to check the growing unbalance.

In an address to the Legislative Council on November 20 1943, the Governor explained that he did not think it wise to plan the future on the basis of an expected revenue greater than £1,500,000, while current expenditure, including wartime expenditure, was about £1,750,000. He said :'In the expansion of our social services we have therefore already passed the point where we may reasonably expect to be able to balance our budget in the post-war years.'

Thus the increased revenues available to government during the war were the source of considerable government saving. Cash balances and investments in government rose :[3]

	Dec. 31, 1939	Dec. 31, 1943	Dec. 31, 1945
	£	£	£
Cash balances	455,045	1,937,298	2,734,887
Investments	613,867	2,692,523	4,708,645
	£1,068,912	£4,629,821	£7,443,532

The straitened circumstances foreshadowed for the post-war period did not form a major source of concern in other respects; the average income derived from this rather considerable amount of current assets was relatively negligible at two-and-a-half to three per cent per annum; by 1945 a total of £1,850,000 had been passed over to the Imperial government in the form of interest-free loans. Another source of income was the low rates of income tax deemed appropriate on copper mines. As these mining companies were domiciled in the United Kingdom, their effective rate of tax was the UK rate; this being at a far higher level than that in Northern Rhodesia gave rise to a major unearned annual windfall to the British Treasury. Thus there were some contradictions between the colonial government point of view on the need to husband the territory's resources and the (implied) need to employ its resources as remuneratively as possible.

1945-53

This was a period of buoyant revenue for the copper mines, for government and for most sectors of the economy. During eight years the value of the main minerals produced in the country increased from less than £15 million to over £95 million. Nearly all these earnings were, as usual, represented by copper. To see these figures in perspective, the following related facts are relevant:

1. In 1953 national income amounted to only £88.7 million, more than £6 million less than sales of copper.
2. Overseas remittance estimated at £25.4 million represented more than twenty-six per cent of net national income.
3. Wages and salaries also increased by some 550 per cent (see Appendix II, Table 2) and the earnings of other sectors of the economy also enjoyed major rises.
4. Traffic receipts of Rhodesia Railways increased from £1,605,000 (1945) to £4,207,000 (1953).
5. Taxable profits of companies registered in Northern Rhodesia other than mines rose from £296,000 (1945) to £1,575,000 (1953)—an indication of the negligible scale of development before 1945.
6. Income from wages and salaries of employees rose from £8,270,000 (1945) to £45,621,000 (1953). Of this amount, European earnings rose from £5,157,000 to £24,921,000, African from £3,112,000 to £20,700,000.

Colonial government was by no means geared to take full advantage of the good fortune represented by a long period of stable earnings. It would have been inconceivable that any overall long-term development plan could have been prepared and promoted earlier in Northern Rhodesia (or in any other colony). Nevertheless there was a growing volume of investment (see Appendix, Table 3). A noticeably high proportion of investment expenditure was, not surprisingly, incurred on behalf of the mining groups, and by central and local government; but all sectors of the economy benefited from the rising level of income.

Since the initial capital which opened up the mines, Northern Rhodesia has never been a major recipient of foreign finance for investment. On the contrary, it has been regarded as lacking investment opportunities. The total amounts of monies entering, particularly from the United Kingdom, have consistently been dwarfed by the sums of dividends and the transfers remitted from Northern Rhodesia to other countries. Still, in 1964, there was no sign that the pattern was likely to change; Zambia will probably receive more foreign capital than in the past, but the great bulk of such capital will in the long run come from the country's own internal resources. The country has neither been a point of first entry for immigrants to Africa nor for investment capital.

To present an impression of the economy as it existed immediately before the Federation of Northern Rhodesia with Southern Rhodesia and Nyasaland, it is best to deal with some of the principal features individually.*

Agriculture

The period from 1945 until Federation was characterised by a marked increase in the acres actively farmed by Europeans and Africans alike. By the 1954–5 season the area under maize production on European farms had risen to 109,292 (1946–7 : 49,000) and the crop amounted to 665,000 bags (bags of 200 lb. each). Meanwhile maize deliveries from African areas rose greatly in the average year, and in the peak year of 1955 amounted to 595,000 bags. It is noteworthy that the estimated production per acre of European maize did not rise during this period. The yield of 6.6 bags to the acre achieved in the 1947–8 season had not been reached again by 1954. No record of African yields is available for this period; but probably maize acreage increased greatly, together with the number of farmers engaged in maize growing. Following a serious maize shortage in 1947, government gave increased encouragement to maize farmers. The resulting rise in production roughly met the increases in domestic demand, but this was at the

---

* Mining is treated elsewhere in the volume.

cost of a maize subsidy which by the early 1950s was running at a rate exceeding £1 million per annum.

No other agricultural product had comparable success. The wheat subsidy rose until in the eighteen months from January 1953 to June 30, 1954 it cost as much as £378,490, but the crop fell to negligible proportions. The Fort Jameson area enjoyed a post-war boom in flue-cured virginia tobacco, but after the 1950-1 season, when nearly 4.5 million lb were produced, declining prices reduced the number of registered growers, the acreages and crop so that by 1964 virginia tobacco production had practically ceased in that area. In the Central and Southern Provinces, virginia tobacco production first exceeded one million lb. in 1948-9; experience in these areas has been much more fortunate, culminating in a crop of some twenty-five million lb. in the 1963-64 season. As an export crop this quantity is of substantial economic significance.

Of animal produce, beef and dairy products have been the most important. But despite having cattle estimated at three-quarters of a million by 1955 (and over one million by 1964) the amount of meat coming on the market has never been enough to make the country independent of meat imports.

Industry

Apart from mining, smelting and refining copper ores, there was little advance in industry in 1945. In that year the *Busschau Report*[4] commented on the unpreparedness of the country for any range of industry, mainly because of the small markets available. Such industry as had been developed was mostly service industry (to the mines, particularly), and industries engaged on production of building materials. In 1950 the government constituted the Northern Rhodesia Industrial Loans Board with an initial capital of £250,000 but there was little demand for these funds. The momentum stimulated by the copper boom, however, did cause a major increase in industrial investment and profits.

Imports and Exports

EXPORTS BY ITEM

	1946	1949	1953
	£m.	£m.	£m.
Copper	10.4	27.8	86.7
Other metals	1.2	3.5	4.2
Tobacco	0.4	0.8	1.6
Other	0.8	0.8	1.2
	12.8	32.9	93.7

IMPORTS BY COUNTRY OF ORIGIN

United Kingdom	2.4	7.3	18.9
Union of S. Africa	2.2	5.6	15.1
Southern Rhodesia	1.7	3.0	7.7
Other	1.8	5.4	10.1
	8.1	21.3	51.8

While Southern Rhodesia was of little importance to Northern Rhodesia as an export market, imports from that country rose steadily during the years immediately preceding Federation.

Before Federation, Northern Rhodesia had a period of marked prosperity, but by the early 1950s there was no sign that distribution of income, economic development within the economy and opportunity for its inhabitants were likely to change much in the ensuing years. Federation served to ossify much of the existing pattern for a decade; it is doubtful whether this pattern would have altered without the political revolution that ended it.

1953-63

The overall economic output of the Federation accentuated the imbalance within the economy. More capital investment was made during the years 1953–63 in the three territories combined than could have taken place if Federation had never occurred. But the accent of economic growth was not in Northern Rhodesia or Nyasaland but in Southern Rhodesia. That the North lost in quantitative terms has been amply demonstrated.

Business will readily move across political and tariff barriers. However, once within a single political area it will so locate itself as to maximise profit. The natural forces that made Southern Rhodesia a more favoured area than Northern Rhodesia for European investment were reinforced during Federation by political circumstances. One gains the impression that the general business climate was better in Southern Rhodesia than in the other territories. For this the attitudes of the governments were partly responsible. That in the South had far more practice in attracting business than the North. Another factor was the lack of cordiality that subsisted in the relationships between Federal government and the government of Northern Rhodesia. The former held all the economic controls, and had a near monopoly of power, and each of the territorial governments was dependent upon the Federal government for capital investment.

Arrangements made for Federation appear to have entirely ignored the economic status of the individual territories or, at best (with the intention that Southern Rhodesia should be permitted to develop freely) to have been based on the assumption that benefit to one would in the long term benefit the others. What is evident is that over the Federal period 1953-63 there were major transfers of income from the North elsewhere, made under the guidance of the Federal government. What is not clear is the attitude of the UK government to this economic pattern. The powers reserved to the Federal government were great and the power of the territorial governments to promote the interests of their own countries were correspondingly limited. No provision was made to check the exploitation of one territory for the benefit of another, even where the stages of development reached in the respective territories were obviously unequal.

It is not suggested that Northern Rhodesian development came to a halt during the period of Federation. But it is clear that her preconditions determined what development took place, and the effects of the country's earlier history still predominated. The tempo of events, determined by the outside world and by sudden access to riches, had not been able to counterbalance the effect of the pre-war void in development; the inability of the indigenous people to advance unaided to fill the demands suddenly created by the economic system had been demonstrated; the need for the influence of immigrants as innovators (however they may have acted subsequently) was evident, the economic disadvantages of the country in spite of the evident riches were perpetuated due to its geographical location.

Mining

During Federation, mining, which means largely copper mining, normally contributed slightly below half the gross domestic product of Northern Rhodesia; in the early years of the copper boom the mining proportion of gross domestic product was as high as 56.8 per cent in 1955, falling to 32.6 per cent in 1959 and recovering by 1960 to 47.5 per cent.*

The price of copper rose to over £400 per ton in 1956 before falling to a low point of £158 per ton in 1958. The fall in income was offset by larger output at the lower price and the effect of the fall was cushioned by dividend reductions. This was the first major

* In money terms the place of mining in the economy is to some extent illustrated by Table eighty-four, Part 1, *National Accounts of Federation of R & N, CSO*

slump in copper since the early 1930s, and was nowhere near so drastic in its effects on the economy, partly because the groups themselves were infinitely more stable financially; in part because the membership of a larger economic unit, the Federation, allowed the shock to be taken in part by other sectors of the economy.

In the past both colonial and Federal governments left the copper companies free to decide output and pricing policy, and the position appears to have been maintained up to the present. In future, close communication between the mining groups and the government will be needed unless misunderstandings are to arise. The present freedom of the mines to forego revenue by restricting price or output is not different from the freedom accorded to any other business. But the status of copper in the economy is such that the loss of government revenue and of foreign exchange earnings that can be caused by private and not unavoidable decisions by the copper companies are material. Price stabilisation remains an experiment at present and a somewhat costly one in the near term (especially for the copper producers themselves). Governments of most developing countries that are major copper producers appear to allow less freedom to the producing companies than has been the case in Zambia. Inadequate revenues from copper could undermine the government's plan to develop the country. The mining companies are certainly well aware of the need to avoid being represented in an unfavourable light: no doubt in the interests of their own relations with government an increasingly high level of consultation on policy will be aimed at in future.

Agriculture

From January 1, 1956, responsibility for European agriculture was transferred from the colonial to the Federal government; development of African agriculture remained the charge of the government of Northern Rhodesia.

Figures for Federal government spending on European agriculture in Northern Rhodesia are not separable from Federal totals. Indications are that the standard of agricultural service available to the European farmer was markedly raised, while at Mkushi new farms for Europeans were made available. The effect of accentuating natural investment in European farms is probably related to the sharp rise in yield per acre for the European-grown maize crop which was over fourteen bags per acre by 1960-1 and has remained at levels of production twice as high as prevailed pre-Federation. Spectacular increases have also been seen in production of flue-cured virginia tobacco (about 25 million lb. in 1964) and cotton.

African agricultural activity has also increased sharply. By

1962 maize deliveries ran to 885,462 bags (of 200 lb. net) while groundnut reports relatively recent development, more of the order of 200,000 bags. Other cash crops undergoing expansion were Burley tobacco and cotton. The additional production in these was achieved to a great extent by increasing the numbers working upon the land. Particularly in the case of maize, the yield per acre remained low.

Expenditure by the territorial government tended to fluctuate with government income, but expenditure by the Ministry rose from £281,316 in 1952 (for European and African combined) to £797,114 in 1963 (African farmers only), an indication of the growing awareness by government that development of sectors of the economy other than copper was urgent.

Commerce, Industry and Finance

Prior to Federation, Salisbury, Johannesburg and even London had controlled many overseas businesses operating in Northern Rhodesia; with the political change the tendency to favour Salisbury was accentuated. No financial centre of any significance could develop in Northern Rhodesia during Federation because with improved communications the predominance of Salisbury was steadily enhanced.

Similarly the principal distributing centres in the Federation were most conveniently sited nearer to the points of first entry than in Northern Rhodesia. No Northern Rhodesian town could rival Bulawayo and Salisbury as distribution centres for wholesalers and manufacturers' representatives. The portion of gross domestic product from distribution in Northern and Southern Rhodesia respectively was:

ESTIMATED VALUE OF DISTRIBUTION SERVICES (£M)

	1954	*1957*	*1961*	*% increase/1961 over 1954*
Southern Rhodesia	20.0	28.6	33.6	68.0
Northern Rhodesia	8.4	10.5	11.6	38.1

[Source: *National Accounts of the Federation of R & N, Cf. P. 104 CSO.*]

The income earned from distribution in Northern Rhodesia increased by only £3.2 millions at a period when territorial income was estimated to have increased by £61.6 millions. The area from which any Northern Rhodesia infant industry principally needed protection was the adjacent Southern Rhodesia, and no such protection could be forthcoming under Federation. It could probably be substantiated that the effect of Federal trade and tariff policy was that effective protection was given mainly to the South and that there resulted an increase of net income in that area and a decrease in net income in the other two territories.

The long term outcome of Federation might have been to bring a greater stability to the component territories; as it happens, both copper and tobacco, the two principal primary sources of cash income had been among the more stable of raw materials; moreover tobacco prices tend more to be independent of most other raw materials. But during the period of Federation the rapid expansion of the economy of Northern Rhodesia that had characterised the post-war period came to a halt. From 1945 to 1953 gross domestic product has risen from £15.4 million to £112.2 million (*National Income and Social Accounts of N.R. 1945-53*); after rising to £194.3 million in 1956 it amounted only to some £204 million by 1962; allowing for a fall of about £10 million in mining which had been offset by a rise of a similar order in the estimated product of agriculture, the remainder of the economy had been remarkably static, in contrast to the economy of Southern Rhodesia which had continued to expand. Indeed, the contrast and the disposition of expenditure of the Federal government were to cause the then Minister of Finance, the colonial civil servant Mr Ralph Nicholson, to complain in the course of his 1959 Budget speech of the inequitable share of total revenue that accrued to Northern Rhodesia. The same theme was taken up in 1960 by the weekly newspaper *Central African Mail* which roundly accused the Federal government of extracting from Northern Rhodesia a total of £63 million more than was spent in that country during the seven years up to 1959.

Henceforward the theme was taken up by A. Hazelwood and P. O. Henderson, two British economists who, in *Nyasaland; The Economics of Federation,* estimated that up to mid-1959 Northern Rhodesia had suffered a net loss in excess of £50 million. The theme became somewhat of a commonplace in Northern Rhodesia during the later years of Federation.

Geographically and historically, the pre-conditions of Federation were such as to make of Northern Rhodesia a hinterland of the more advanced South as soon as the two countries became a part of a single entity. When existing influences were reinforced by the political decisions on siting of the capital and on provision of services generally, so as to reinforce the most profitable sectors of the economy, the pattern of Federal development was determined until such time as that political entity was to come to an end.

10

Economic Prospects

TOWARDS the close of 1963 the embryonic state of Zambia began to come into focus. Under Federation the country had grown into a larger political entity, participating in common services with assumed economies from sharing these with other territories. Moreover, financial institutions had been moulded and trading patterns established both internally and externally. In determining the infrastructure also the die seemed to have been cast; Rhodesia Railways running up from South Africa and Portuguese East Africa was the dominant freight route to the detriment of developing alternative access to the sea and the outside world. Electric power production was centralised on the south bank of the Kariba dam in Southern Rhodesia—and the bulk of the country's electricity supply was therefore imported.

The pattern of economic development of North and South seemed so closely interwoven that mutual damage appeared probable from the tearing apart in December 1963. In the event this danger was avoided, at least in the short term. The flow of commerce and economic inter-relationships continued. In June 1964 Southern Rhodesia remained by far the largest supplier of goods of all kinds to Zambia and economic connections were largely adjusted without dislocation.

While the resumption of responsibility by the Northern Rhodesia government for the economic ministries was effected smoothly, the new centre of economic control threw into relief the imbalance in the country's development. This theme is stressed in the principal reports on the territory's economy, particularly the report of the UNESCO Planning Mission on Education in Northern Rhodesia,[1] which notes in Chapter 1, paragraph 2: 'The most striking feature of Northern Rhodesia society is the sharpness of the division within it, and it is this feature which is now directly challenged. There is a marked inequality of access to positions of responsibility, power and wealth and, related to this, unequal access to the education and skill needed to fill them. The contrasts sit awkwardly with the final political equality that will exist early in 1964.' Though the report was specifically upon education it was nonetheless necessary to include a section entitled 'Contrasts in the Northern Rhodesia Economy'.

This imbalance was authoritatively described by the Economic Survey Mission of UN/ECA/FAO. In March 1964 the Mission prepared a blue-print for a plan covering all principal economic aspects of the country's development. Quite apart from the wide gulf in living standards between white and black, the Mission pinpointed equally significant discrepancies between town and country; between areas on the line-of-rail and those remote from the main lines of communication; between development of copper production and development of all other primary sources of economic wealth. All these contrasts constitute economic sources of weakness which can lead to social and political instability, and one-sided development accentuates the dangers of a 'mono-economy'. Primary products, with swings in demand and relatively inelastic supply, are a notoriously awkward mainspring for economic growth. In 1961, copper mining, at £95 million, provided 46.5 per cent of the gross domestic product (See Appendix II, Table 5A), while in 1962 the proportion, at £93.8 million, was 45.8 per cent. Table 5A indicates the extent to which the country's considerable foreign exchange receipts depended upon copper in 1961—a year in which the value of copper exports was not higher than average. These figures show how the economy has remained copper-orientated to so great an extent for twenty-five years from the time when copper first dominated the territory.

The Government Balance Sheet, 1964

The present whipping boy for all this imbalance in the territory's development is, conveniently, the Federation or the Federal government, neither of which is in any position to answer back. But it was the colonial government which held the economic controls for all but the last ten years of this period. Its record both then and during Federation gives no indication that, in the absence of Federation, national policy would have been geared to decisive government intervention in the territory's development. The first government of the Republic of Zambia had a number of points of especial strength, particularly by contrast with other new African states.

1. In copper there was a source of remarkably high foreign exchange earnings, amounting per head of population to nearly £30.
2. The country had many highly skilled immigrants, equipped to supply all the goods and services required by the developed parts of the economy.
3. The basic services needed for development—rail and road communication and power supply—were available.
4. Although little advantage had been taken of the experience of other newly independent African states, there was available a fund of information about their recent (and in some respects parallel) development.

Some of these advantages had built-in drawbacks. In addition to the weakness of reliance upon the single commodity, copper, other liabilities of the government balance sheet were:

1. The instability of the government machine which was being taken over. Later we will refer to the likely shortage of manpower both within and without government. Here we need only remark on the upheaval in all sections of the civil service coming at a time when the responsibilities of government were being enhanced by the return of the ex-Federal departments. This was caused by the unprecedented volume of resignations, retirements, promotions and transfers taking place while an inexperienced group of ministers were assuming the responsibilities of power.
2. The limitations of the administration as an instrument for developing the country. It has already been observed that with the colonial government, this task of innovation and development of the economy had a relatively low place. It was therefore inevitable that a government pledged to promote the use of the country's resources—material, financial and human—should find the established usages of government not wholly relevant to the job at hand.
3. By the same token that the country's skills were largely provided by expatriates, it had been thought unnecessary to develop the skills of the indigenous population. As a result, the country lacked the professional personnel who were already available in countries farther north. Since a large proportion of qualified persons were domiciled elsewhere, there lay here a major source of potential instability.
4. The uneven pattern of development had awakened many

people to desires which they could not readily fulfil. The spread of knowledge and ideas were bringing about a revolution in social outlook now canalised in the immediate demands of the new electorate. At present, the greatest single strain on society seems to come from unemployment. A growing number of people have been reaching their twenties with several years' education but with no experience of the discipline of a regular job or of the stability of a regular wage.

5. On the border of the Copperbelt, only a few miles from the copper mines, lies the Congo. This unstable country, with a fragmentary local administration and the most sketchy hold upon law and order, was an obvious source of instability.

To summarise: foreign exchange reserves were available in relative abundance, but skills were inadequate. The resources showed wide promise, but a plan and a policy were needed to put them to work.

THE STRATEGY OF DEVELOPMENT

The lack of balance in the economy is exemplified by the spectacular inequalities between European and African, town and country, also within the towns. The best paid and most senior jobs, whether in public service or in the private sector, are almost all held by Europeans. But the country now has its first popular government, and it is a condition of future progress that the new hopes of the people should be met as far as possible.

One of the least satisfactory features of the economy had been inability to provide increased employment opportunities for the expanding population. The historical background to development in the country goes far towards explaining this feature but to the Mission the stagnation in employment for so long a period was surprising; 'It can be explained', they write, 'only by reference to the declining labour force in the mines (accompanied by higher labour costs, increased output and greatly enhanced output per worker) on the one hand, and on the other by the spectacular transfers of income from the north to other territories which occurred during Federation'. This lack of employment openings is directly related to the accentuation of economic growth within Southern Rhodesia which, as already indicated, was a natural and predictable outcome of political federation. It is surprising that the

Report ignores the considerable increases in wages that have taken place during the historical period examined in the course of the Survey.

The Report pinpoints 'the possibility of a surge forward' based upon the immediate fiscal gains, both directly through the return of revenues and indirectly from the increased purchasing power generated by ex-federal services now to be paid for in Zambia. Possibly even more important, the government has regained the economic powers needed to expand and develop the economy, namely direct taxation, control over external trade, and the ability to deal with other countries and international agencies as a sovereign power. Finally it recognises the special position in popular esteem of the first elected nationalist government—the first government to have any chance of widespread goodwill.

Aims of the Plan

Discussion with the government crystallised the general aims of economic policy. These were :

1. To increase employment quickly.
2. To promote greater equality of living standards, having particular regard to the poorer provinces and to the greater 'Africanisation' of employment.
3. To avoid social disruption by building upon existing forms when possible.
4. To promote the development of Zambia as part of the pattern of African development.
   'On the question of public or private enterprise, the government's attitude appears to be pragmatic'—but there was recognition that government would in any case depend on private enterprise for many years and nationalisation of the copper mines was regarded as being out of the question.

The first of these aims is vital for political and economic stability. The range of employment avenues for Africans must be broadened to admit Africans to all the main classes of employment. The country cannot permanently afford the cost of development with an establishment of salary scales geared to expatriate terms. Related to this, there is a thorny problem on which the Report is silent: how to produce, in a fairly short period of Africanisation, a sufficient number of African entrepreneurs and individual businessmen.

The quantitative estimates of the Mission were based upon

a sketch of the sort of economic structure which would satisfy the following criteria by 1970:

1. to provide at least 150,000 more jobs than there are today;
2. to be such that the advance would continue in the 1970s;
3. to imply significant improvements in living standards, especially for Africans;
4. to be, to the best of expert judgment, physically feasible;
5. to be viable, in the sense of being compatible with a balance in foreign payments and price stability.

Internal consistency is claimed for the set of projections which also add up to a comprehensive program in the sense that if one sector fails other sectors will be seriously affected; higher imports would become necessary if the agricultural or industrial programs failed; while a failure in income of any sector would cut into the prospective market for home-produced goods and products, and thereby undermine the dependent producer.

The Plan's operation: Employment and investment

Financed by rising income and buttressed by increased foreign exchange, government consumption and investment would grow by about fifty per cent and seventy-five per cent respectively between 1965 and 1970. Employment would rise, geared both directly and indirectly to increased government expenditure, and by 1970 the increase in government current expediture would have risen to an annual rate of £32 million coupled with an increase from mining production estimated at £16 million; total GDP should have risen by a total of £93 million. The balance above the mining product would represent the additional contribution of other sectors of the economy. The estimated resultant effect on the employment situation would be a total of 164,000 jobs for Africans by 1970, in addition to those available in 1963. The Report also notes that in that year an additional 20,000 Africans, aged sixteen or over, should still be at school or university because of the much increased program of education. Given the present estimate of urban unemployed males of 57,000 and a natural increase by 1970 of 40,000—a total of 100,000 additional jobs to be found—the total increase in places should theoretically suffice to contain the unemployment problem. This calculation is supported by the planned resettlement of 30,000 families in the rural areas, dependent on agriculture. Nevertheless the extent of the future drift to the towns can be estimated only in the most approximate terms, to say nothing of the effect of returning Zambians from neighbouring territories, immigrants from those territories and the tendency, observable everywhere else, for women to compete with men for paid employment.

To enable this increase in income, production and employment to take place, a major rise in investment is required amounting over the six years 1965-70 to somewhat over £450 million. Some thirty per cent of this amount is to be provided by government; for the remaining seventy per cent reliance is placed upon the private sector (perhaps twenty-five per cent from additional capital expenditure by the copper mining groups, forty-five per cent from commerce, industry and all other private sources). Such a program would imply the import by the private sector of very considerable amounts of capital, although in the absence of the Report's estimate of depreciation quotas and non-mining profits retentions, the amount of such capital cannot readily be estimated.

THE CENTRAL ISSUES OF POLICY

Having laid down its main thesis, the Mission proceeds to outline a series of political decisions that will have to be taken as adjuncts to the plan and to ensure its success. It is problematic whether the pre-conditions stipulated will all be realisable by a free society in the 1960s in a newly independent African state, for they do not lend themselves to easy fulfilment.

I. *Copper Production*

Copper production needs to rise from the present figure of some 700,000 short tons in 1964 to at least 800,000 by 1970. This will entail heavy capital investment by the mining groups. But the Report points out that there is no reason why the interests of the mining companies, over plans for development, should coincide with the government's interests. The companies represent private shareholders, few of whom are domiciled in Zambia, and the companies may well prefer to distribute all their profits or to reinvest in other countries; it is implied that development plans of the mining groups are not likely to measure up to national requirements. And yet copper is far too important to the country for mining policy to be decided without regard to the country's interests. Some kind of agreement between the companies and the government appears essential to ensure the integration of this primary source of earning power into the general economic plan of an independent country.

II. *Foreign Exchange and Taxation*

If the plan is to be promoted, foreign exchange earnings, considerable as they already are, need to be augmented and husbanded. As internal income grows, part of this increase will be reflected in more imports, so exports will need to be stepped up. Foreign exchange can be strengthened further by reducing internal income (a large part of which is represented by remittances to other countries).

III. *Wages and Prices*

On the subject of wages, the Report warns that Zambia 'can have big increases in wages or big increases in employment, *not both*'. There is no question of the country's being able to afford minimum wages on the scale demanded by some trade unionists (£22 per month). Wage increases already granted to unskilled workers, modest enough though they are by Europeans standards, are already eliminating labour-intensive production methods. This applies especially where handling of materials can be mechanised, and without government intervention to provide jobs, it is likely that employment would be reduced.

Another major problem is that Africans moving into European jobs expect to be paid the same high salaries. This, it is pointed out, would increase the inequalities in income distribution which it is the policy of government to reduce. The Mission believes strongly that wages and salaries should not be permitted to rise rapidly during the coming six years, if the program is to be carried out safely. The cabinet have announced voluntary salary cuts of £100 per minister and £50 per parliamentary secretary, the monies saved to be returned to government revenue. The avoidance of wage-induced inflation is perhaps the most difficult task facing government.

IV. *High-Level Manpower : The Europeans*

The negligible number of Africans with higher educational qualifications cannot be rapidly increased, although Africanisation of salaried employment in the very near future is inevitable. Therefore, a supply of non-Africans will be vital to the economy for many years to come in the technical and professional fields. The Report recognises that, should a particular class of service at present supplied almost exclusively by Europeans—medical services, for instance—collapse through lack of staff, other Europeans will be likely to leave and a cumulative decline ensue. Steps are recommended to recruit personnel from overseas as early as possible, and to attempt to obtain undertakings from the United

Kingdom and/or the Commonwealth that staff would be provided to prevent a breakdown in any essential service.

V. *Trade Links*

Passing reference only is made to the development of Zambia as part of the greater sub-region of East and Central Africa and to the recent ECA Report on that topic. The more promising near term course of bilateral agreements with Congo-Leopoldville and with Malawi are referred to, and the opportunity is taken to point out that in early 1964 both South African and South Rhodesian goods came in on preferential terms. Attention was paid to this political embarrassment in May 1964 when the rebate on a wide range of Southern Rhodesian goods was cancelled; at the end of the year it was announced that no new trade agreements would be negotiated with either country. President Kaunda and his colleagues were constrained to explain to other African leaders the impossibility of Zambia's joining in a trade boycott of South Africa, but at the same time importers were urged to look for other sources of supply. A re-orientation would have to be gradual to avoid a sudden rise in living costs; another material factor was that delivery dates from manufacturers in southern Africa were normally shorter, so that extra finance was needed to switch to more distant suppliers. Hope of escape from this dilemma was aroused by an ECA conference at Nairobi in February 1965 in which proposals were made for a common market covering Zambia, Malawi and East Africa. Finance Minister Arthur Wina forecast that Zambia would play a leading role in such an economic association. The idea gave new stimulus to discussions about building a railway from Zambia to Dar es Salaam, for without such a link Zambia could scarcely join in a common market with East Africa. However, it was estimated that the railway would take four years to build and might cost £60 million.

VI. *Agriculture*

One of the very infrequent attempts by the colonial government of Northern Rhodesia to plan the economic development of the territory, was concerned with the imbalance between development in rural and urban areas. Although a 1961 report stressed the scope for national investment in agriculture, the recommendations were never implemented because the necessary funds were never found. But the document did promote the claims of the rural areas to a major part of government expenditure and did enunciate the principle of concentrating investment and effort upon the areas where the return per unit of expenditure was the greatest. The section on Agriculture in the UN Report does not attempt to answer the very germane question: 'Should resources be used where the income return is greatest?' In the light of the known great shortage of agricultural extension specialists, this question is urgent. However, basic objectives for policy are:

1. There should be some development in every province (irrespective of agricultural potential).
2. The resettlement of families, both of recent urban arrivals who are unemployed and of rural families from areas where overcrowding or soil erosion is taking place.
3. Migration to the towns should be discouraged in the long run. It is recognised that no policy for agriculture is likely to act as an important discouragement to migration in the forseeable future.
4. Agricultural produce from 1965 to 1970 should be increased as indicated in Table 9 (see Appendix): the additional African £6.6 million represents output resulting from the mission's recommended program.

This would involve production of most of the nation's food supplies, an increase by value of £10 million in exports, and very considerable savings in foreign exchange.

VII. *Obstacles to Industrialisation*

No first-class industrial opportunity in Zambia has ever failed to be promoted through lack of funds. Hitherto the opening and particularly a protected market have been lacking. For the time being, therefore, undue emphasis on availability of finance is misplaced. What are lacking are the components of an industrial background and tradition. It would seem probable that industrial progress will be influenced by future relationships with industrialists in Southern Rhodesia and South Africa, and by the policies, including exchange control regulation, of those countries. An obstacle not stressed by the Report is the effect of the remoteness of Zambia. Delivery dates are long, costs have a tendency to be raised and working capital is often needed on a scale not known in countries better placed geographically. The diversification of product practised by manufacturers in highly industrialised countries, through fragmentation of demand, also gives rise to difficulties in industrialisation with a small market.

There is virtually no African enterprise in industry as yet. The Report recommended the co-operative movement as a suitable vehicle for this (as for many other economic activities). In practice, it seems likely that the African advance into industry will follow the pattern clearly established elsewhere and take place via commerce, arriving at manufacturing through retail and wholesale trading.

MANPOWER

'Zambia at the moment is at a critical juncture—with possibilities that could lead to a cumulative uprising, or the reverse. The availability of the necessary manpower will largely determine the outcome, and a month or two either way in recruitment could make all the difference.'

These words closed the section on manpower in the UN/ECA/FAO report. They illustrate the extreme hazards to be overcome by development planning for the first several years of independence. The origin of the manpower problem is the same as that of most other economic problems here discussed—the speed with which the economy has developed and the extreme lack of balance between different sectors of the economy. This is manifest in educational facilities available:

1. to European and African;
2. between line-of-rail and rural areas;
3. between males and females;
4. between children of the 1960s and persons ten or more years older.

The manpower problem can conveniently be classified in relation to employment under three general heads:

(a) The top positions, administrative, professional, executive, whether public or private;
(b) the intermediate positions requiring skill and in many cases formal qualifications;
(c) the remaining majority of jobs and the super-abundant labour supply.

(a) The top positions are widely spread among the civil service, local authorities and all parts of the private sector of the economy. With the government poised to initiate large-scale development policies creating unprecedented demands for highly qualified personnel, the number of Zambian African graduates is estimated at not more than one hundred; personnel possessing other professional qualifications are likewise scarce.

(b) In assessing manpower available for the second echelon jobs, requiring less than the highest qualifications and experience, the position is similar. Indeed, here the sheer disparity between numbers available and numbers required is far greater, and the nature of the jobs is such that expatriates cannot be used to fill them even if the number of vacancies were not so great as to make such a solution impossible. Thus the middle ranks of the civil service, the staff of the many small local authorities upon which such heavy demands are shortly to be made if the development plan is to have effect, cannot be built up except on a cadre of experienced and educated Africans. The projected shortfall in numbers of school-certificate holders can be expected to grow during the coming five years and only lessen to a small degree by 1975.

(c) Unskilled and semi-skilled labour, of illiterates or semi-literates, provides by far the greatest part of the available force. Although most African workers are in occupations which draw employees from unskilled labour or semi-skilled labour, it is these classes, overwhelmingly the largest in the labour force, which contain the largest numbers of unemployed, both absolutely and proportionately. The pattern already noted of migration from rural to urban areas augments the numbers of unskilled (in relation to urban requirements) and it is this class, uneducated, urbanised or undergoing urbanisation, which forms the unemployment problem.

The near-term 'Emergency' period 1965-1970

The Mission's proposed educational program will not provide major dividends to the economy until after the 'Emergency' period. This is especially true of the top positions to be filled. Thus despite the imminent establishment of a university at Lusaka following the proposals of the Lockwood Report,[2] the Mission estimates that 'the number of Africans of Zambia holding degrees in 1970 cannot exceed 500 and will probably be much less'. A continuing and increasing need for expatriates is inevitable and provision is made accordingly in proposals for government expenditure, but although there may be an available supply of suitably trained English-speaking personnel, the cost will be vastly greater if employment offered is only secure for a period of five or ten years.

The Long Term—1971 and after

Manpower needs until 1980 estimated in a projection that suggests gross needs for school-certificate holders for educational plans alone range from 2,300 in 1965 to 13,500 in 1980, but the Mission returns to the need for a detailed manpower survey before definitive figures of requirements can be produced.

On finance, the costs of the program will rise from £11.5 million in 1965 to £14.5 million in 1970. This figure is noted to be only of the order of 4.5 per cent of gross domestic product and well below the amounts spent by many countries on education though well above what is normal for states in Africa.

THE CHALLENGE IN SUMMARY

The year 1964 marked the most significant political development in the history of Zambia. It started with the demise of Federation and proceeded with the rapid widening of the functions controlled by the nationalist government up to independence. Turning points in economic history are frequently less striking, but in this instance there are two main reasons for believing that the economic prospects for Zambia have undergone major change.

First, the end of Federation made it possible for the country to be developed as an entity and for its own primary benefit. No longer are economic affairs of Zambia to be considered aspects of varying importance in a wider picture. Transfers of income (exploitation) take place naturally when a country with Zambia's peculiar combination of advantages and disadvantages is linked politically with a neighbour economically more advanced and geographically better placed. From the outset of 1964 Zambia was in charge of her own economic affairs and possessed the powers to protect her agriculture and industry like any other developing state, while she will now also be able to direct national investment to spend her income for her own exclusive benefit.

Secondly, the change of government from colonial rule has made possible an entirely fresh approach to economic policy making.

The future of Zambia will be moulded by the change in government and the change in approach. Given these facts, there are numerous guides both in the Report and in evidence generally available from government statements, the various statistical indices and elsewhere, of what the future is likely to hold.

It is clear that the country and the government will have more money available than the average independent country, both in terms of income per head and taxable capacity and, especially, in foreign exchange earnings.

The time available in which to bring about change is, however, short. The time limiting factors are the rapidly expanding population and the forseeable future during which copper can reasonably be expected to retain its present high rate of earnings. No government can leave development to chance in these circumstances. Indeed the government must both satisfy popular expectation and ensure that the country's resources are used in her best interests.

Government expenditure is the starting point of the stimulus to development. There will be expenditure on agriculture, education and all other functions of government. From such public expenditure the money will come out predominantly in salaries and wages paid directly, in buildings and roads (in which salaries and wages are sunk in local material costs), in some plant and in loans and advances. Budgeted revenue for 1964-5 is £56 million including a surplus on current account; by 1970 revenue is likely to be running at a rate of £80 million or more.

A corollary to increased government expenditure is increased internal control measures over the economy and the near certainty of increased rates of taxation. Exchange control, control of interest rates and physical control of credit are likely to be among measures used. Increased expenditure by increasing incomes will tend to inflate the internal economy. Internal price inflation will need to be checked in order to avoid the reinforcing effect of wage inflation. Furthermore, because of Zambia's inevitably high propensity to import, a large proportion of new income will result in increased imports and foreign exchange requirements. Protective measures will be needed to ensure the Zambian balance of payments. With relatively copious foreign exchange earnings the prospect of balance of payments difficulties may seem to be remote. The Report proposes plans for expenditure on development at such a rate that Zambia's earning power should be fully extended. Furthermore, it is safe to assume that any government will be pressed by opposition and electorate to spend up to and possibly beyond the point at which foreign exchange resources are adversely affected. So exchange control and other known devices to control the economy of a new state will be needed.

An unknown factor which could be of importance will be relations with neighbouring states. An early change to majority rule in the government of Southern Rhodesia would only bring marginal changes in economic policy; a customs union would be impracticable without the economic pattern of the Federation redeveloping. There would be—as there is at present—scope for bargaining over markets and tariff rates but with few exceptions the balance of long-term advantage would still lie to the South.

In combination with the proposed East African Federation there are two possible lines of approach. The first is that Kenya with its more developed agriculture, and Dar es Salaam with better communications, might well be potential low-cost producers of a wide range of the goods that could be economically produced in

Zambia and the pattern of the Federation might be reproduced with Zambia proving to be too high cost an area to benefit from amalgamation with a larger economic unit. The alternative possibility has particular reference to industry and foreign capital investment. These could locate themselves in certain circumstances wherever political stability was demonstrably greatest. Should Zambia be an area of exceptional political stability north of Zambezi, it might be an especially favoured location for many lines of development.

The other region with which Zambia's economic links are especially strong is Katanga. Were it a political possibility, a wide area of economic agreement between the Congo and Zambia might be of more advantage than any other case. The frontier runs almost entirely through areas of joint economic interest, dividing markets, setting up barriers between producer and purchaser, causing unnecessary delay in communications and chaos in foreign exchange relationships. Although the convulsions of that unhappy state are not yet over, Zambia has little to lose and much to gain from the friendliest of relations with the Congo and the closest of economic ties with whatever government controls Katanga.

The other country from which great benefits might be derived is the Republic of South Africa. In so far as foreign enterprise and investment are sought, this country is by far the best placed to supply them. The problems of operation on this continent are without doubt better understood by businesses already established in Africa; communications are better understood and forms of organisation need to take a pattern quite different from whatever may be suitable, for example, in Britain. A large proportion of the companies which would normally be interested in setting up businesses in Zambia are either from South Africa or already have subsidiaries and associates there under whose sphere of influence or selling areas Zambia would tend to fall. It is of some relevance that, to businessmen in the Republic, Zambia should appear to be a stable country with a climate conducive to investment. The Republic is also highly important as a potential source of skilled manpower both for public or private enterprise. Whatever the relationship between the two countries at government level, there is a very material potential gain or loss for Zambia in the vital fields of investment and personnel.

It seems appropriate to conclude by a brief summary of the most likely economic picture ten years from now. Population will have risen to between 4.5 million and 5 million. Provided no major recession in copper prices has occurred, national income should be at least 50 per cent higher than at present, and income per head should be somewhat higher. Agricultural output is likely to have increased but the biggest increase is looked for in areas which are already most developed agriculturally. The unemployment problem may have been contained but is unlikely to have been solved, so that continued efforts will still be needed to create employment opportunities.

The speed of growth in industry depends on the economic associations that are made. Industry will not be in a state in which it can attempt to sustain itself technologically : it will still be what the Report calls a branch-plant economy. Whether or not Zambia will become once more the hinterland of a better situated industrial area depends upon political decisions that will be taken during the coming years.

There will still be non-African people in Zambia in considerable numbers, though it is difficult to envisage a settled population of Europeans; rather one could expect to find a decisive increase in the proportion of expatriates. It is greatly to be hoped that a strong class of African businessman will have been created, though the time for its evolution is so short.

The country starts from its unique and somewhat paradoxical position with a vision of whither it should go, a method of approach suitable to its circumstances and resources potentially sufficient to raise its standards. It is more favoured than most of its contemporaries.

APPENDIX I

Zambia's Constitution

The President

ZAMBIA will have a President who will be head of State and Commander-in-Chief of the Armed Forces.

The President will be elected at the same time as the general election of members of the National Assembly after any dissolution of Parliament. Each presidential candidate must be nominated by at least 1,000 registered voters. Every candidate for election to the National Assembly will declare in advance which presidential candidate he supports. Constituency ballot papers will show the name of the presidential candidate each parliamentary candidate supports. Each voter will then be able to vote simultaneously for the parliamentary candidate of his choice and the presidential candidate supported by that candidate. The President elected will be the candidate who receives the greatest number of votes from the electorate as a whole.

[During August 1964, there was a campaign to make Kaunda the President of Zambia for life. But he rejected the proposal, saying that he wanted Zambia to be a 'liberal democracy'.]

Cabinet

There will be a Cabinet, the chairman of which will normally be the President, consisting of a Vice-President, who will be the President's principal assistant, and the Leader of the House in Parliament, and not more than fourteen Ministers. The President will appoint the Vice-President and the Ministers (and also Parliamentary Secretaries) from among the members of the National Assembly and will have the power to remove them from office.

Subject to the powers of the President as head of State, the Cabinet will be responsible for government policy and will advise the President on all matters referred to.

Legislature

The legislative powers of the Republic will be vested in a Parliament consisting of the President and a National Assembly of seventy-five elected members. The President will have powers to nominate up to five persons as special members of the National Assembly in order to enhance the representative character of the Assembly or to obtain the services of persons with special qualifications or particular value.

The President will not be a member of the National Assembly

but will have the power to address it at any time. The normal life of a Parliament will be five years, but Parliament will have the power to vary in special circumstances, such as war or an emergency. The President will be able to summon the National Assembly to meet at any time.

Bills will not become law until they have been passed by the National Assembly and assented by the President. If the President is unwilling to give his assent he will be able to return a Bill to the Assembly, in which case it will not be presented again for presidential assent unless within six months it receives the support of a two-thirds majority of all the members of the Assembly. Where this occurs the President must either dissolve Parliament or give his assent within twenty-one days.

Amendment of the Constitution

Parliament will have the power to alter the constitution provided that the proposed amendment has the support of two-thirds of all members of the National Assembly at the second and third readings of the Bill containing it. Thirty days must elapse between the publication of a Bill to amend the constitution and its first reading.

Where any Bill relates to the code of human rights (see below) the judiciary or the procedure for amending the constitution, its proposals must in addition be approved by a simple majority of the total electorate at a referendum.

Human Rights

If not less than seven members of the National Assembly give written notice to the Speaker within three days of the final reading of any Bill, a tribunal of two High Court judges will be appointed to consider whether the Bill is inconsistent with the code of human rights, and report to the President and the Speaker. If the Bill appears inconsistent to the tribunal the President would be able to assent or refuse his assent to the Bill, or return it to the Assembly. A similiar procedure would apply to a statutory instrument and the President would be able to make an order affirming or annulling it.

Electoral Provisions

The franchise will be based on universal suffrage for all persons aged not less than twenty-one years who are citizens of Zambia and not otherwise disqualified.

An Electoral Commission consisting of a chairman and two members appointed by the President will prescribe constituency boundaries and carry out periodical reviews of the division of the country into constituencies, the number of which will correspond with the number of elected seats in the National Assembly. Constituencies, each of which will have approximately the same total population, will each have one member.

House of Chiefs

Provision for the composition, functions and procedure of the House of Chiefs will be substantially the same as those in the previous constitution.

The Judiciary

The provisions of the existing constitution relating to the High

Court will remain substantially unaltered. There will continue to be a Court of Appeal, and the President will be empowered to make an order declaring that the Judicial Committee of the Privy Council shall be a Court of Appeal for Zambia.

The Chief Justice will be appointed by the President; all other judges will be appointed by the President on the recommendation of the Judicial Service Commission. A judge will be removed by the President only on the report of a tribunal of three persons with judicial experience set up by the President.

Public Service

The President will be responsible for appointing members of the public service and for their disciplinary control and removal from office. Where the offices of Permanent Secretary, Secretary to the Cabinet or the Commissioner of Police are concerned, the President will act after consultation with the Public Service Commission.

Citizenship

The constitution makes provision for citizenship by birth and by registration, for Commonwealth citizenship on the part of Zambia nationals, and for reciprocal privileges between citizens of Zambia and citizens of any Commonwealth country and of any foreign country specified by the Zambia government.

APPENDIX II

Statistical Tables

TABLE I. ACTUAL RECURRENT EXPENDITURE

Expenditure Heads	1924-5 Actual £	1925-6 Actual £	1926-7 Actual £	1927-8 Actual £
Recurrent Expenditure:				
Charges on account of Public Debt ...	—	—	—	—
Pensions and gratuities	14,018	15,855	17,981	29,081
The Governor	5,971	6,261	5,886	5,937
Administrator-general	*Included in Judicial until 1936*	—	—	—
Agriculture	3,434	5,301	9,832	10,289
Audit	1,592	2,548	3,045	2,868
Customs	4,380	4,903	5,314	6,811
European education	7,722	10,591	13,487	15,801
Health	28,746	34,634	38,969	45,571
Income Tax	2,320	1,969	1,994	2,178
Judicial	3,511	4,436	4,304	4,410
Lands, mines, and surveys	9,704	8,439	10,618	14,284
Legal	2,803	3,648	3,535	4,128
Miscellaneous services	8,381	25,164	23,169	27,460
Native affairs	*Included in Secretariat*	6,037	6,282	6,651
Native education	348	3,995	6,603	6,593
Northern Rhodesia Police	17,746	17,825	19,832	22,060
Northern Rhodesia Regiment	29,967	30,670	29,212	32,374
Percentage of tax and licences	5,423	5,500	6,300	8,100
Posts and telegraphs	21,111	24,698	28,302	31,331
Printing and stationery	4,280	5,165	5,483	6,370
Prisons	12,711	13,374	12,863	13,867
Provincial administration	87,585	89,693	101,897	104,380
Public Works department	4,694	5,761	8,061	7,234
Public Works recurrent	13,130	15,287	18,701	25,224
Secretariat	8,022	6,583	7,027	7,427
Stores and transport	3,092	3,335	4,026	4,853
Subventions	330	490	656	1,567
Treasury	9,437	7,800	8,652	9,242
Veterinary	14,723	16,009	19,553	19,084
Ndola electricity and water undertaking ...	—	—	—	—
Lusaka electricity and water undertaking ...	—	—	—	—
Northern Rhodesia Volunteer Force ...	957	—	—	—
Total annually recurrent expenditure	325,778	375,971	421,584	475,175

In order to maintain a uniform basis throughout expenditure items have been

UNDER THE MAIN HEADS FOR THE YEARS 1924-1936

1928-9 Actual £	1929-30 Actual £	1930-1 Actual £	1931-2 Actual £	1932-3 Actual £	1933 Actual £	1934 Actual £	1935 Actual £	1936 Actual £
3,861	6,900	5,744	17,331	64,670	70,982	83,115	106,226	120,604
30,632	24,949	30,903	34,625	50,773	68,568	72,694	62,972	74,771
6,963	6,339	6,936	5,347	6,997	7,430	8,111	7,496	7,845
—	—	—	—	—	—	—	—	1,577
11,485	15,281	18,797	30,918	16,506	14,020	6,839	9,016	9,521
3,483	3,489	3,642	4,152	4,002	3,379	3,798	4,685	4,459
6,446	7,966	9,760	11,230	12,231	10,795	10,097	10,593	11,272
19,141	20,697	27,001	33,110	30,279	28,852	27,146	29,017	29,934
47,742	54,716	59,734	68,949	64,470	63,029	56,836	60,429	65,091
1,507	2,167	2,670	2,736	2,962	3,106	3,332	3,330	3,560
5,237	6,445	7,846	9,438	9,884	9,594	9,622	10,671	8,992
14,380	17,055	20,362	22,197	21,204	19,160	15,910	17,706	17,140
4,222	4,425	5,034	5,316	4,323	3,707	3,996	4,180	4,452
29,920	23,835	46,896	84,734	64,902	64,228	44,431	58,777	65,458
6,790	6,412	3,384	3,450	2,214	1,910	1,259	*Included in Secretariat*	—
8,493	12,297	14,447	21,905	21,748	29,237	20,319	24,871	24,842
26,273	29,161	37,200	46,388	49,302	43,206	37,767	44,198	45,726
33,553	31,311	32,931	32,143	27,943	25,317	20,403	21,354	20,059
8,400	8,650	10,514	10,591	6,053	8,941	5,611	5,507	5,243
31,496	37,120	49,574	52,651	50,240	44,395	46,053	49,415	50,038
6,611	8,488	8,690	10,920	8,689	7,774	7,098	8,304	9,525
12,659	12,946	12,693	14,353	16,145	14,515	11,982	11,552	11,734
105,036	111,055	125,561	128,855	120,988	111,320	100,830	107,623	111,583
7,586	6,927	8,389	9,140	7,871	6,620	3,259	5,645	8,214
21,477	26,018	39,336	48,997	38,967	32,432	27,031	31,855	40,202
8,409	9,468	11,089	13,411	13,141	11,752	9,778	11,414	12,895
4,263	5,348	5,899	6,141	6,042	5,605	5,103	5,598	5,289
1,425	2,371	7,350	7,915	9,553	7,412	7,411	6,856	12,205
9,903	9,956	10,248	10,400	11,560	9,884	9,202	8,576	9,143
19,007	20,575	22,334	21,741	19,544	18,032	22,745	21,189	19,281
—	—	—	—	—	—	12,638	8,572	8,035
—	—	—	—	—	—	—	5,106	8,134
496,339	532,367	644,964	769,084	763,203	745,202	694,416	762,733	826,824

regrouped to conform, as far as possible, to present departmental organisations.

TABLE 2—NATIONAL INCOME, 1945-53—(£ million)

INCOME	A.A.	1945	1946	1947	1948	1949	1950	1951	1952	1953[3]
IN THE MONEY ECONOMY:										
1. *Wages and Salaries*:										
(a) European, Asiatic and coloured	a	5.2	5.6	7.0	8.8	10.8	12.8	16.5	20.2	24.9
(b) African	a	3.1	3.4	4.0	4.8	6.2	7.6	10.6	13.2	20.7
TOTAL WAGES AND SALARIES[1]:		8.3	9.0	11.1	13.6	17.1	20.4	27.1	33.4	45.6
2. *Money income from unincorporated enterprise*:										
(a) European	c	0.9	1.1	1.4	1.7	2.3	2.6	3.0	3.4	3.7
(b) African	d	0.2	0.2	0.2	0.6	0.4	0.8	0.8	1.1	1.4
TOTAL MONEY INCOME FROM UNINCORPORATED ENTERPRISE:		1.1	1.3	1.6	2.3	2.7	3.4	3.8	4.5	5.1
3. *Company incomes*:										
(a) Mining and refining companies	a	2.8	3.9	9.8	12.1	16.1	24.3	40.3	39.9	42.6
(b) Other companies	c	1.0	1.1	1.3	1.3	1.6	1.9	2.4	2.8	3.2
(c) Royalties	a	0.3	0.6	1.6	2.3	3.0	4.5	7.3	8.8	10.3
TOTAL COMPANY INCOMES[1]:		4.1	5.6	12.6	15.8	20.8	30.7	50.0	51.5	56.3
4. Miscellaneous European income from property, n.e.i.	c	0.1	0.1	0.1	0.1	0.1	0.1	0.1	0.2	0.2
5. Government income from property	a	0.1	0.1	0.1	0.2	0.3	0.3	0.4	0.5	0.5
6. *Net domestic output*:		13.7	16.1	25.5	32.0	41.0	54.9	81.4	90.1	107.7
7. *Add* Net interest, dividends and profits received from abroad	b	0.1	0.2	0.2	0.2	0.2	0.2	0.5	0.9	1.4
8. *Less* Net interest, dividends and profits remitted abroad	a	2.4	4.0	10.5	11.7	13.8	22.2	27.7	26.6	25.4
9. *Net national income in money economy*:		11.4	12.3	15.2	20.5	27.4	32.9	54.2	64.4	83.7
GENERATED IN THE SUBSISTENCE ECONOMY:										
10. African Subsistence Income (Nominal)[2]	e	5.0	5.0	5.0	5.0	5.0	5.0	5.0	5.0	5.0
NET NATIONAL INCOME:		16.4	17.3	20.2	25.5	32.4	37.9	59.2	69.4	88.7

[1]Individual items do not necessarily add to totals because of rounding.
[2]These are nominal entries based on experience in Southern Rhodesia.
[3]Provisional. All 1953 figures in this report are provisional.
Note.—A.A. = 'Assessed Accuracy'.

TABLE 3—INVESTMENT, 1945-53—(£ million)

	A.A.	1945	1946	1947	1948	1949	1950	1951	1952	1953
INVESTMENT:										
Home Investment:										
11. Mines and refineries	a	−215	−248	1,005	3,214	4,196	5,331	7,776	9,449	12,700
12. Railways	a	−82	26	152	209	427	465	434	624	632
13. Other private	e	326	480	507	813	859	1,031	1,075	1,612	1,600
14. Central government	a	263	424	991	2,301	3,392	3,898	5,050	7,460	6,721
15. Local government	c	32	61	76	132	257	545	652	1,102	2,610
16. TOTAL		324	743	2,731	6,669	9,131	11,270	15,987	20,247	24,263
Foreign Investment:										
17. Mines and refineries	a	+215	248	−3,505	−3,185	−5,196	−7,339	−14,549	283	−4,260
18. Railways	a	+82	−26	−152	−209	−427	−465	−434	−624	−632
19. Other private	d	435	222	3,112	666	3,268	3,123	18,988	977	−4,779
20. Central government	a	1,036	329	−579	−1,047	−1,497	704	932	1,714	12,593
21. Local government	d	8	27	40	37	30	11	20	30	40
22. TOTAL		1,776	800	−1,084	−3,739	−3,822	−3,966	4,957	2,380	2,962
23. TOTAL HOME AND FOREIGN ...		2,100	1,543	1,647	2,930	5,309	7,304	19,944	22,627	27,225
24. Statistical discrepancy		−70	+256	−32	+410	+222	−502	+132	+575	+464
25. TOTAL INVESTMENT		2,030	1,799	1,615	3,340	5,531	6,802	20,076	23,202	27,689

TABLE 4—VALUE OF MAIN MINERALS PRODUCED IN NORTHERN RHODESIA, 1945-53

	Copper (Blister)	Copper (Electrolytic)	Lead	Zinc	Cobalt and cobalt alloy	Total all minerals
	£	£	£	£	£	£
1945 ...	7,431,857	3,814,693	63,560	696,218	672,148	12,962,522
1946 ...	8,469,885	3,855,825	486,225	869,512	475,674	14,503,196
1947 ...	13,944,787	6,445,240	1,296,755	1,301,496	399,039	23,521,483
1948 ...	18,161,258	7,694,797	1,243,330	1,700,397	434,491	29,771,862
1949 ...	23,548,968	7,706,200	1,403,505	1,972,558	645,273	35,579,543
1950 ...	30,678,420	12,731,944	1,537,559	3,126,650	1,096,337	49,323,187
1951 ...	41,166,736	21,043,091	1,364,373	5,928,360	1,387,682	72,161,125
1952 ...	45,371,488	26,463,604	1,740,500	3,792,975	1,119,607	79,254,907
1953 ...	51,749,000	38,263,875	1,047,093	1,897,030	1,836,272	95,014,411

TABLE 5—COMMERCIAL REVENUE AND EXPENSES

[From the UN/ECA/FAO Report, March 1964]

A—Gross Domestic Product, by Sector of Origin, 1961

(£ million)

Copper mining ...	95
Other mining ...	3
Commercial agriculture (a) ...	8
Manufacturing ...	10
Construction ...	9
Electricity and Water ...	2
Transport and Communications ...	11
Distribution ...	14
Government service (b) ...	13
Other services ...	13
TOTAL COMMERCIAL PRODUCT ...	178
Subsistence agriculture ...	21
Other subsistence ...	5
GROSS DOMESTIC PRODUCT ...	204

(a) includes forestry and fishing.
(b) includes Federal Government services in Zambia.

[Source: *National Accounts of the Federation of Rhodesia & Nyasaland* 1954-62 and supplementary information provided by the C.S.O., Salisbury.]

TABLE 5, B—Copper Industry: Operating Account, 1961

(£ million)

Receipts		*Expenditure*	
Exports ...	111	African wages ...	12
Addition to inventories ...	7	Non-African wages ...	20
Sales of electricity ...	1	Imported supplies (a) ...	20
Housing services ...	2	Purchases of electricity ...	6
Mine development ...	5	Local purchases ...	5
		Direct taxes (b) ...	26
		Net profits and royalties ...	37
TOTAL ...	126	TOTAL ...	126

(a) includes £0.5 million customs duties.
(b) includes Government share of royalties.

[Source: Same as Table A above.]

TABLE 5, C—Balance of Payments, 1961

(£ million)

Receipts		*Payments*	
Exports—copper	116	Imports of goods	101
other minerals ...	3	Dividends and royalties ...	25
farm products ...	5	Current account surplus ...	1
manufactures ...	1		
Net current transfers and tourist receipts	2		
TOTAL RECEIPTS	127	TOTAL PAYMENTS	127

[Source: as Table A.]

TABLE 5, D—Employment by race and sector, 1954 to 1962

(annual averages, thousands)

19...........	54	55	56	57	58	59	60	61	62
A. *African*									
Mining ...	44	43	46	47	40	41	43	42	41
Agriculture (a)	39	37	35	36	36	37	37	38	39
Manufacturing	18	20	22	21	22	20	20	19	17
Construction ...	56	59	65	66	62	45	36	30	24
Transport and communications	7	7	8	9	10	10	10	10	10
Private domestic service ...	30	32	35	35	35	36	36	36	36
Other ...	47	51	54	58	59	62	65	64	63
TOTAL ...	241	249	265	272	264	251	247	238	230
B. *Non-African*									
TOTAL ...	25	27	29	32	32	33	33	32	33

(a) Including forestry and fishing.
[Source: *Monthly Digest of Statistics*]

TABLE 6—MINES PRODUCTION

	Productive Capacity Short tons	Number of Employees	Ore-Reserves Million short tons	Grade % Cu.	Gross Profit from Sales of Copper 1963 £ million
	a	b	c	d	e
Rhokana	110,000	9,700	125	2.92	6.2
Nchanga	250,000	7,000	232	4.39	16.1
Bancroft	55,000	5,400	98	3.66	1.1
Roan Antelope ...	100,000	8,000	93	2.92	2.9
Mufulira	180,000	9,600	176	3.34	8.8
Chibuluma ...	25,000	2,000	10	4.60	0.7
Chambishi ...	30,000	—	35	3.35	—

TABLE 7—EDUCATION IN TWO STREAMS

	Government Expenditure on Education		School Enrolment	
	African	*European*	*Government and Aided African Schools*	*European*
1925	£3,994	£12,239	n.a.*	397
1930	£14,547	£27,001	20,146*	774
1935	£24,871	£29,017	22,695	1,053
1940	£55,183	£44,548	58,792	1,284
1945	£149,450	£75,289	117,123	2,485
1950	£504,176	£445,353	143,398	4,748

*Enrolment in schools open at least 120 days in the year and following the Government code.

[Sources: Northern Rhodesia *Blue Books* and *Annual Reports* of the Departments of African and European Education.]

TABLE 8—EXPENDITURE ON AFRICAN EDUCATION

	Ministry of African Education	Total Recurrent Expenditure	Percentage Total
	£	£	
1951	458,019	15,830,760	2.9
1952	565,249	24,659,447	2.3
1953	642,334	28,221,596	2.3
½ year to June 1954	638,424	10,684,930	6.0
1954/55	1,054,675	13,576,184	7.8
1955/56	1,717,158	16,654,221	10.6
1956/57	1,699,816	18,502,005	9.2
1957/58	1,865,120	16,726,963	11.1
1958/59	1,843,845	14,804,802	12.5
1959/60	2,130,047	16,204,830	13.1
1960/61	2,591,115	18,293,319	14.2
1961/62	3,028,057	19,665,928	15.4
1962/63	3,515,995	20,814,988	16.9

Note: from 1954 onwards total recurrent expenditure does not include European education. Figures before and after are therefore not comparable.

TABLE 9—COMMERCIAL AGRICULTURAL SUPPLIES 1965-70

(£ MILLION AT 1965 PRICE)

Supply	1965	1970	*Per cent increase* 1965-70
African	5.9	9.6	63
European	8.5	12.2	44
Additional African from Mission's program ...	—	6.6	
Total domestic commercial supplies at producer prices	14.4	28.4	97
Distribution costs	5.2	7.9	
Final imports	2.2	2.0	
Supplies at market prices	21.8	38.3	
Less: Private and Government consumption ...	8.2	11.2	
Sales to other sectors ...	7.7	10.8	
Exportable surplus	5.9	16.3	

APPENDIX III

Ownership of Mines

APPENDIX IV

Principal Towns of Zambia

ABERCORN: Small agricultural and fishing centre, twenty-five miles from Lake Tanganyika and port Mpulungu. Above sea level 5,400 ft.

BANCROFT: Small Copperbelt town serving Bancroft mine. Population, 25,000; non-African, 2,300.

BROKEN HILL: One of the oldest established towns. Railway headquarters, also headquarters of Central African Road Services. Mining lead and zinc. Strategically placed close to 'turn-off' for East Africa, and half way between the capital, Lusaka, and the Copperbelt. Population, 40,000; non-African, 5,500.

CHINGOLA: Copperbelt town serving Nchanga mine. Population, 48,000; non-African, 6,000.

FORT JAMESON: Administrative centre near border of Zambia and Malawi, in prosperous farming region.

KITWE: Centre of the Copperbelt, serving Nkana mine. Population, 90,000; non-African, 11,000.

LIVINGSTONE: On northern bank of Zambezi river, near Victoria Falls. An important railway junction and distribution centre for adjacent agricultural and timber area. Population, 33,000; non-African, 4,600.

LUANSHYA: Copperbelt town, serving Roan Antelope mine. Population, 62,000; non-African, 6,000.

LUSAKA: Capital of Zambia. Main line-of-rail from south to Congo; centre of territorial road system north from Southern Rhodesia to Tanzania and the Congo, and east to Malawi and Portuguese East Africa. Population, 92,000; non-African, 14,000.

MUFULIRA: Copperbelt town serving Mufulira mine. Ten miles from the Congo border. Population, 73,000; non-African, 7,000.

NDOLA: Main distribution centre for consumer goods. Close to the Copperbelt, with large copper refinery on outskirts. Population, 89,000; non-African, 11,500.

Principal Newspapers and Journals

Broken Hill Observer: Box 131, Broken Hill (***weekly***).
Central African Mail: Box 1421, Lusaka (***weekly***).

Financial Mail of Zambia: Box 1059, Lusaka (*monthly*).
Livingstone Mail: Box 97, Livingstone (*weekly*).
Zambia News: Box 69, Ndola (*daily*).
Zambia Star: Box 8091, Woodlands, Lusaka (*fortnightly*)
Zambia Review: 201, Security House, Ndola (*monthly*).

Some Proclaimed Ancient Monuments

NORTHERN PROVINCE

Kalambo Falls, Abercorn: At 726 ft., highest waterfalls in Africa, twelfth highest in the world. Important archaeological site revealing full succession from early Stone Age to Iron Age.

Niamkolo Church: Built by the London Missionary Society in 1895 on the shore of Lake Tanganyika. Oldest surviving stone-built church.

'Good News' Monument: Commemorating launching in 1884 of the *Good News,* the first steamship on Lake Tanganyika.

WESTERN PROVINCE

Collier Monument, Luanshya: A copper obelisk on the site where Collier discovered the Roan Antelope copper mine in June 1902.

Old Slave Tree, Ndola: Ancient mupapa trees where Swahili slave-traders celebrated victories and shared out spoils.

CENTRAL PROVINCE

Nsalu Cave, Kanona area: Long occupied during the Stone Age, the cave contains schematic paintings in colour, stone implements and later burials.

Livingstone Memorial, Chitambo: This stands on the site in the Serenje district where Livingstone's heart was buried on May 1, 1873.

Big Tree, Broken Hill: A giant fig, the central meeting place for European townsfolk during the earliest days of settlement here.

SOUTHERN PROVINCE

Chirundu Fossil Forest, Gwembe district: A large area of fossils of the Secondary Age. Also middle and late Stone Age industrial settlements.

Fort Monze and Cemetery, Monze: One of the earliest police posts, established by British South Africa Police in 1898. Graves of early administrators and police.

Administrator's House, Kalomo: Residence of Coryndon, administrator of North-Western Rhodesia, until the capital was transferred to Livingstone. Built 1903.

Old Government House, Livingstone: Built in 1907. Became the Residency and headquarters of the British South Africa Company's administrator of North-Western Rhodesia, then of the governors of Northern Rhodesia from 1924 until 1935 when the capital was transferred to Lusaka.

APPENDIX V

Further Reading: A Select Bibliography

GENERAL HISTORY

AXELSON, ERIC V. *The Portuguese in South-East Africa.* Johannesburg: Witwatersrand University Press, 1960.

BERTRAND, ALFRED. *Upper Zambezi: The Kingdom of the Barotse.* London: Unwin, 1899.

BRELSFORD, W. V. *The Tribes of Northern Rhodesia.* Lusaka: Government Printer, 1957.

CLARK, J. DESMOND. *The Prehistory of Southern Africa.* Harmondsworth: Penguin, 1959.

COOLEY, WILLIAM DESBOROUGH. *Inner Africa Laid Open.* London: Longmans, 1852.

COUPLAND, SIR REGINALD. *East Africa and Its Invaders from the Earliest Times to the Death of Seyyid Said.* Oxford: Clarendon Press, 1938.

DUFFY, JAMES. *Portuguese Africa.* Cambridge, Mass.: Harvard University Press, 1959.

DUFFY, JAMES. *Portugal in Africa.* Harmondsworth: Penguin; Cambridge, Mass.: Harvard University Press, 1962.

FREEMAN-GRANVILLE, G. S. P. *The Medieval History of the Coast of Tanganyika.* London: Oxford University Press, 1962.

GANN, L. H. *A History of Northern Rhodesia.* London: Chatto & Windus, 1964.

GANN, L. H. *The Birth of a Plural Society: The Development of Northern Rhodesia Under the British South Africa Company.* Manchester: Manchester University Press, 1958.

GELFAND, MICHAEL. *Northern Rhodesia in the Days of the Charter.* Oxford: Blackwell, 1961.

GIBBS, PETER. *A Flag for the Matabele.* London: Muller, 1955.

HANNA, A. J. *The Beginnings of Nyasaland and North-Eastern Rhodesia.* 1859-1895. Oxford: Clarendon Press, 1956.

HANNA, A. J. *The Story of the Rhodesias and Nyasaland.* London: Faber, 1960.

HOLE, HUGH MARSHALL. *The Making of Rhodesia.* London: Macmillan, 1926.

JOHNSTON, SIR HARRY H. *British Central Africa.* London: Methuen, 1898.

OLIVER, ROLAND, AND FAGE, J. D. *A Short History of Africa.* Harmondsworth: Penguin, 1962.

OLIVER, ROLAND, AND MATHEW, GERVASE (Ed.). *History of East Africa.* Oxford: Clarendon Press, 1963.

ROBINSON, RONALD, GALLAGHER, JOHN, AND DENNY, ALICE. *Africa and the*

Victorians. London: Macmillan; New York: St Martin's Press, 1961.

SAMPSON, RICHARD. *So This Was Lusaakas*. Lusaka: 1960.

TANSER, G. H. *British Central African Territories: Southern Rhodesia, Northern Rhodesia and Nyasaland*. Cape Town: Juta, 1952.

THOMSON, J. MOFFAT. *Memorandum on the Native Tribes and Tribal Areas of North-Eastern Rhodesia*. Lusaka: Government Printer, 1934.

POLITICAL HISTORY

BALFOUR, PATRICK, LORD KINROSS. *Lords of the Equator: An African Journey*. London: Hutchinson, 1937.

CECIL, LADY GWENDOLEN. *The Life of Robert, Marquess of Salisbury*. London: Hodder & Stoughton, 1921–32.

CLEGG, EDWARD. *Race and Politics: Partnership in the Federation of Rhodesia and Nyasaland*. London: Oxford University Press, 1960.

CREIGHTON, T. R. M. *Southern Rhodesia and the Central African Federation: The Anatomy of Partnership*. London: Faber, 1960; New York: Praeger, 1961.

EHNMARK, ANDERS AND WÄSTBERG, PER. *Angola and Mozambique*. London: Pall Mall Press; New York: Roy, 1963.

EPSTEIN, A. L. *Politics in an Urban African Community*. Manchester: Manchester University Press, 1958.

FRANCK, THOMAS M. *Race and Nationalism: The Struggle for Power in Rhodesia-Nyasaland*. New York: Fordham University Press; London: Allen & Unwin, 1960.

FRANKLIN, HARRY. *Unholy Wedlock*. London: Allen & Unwin, 1960.

GIBBS, PETER. *Avalanche in Central Africa*. London: Arthur Barker, 1961.

GRAY, RICHARD. *The Two Nations: Aspects of the Development of Race Relations in the Rhodesias and Nyasaland*. London: Oxford University Press, 1960.

KAUNDA, KENNETH. *Zambia Shall Be Free*. London: Heinemann, 1962; New York: Praeger, 1963.

LEYS, COLIN, AND PRATT, CRANFORD. *A New Deal in Central Africa*. London: Heinemann; New York: Praeger, 1960.

LUCAS PHILLIPS, C. E. *The Vision Splendid*. London: Heinemann, 1960.

LUGARD, FREDERICK, J. D., LORD. *The Dual Mandate in British Tropical Africa*. Edinburgh and London: Blackwood, 1922.

MACKENZIE, D. W. *John Mackenzie*. London: Hodder & Stoughton, 1902.

MACKENZIE, J. *Austral Africa, Losing It or Ruling It*. London: Sampson Low, 1887.

MASON, PHILIP. *The Birth of a Dilemma: The Conquest and Settlement of Rhodesia*. London: Oxford University Press, 1958.

MASON, PHILIP. *Year of Decision*. London, New York: Oxford University Press, 1960.

MULFORD, D. C. *The Northern Rhodesia General Election*. London: Oxford University Press, 1964.

SANGER, CLYDE. *Central African Emergency*. London: Heinemann, 1960.

SHEPPERSON, GEORGE, AND PRICE, THOMAS. *Independent African*. Edinburgh: Edinburgh University Press, 1958.

STONEHOUSE, JOHN T. *Prohibited Immigrant*. London: Bles, 1960.

THOMSON, H. C. *Rhodesia and Its Government*. London: Smith, Elder, 1898.

WELENSKY, SIR ROY. *Welensky's 4,000 Days*. London: Collins, 1964.

Wheare, K. C. *Federal Government.* London: Oxford University Press, 1963.

BIOGRAPHIES AND MEMOIRS

Brode, Heinrich. *Tippoo Tib.* London: Arnold, 1907.

Burnham, Frederick Russell. *Scouting on Two Continents.* New York: Doubleday, Page, 1927.

Dundas, Sir Charles. *African Crossroads.* London: Macmillan; New York: St Martin's Press, 1955.

Gross, Felix. *Rhodes of Africa.* London: Cassell, 1956; New York: Praeger, 1957.

Hall, R. S. *Kaunda: Founder of Zambia.* London: Longmans Green, 1964.

Harding, Colin. *In Remotest Barotseland.* London: Hurst & Blackett, 1905.

Harding, Colin. *Far Bugles.* London: Simpkin Marshall, 1933.

Johnston, James. *Reality Versus Romance in South Central Africa.* London: Hodder & Stoughton, 1893.

Le Roux, Servaas D. *Pioneers & Sportsmen of South Africa.* Salisbury: Privately published, 1939.

Letcher, Owen. *Big Game Hunting in North-Eastern Rhodesia.* London: Long, 1911.

Michell, Sir Lewis. *Life of Rhodes.* London: Arnold, 1910.

Millin, Sarah Gertrude. *Rhodes.* Rev. ed.; London: Chatto & Windus, 1952.

Oswell, W. Edward. *William Cotton Oswell: Hunter and Explorer.* London: Heinemann; New York: Doubleday, Page, 1900. 2 vols.

Sharpe, Sir Alfred. *The Backbone of Africa.* London: Witherby, 1921.

Stephenson, J. E. *Chirupula's Tale.* London: Bles, 1937.

Tanser, G. H. *Founders of Rhodesia.* London: Oxford University Press, 1950.

Taylor, Don. *The Rhodesian: Life of Sir Roy Welensky.* London: Museum Press, 1955.

Thomson, J. B. *Joseph Thomson, African Explorer.* London: Sampson Low, 1896.

Verbeken, A. *Msiri, Roi du Garenganza.* Brussels, 1956.

Williams, Basil. *Cecil Rhodes.* London: Constable, 1921.

Woodhouse, C. M., and Lockhart, John G. *Cecil Rhodes.* London: Hodder & Stoughton; New York: Macmillan, 1963.

RACE RELATIONS, ANTHROPOLOGY AND SOCIAL STUDIES

Barnes, James A. *Politics in a Changing Society.* London: Methuen, 1897; Cape Town and New York: Oxford University Press, 1954.

Bettison, D. G. *Numerical Data on African Dwellers in Lusaka, Northern Rhodesia.* Livingstone: Rhodes Livingstone Institute, 1960.

Campbell, Dugald. *In the Heart of Bantuland.* London: Seeley, Service, 1922.

Colson, Elizabeth. *The Plateau Tonga of Northern Rhodesia: Social and Religious Studies.* Manchester: Manchester University Press; New York: Humanities Press, 1962.

Cunnison, I. G. *The Luapula Peoples of Northern Rhodesia: Custom and History in Tribal Politics.* Manchester: Manchester University Press, 1959.

DOKE, CLEMENT M. *The Lambas of Northern Rhodesia.* London: Harrap, 1931.

GLUCKMAN, MAX, AND COLSON, ELIZABETH. *Seven Tribes of British Central Africa.* Manchester: Manchester University Press, 1959.

HOWARTH, DAVID. *Shadow of the Dam.* London: Collins; New York: Macmillan, 1961.

JOSEPHINE. *Tell Me, Josephine,* ed. Barbara Hall. London: Deutsch; New York: Simon and Schuster, 1964.

MERLE-DAVIS, J. *Modern Industry and the African.* London: Macmillan, 1933.

MORRIS, COLIN M. *The Hour After Midnight.* London: Longmans, 1961.

POWDERMAKER, HORTENSE. *Copper Town: Changing Africa. The Human Situation on the Rhodesian Copperbelt.* New York: Harper & Row, 1962.

RICHARDS, AUDREY I. *Land, Labour and Diet in Northern Rhodesia.* London: Oxford University Press, 1939.

RICHARDS, AUDREY I. *Chisungu.* London: Faber; New York: Grove Press, 1956.

SMITH, EDWIN W., AND DALE, ANDREW MURRAY. *The Ila-Speaking People of Northern Rhodesia.* London: Macmillan, 1920.

TAYLOR, JOHN VERNON AND LEHMANN, D. A. *Christians of the Copperbelt: The Growth of the Church in Northern Rhodesia.* London: Student Christian Movement Press, 1961.

WATSON, WILLIAM. *Tribal Cohesion in a Money Economy.* Manchester: Manchester University Press, 1958.

WOOD, ANTHONY ST. JOHN. *Northern Rhodesia: The Human Background.* London: Pall Mall Press, 1961.

YOUNG, C., AND BANDA, HASTINGS KAMUZU (Ed.). *Our African Way of Life.* London: Lutterworth, 1964.

ECONOMIC AND FINANCIAL DEVELOPMENT

BANCROFT, JOSEPH A. *Mining in Northern Rhodesia.* London: British South Africa Co., 1961.

BARBER, WILLIAM J. *The Economy of British Central Africa.* Stanford: Stanford University Press, 1961.

BRADLEY, KENNETH. *Copper Venture.* London: Mufulira Copper Mines, 1952.

GOULDSBURY, CULLEN, AND SHEANE, H. *The Great Plateau of Northern Rhodesia.* London: Arnold, 1911.

GREGORY, SIR THEODORE. *Ernest Oppenheimer and the Economic Development of Southern Africa.* Cape Town and New York: Oxford University Press, 1962.

HAILEY, WILLIAM MALCOLM, LORD. *An African Survey.* London and New York: Oxford University Press, 1957.

HARRIS, J. H. *The Chartered Millions.* London: Swarthmore Press, 1921.

LETCHER, OWEN. *South Central Africa.* Johannesburg: Africa Publications, 1932.

MALCOLM, SIR DOUGAL O. *The British South Africa Company.* London: Privately printed, 1939.

PIM, SIR ALAN W. *Financial and Economic History of the African Tropical Territories.* London and New York: Oxford University Press, 1940.

SAFFERY, A. LYNN. *Some Aspects of African Living: Conditions on the Copperbelt.* Lusaka: Government Printer.

Thompson, Cecil Henry, and Woodruff, Henry Wells. *Economic Development in Rhodesia and Nyasaland.* London: Dobson, 1955.

Trapnell, C. G. *The Soils, Vegetation and Agriculture of North-Eastern Rhodesia.* Lusaka: Government Printer, 1943.

Trapnell, C. G., and Clothier, J. N. *The Soils, Vegetation and Agriculture of North-Western Rhodesia.* Lusaka: Government Printer, 1937.

EXPLORATION

Burton, Sir Richard F. *Lacerda's Journey to Cazembe.* London: John Murray, 1873.

Chapman, James. *Travels in the Interior of South Africa.* London: Bell & Daldy, 1868.

Coupland, Sir Reginald. *Livingstone's Last Journey.* London: Collins, 1945; New York: Macmillan, 1947.

Gibbons, A. St. *H. From North to South through Barotseland.* London: John Lane, 1904.

Guyot, P. *Voyage au Zambèse.* Paris: André, 1895. Reprinted from *Bulletin de la Société de Geographie de l'Est,* Nancy, 1882-6.

Livingstone, David. *Missionary Travels and Research in South Africa.* London: John Murray, 1857.

Livingstone, David. *The Last Journals of David Livingstone.* London: John Murray, 1874; New York: Harper, 1875.

Moorehead, Alan. *The White Nile.* London: Hamish Hamilton; New York: Harper, 1960.

Pedroso Gamitto, A. C. *King Kazembe and the Marawe, Cheva, Bisa, Bemba, Lunda and other Peoples of Southern Africa* (2vv.). Lisbon: Junta de Investigaçôes do Ultramar, 1960.

Perham, Margery, and Simmons, J. *African Discovery.* London: Faber, 1961; Evanston: Northwestern University Press, 1963.

Rego, A. da Silva. *Portuguese Colonisation in the Sixteenth Century.* Johannesburg: University of Witwatersrand, 1959.

Wallis, J. P. R. (Ed.) *The Zambezi Expedition of David Livingstone.* London: Chatto & Windus, 1956.

MISSIONARY HISTORY

Coillard, François. *On the Threshold of Central Africa.* London: Hodder & Stoughton, 1897.

Crawford, Dan. *Thinking Black.* London: Morgan & Scott, 1912.

Crawford, Dan. *Back to the Long Grass.* London: Hodder & Stoughton, 1921.

Jack, J. W. *Daybreak at Livingstonia.* London: Oliphant, Anderson Ferrier, 1901.

Livingstone, David. *Livingstone's Private Journals.* Ed. Isaac Schapera. London: Chatto & Windus; Berkeley: University of California Press, 1960.

Mackintosh, C. W. *Coillard of the Zambezi.* London: Unwin, 1907.

Moffat, Robert. *Missionary Labours and Scenes in Central Africa.* London: John Snow, 1842.

Moffat, Robert. *Matabele Journals of Robert Moffat.* London: Chatto & Windus, 1945.

Seaver, George. *David Livingstone.* London: Lutterworth, 1957.

Smith, Edwin W. *The Way of the White Fields in Rhodesia.* London: World Dominion Press, 1928.

SWANN, A. J. *Fighting the Slave Hunters in Central Africa.* London: Seeley, 1910.

MISCELLANEOUS

BRELSFORD, W. V. *The Story of the Northern Rhodesia Regiment.* Lusaka: Government Printer, 1954.

DARLING, FRANK F. *Wild Life in an African Territory.* London and New York: Oxford University Press, 1960.

FANSHAWE, D. B. *Fifty Common Trees of Northern Rhodesia.* Lusaka: Government Printer, 1962.

FRAENKEL, P. J. *Wayaleshi.* London: Weidenfeld & Nicolson, 1959.

INGRAM, DEREK. *Commonwealth for a Colour-Blind World.* London: Allen & Unwin, 1965.

KEATLEY, PATRICK. *The Politics of Partnership.* Harmondsworth: Penguin, 1963.

LEGUM, COLIN. *Pan-Africanism.* Rev. ed.; London: Pall Mall Press; New York: Praeger, 1965.

MANNIX, DAVID, AND COWLEY, MALCOLM. *Black Cargoes: A History of the Atlantic Slave Trade.* London: Longmans, 1963.

OTHER MATERIAL

Much of interest can be found in the *Northern Rhodesia Journal* and the *Rhodes-Livingstone Journal* as well as in the *Occasional Papers* of the Rhodes-Livingstone Museum. Articles relating to the history of Zambia appear from time to time in such publications as the *Journal of African History, Current Anthropology,* and the *South African Archaeological Bulletin.* Papers delivered to the conference of the History of the Central African Peoples in 1963 are available at the Rhodes-Livingstone Institute.

Notes and References

Abbreviations used in the Notes

African S.	Correspondence of the Colonial Office concerning southern Africa (White Books)
BSA Coy.	British South Africa Company (the 'Chartered')
C.	Command Paper
Colonial No.	Colonial Office Paper
CBHT	*Central Bantu Historical Texts*
CHCAP	Conference of the History of the Central African Peoples —held at Lusaka, 1963
CT	Cape Town Office of British South Africa Company
JAH	*Journal of African History*
JAS	*Journal of the African Society*
JRAI	*Journal of the Royal Anthropological Institute*
NJ	*Nyasaland Journal*
NRJ	*Northern Rhodesian Journal*
RLI	Rhodes-Livingstone Institute
RLP	*Rhodes-Livingstone Papers*
SAAB	*South African Archaeological Bulletin*
SALJ	*South African Law Journal*

There are 'Hansards' for S. Rhodesia, N. Rhodesia and there was a 'Hansard' for the Federal Assembly. It will be evident from the text which one is quoted. *Official Reports of Debates* at Westminster are always given as H.C. Hansard or H.L. Hansard.

Works cited in the Bibliography are given in abbreviated form in the Notes (author, title and date). For full details see above.

1: The Land and its Peoples

I GENERAL FEATURES

[1] Sir Charles Dundas, *African Crossroads*, 1955, pp. 163–4. Sir Charles was Chief Secretary, 1934–7.

[2] See Trapnell and Clothier, *Soils, Vegetation and Agriculture of North-Western Rhodesia,* and the companion volume by Trapnell for *North-Eastern Rhodesia,* 1937 and 1943.

[3] See *Northern Rhodesia Handbook,* 1953 edition, pp. 203–8 for a brief readable article on the country's forests; also D. B. Fanshawe, *Fifty Common Trees of Northern Rhodesia,* 1962.

[4] C. M. Doke, *The Lambas of Northern Rhodesia,* 1931, pp. 21–2.

[5] The outstanding work on Northern Rhodesia's *fauna* is F. Fraser Darling, *Wild Life in an African Territory,* 1960.

II OUTLINES OF GEOLOGY

[1] See Felix Mendelssohn (Ed.) *Geology of the Northern Rhodesian Copperbelt,* 1961. The only general account of the region's geology is to be found in *Memoir No. 2* of the Department of Geological Survey, Government Printer, Lusaka 1964. A bibliography by G. J. Snowball of works on the region's geology is in *Records of the Dept. of Geological Survey,* 1959.

[2] *Northern News,* October 25, 1962.

III TRACES OF EARLY MAN

[1] Much of the material in this section is derived from Dr Desmond Clark, *The Prehistory of Southern Africa,* 1959.

[2] The whole question of *Homo habilis* and his relationship to the Australopithecine man-apes is still in dispute. See *Nature,* April 1964, pp. 3–9; National Geographical Society *News Bulletin,* April 3, 1964; *National Observer,* March 25, 1962; *New York Times,* April 4, 1964, and June 7, 1964.

[3] For a discussion, see Sonia Cole in *History of East Africa,* Ed. R. Oliver and G. Mathew, 1963, pp. 24–9.

[4] Clark, op. cit. table 5, p. 54.

[5] Ibid. p. 130.

[6] *NRJ,* Vol. 2, No 4, pp. 55–6.

[7] Clark, op. cit. pp. 166–184.

[8] For detailed list, see *Annual Report,* Commission for the Preservation of Natural and Historic Monuments and Relics, Lusaka: Government Printer, 1964.

IV THE FIRST FARMERS

[1] A concise account of this culture is found in Dr Brian Fagan's article in the *South African Archaeological Bulletin* (*SAAB*), Vol. XVIII, No 69, pp. 4–5.

[2] Merrick Poznansky, *SAAB,* Vol. XVI, No 64, pp. 136–8.

[3] Conference of the History of the Central African Peoples (Lusaka 1963) (CHCAP) K. R. Robinson, 'Archaeology of the Rozwi', p. 3. The relationship of early Iron Age cultures north and south of the Zambezi is discussed in Dr Fagan's comprehensive 'Iron Age Peoples in Northern Rhodesia' in *Current Anthropology,* Chicago, 1964.

[4] Clark, op. cit. p. 21.

V TRADE WITH THE EAST

[1] The most complete account of discoveries relating to this culture is Dr Brian Fagan's article previously mentioned: 'The Kalomo Choma

Iron Age Project (1960–3) Preliminary Report,' in *SAAB* Vol. XVIII, No 69, pp. 5–12.

[2] For a general summary of early settlements on Africa's east coast, see Roland Oliver and J. D. Fage, *A Short History of Africa,* 1962, pp. 96–8. See also W. E. F. Ward, *A History of Africa,* Book II, 1963, pp. 199–203, for a simple account.

[3] G. S. P. Freeman-Granville, *Medieval History of the Coast of Tanganyika,* 1962, passim.

[4] Fagan, op. cit. pp. 12–14.

[5] J. P. R. Wallis (Ed.) *Zambezi Expedition of David Livingstone,* Vol. II, 1956, p. 395. The Portuguese Father Monclaro mentioned cotton spinning and weaving by Africans about 1570.

[6] *Lochinvar Research Project,* cyclostyled, circulated by the Rhodes-Livingstone Museum, October 1963.

VI THE LEGENDS OF THE TRIBES

[1] For a general account, see W. V. Brelsford, *The Tribes of Northern Rhodesia,* 1956.

[2] C. M. Doke, op. cit. Harrap 1931, pp. 20, 21.

[3] Ibid. pp. 228–9.

[4] J. J. Munday, 'Kankomba' in *Central Bantu Historical Texts* (*CBHT*) I, Rhodes-Livingstone Institute (RLI) Lusaka 1961, p. 1.

[5] Op. cit. p. 5.

[6] See genealogy of the Lozi in Max Gluckman's paper in *Seven Tribes of British Central Africa,* ed. Max Gluckman and Elizabeth Colson, 1959.

[7] 'Mwata Kazembe XIV', translated by Ian Cunnison, in *CBHT* II, RLI, Lusaka 1961.

VII MIGRATION AND CONQUEST

[1] Max Gluckman and Elizabeth Colson (eds.) op. cit. p. 100.

[2] J. Moffat Thomson, *Memorandum on the Native Tribes and Tribal Areas of North-Eastern Rhodesia,* 1934. For a general account of the Ila see E. W. Smith and A. Dale, *The Ila Speaking People of Northern Rhodesia,* 1920.

[3] Invaluable work on the early history of tribes along the middle Zambezi has been done by D. P. Abraham. See his 'Tasks in the Field of Early History,' a paper read to CHCAP, May 1963. Professor J. D. Clark has suggested (*NRJ,* No 2, 1950, pp. 42–52) that the Ila and Tonga immigrated down the eastern side of the Nyasa and up the Zambezi.

[4] E. Axelson, *The Portuguese in South-East Africa,* 1960.

[5] W. H. I. Rangeley in 'Notes on Cewa Tribal Law', (*Nyasaland Journal* (*NJ*) Vol. I, No 3, Blantyre 1948) suggests *c.* 1550 for the arrival of the tribe. Other authorities (e.g. E. H. Lane-Poole) suggest a considerably earlier date.

[6] For the history of the Nsenga, see article by Dr R. Apthorpe in *RLP,* XXVIII, pp. 47–67.

VIII THE LUNDA EMPIRE AND THE PORTUGUESE

[1] Studies of the Bemba and Lozi tribes may be found in Max Gluckman and Elizabeth Colson (eds.) op. cit. The anthropologist Audrey Richards, writing in 1931, said that Luba words unknown to commoners were still retained for Bemba royal rituals.

[2] R. Oliver and J. D. Fage, *A Short History of Africa*, 1962, p. 48.

[3] Leon Duysters, 'Histoire des Aluunda' in *Problèmes d'Afrique Centrale,* Brussels 1958, pp. 79–82.

[4] *CBHT* (II) pp. 3–4. Also, Duysters, op. cit. pp. 82–3.

[5] There was a Chieftainess Luweji in Zambia's Balovale District until October 1963. She was installed in Chavuma by her late father, Mwata Yamvo (father-in-law of Moise Tshombe of Katanga) in 1957. Wearing a necklace of genital organs, Mwata Yamvo crossed from the Congo at the invitation of the Northern Rhodesian Government to enthrone his daughter, thus settling a Lunda-Luvale succession dispute. Luweji retired to the Congo because of agitation against her by the United National Independence Party (UNIP).

[6] See James Duffy, *Portugal in Africa*, 1962, pp. 37–45.

[7] B. M. Fagan, 'A Collection of 19th-century Ironwork from the Lusaka area, N. Rhodesia,' *Journal of the Royal Anthropological Institute* (*JRAI*), Vol. 91, 1961.

[8] A useful list of staple African crops and their origins is given in W. E. F. Ward, op. cit. Bk. II, p. 244.

[9] A. da Silva Rego, *Portuguese Colonisation in the Sixteenth Century,* 1959, p. 105.

[10] D. P. Abraham, paper presented to CHCAP, May 1963, footnote.

IX THE COMING OF THE BEMBA

[1] R. Apthorpe, op. cit. p. 51. Writing in 1831, the Portuguese army officer Pedroso Gamitto said: 'The Bemba are generally characterised by their bad faith, their ferocity and their rapacious spirit'—*King Kazembe,* 1960, Vol. II, p. 160.

[2] W. Lammond, 'The Luapula Valley', in *NRJ* Vol. 2, No 5, p. 51

[3] Ann Tweedie, 'Towards a History of the Bemba from Oral Tradition', paper to CHCAP, p. 4.

[4] *CBHT* (I), Part 1, p. 8.

[5] Tweedie, op. cit. p. 5.

[6] According to Brelsford, op. sit. p. 33, Mwase's tattooed chest and stomach skin are even today among the Bemba royal relics.

[7] Captain Pedroso Gamitto gives an eye-witness account. See also F. M. Thomas, 'Historical Notes on the Bisa Tribe', RLI, 1956.

[8] I. G. Cunnison, *The Luapula Peoples of Northern Rhodesia,* 1959, pp. 37–42.

X THE LOZI ENTER THE VALLEY

[1] For a detailed discussion of this formerly vexed topic, see the papers delivered to the CHCAP by Mutumba Mainga and Lishomwa Muuka.

[2] G. C. Clay postulates a Luba origin for the Nkoya. See *History of the Mankoya District,* RLI 1946.

[3] This subject is discussed in Chapter 4, p. 92. It is noteworthy that the Lovale chieftainess Nyakatoro (pre-1900) described Lewanika of the Lozi as a 'blood relation' and declared that both tribes came from north of the Kasai river. Nyakatoro nonetheless denied being under Lozi rule and her country subsequently became part of Angola. See Colin Harding, *In Remotest Barotseland,* 1905.

[4] S. J. Chibanza in 'Kaonde History', *CBHT* (I), p. 43. 'Chiboko was the first man to be appointed as a chief by the general approval and consent of the Paramount Chief Musokantanda and by confirmation of

the African king, Mwata Yamvo. He therefore settled on a river called Kaonde (in what was formerly the Belgian Congo). It is from there that the tribe derived the word Kaonde....'

[5] See M. Mainga, op. cit., for a variety of legends about the early Luyana rulers.

[6] *CBHT* (II), pp. 14–23.

[7] See Brelsford, op. cit., pp. 8–17.

[8] G. C. Clay, 'Barotseland between 1801 and 1864', paper to CHCAP, p. 3.

XI MWATA KAZEMBE AND LACERDA

[1] W. Lammond, *NRJ,* Vol. 11, No 5, p. 52.

[2] *CBHT* (II), pp. 31–2.

[3] Ibid. p. 53. This version says Nkuba made a chair of the skin, but a door-mat is a more popular version.

[4] Ibid. pp. 65–6.

[5] For a description of eighteenth-century Zumbo, see M. D. D. Hewitt's paper to CHCAP, p. 13.

[6] Ibid. p. 12.

[7] The prazo-holders were feudal lords along the Zambezi. There are still legends of the 'negresses' labouring to produce gold among the Luangwa valley people. J. Scott-Prentice, personal communication.

[8] Captain-major Albino Pacheco, whose diary on a journey up the Zambezi (1861–2) gives an account of Fr Pedro, is quoted in Paul Guyot, *Voyage au Zambèse,* 1895.

[9] Ibid. The dating is uncertain.

[10] E. Axelson, op. cit., passim.

[11] J. Duffy, *Portuguese Africa,* 1959, pp. 145–6. Dutch privateers halted the Angola slave-trade for some years.

[12] R. F. Burton, *Lacerda's Journey to Cazembe,* 1873, gives the full translation of Lacerda's diary, with other early Portuguese journeys in the African interior. See also: I. Cunnison in *JAH,* Vol. II, No 1.

[13] Ibid. p. 13.

[14] Ibid. pp. 24–5n.

[15] David Livingstone, *Livingstone's Private Journals,* ed. I. Shapera, 1960, p. 41.

[16] Burton, op. cit., p. 20.

[17] Lacerda called Pereira an 'old backwoodsman'. He was also called 'a Terror'.

XII 'THE INSOLENCE OF THE CAFFRES'

[1] Burton, op. cit. p. 78.

[2] Ibid. p. 95.

[3] Ibid. p. 99.

[4] Ibid. p. 115.

[5] Ibid, pp. 148–164, passim.

[6] Translated in Burton op. cit., after the Lacerda diary, by B. A. Beadle.

[7] See Pedroso Gamitto, *King Kazembe,* 1960.

XIII THE NGONI INVADERS

[1] Brelsford, *The Tribes of Northern Rhodesia,* p. 89.

[2] Southern Rhodesia Information Department leaflet on Sinoia Caves.

[3] See J. A. Barnes, 'Seven Tribes of Central Africa', CHCAP.

[4] Tweedie, 'Towards a History of the Bemba', CHCAP, p. 196.

[5] Heinrich Brode, *Tippoo Tib*, 1907, p. 30.
[6] Tweedie, op. cit.
[7] Details supplied by Henry Mulenga of Chinsali.
[8] Barnes, op. cit. p. 194.
[9] It has been suggested that an Arab from Zanzibar helped to direct the Bemba tactics.

XIV SEBITUANE CONQUERS BAROTSELAND

[1] Gluckman and Colson (eds.), op. cit., p. 1.
[2] Now in the Caprivi Strip, S.W.A.
[3] A. St. H. Gibbons, *From North to South through Barotseland*, 1904, pp. 148–9.
[4] Gluckman and Colson (eds.), op. cit.
[5] Ibid. for genealogy of Lozi 'royal' family.
[6] Clay, paper to CHCAP, 'Barotseland between 1801 and 1864', p. 3.
[7] James Chapman, *Travels in the Interior of South Africa*, Vol 1, 1868, p. 168.
[8] Brelsford, *Tribes of N. Rhodesia*, p. 7.
[9] Ibid.
[10] Gibbons, op. cit., p. 147–8

2: Contending Forces of the Nineteenth Century

I LIVINGSTONE, 1851–60

[1] The London Missionary Society's missionaries' complete lack of information at this period about northern Bechuanaland and beyond is shown by the map facing p. 18 in R. Moffat's *Missionary Labours and Scenes in Central Africa*, 1842.
[2] D. Livingstone, *Missionary Travels*, 1852, p. 119.
[3] Ibid. pp. 54–73.
[4] Livingstone, *Private Journals*, Ed. Isaac Shapera, 1960, p. 16.
[5] W. E. Oswell, *William Cotton Oswell*, London 1900, Vol. 1, p. 245.
[6] *Private Journals*, p. 15.
[7] Ibid. p. 26.
[8] *Missionary Travels*, p. 89.
[9] *Private Journals*, p. 24.
[10] Ibid. p. 25.
[11] Ibid. p. 28.
[12] This is the date for the 'discovery' of the Zambezi given in *Private Journals* (p. 38). In *Missionary Travels* (p. 90), Livingstone said 'the end of June', which was probably wrong.
[13] *Private Journals*, pp. 40–1.
[14] *Missionary Travels*, p. 92.
[15] *Private Journals*, p. 13.
[16] Ibid. p. 184. It is interesting that until recent times, syphilis remained endemic among the Ila, despite constant efforts of the health authorities to stamp it out.
[17] He was impressed with the great hospitality shown him by the Portuguese, but realised that no waggon route was possible. Also the Mambari had too tight a grip on the transcontinental routes (see *JAH*, Vol. III, No 3, for article 'Long distance trade routes in Central Africa', by J. Vansina).

[18] A type of palanquin carried on poles.

[19] 'For the first time in my life I feel willing to die', Coupland, *Livingstone's Last Journey*, 1945, p. 14.

[20] *Missionary Travels*, p. 518.

[21] Ibid. p. 524. The Zambezi is still called Liambai in Barotseland. The name Zambeze existed at least as early as 1600, when the lower reaches were called the Cuamo by the Portuguese. See E. Axelson, op. cit. passim, and material facing p. 129.

[22] Ibid. p. 520.

[23] Ibid. p. 513.

[24] Ibid. pp. 681–3.

[25] See *The Zambezi Expedition of David Livingstone*, J. R. R. Wallis (Ed.), 1956, especially dispatches in Vol II.

[26] Livingstone was often called *Monare* or *Munali*, the meaning of which has been much debated. It was probably derived from the Boer *Mjinheer*. Livingstone was also called *Njereza*, a corruption of *ngelezi* (English). Sometimes he was addressed by his African companions simply as David, which disgusted Brode. (See *Tippoo Tib*, p. 38)

[27] For a brief account of this visit, see G. C. Clay's paper to CHCAP, pp. 9–10.

II THE ARABS AND THE YEKE

[1] Burton, *Lands of Cazembe*, p. 37.

[2] Pedroso Gamitto, *King Kazembe*, Vol. II, pp. 119–20.

[3] Ibid. Vol. II, p. 87.

[4] See Captain Thomas Smee's account, quoted by Alan Moorhead in *The White Nile*, 1960.

[5] H. Brode, *Tippoo Tib*, 1907, p. 9.

[6] R. Robinson, J. Gallagher and A. Denny, *Africa and the Victorians*, 1961, p. 42 et seq.

[7] For a full account of Seyyid Said, see Sir Reginald Coupland's *East Africa and its Invaders, from the Earliest Times, to the Death of Seyyid Said in 1856*, 1938.

[8] A. Smith, *History of East Africa*, Vol 1, 1963, p. 267 et seq.

[9] *Missionary Travels*, p. 223. This did not displease Livingstone, who always thought dark skin more beautiful than light.

[10] See in Roland Oliver and J. D. Fage (eds.), *History of East Africa*, passim.

[11] Livingstone, *Private Journals*, pp. 227–8 and *Last Journal*, 1874, Vol. I, pp. 282, 335.

[12] *CBHT* (I), p. 37.

[13] Oliver and Fage (eds.), *History of East Africa*, pp. 277 et seq.

[14] *Msiri* means 'mosquito'—doubtless a comment on the activities of his raiders. The fullest account of this personality is in A. Verbuken's *Msiri, Roi du Garenganza*, 1956.

[15] *CBHT* (II), pp. 82–3.

[16] Ibid. p. 34n.

[17] The lieutenants were detribalised warriors who wore red cloaks, feathered headdresses and copper ornaments. They were the products of the Ngoni invasions, and like their mentors, the Ruga Ruga used the stabbing spear devastatingly.

[18] Dan Crawford, *Thinking Black*, 1912, p. 295.

[19] Brelsford, *Tribes of Northern Rhodesia*, p. 108.

[20] *CBHT* (I), p. 38.
[21] Doke, *The Lambas of Northern Rhodesia,* p. 41–2.
[22] *General List of Chiefs,* Government Printer, Lusaka 1960, p. 12.

III TIPPOO TIB

[1] In *The White Nile,* Moorehead incorrectly gives Tippoo Tib's name as Mohammed bin Sayid.
[2] Livingstone, *Last Journal,* 1874, p. xx.
[3] Tippoo Tib's autobiography (with English translation) appears in 'Maisha ya Hamed bin Muhammed el Murjebi yaani Tippu Tib', *East African Swahili Committee Journals.*
[4] Alfred J. Swann, *Fighting the Slave Hunters in Central Africa,* 1910, pp. 173–7.
[5] Brode, op. cit.
[6] D. Campbell, *In the Heart of Bantuland,* 1922, p. 258.
[7] The account that follows is derived mainly from Brode, op. cit.
[8] Brelsford, *Tribes of Northern Rhodesia,* p. 74.
[9] *CBHT* (II), p. 88.
[10] Ibid. and Brode, op. cit.
[11] D. Frost, quoted in *Tribes of Northern Rhodesia,* p. 103–4.
[12] *Nshila,* Government Printer, Lusaka.

IV LIVINGSTONE AND HIS FOLLOWERS

[1] G. Seaver, *David Livingstone,* 1957, p. 251.
[2] For an outline of missionary penetration, see L. Gann, *The Birth of a Plural Society,* 1958, pp. 19–43.
[3] Holub's account appears, translated into English, in R. Sampson, *So This Was Lusaakas,* 1960, pp. 6–10.

V 'NORTHERN ZAMBEZIA' AND THE SCRAMBLE FOR AFRICA

[1] See Lady Gwendolen Cecil, *Life of Robert, Marquess of Salisbury,* 1921–32.
[2] *History of East Africa,* Vol. 1, p. 374.
[3] G. Seaver, *David Livingstone,* p. 292.
[4] J. W. Jack, *Daybreak at Livingstonia,* 1901, pp. 227–35.
[5] R. Robinson, J. Gallagher and A. Denny, *Africa and the Victorians,* 1961, p. 224.
[6] Ibid. p. 226.
[7] *Letters of Queen Victoria,* Third Series, Vol. 1, p. 543.
[8] J. Duffy, *Portuguese Africa,* 1959, p. 194, and D. Crawford, *Thinking Black,* p. 74.

3: Concession Hunters and a Queen's Protection

I GENESIS OF THE BRITISH SOUTH AFRICA COMPANY

[1] Of nearly a score of Rhodes biographies, the most recent (and one of the most sympathetic) is by C. M. Woodhouse and J. H. Lockhart, *Cecil Rhodes,* 1963.

[2] For a useful account of this feat, see *The British South Africa Company* by Sir Dougal O. Malcolm, privately printed, London 1939.

[3] Mackenzie summed up his long experience and views in *Austral Africa, Losing It or Ruling It,* 1887. For a biography, see D. W. Mackenzie's *John Mackenzie,* 1902.

[4] H. M. Hole, *The Making of Rhodesia,* 1926, Ch. 4.

[5] See F. Gross, *Rhodes of Africa,* 1956, passim.

[6] See P. Gibbs's *A Flag for the Matabele,* 1955, p. 150, for a brief study of Sir Hercules.

[7] For Sir Sidney Shippard see frequent references in Sarah Gertrude Millin's *Rhodes* and other works quoted. See 'A Few Notes on Sir Sidney Shippard', *S.A. Law Journal,* 1902. It is noteworthy that Harris, secretary of the British South Africa Company, used Shippard's second name, Godolphin, as code signature in one of the historic Jameson Raid telegrams.

[8] Gross, op. cit. p. 151.

[9] Ibid. p. 146.

[10] C.5534.

[11] A comprehensive account of negotiations for the Rudd Concession is given by several authors previously quoted—e.g. Millin, Hole, Gross. The most recent is Woodhouse and Lockhart, *Rhodes,* pp. 132–157.

[12] A facsimile of the Concession is in Malcolm, op. cit.

[13] Hole, op. cit. p. 97 et seq.

[14] Shippard was seconded in this argument by the Rev. Charles Helm. Shippard also advocated giving arms to Khama, to maintain the balance of power (see C.5918).

[15] See biographies, for Rhodes's relations with Parnell and the Liberals.

[16] See R. Robinson, J. Gallagher and A. Denny, *Africa and the Victorians,* pp. 234–53 for a masterly account of the charter negotiations.

[17] Dictionary of National Biography.

[18] Gifford's letter and Knutsford's reply are quoted in full by Hole, op. cit., Ch. 8.

[19] Author's italics.

[20] Facsimile in Hole, op. cit. facing p. 107.

[21] The full text of the charter forms appendix to Vol. I of Sir Lewis Michell's *Life of Rhodes,* 1910.

[22] The British South Africa Company did not buy the Lippert Concession until 1892. This purported to give land rights, but was declared valueless in 1918.

[23] *Evening Standard,* Salisbury, S. Rhodesia, August 17, 1959.

[24] The British South Africa Company shares were 12s. in 1892; in 1890 they had been £3.15.0d.

[25] The *Financial Times* stated, in 1892, that Rhodes was doing all he could to 'provoke' Lobengula.

[26] Gross, op. cit. p. 233.

[27] It is rewarding to compare accounts of this incident in Hole, op. cit. pp. 313–5, and Millin, op. cit. pp. 192–5.

[28] Paragraph seven of 'Fort Victoria Agreement'.

[29] Dr G. W. H. Knight-Bruce, formerly the Bishop of Bloemfontein, who had visited Lobengula's kraal shortly before the Rudd Concession was obtained.

[30] Hole, op. cit. p. 310.

[31] The two men were tried several years later, sentenced to fourteen years in jail, then freed after two years.

[32] Cf. H. Labouchere, MP, in *Truth*, December 14, 1893. 'The war was forced on these people in order to rob them. The Queen's specific pledges to their king have been ignored.' A revealing account of the British South Africa Company's role in Southern Rhodesia is given in John H. Harris's *The Chartered Millions*, 1921.

II THE LOCHNER CONCESSION OF 1890

[1] Hansard, No 60, 366 et seq.
[2] Ibid. 374–6
[3] However, Max Gluckman holds a contrary view. See his foreword (p. x) to Gann's *The Birth of a Plural Society*, op. cit.; cf F. Coillard, *On the Threshold of Central Africa*, 1897, p. 218, et seq.
[4] C. W. Mackintosh, *Coillard of the Zambezi*, 1907.
[5] F. Gross, *Rhodes*, p. 268. The British South Africa Company demanded the whole of Bechuanaland in 1895, but there was such a violent reaction that Rhodes admitted that he was 'utterly beaten by these niggers'.
[6] T. W. Baxter in *NRJ*, No 3, p. 39.
[7] Ibid. p. 42.
[8] Ibid. p. 40.
[9] Coillard, op. cit. p. 356–8.
[10] Hole, op. cit. pp. 129 and 215.
[11] Mackintosh, op. cit. p. 383.
[12] Shippard's active interest in the company's progress is once again apparent. He wrote to the King in November 1889 (CT 1/4/5) supporting the British South Africa Company.
[13] *NRJ*, No 3, p. 40.
[14] Hole, op. cit. p. 215.
[15] Coillard, op. cit. p. 385.
[16] Gann, *The Birth of a Plural Society*, p. 56.
[17] *NRJ*, No 3, p. 43.
[18] S. D. Le Roux, *Pioneers and Sportsmen of S. Africa*, 1939, p. 349.
[19] This letter was perhaps delivered by Lochner and is not traced. But Coillard refers to it in his reply of April 8, 1890.
[20] Mackintosh, op. cit. p. 383.
[21] Ibid. p. 384.
[22] *NRJ*, No 3, p. 43.
[23] Coillard to British South Africa Company, June 5, 1891.
[24] Middleton to Colonial Office, November 1890. (*NRJ*, No 3, p. 44)
[25] See record of directors in *British South Africa Company* by Sir Dougal O. Malcolm.
[26] Letter to British South Africa Company, June 5, 1891. For Coillard's lack of understanding, noteworthy is his statement about the Company in May 1890: 'It has already extended its protectorate over the Matabele country.'
[27] James Johnston, *Reality Versus Romance in South Central Africa*, 1893, p. 148.
[28] See Hailey, *An African Survey*, 1957 edition.
[29] Coillard, op. cit. p. 386.
[30] A photograph of the scene by Coillard is in Mackintosh's *Coillard of the Zambezi*, facing p. 384.
[31] Hole, op. cit. p. 215.
[32] Ibid.

[33] Lochner to British South Africa Company, November 27, 1889: 'Khama is sending a special embassy with me taking valuable presents to Lewanika.'
[34] Coillard, op. cit. p. 388.

III THE MEANING OF THE CONCESSION

[1] No 320. African S., 392.
[2] Hole, op. cit. p. 218.
[3] Bradley, *Copper Venture*, 1952, p. 49.
[4] Coillard, op. cit. p. 388.
[5] Enclosure in No 320 of African S., 392.
[6] Coillard, op. cit. p. 387.
[7] Coillard Papers, 5/5.
[8] Coillard, *Threshold*, p. 388.
[9] J. Johnston, op. cit. p. 148.
[10] No 320, African S., 392.
[11] No 254, African S., 414.
[12] *JAS*, Vol. I, No cxx, July 1931.
[13] No 320, African S., 392.
[14] Coillard Papers.
[15] Ibid.
[16] Coillard, *Threshold*, p. 388.
[17] Coillard Papers.
[18] No 320, African S., 392.
[19] C. 5/5.
[20] J. Johnston, op. cit. p. 145, and Coillard's *Journal*, June 4, 1891.
[21] It is interesting to note that Westbeech thought very highly of Middleton and praised him for his generosity. See E. C. Tabler, ed., *Trade and Travel in Early Barotseland*, London: Chatto & Windus, 1963.
[22] Mackintosh, op. cit. p. 386.
[23] No 245, African S., 414.
[24] Enclosure to No 146, African S., 414.
[25] No 317, African S., 392.
[26] No 146, African S., 414.
[27] No 10 and No 121, African S., 414
[28] No 161, African S., 414
[29] No 77, African S., 414.
[30] Later Sir Harry Johnston, author of *British Central Africa*, 1898.
[31] C. 7637.
[32] No 187, African S., 414.
[33] See Gann, *Plural Society*, p. 54 for a succinct account of Rhodes's interest in Nyasaland.
[34] No 254, African S., 414.
[35] No 245, African S., 414.
[36] See Mackintosh, op. cit. p. 390, for Coillard's account.
[37] Coillard, *Threshold*, p. 407.
[38] This letter cannot be traced but apparently it was in strong terms.
[39] No 47, African S., 426.
[40] Coillard, op. cit. p. 437.

IV REVELATIONS OF JOHNSTON AND THOMSON

[1] Dr James Johnston was later a member of the Jamaica Legislative Council. Except where otherwise stated, material for this section is

derived from his book *Reality Versus Romance in South Central Africa*, 1893. Dr Johnston was no relation to Sir Harry Johnston.

[2] Coillard, op. cit. p. 445.

[3] H. C. Thomson, *Rhodesia and Its Government*, 1898.

[4] Ibid. p. 8.

[5] Ibid. p. 245.

[6] Ibid. p. 85.

V WINNING THE NORTH-EAST

[1] See A. Bertrand, *Upper Zambezi: The Kingdom of the Barotse*, 1899, p. 272.

[2] A. J. Hanna, *The Beginnings of Nyasaland and North-Eastern Rhodesia*, 1956, passim.

[3] A. J. Hanna, *The Story of the Rhodesias and Nyasaland*, Faber 1960, pp. 111–2.

[4] Ibid. p. 111.

[5] K. Bradley, op. cit. p. 32.

[6] R. Robinson, J. Gallagher and A. Denny, op. cit. p. 447.

[7] See Sir Alfred Sharpe, *The Backbone of Africa*, Witherby 1921.

[8] His biography is given in *Joseph Thomson, African Explorer*, by his brother Rev. J. B. Thomson, Sampson Low 1896.

[9] Hanna, op. cit. p. 114.

[10] J. B. Thomson, op. cit., p. 269.

[11] See T. W. Baxter, *Occasional Papers of the National Archives of Rhodesia and Nyasaland*, No 1, Salisbury 1963. p. 27. This paper gives texts of some of the treaties.

[12] Ibid. p. 29.

[13] Ibid. pp. 35–7.

[14] M. Gelfand, *Northern Rhodesia in the Days of the Charter*, 1961, p. 87.

[15] *CBHT* (II), pp. 110–1.

[16] Crawford, *Thinking Black*, pp. 300–1, and pp. 306–8.

[17] For observations in this vein, see article by Mr Justice J. B. Thomson (no connection with the Thomsons of note 8 above), in *NRJ* No 6, Vol. 2, pp. 67–8.

[18] Map in Rev. J. B. Thomson, op. cit., facing p. 249.

[19] Ibid. p. 245 et seq.

[20] See *Geographical Journal*, Vol. 1, No 7, February 1893, p. 97 for Joseph Thomson's account.

[21] C. M. Doke, *The Lambas of Northern Rhodesia*, 1931, p. 43.

[22] No 403, African S., 197.

[23] L. H. Gann, *Plural Society*, p. 57.

[24] A. J. Hanna, *The Story of the Rhodesias and Nyasaland*, p. 115.

[25] W.1/3, *Lusaka Archives*. The frailty of these treaties was never fully disclosed until the publication of a White Paper: *The British South Africa Company's Claims to Mineral Royalties in Northern Rhodesia*, Lusaka: Government Printer, 1964.

[26] Baxter, op. cit. pp. 23–4.

[27] Rev. J. B. Thomson, op. cit. p. 296.

4: Three Decades of Chartered Rule

I THE FIRST WHITE ADMINISTRATORS

1 Hanna, *The Beginnings of North-Eastern Rhodesia and Nyasaland,* passim.
2 *Life and Work in British Central Africa, October* 1890 quoted by A. C. Ross in 'The African—Child or a Man', paper to CHCAP.
3 No 366a, African S., 403.
4 C. 7637.
5 H. H. Johnston, *British Central Africa,* p. 97.
6 *NRJ,* Vol. 2, No 6, p. 68.
7 Report of the Administrators, 1896. In the British South Africa Company Report, 1899, the map still shows Fort Rosebery as being on the Luapula river.
8 Gann, *Plural Society,* p. 62. The Barotseland—North-Western Rhodesia Order in Council was ultimately signed in November 1899, and the Order in Council for North-Eastern Rhodesia two months later.
9 FO.84/2052. See also p. 4 of E. Stokes's paper to CHCAP.
10 Gelfand, op. cit. pp. 85–9.
11 The most detailed account of the overthrow of Mpezeni is in J. A. Barnes's, *Politics in a Changing Society,* 1954, especially pp. 83–96. Also, J. K. Rennie, 'The Angoni States', paper to CHCAP, pp. 14–8.
12 Gelfand, op. cit. p. 92.

II LEWANIKA AND THE LAND

1 No 242, African S., 426, enclosure, Lochner-Knutsford.
2 See F. Coillard, op. cit. pp. 530–1, for footnote giving A. Jalla's eye-witness account.
3 See F. R. Burnham's *Scouting on Two Continents,* 1927, p. 211.
4 Coillard Papers, S.R. Archives, CO/5/5.
5 Ibid.
6 Hanna, *The Story of the Rhodesias and Nyasaland,* p. 132. Also, C.7032.
7 C. M. N. White, 'The Re-Writing of African History during the Scramble', paper to CHCAP.
8 C. Harding, *In Remotest Barotseland,* 1905, pp. 83–5 and 110, 118.
9 Hanna, op. cit. p. 133.
10 No 101, African S., 686.
11 CO/5/5.
12 See T. W. Baxter in Occasional Papers, C.A. Archives, June 1963, p. 12.
13 Ibid. pp. 12–19.
14 Article by A. Lawley in *British South Africa Annual Report,* 1899.
15 C. Harding, *Far Bugles,* 1933, p. 97.
16 C. Harding, *In Remotest Barotseland,* p. 277.
17 Harding, *Far Bugles, p.* 123.
18 See Baxter, op. cit. p. 20.
19 Minutes of this meeting are in Box N, RLI, Lusaka.
20 No 186, African S., 872.
21 No 48, African S., 899.
22 Lusaka archives, N-W.R., 3/19/40.

III EMBERS OF A SOCIAL SYSTEM

1 See full-length study by J. A. Barnes, op. cit.

[2] E. Clegg, *Race and Politics,* Oxford University Press 1960, p. 30.
[3] See Gluckman and Colson, op. cit., for accounts of tribal structures.
[4] *NRJ,* Vol. 2, No 5, p. 65.
[5] Clegg, op. cit. p. 31.
[6] W. H. G. Rangeley, *Nyasaland Journal,* No 3, p. 18.
[7] C. Gouldsbury and H. Sheane, *The Great Plateau of Northern Rhodesia,* 1911, p. 126.
[8] C. M. Doke, op. cit. p. 66 et seq.
[9] *NRJ,* Vol. 2, No 4, p. 94.
[10] Doke, op. cit. p. 119–122.
[11] Personal communication, Paul Mwanza, Chinsali.
[12] *RLP,* No 32, 'Elements in Luvale Beliefs and Rituals', p. 12.
[13] Doke, op. cit. pp. 142–3.
[14] A. J. Swann, *Fighting the Slave Hunters in Central Africa,* 1910, p. 283.
[15] A lucid explanation of *chisolo* is in E. W. Smith and A. M. Dale, *The Ila-speaking People of Northern Rhodesia,* 1920, Vol. 2, pp. 232–7
[16] W. V. Brelsford, *The Tribes of Northern Rhodesia,* 1957, p. 55.

IV WAR IN THE BUSH

[1] Material for this section is largely derived from W. V. Brelsford, *Story of the Northern Rhodesia Regiment,* 1954.
Also, see article by C. E. Hamshere in *History Today,* April 1965, pp. 249–58.

5: Colonialism and the Roots of African Nationalism

I THE DILEMMAS OF INDIRECT RULE

[1] E. G. H. Marshall Hole in memorandum of January 1921, A7/3, Lusaka Archives.
[2] Lord Hailey, op. cit. p. 452.
[3] John X. Merriman to Sir F. D. Chaplin. A3/4/1, Lusaka Arch.
[4] Lord Lugard, *The Dual Mandate in British Tropical Africa,* 1922.
[5] See Sir Alan Burns, *History of Nigeria,* London: Allen & Unwin 1955.
[6] Tagart was described as a 'sound native man' shortly before his appointment as Secretary for Native Affairs in 1921. B1/1/A378, Lusaka Arch.
[7] Hansard No 9, March 1929.
[8] See Hailey, op. cit. pp. 527–45, for an analysis of indirect rule.
[9] C. 3574: 1930.
[10] See appendix to Hansard No 12, November 1930.
[11] Hansard No 26, May 1936.
[12] Hansard No 43, September 1942.
[13] H. Franklin, personal communication.
[14] A3/2/1, Lusaka Arch.
[15] B1/7(Nat. F/1/2), Lusaka Arch.
[16] See C. 5009, 1930.
[17] C. Dundas to Sir H. Young in SEC/LAB/177, Lusaka Arch.
[18] S.P.C. to C.S., June 1936, SEC/E/41.

[19] Hailey, op. cit. p. 461.
[20] Hansard, No 26, May 1936.
[21] Hansard, No 53, March 1946.
[22] Hansard, No. 56, November 1946.
[23] Ibid.

II THE FIRST AFRICAN POLITICIANS

[1] See Major G. St.-J. Orde Browne, 'Labour Conditions in Northern Rhodesia', Colonial No 150, 1938, pp. 9–13, for background and statistics.
[2] Gann, *A History of Northern Rhodesia*, pp. 166–7.
[3] Cullen Young and Hastings Banda, editors, *Our African Way of Life*, 1946, pp. 26–7.
[4] Information supplied by Donald Siwale and the Rev. James R. Wilkie of Mwenzo Mission, 1964. On the North Nyasa Native Association, see Richard Gray, *The Two Nations*, pp. 171–2.
[5] ZA/4/1/11/9, Lusaka Arch.
[6] ZA/4/1/12/8, Lusaka Arch.
[7] O. Letcher, *Big Game Hunting in North-Eastern Rhodesia*, 1911, pp. 229–30.
[8] *Native Affairs Report* 1928. Moffat Thomson, Secretary for Native Affairs, remarked: 'This is to be regretted as it served a useful purpose by providing a means of expression for native views on social and political matters....'
[9] Report of Commission of Enquiry into Disturbances in the Copperbelt, Lusaka: Government Printer 1935.
[10] *Native Affairs Report* 1930, p. 9.
[11] The Secretary for Native Affairs was Moffat Thomson.
[12] Sir Charles Dundas, *African Crossroads*, 1955, p. 175.
[13] An account of sexual relations between European men and African women in the first part of this century may be found in *NRJ*, Vol. 5, No 2, p. 106.
[14] Report of Commission, 1935, op. cit. pp. 416–7.
[15] For an authoritative account, see Gann, op. cit. pp. 237–404, passim.
[16] Minutes of the Northern Rhodesia Advisory Council, 1920.
[17] SEC/NAT/321, Lusaka Arch.
[18] For a biography of Garvey, see Edmund C. Cronon, *Black Moses*, University of Wisconsin Press, 1962.
[19] G. Shepperson and T. Price, *Independent African*, 1958.
[20] A relation of the Barotse royal family, Godwin (Lewanika) Mbikusita later became a Federal MP and secretary of the 'white collar' Mines African Staff Association. His right to use the name Lewanika is questioned by some.
[21] C. Dundas, op. cit. p. 174.
[22] SEC/NAT/348, Lusaka Arch.
[23] Report published as C. 5949 of 1939. For a valuable commentary see Richard Gray, *The Two Nations*, 1960, pp. 150–194.
[24] See 'Statement by the Governor of Northern Rhodesia on the Recommendations of the Report of the Copperbelt Commission, 1940', dated February 18, 1941, p. 3.
[25] A history of UACS is given in A. L. Epstein's *Politics in an Urban African Community*, 1958.
[26] The 'tribal elders' system and Boss Boys' Committee were management

attempts to create avenues of communication with mineworkers. See *Forster Report* (1940), pp. 41–3, and Epstein, op. cit. pp. 63–6.

27 For excerpts from an early speech by Nkumbula, see E. Clegg, op. cit. pp. 114–5.

28 Hansard, No 46, November 1943.

29 SEC/NAT/311, Lusaka Arch.

30 Ibid.

31 Hansard, No 61, June 1948.

32 J. Sokoni, personal communication.

33 SEC/NAT/477, Lusaka Arch.

34 *Northern News,* May 26, 1964; Welensky bought a major holding in the paper in 1947, and sold it to the Argus Group in 1950.

35 J. Sokoni, personal communication.

36 Hansard, No 59, January 1948. For the background, see Clegg, op. cit. pp. 133–7.

37 Sir Roy Welensky, *Welensky's 4,000 Days,* 1964, p. 24.

38 *Central African Post,* April 4, 1948.

39 *Central African Post,* June 11, 1948; see also Gann, *A History of Northern Rhodesia,* pp. 402–4.

III LAND AND LABOUR

1 For a valuable sociological survey of conservative rural people (the Mambwe) and their subsistence farming, see W. Watson, *Tribal Cohesion in a Money Economy,* 1958.

2 H. Mulenga, personal communication.

3 Colonial No 145, 1938.

4 Colonial No 150, 1938. See p. 6: 'Considering now the actual conditions of life in the village, two sinister elements are conspicuous—undernourishment and disease.'

5 A. Lynn Saffery, *Some Aspects of African Living: Conditions on the Copperbelt,* n.d., p. 19.

6 Estimates for the whole country are given on Map 2, Colonial No 150, 1938.

7 For an exhaustive study of Bemba village life, see Audrey Richards, *Land, Labour and Diet in N. Rhodesia,* 1939.

8 Hailey, *An African Survey,* 1938, p. 1553.

9 B. Luwo, personal communication.

10 H. Franklin, *The Saucepan Special,* Lusaka: Government Printer 1950.

11 The newspaper reached a peak circulation of 18,000 in the War years.

12 Saffery, op. cit. passim.

13 Orde-Browne, op. cit. p. 67.

14 J. Merle-Davis, *Modern Industry and the African,* 1933, pp. 76–7.

15 Orde-Browne, op. cit. p. 67.

16 J. Lewin, *The Colour-Bar in the Copperbelt,* S.A. Institute of Race Relations, 1941, pp. 5–6.

17 Ibid.

18 Annual Report, Department of Native Affairs, 1928, p. 17.

19 Report on Disturbances in the Copperbelt, 1935, pp. 494–500.

20 Ibid. p. 647. The governor, Sir Hubert Young, said there might have been a demand for more money, but no justification for it.

21 Lewin, op. cit. p. 4.

22 For an official account, see Commission Report, July 1940, pp. 11–25.

23 Ibid. p. 64.

24 Saffery, op. cit. p. 11.
25 Ibid. p. 22.
26 Copy in Lusaka Arch.
27 Sir S. Gore-Browne, personal communication.
28 See A. L. Epstein, op. cit. passim.
29 Ibid. p. 63.
30 See G. Shepperson and T. Price, op. cit. p. 412.
31 For the 'Elwell affair' see SEC/NAT/311, Lusaka Arch.
32 Epstein, op. cit. pp. 91–3.
33 *Dalgleish Report*, Government Printer, Lusaka 1948.

IV EDUCATION: THE TWO STREAMS

1 See Table 7, Appendix

V CHALLENGES TO THE CHARTERED COMPANY

1 B1/7—NAT/4/1/7, Lusaka Arch.
2 B1/7—NAT/H/5, Lusaka Arch.
3 Hansard, No 31, December 1938.
4 J. E. Stephenson, *Chirupula's Tale*, 1937.
5 *Pim Report,* Colonial No 145, 1938.
6 Sir Alan Pim, *Financial and Economic History of the African Tropical Territories,* 1940, p. 191.
7 Speech by Sir Dougal Malcolm, Salisbury, April 14, 1949.
8 General Notice 118 of 1939, published in the *Government Gazette,* Lusaka, March 10, 1939. For a searching analysis, see the Northern Rhodesia White Paper, *The British South Africa Company's Claim to Mineral Royalties,* 1964.
9 The report of the commission has never been made public.
10 Hansard, No 46, December 1943.
11 For an account of the negotiations, see L. H. Gann, *A History of Northern Rhodesia,* pp. 392–7.
12 Hansard, No. 57, December 1947.
13 Hansard, No 59, January 1948.
14 G. Beckett, personal communication.
15 Colonial No 272, 1951.

6: Federation—Genesis and Exodus

I THE IRRESISTIBLE PROGRESS

1 *Bulawayo Chronicle,* February 18, 1949.
2 *Central African Post,* March 3, 1949. In 1949, Northern Rhodesia had a favourable visible trade balance of £12,000,000; by 1952 this had risen to more than £42,000,000.
3 Dated March 8, 1949, MS/1013/1/1, Lusaka Arch.
4 Hansard, No 62, November 1948.
5 Welensky, op. cit. p. 35.
6 Minutes African Representative Council (ARC), 1948.
7 'I am convinced that the only hope for Africa lies, not in segregation or dyarchy, not in repression by a dominant race, not even in some benevolent autocracy, but in co-operation between the white and black races, slowly and patiently achieved.'
8 Sir Stewart Gore-Browne, Hansard, No 62, November 1948.

[9] MS/1013/1/1, Lusaka Arch.
[10] Ibid.
[11] Ibid.
[12] Welensky, op. cit. p. 34.
[13] MS/1013/1/1, Lusaka Arch.
[14] Hansard, No. 66, November 1949.
[15] Welensky, op. cit. p. 36.
[16] *Northern News,* July 28, 1959.
[17] Welensky, op. cit. p. 37.
[18] C. No 8233.
[19] A comprehensive analysis of the proposals and subsequent constitutional formulae up to 1953 appears in Thomas M. Franck, *Race and Nationalism,* 1960, pp. 40–63.
[20] S. Kapwepwe, personal communication. See also K. D. Kaunda, *Zambia Shall Be Free,* 1962, p. 43.
[21] *The Times,* November 21, 1951.
[22] Epstein, op. cit. p. 160.
[23] Kaunda, op. cit. p. 47.
[24] World Church Group, Edinburgh, February 1952 (cyclostyled).
[25] C. No 8573.
[26] *The Times,* April 27, 1952.
[27] *Draft Statement and Principles of Inter-Racial Policy,* July 20, 1953 (cyclostyled).
[28] Confidential report of discussions, dated August 24, 1953.
[29] C. No 8754.
[30] Quoted in *East Africa and Rhodesia,* April 23, 1953, at p. 1085.
[1] HL Hansard, April 2, 1953.
[32] Hansard, June 26, 1952.
[33] Quoted in *Central African Mail,* February 24, 1960.
[34] *East Africa and Rhodesia,* March 5, 1953 at 857.
[35] Hansard, No 77, April 1953.
[36] Quoted in Epstein, op. cit. p. 761.
[37] April 20, 1953.
[38] The previous year, Chitimukulu had gone to London with a delegation paid for by Congress.
[39] F. Barton, personal communication.

II THE PROUD YEARS

[1] K. C. Wheare, *Federal Government,* 1963, p. 28.
[2] N.R. Chamber of Mines *Yearbook,* 1958 edition, relates these figures to the contribution of the copper mines.
[3] The peak was 29.1 per cent in 1955.
[4] National Accounts of the Federation, 1954–61.
[5] See statement by E. D. Hone in Hansard No 91, March 1957.
[6] *Monckton Report,* p. 90.
[7] Hansard, No 80, November 1955.
[8] Ibid.
[9] Hansard, No 84, March 1955.
[10] Hansard, March 1955.
[11] *East Africa and Rhodesia.*
[12] H. Franklin, *Unholy Wedlock,* 1960, p. 114.
[13] *Central African Post,* March 7, 1955.
[14] Hansard, No 72, December 1951.

[15] T. M. Franck, op. cit. p. 313.
[16] Hansard, August 1956.
[17] Welensky, op. cit. p. 73.
[18] Ibid. p. 77.
[19] Hansard, No 91, March 1957.
[20] *East Africa and Rhodesia,* May 1, 1958, p. 1094.
[21] See Franck, op. cit. pp. 173 et seq.
[22] Welensky, op. cit. p. 71.
[23] Ibid. pp. 92, et seq.

III THE MEANING OF DISCRIMINATION

[1] Hansard, July 1954.
[2] Hansard, No 82, July 1954.
[3] Hansard, No 84, March 1955.
[4] *Central African Post,* March 25, 1955.
[5] Hansard, No 98, July 1959.
[6] *Nshila,* September 15, 1959.
[7] *Central African Mail,* September 6, 1960.
[8] *Guillebaud Report* (cyclostyled), January 1953.
[9] *Forster Report,* Government Printer, Lusaka 1954.
[10] *Central African Post,* January 17, 1955.
[11] For an analysis see Franck, op. cit. pp. 273 et seq.
[12] N.R. Chamber of Mines *Yearbook,* 1956–60 editions.
[13] See D. G. Bettison, *Numerical Data on African Dwellers in Lusaka, N. Rhodesia,* RLI, 1960.
[14] National Accounts of the Federation, 1954–61, Central Statistical Office, Salisbury.
[15] *Central African Post,* July 8, 1948.
[16] November 8, 1952.
[17] See *African Affairs Report,* 1958.
[18] *Central African Examiner,* February 1962, p. 15.
[19] *African Education Report,* 1958.

IV THE AFRICAN REVIVAL

[1] *Central African Post,* April 14, 1953.
[2] *Rhodesia Herald,* April 8, 1953.
[3] *Central African Post,* April 24, 1953.
[4] *African Affairs Report,* 1953.
[5] K. D. Kaunda, op. cit. pp. 186–96.
[6] Hansard, No 78, April 1953.
[7] *African Times,* January 31, 1958.
[8] Report No 13, African Representative Council, June 8, 1955, cols. 317–22.
[9] Ibid.
[10] For a comprehensive account of this affair, see *Central African Examiner,* January 17, 1959.
[11] Kaunda, op. cit. pp. 31–4.
[12] A. L. Epstein, op. cit. p. 162.
[13] *Central African Post,* April 9, 1956.
[14] P. Mason, *Year of Decision,* 1960, pp. 115–6.
[15] Hansard, No 88, July 1956.
[16] *Ibid.*
[17] C. Sanger, *Central African Emergency,* 1960, p. 220.

[18] *Central African Post,* January 28, 1956.
[19] S. Kapwepwe, personal communication.
[20] *Central African Post,* June 3, 1955.
[21] *Branigan Report,* Government Printer, Lusaka 1956, p. 16.
[22] *Central African Post,* June 29, 1955.
[23] Hansard, No 89, October 1956.
[24] Welensky, op. cit. p. 74.
[25] Ibid. p. 77.
[26] *Ridley Report,* cyclostyled Lusaka 1959, p. 11.
[27] C. Leys, C. Pratt, *A New Deal in Central Africa,* 1960, p. 127.
[28] Kaunda, op. cit. p. 83.
[29] Ibid.
[30] R. S. Hall, *Kaunda: Founder of Zambia,* Longmans Green 1964, p. 24.
[31] Sanger, op. cit. p. 241.
[32] Welensky, op. cit. p. 88.
[33] Hansard, No 93, November 1957.
[34] *African Times,* February 2, 1958.
[35] *African Times,* December 13, 1957.
[36] *African Times,* December 6, 1957.
[37] *African Times,* January 17, 1958.
[38] *African Times,* February 7, 1958.
[39] *African Affairs Report,* 1957, said there were 10,000 unemployed on the Copperbelt.
[40] Kaunda, op. cit. p. 91.
[41] *African Times,* February 7, 1958.
[42] *Ridley Report,* p. 8.
[43] *Northern News,* November 7, 1958.
[44] Ibid.
[45] *Northern News,* October 11, 1958.
[46] *Northern News,* November 14, 1958.
[47] *African Eagle,* November 23, 1958.
[48] *Northern News,* October 27, 1958.
[49] Kaunda, op. cit. p. 97.
[50] *Northern News,* October 28, 1958.
[51] Ibid.
[52] C. Legum, *Pan-Africanism,* 1965, pp 42–5.
[53] *Northern News,* December 20, 1958.
[54] *Northern News,* December 22, 1958.
[55] *Northern News,* December 24, 1958.
[56] *Northern News,* January 19, 1958.

V ACCRA AND AFTER

[1] Federal Hansard, April 1959.
[2] *Central African Examiner,* January 17, 1959.
[3] Hansard, No 96, December 1958.
[4] 'The Africa of Today and Tomorrow', Royal Africa Society, April 1959, p. 60.
[5] Hansard, April 1959.
[6] *Northern News,* December 29, 1958.
[7] Hansard, No 95, October 1958.
[8] *Northern News,* January 6, 1959.
[9] *Northern News,* February 19, 1959.
[10] H. Franklin, *Unholy Wedlock,* p. 145.

[11] Welensky, op. cit. p. 116.
[12] *Northern News,* January 30, 1959.
[13] Welensky, op. cit. p. 120.
[14] Ibid.
[15] *Ridley Report,* p. 20.
[16] *Northern News,* March 12, 1959.
[17] *Ridley Report,* p. 26.
[18] *Rhodesia Herald,* February 16, 1959.
[19] See analysis issued by Lusaka Secretariat, March 26, 1959.
[20] *African Affairs Report,* 1959.
[21] *Central African Examiner,* October 24, 1959.
[22] Hansard, No 99, January 1960.

7: The Creation of Zambia

I MONCKTON AND THE SECESSION STORM

[1] Welensky, op. cit. p. 141.
[2] *East Africa and Rhodesia,* May 7, 1959.
[3] Report of the Nyasaland Commission of Enquiry, July 1959, C. 814.
[4] HC Hansard, July 1959.
[5] See, for example, A. J. Hanna, *The Story of the Rhodesias and Nyasaland,* p. 268.
[6] Welensky, op. cit. p. 138.
[7] HC Hansard, July 1959.
[8] Report of the Advisory Commission on the Review of the Constitution of Rhodesia and Nyasaland, C. 1148, p. 8.
[9] *Sunday Times,* May 3, 1959.
[10] For a report of this conference, at which the Northern Rhodesian delegate was Mainza Chona, see C. Hoskyns, *Africa South in Exile,* Vol. 4, No 4.
[11] *Central African Mail,* March 1, 1960.
[12] C. 1151–1, 1960.
[13] *Central African Mail,* August 9, 1960.
[14] For a survey of the Federation's military build-up, see *Central African Examiner,* May 1962.
[15] C. E. Lucas Phillips, *The Vision Splendid,* 1960.
[16] Hansard, March 28, 1960.
[17] *Monckton Report,* C. 1148, p. 16.
[18] Welensky, op. cit. pp. 267–83.
[19] Hansard, October 25, 1960.

II THE ADVANCE OF THE UNITED NATIONAL INDEPENDENCE PARTY

[1] Kaunda, op. cit. p. 103.
[2] *Central African Mail,* August 23, 1960.
[3] Kaunda, op. cit. pp. 138–9.
[4] UNIP 'Welcome Address', January 10, 1960.
[5] *Central African Mail,* February 23, 1960.
[6] See *Harrigan Commission of Inquiry,* Lusaka: Government Printer 1960; and *Central African Examiner,* May 7, 1960.
[7] *Annual Report,* Northern Rhodesian Police 1960.
[8] Kaunda, op. cit. p. 140.

[9] *Annual Report,* Northern Rhodesian Police 1960.
[10] D. C. Mulford, *The Northern Rhodesia General Election,* 1964, p. 117.
[11] *Central African Mail,* June 21, 1960.
[12] Welensky, op. cit. p. 196.
[13] *Central African Mail,* June 21, 1960.
[14] Ibid. September 6, 1960.
[15] *Commonwealth Survey,* Vol. 6, No 21. See also, H. Franklin, *Unholy Wedlock,* p. 197.
[16] *Northern News,* March 3, 1960.
[17] Welensky, op. cit. p. 276.
[18] *Commonwealth Survey,* Vol. 7, No 2.
[19] Welensky, op. cit. p. 191.
[20] On this issue, the Dominion Party had made a pact with the UFP.
[21] HC Hansard, October 19, 1961, col. 267.
[22] *The Times,* February 13, 1960.
[23] Franklin, op. cit. p. 197 et seq.
[24] *Central African Examiner,* March 1961.
[25] Welensky, op. cit. p. 296, and Franklin, op. cit. p. 204.
[26] *Central African Mail,* February 14, 1961.
[27] Welensky, op. cit., p. 300.
[28] *Central African Mail,* February 14, 1961.
[29] Welensky, op. cit., p. 303.
[30] *Rhodesia Herald,* February 20, 1961.
[31] Hansard, March 2, 1961.
[32] C. 1295 and C. 1301, February 1961.
[33] *Commonwealth Survey,* Vol. 7, No 7.
[34] HC Hansard, July 27, 1953.
[35] Welensky, op. cit., p. 306.
[36] HL Hansard, February 9, 1961.
[37] *An Account of the Disturbances in N. Rhodesia, July-October* 1961, Government Printer, Lusaka, p. 1.
[38] C. 1403, June 1961.
[39] See *Constitutional Changes—the Scheme Explained,* Government Printer, Lusaka 1961.
[40] See report of Commons debate in *The Guardian,* June 27, 1961.
[41] *Bulawayo Chronicle,* July 1, 1961.
[42] Katilungu replaced Nkumbula in the Legislative Council, July 1961; he was killed in a car accident in the Congo, November 1961.
[43] Hansard, 103, June 1961.
[44] *Central African Mail,* July 4, 1961.
[45] *The Guardian,* July 8, 1961.
[46] Hansard, 103, July 1961.
[47] *Central African Mail,* July 11, 1961.
[48] *The Times,* July 18, 1961.
[49] *The Scotsman,* July 28, 1961.
[50] See *Account of the Disturbances. . . .* op. cit.
[51] *Daily Mail,* August 10, 1961.
[52] See *A Grim Peep into the North,* published by UNIP, October 1961.
[53] Welensky, op. cit., p. 314.
[54] Ibid. loc. cit.

III THE FATEFUL ELECTION

[1] For an expression of this uncertainty, by a journalist close to Macleod,

see: D. Ingram, *The Commonwealth Challenge,* London: Allen and Unwin 1962, p. 110.

[2] HC Hansard, October 19, 1964 cols. 479–80.

[3] *Northern News,* September 23, 1961.

[4] Appendix C (Private and Confidential), Minutes of the UFP Emergency Conference, September 1961.

[5] UFP (Private and Confidential). NRD/CIR/156/6i.

[6] HC Hansard, October 19, 1964, col. 370.

[7] Appendix B (Private and Confidential), Minutes of the UFP Emergency Conference, September 1961.

[8] See letter by Sir Albert Robinson, *The Observer,* July 9, 1964.

[9] ANC circular, August 16, 1961.

[10] Subsequently Minister of Finance.

[11] *Central African Mail,* December 5, 1961.

[12] Welensky, op. cit. pp. 317–22.

[13] *Daily Express,* February 21, 1962.

[14] Hansard, March 6, 1962.

[15] *Central African Mail,* April 24, 1962.

[16] *Report of the Delimitation Commission,* September 1962.

[17] For an analysis of the Liberals' difficulties, see D. M. Mulford, *The Northern Rhodesia General Election,* p. 95.

[18] Mulford, op. cit. passim.

[19] Both Gore-Browne and Desai had spoken before the United Nations with Kaunda the previous March.

[20] *UNIP Policy,* Lusaka, September 1961.

[21] *Northern News,* September 8, 1962.

[22] *Northern News,* September 28, 1962.

[23] Out of 100 persons selected at random three weeks before the election, only twelve Africans and one Eurafrican correctly answered six basic questions on the constitution (*Central African Mail,* October 9, 1962).

[24] Mulford, op. cit. pp. 115–9.

[25] *Northern News,* October 29, 1962.

IV THE AFRICAN COALITION

[1] *Central African Mail,* November 6, 1962.

[2] Ibid. November 20, 1962.

[3] D. C. Mulford, op. cit. p. 165.

[4] Ibid. pp. 174–80.

[5] *Central African Mail,* March 2, 1963.

[6] *Central African Mail,* June 1, 1963.

[7] *Central African Mail,* August 3 and 10, 1963.

[8] *Central African Mail,* August 24, 1963.

[9] *Report of the Commission of Enquiry into Unrest on the Copperbelt,* cyclostyled, August 1963.

[10] Welensky, op. cit. pp. 351 et seq.

[11] *The Times,* February 14, 1963.

[12] HC Hansard, April 30, 1963.

[13] C. 1948 of 1963.

[14] See *Report of the Central African Conference,* 1963, Government Printer, Lusaka.

[15] C. Fed., 246 of 1963.

[16] *Central African Mail,* June 7, 1960.

[17] *Analysis of Polling,* issued by Elections Office, Lusaka 1964.

V THE REPUBLIC OF ZAMBIA

[1] Eight of the forty-three ministers had been detained when ZANC was banned in 1959.
[2] Kaunda, loc. cit.
[3] For a study of the Lumpa Church, see R. Rotberg, 'The Lenshina Movement', *RLJ,* No 29, June 1961.
[4] *Central African Mail,* June 15, 1963.
[5] *N.R. Court of Appeal,* Nos 66–9 of 1964. The sentence was later commuted.
[6] *Central African Mail,* August 14, 1964.
[7] British South Africa Company letter to shareholders, December 22, 1964.
[8] *Central African Mail,* April 3, 1964.
[9] British South Africa Company's letter to shareholders.
[10] Hansard, August 1964.
[11] *The Times,* September 16, 1964.
[12] *The British South Africa Company's Claims to Mineral Royalties in Northern Rhodesia,* Government Printer, Lusaka 1964.
[13] *The Times,* September 30, 1964.
[14] British South Africa Company, letter to shareholders.
[15] Kaunda, loc. cit. For an account of Kaunda's role in PAFMECSA see Richard Cox, *Pan-Africanism in Practice* (*PAFMECSA*). London and New York: Oxford University Press, 1964.
[16] *External Trade Statistics,* 1964. Central Statistical Office, Lusaka.
[17] UN/ECA/FAO Report, p. 32.
[18] *The Challenge to the Construction Industry,* Central Planning Office, Lusaka, October 1964.

VI THE INTEGRATION OF BAROTSELAND

[1] *Monckton Report,* pp. 45–6.
[2] Evidence given to Macdonell Commission, and Report KDE/2/3/1-15, Lusaka Arch.
[3] Franklin, op. cit. p. 220.
[4] *Nshila,* June 9, 1959.
[5] Hansard, No 97, April 1959.
[6] August 16, 1960.
[7] Hansard, No 101, November 1960.
[8] *Central African Mail,* November 22, 1962.
[9] *Commonwealth Survey,* May 9, 1961, p. 493.
[10] Franklin, op. cit. pp. 217–9, *The Times,* March 6, 1962, and *Central African Mail,* February 20, 1962.
[11] Welensky, op. cit. pp. 360–1.
[12] *Central African Mail,* August 31, 1963.
[13] C. 2366 of 1964.

VII ZAMBIA'S EDUCATIONAL NEEDS

[1] See Table 8 in Appendix and references in Chapters 9, 'The Economic History of Zambia' and 10, 'Economic Prospects'.
[2] Penal Code (Amendment) Bill, 1964.

8: *The Copperbelt*

I THE ANCIENT MINERS

[1] Sir Richard Burton, *Lacerda's Journey to Cazembe,* p. 222.
[2] J. A. Bancroft, *Mining in Northern Rhodesia,* 1961, p. 26.
[3] Kenneth Bradley, *Copper Venture,* p. 61.
[4] Article in *Horizon,* published by Rhodesian Selection Trust, Salisbury, March 1961, p. 13.
[5] Bancroft, op. cit. p. 27.
[6] *Mining in Rhodesia,* printed for information of shareholders of the British South Africa Company.
[7] Bancroft, op. cit. p. 27.
[8] The descriptions which follow are mainly derived from Bancroft, op. cit. pp. 28–34, and Bradley, op. cit. pp. 33–8.
[9] C. M. Doke, *The Lambas of Northern Rhodesia,* p. 347.
[10] Monsignor J. de Hemptinne, quoted by Bancroft.

II THE ELUSIVE ORE-BODIES

[1] Speech by Sir Ronald Prain to the Non-Ferrous Club, Birmingham, England, January 3, 1962.
[2] *Horizon,* May 1959, p. 13.
[3] M. Gelfand, *Northern Rhodesia in the Days of the Charter,* 1961, p. 91; also, E. H. Lane-Poole, in *NRJ* Vol. 15. No 3, pp. 221–3.
[4] *Horizon,* May 1959, p. 11.
[5] J. A. Bancroft, op. cit. p. 56.
[6] O. Baragwanath in *NRJ,* Vol. 5, No 3, pp. 209–220.
[7] Bancroft, op. cit. pp. 38–9.
[8] Gann, *A History of Northern Rhodesia,* p. 121.
[9] Bancroft, op. cit. pp. 112–113.
[10] K. Bradley, op. cit. pp. 64–70
[11] For the career of this remarkable adventurer, see C. M. Doke, *The Lambas of Northern Rhodesia,* pp. 43–7.
[12] *NRJ,* Vol. 5, No 3, p. 279.
[13] *NRJ,* Vol. 2, No 3, pp. 23–5.
[14] O. Letcher, *South Central Africa,* 1932, frontispiece.
[15] *Typescript history of Kansanshi* by Anglo-American Corporation, dated September 1955.
[16] Letcher, op. cit. p. 133, quotes letter from Jameson to Williams.
[17] *African World,* December 1905.
[18] Sir Ronald Prain, lectures to Royal School of Mines, London, November 1957 (published R.S.T.), pp. 27–33, for resumé of advances in copper production, 1900–10.
[19] Bancroft, op. cit. p. 123.
[20] Ibid. p. 145. Bancroft suggests that Chief Nkana showed Thomson the outcrop.

III PROSPECTORS AND FINANCIERS

[1] Copies in Lusaka Arch.
[2] Sir R. Prain, Lectures to Royal Society of Mines, London, R.S.T., 1957, pp. 34–5.
[3] K. Bradley, op. cit. pp. 78–9.

[4] R. Brooks, 'How the Northern Rhodesia Coppers were Found', *NRJ*, Vol. 1, No 1, p. 44.
[5] J. A. Bancroft, op. cit. pp. 146–8.
[6] O. Letcher, *South Central Africa,* p. 83.
[7] Bancroft, op. cit. p. 148.
[8] See detailed map of Nkana Concession in Bradley, op. cit. pp. 84–5.
[9] See *Horizon,* September 1960, p. 17.
[10] C. M. Doke, op. cit. p. 21.
[11] Brooks, op. cit. p. 30.
[12] See Northern Rhodesia *Chamber of Mines Yearbook,* 1962, pp. 27 and 54–5.
[13] *Horizon,* October 1962, pp. 16–8.
[14] Sir Theodore Gregory, *Ernest Oppenheimer,* 1962, pp. 385 and 408.
[15] Bancroft, op. cit. pp. 386–9.
[16] Gregory, op. cit. pp. 386–9.
[17] Bradley, op. cit. passim.
[18] Gregory, op. cit. Ch. 7.
[19] Brooks, article 2, op. cit. pp. 33–4. This was the American Smelting and Refining Company's attempt at penetration which Oppenheimer beat off with the aid of the Rio Tinto Company and other 'imperial' concerns. See Gregory op. cit. pp. 422–30.
[20] Ibid. p. 383.
[21] Bancroft, op. cit. p. 151.
[22] Gregory, op. cit. p. 405.
[23] Brooks, article 1, op. cit. p. 47.
[24] Ibid. article 3, p. 34.
[25] Bancroft, op. cit. passim.
[26] Brooks, article 2, p. 33.
[27] Ibid. p. 34.
[28] R. Brooks, personal communication.
[29] Bancroft, op. cit. p. 79.
[30] Brooks, article 2, p. 29.

IV YEARS OF TRANSFORMATION

[1] Gregory, op. cit. pp. 406–15.
[2] *NRJ,* Vol. I, No 1, p. 44.
[3] Bancroft, op. cit. p. 124.
[4] *Report of Pim Commission,* Colonial No. 145, 1938, passim.
[5] *Report of Forster Commission,* Government Printer, Lusaka 1940, p. 8.
[6] Bancroft, op. cit. p. 77.
[7] *Colonial Annual Report,* population table.
[8] J. Thomson, personal communication.
[9] Gregory, op. cit. pp. 436–43.
[10] See statistical tables, N.R. Chamber of Mines *Year Book,* 1963. More than 3,000 miles of underground workings had been driven on the Copperbelt by 1960.
[11] See *Financial Mail of N. Rhodesia,* January 1964, p. 1.
[12] Speech at Savoy Hotel, London, March 26, 1963.

VII GEOLOGY OF THE COPPERBELT

[1] For an illustrated explanation of Copperbelt geology, see W. G. Garlick's articles in *Horizon,* August and September 1959.

[8] A short account appears in *The Story of the Anglo-American Corporation in Rhodesia,* company publication, undated. Other company publications, e.g. *Summary of Operations, Mufulira Copper Mines Ltd,* describe particular deposits.

9: The Economic History of Zambia

[1] *Report of the Commission Appointed to Enquire into the Financial and Economic Position of Northern Rhodesia,* Colonial No 145, 1938.
[2] *Report of the Working Party on Rural Economic Development,* Lusaka: Government Printer 1961.
[3] *Synopsis of Extracts from Financial Reports of N. Rhodesia.*
[4] W. J. Busschau, *Report on the Development of Secondary Industries in Northern Rhodesia,* Lusaka: Government Printer 1945.

10: Economic Prospects

[1] *Education in N. Rhodesia—Report and Recommendations prepared by* UNESCO *Planning Mission,* 1963. Government Printer, Lusaka 1964.
[2] *Report on the Development of a University in Northern Rhodesia,* Lusaka: Government Printer 1964.

Index

DATE DUE

GAYLORD			PRINTED IN U.S.A.